DEATH IN THE
HAYMARKET

DEATH IN THE
HAYMARKET

A Story of Chicago,
the First Labor Movement
and the Bombing
That Divided
Gilded Age America

JAMES GREEN

PANTHEON BOOKS, NEW YORK

Pantheon Books and colophon are registered trademarks of Random House, Inc.

Library of Congress Cataloging-in-Publication Data
Green, James R., [date]
Death in the Haymarket : a story of Chicago, the first labor movement and the
bombing that divided gilded age America / James Green.
p. cm.
Includes bibliographical references and index.
ISBN 0-375-42237-4
1. Labor movement—Illinois—Chicago—History—19th century.   2. Haymarket
Square Riot, Chicago, Ill., 1886.   3. Working class—Illinois—Chicago—
History—19th century.   4. Chicago (Ill.)—Social conditions.   5. Social
conflict—United States—History—19th century.   I. Title.

HD8085.C53G74 2006
977.3'11041—dc22   2005051844

www.pantheonbooks.com

Printed in the United States of America

First Edition

9 8 7 6 5 4 3 2

To Janet and Nick

Contents

Maps

DEATH IN THE
HAYMARKET

Prologue

AS THE SUN ROSE over Lake Michigan on May 5 in 1886, Chicagoans beheld one of the brightest mornings in memory. In the early light of day, merchants, managers and brokers boarded horse-drawn streetcars on the South Side and headed north on Michigan Avenue toward the business district. Along the way they encountered a few high-hatted rich men, like the great manufacturer George Mortimer Pullman, being driven uptown in fancy carriages from their mansions on Prairie Avenue. Marring the commuters' eastward view of Lake Michigan's azure blue reaches, black freight trains rolled along the shoreline laden with baled cotton from the Mississippi River delta, cut lumber from the piney woods of Texas and soft coal from the mines of southern Illinois—all crucial ingredients in the city's explosive industrial growth during the 1880s. Indeed, the businessmen who went to work in Chicago's financial district that spring day in 1886 were in the midst of a golden decade of profit, when the net value of goods produced by the city's leading industries multiplied twenty-seven times, ten times faster than the average yearly wage.[1]

But that first Wednesday in May when commuters gazed west over the widest industrial landscape in the world, they saw something unusual: a clear sky above the prairie horizon. Gone was the cloud of thick smoke that always hung over the city. The only signals of industrial activity came from the tall chimneys of the huge McCormick Reaper Works two miles away, where strikebreakers, guarded by Chicago police, kept the factory in operation. Scores of other plants and shops remained shut down on this fifth day of a mammoth general strike for the eight-hour day that had begun on May 1.

As the black-coated businessmen entered the downtown area, they could see knots of pickets around the soot-blackened warehouses that stretched along State Street all the way up to the Dearborn Station. Striking freight handlers had stanched the flow of interstate commerce through Chicago's immense grid of iron rails. In solidarity, switchmen had refused to switch trains in one central railyard, crippling the mighty Chicago, Burlington & Quincy Railroad, the city's largest freight handler.[2] Trains still chugged into the city that day, but when the locomotives reached the depots, they sat idle, stuck on the tracks with unloaded cargoes.

Looking back into the rising sun, the businessmen would have seen hundreds of boats riding at anchor in the outer harbor. The captains of side-wheel steamers had banked their boilers, and sailors on lake schooners had struck their sails under orders from the alarmed vessel owners. A vast quantity of wheat and cut lumber awaited shipment, and there were lucrative tons of iron ore and anthracite coal to be unloaded, but the spring shipping season had been ruined by the storm of strikes that had swept over the city. Vessel owners feared for the safety of their ships if they ventured down the South Branch of the Chicago River to unload in the industrial zone because angry strikers, many of them Bohemian lumber shovers, had taken over the lumberyards and could, at any moment, put a torch to their wooden boats and the acres of dry lumber nearby.[3]

The strike wave even reached outside the city, to the enormous railroad car shops in the model town George Pullman had built to escape the turmoil of Chicago. Seemingly unconcerned with labor unrest in the city and in the town he owned, Pullman arrived for work as usual at his palatial company headquarters on Michigan Avenue. Stepping out of a carriage driven by a well-dressed black man who wore his own high hat, the world-renowned industrialist and city builder entered his office building looking as he did every morning, walking purposefully and wearing his usual outfit—a Prince Albert coat, striped trousers and patent-leather shoes.[4]

Yet, beneath his businesslike demeanor, George Pullman suffered from feelings of uncertainty. "My anxiety is very great," he wrote to his wife, "although it is said that I appear very cool and unconcerned about it." The stunning breadth of the eight-hour strike shocked him. He had constructed his company town nine miles from industrial Chicago, where poverty and despair had poisoned relations between manufacturers and their hands and caused frequent strikes, lockouts and riots. In Pullman's model community, carefully selected workmen earned high wages, rented comfortable new houses and lived a healthy life in a clean place. Now the toxic fumes of class antagonism were wafting through the streets of his planned community. "Some change must occur very soon now," he told his wife, "but I cannot yet predict what it will be."[5]

Like George Pullman, other businessmen headed for work on May 5 just as they always did and with their usual frantic energy. When they arrived downtown, these men usually stopped to buy the morning edition of the *Chicago Daily Tribune,* the self-proclaimed businessman's paper. But on this Wednesday, men grabbed the paper eagerly because they had heard rumors about a riot on the West Side the night before in which many policemen were hurt, and no one knew with any certainty what had happened. When they read the morning headline, they were stunned because it carried news of an event far worse than any of them imagined.

A HELLISH DEED

A Dynamite Bomb Thrown into a Crowd of Policemen.

It Explodes and Covers the Street with Dead and Mutilated Officers—A Storm of Bullets Follows—The Police Return Fire and Wound a Number of Rioters—Harrowing Scenes at the Desplaines Street Station—A Night of Terror.

The editors used all seven columns of the front page to describe the shocking events of May 4 in elaborate detail. A bomb thrown into the midst of six police divisions took an awful toll: at least fifty patrolmen had been wounded; several were near death, and one of them, Mathias Degan, had already expired in the arms of a fellow officer. The list of injured men was long, and the descriptions of their wounds were sickening.[6]

The news story explained that the bombing occurred at the end of a meeting called by the city's socialists on Tuesday evening, May 4, in order to denounce the police for killing four strikers at the McCormick Reaper Works in a skirmish that took place the previous afternoon. Roughly 1,500 people had gathered for a rally that began that Tuesday at 7:30 p.m. on Desplaines Street, quite close to Randolph Street, where it widened to become the Haymarket, a busy place where farmers sold their produce by day. August Spies, the city's leading German socialist, had called the meeting to order and then had introduced the renowned labor agitator Albert R. Parsons, who spoke for nearly an hour.

By the time the last speaker mounted a hay wagon to close the meeting, only 600 people remained, according to the news report. Samuel Fielden, a burly stone hauler, had begun his speech by noting premonitions of danger obvious to all. He told the crowd to prepare for the worst, claiming that since the police had shown no mercy to the unarmed workers they gunned down at McCormick's, then the police deserved no mercy in return. "Defend yourselves, your lives, your futures," Fielden shouted to a crowd the *Tribune* described as composed of Germans (who were the most enthusiastic), along with Poles, Bohemians and a few Americans.

At this point, "[a] stiff breeze came up from the north and, anticipating rain, more of the crowd left, the worst element, however, remaining," according to the *Tribune*'s lead reporter. Fielden was winding up his address when witnesses saw a dark line of men forming south of Randolph in front of the Desplaines Street Police Station. A few minutes later the line started to move, and men on the outskirts of the rally whispered, "Police." The large contingent of 176 officers moved rapidly down the street, marching double-time, like soldiers. The silver stars and buttons on the policemen's blue coats glittered in the light cast off from the nearby Lyceum Theater, the only building in this dark grid of streets that glowed with electric lights. The police column was so broad that it filled the width of Desplaines Street, forcing onlookers to move onto the wooden sidewalks.

When the first division of police stopped just before the wagon, the officer in charge said to Fielden in a loud voice, "In the name of the law, I command you to disperse." Then, said the *Tribune*, came the "response." With no warning "something like a miniature rocket suddenly rose out of the crowd on the east sidewalk." It gave off a red glare as it arced about 20 feet in the air before falling in the middle of the street among the police. The bomb lay on the ground for a few seconds and then "exploded with terrific force, shaking buildings on the street and creating havoc among the police." The blast stunned the officers and, before they could come to their senses, the newspaper reported, another shocking scene unfolded as "the anarchists and rioters poured a shower of bullets into the police."

The patrolmen immediately let loose with their pistols and kept up an incessant shooting for nearly two minutes as the dark sky above the street glowed with the flashes of gunfire. The civilians gathered on Desplaines Street ran for their lives. Some went west on Randolph and others east toward the Chicago River. Either way, those in flight ducked as bullets whizzed past them, and many of them dropped on the streets before they could escape. "The groans of those hit could be heard above the rattle of revolvers," wrote one reporter. Some of those who fled took refuge in the halls or entrances of houses and in saloons. When the shooting stopped, they cautiously ventured forth, only to face more gunfire from the police.

After this second assault ended, reporters saw men crawling on their hands and knees. Others tottered "along the street like drunken men, holding their hands to their heads and calling for help to take them home." Many victims had their wounds dressed in drugstores and on wooden sidewalks, while others boarded streetcars going in every direction and containing wounded people fleeing from the Haymarket.

At this point the journalists on the scene ran across the river to "newspaper alley" seven blocks away so they could file the biggest story of their lives. The news of the sensational events at the Haymarket flew across telegraph lines to newsrooms all over the nation and across the Atlantic to Europe as well. Every paper in London reported the event, and several even published long and graphic special sections with reports rendered in minute detail. Overnight, the Haymarket event became the biggest news story since Lincoln's assassination twenty-one years earlier. "No disturbance of the peace that has occurred in the United States since the war of rebellion," said the *New York Times,* "has excited public sentiment throughout the Union as it is excited by the Anarchists' murder of policemen in Chicago on Tuesday night."[7]

At 11:30 p.m. police wagons rumbled into the Haymarket district from other precincts carrying reinforcements who cleared the streets around the station and "mercilessly clubbed all who demurred at the order to go." After patrolmen drove all pedestrians from the area, the West Side fell silent, and "Desplaines Street looked black and deserted, save where the gas-lamps showed blood on the sidewalks and the curbstones."

The *Tribune*'s account then described the scene at the Desplaines Street Station: a "harrowing spectacle of wounded and dying men on the floor oozing blood that flowed literally in streams" until almost "every foot of the space was red and slippery." Officers stoically bandaged up their own wounds but reportedly never moaned, according to one reporter who wrote that he had never seen such heroism.

The station's basement was filled with wounded civilians who were scattered around on the floor, some with serious wounds. One of them moaned and screamed, "but the remainder were as quiet as the death which was settling down upon quite a few of their number." Thomas Hara of Eagle Street near the Haymarket, one of those shot in the back as he fled the melee, "claimed to be an unoffending citizen" but was probably a rioter, according to the *Tribune* reporter. Policemen interviewed at the station expressed no sympathy for the men in the basement who were suspected rioters, including socialists and anarchists who had been "preaching dynamite for years."

Reporters finally buttonholed Chief Inspector John Bonfield, who had ordered the police advance on the protest rally. "The Communists were bent on mischief" for some time, he explained, and therefore the police, anticipating "the hellish intent of the Haymarket meeting," had massed most of the city's force at the Desplaines Street Station the previous night. When the meeting started, the inspector sent officers in civilian clothes out into the crowd with orders to report back to him if the speeches became dangerous. "When finally the speakers urged riot and slaughter" to seek revenge for the deaths of the strikers killed at McCormick's, the inspector said he issued his fateful order to march on the meeting.

NONE OF THE businessmen who read this terrifying story in the *Tribune* on May 5 had any reason to doubt the reporters' accounts. The news appeared in their paper, the city's paper of record, which was edited by Joseph Medill, perhaps the most respected journalist in the nation. An early champion of Lincoln and of war against the southern secessionists, Medill had served a term as a reform mayor of Chicago, and by 1886 he was a powerful force in the Republican Party and an influential voice in the business community.[8]

For all these reasons, the *Tribune*'s account of the events of May 4 provided a governing narrative for the city's propertied classes and for the state's attorney who would prosecute the alleged perpetrators. The news reported on May 5 carried an aura of authority and objectivity, but it also contained some curious inconsistencies and contradictions that would come into sharper focus when the smoke cleared from the streets, leaving more than a few people wondering what really happened in the Haymarket that terrible night.

In the immediate aftermath, the *Tribune* called for severe action against those aliens responsible for the massacre. The riot in the market would not have occurred, the editor added, but for "the excessive, ill-conceived toleration" the mayor and city officials accorded to radical agitators. A bloody lesson had been learned; the government must deport these "ungrateful hyenas" and exclude any other "foreign savages who might come to America with their dynamite bombs and anarchic purposes."[9]

These staunch opinions failed, however, to reassure the public that law and order would prevail. City residents were seized with panic as fantastic rumors swept through the city. Remembering this moment during her difficult time as a widowed dressmaker in Chicago, Mother Jones wrote that "the city went insane and the newspapers did everything to keep it like a madhouse." On the morning after the violent encounter, one observer said, he passed many groups of people on the streets engaged in excited conversation about the events of the previous night. Everyone assumed that the speakers at the Haymarket meeting and other "labor agitators" had perpetrated the horrible crime. The air was charged with hatred and cries of "Hang them first and try them afterwards!"[10]

It was no time for careful public discussion of what had actually taken place in the Haymarket. In those first days of rage over the bombing, the daily press not only shaped but also reflected a popular certainty about who was to blame for the tragedy. There would be no discussion about why this catastrophe had occurred in Chicago, no talk of what might have been done to prevent it. Filled with horror at accounts of an unspeakable crime, citizens demanded an immediate response from the state, one that would punish not only the "dynamite orators" responsible for the bombing, but also those who sheltered and encouraged them.[11]

And yet affixing blame for the tragedy did little to diminish the acute anxiety that swept the nation after the bombing. Indeed, identifying the anarchists as secret conspirators responsible for the lethal deed led to wild exaggerations of the menace these subversives posed to social order. In New York City, for example, the *Times* reported that workers who "placed responsibility for their poverty upon the bourgeoisie" were armed with rifles and bombs and were prepared with plans to bring down "the ruling class." Even after these rumors disappeared from the press, the specter of radicalism would remain alive in "the bourgeois imagination."[12]

The Haymarket bombing confirmed the worst fears of violent class warfare wealthy urban dwellers had harbored ever since the railroad strikes of 1877, when more than 100 workers and civilians were killed by policemen and militiamen. In all the street fighting that broke out episodically for the next nine years, strikers and rioters had been put down by the superior forces of state and local government, whose officers had suf-

fered no fatalities of their own. Then on May 4, when one bomb thrown by
a single hand shredded the ranks of the nation's strongest police force,
many citizens reacted hysterically, experiencing a kind of fear they had
never known before. The invention of dynamite had changed the calculus
of power. Now the weakest, most wretched elements of society had a
weapon that could inflict incalculable damage.

Politically motivated bombings had occurred the year before in London, where Irish-American nationalists attacked British colonial targets,
and earlier in other European cities, where anarchists targeted imperial
rulers, but nothing like this had ever happened in post–Civil War America. There had been many riots in the nation's cities, but now, "for the
first time in the history of the Republic," the *New York Times* observed,
law officers had been "killed by citizens attacking the right to private
property." As a result, the Haymarket affair generated emotional shock
waves that would reverberate through the country for years to come.[13]

As the frenzy of panic that gripped Chicago spread across the nation,
it became clear that Americans were reacting to more than a single terrifying attack on the forces of law and order. No event since the Civil War
had produced such profound excitement as the Haymarket violence, a
perceptive Chicago minister observed. This was not just because this
warlike act occurred during peacetime, but because the catastrophe provoked the widespread fear that the bombing was but "the first explosion
of a deep discontent on the part of millions of poor people in this and
other countries."[14]

THE BOMB BLAST on May 4 triggered an avalanche of events: a police riot
in which at least three protesters died, a wave of hysteria in which police
and prosecutors violated civil liberties, a sensational show trial of the
eight workers accused of the bombing and the intensely publicized hanging of four anarchists accused of committing the crime of the century.
Indeed, the whole Haymarket affair, lasting from May 4, 1886, until
November 11, 1887, when the anarchists swung from the gallows in the
Cook County Jail, produced what one historian called "a drama without end."[15]

The hangings did not bring down the curtain on this drama, however.
The Haymarket affair troubled the consciences of many citizens for
years, and for the next two decades and beyond as jurists, trade union-

ists, journalists and other writers, even elected officials, kept trying the case over and over. The whole violent string of events in Chicago left a bitterly divided memory as its legacy. To most Americans, the dead anarchists were, as Theodore Roosevelt put it, "the foulest sort of murderers." But to other people, especially immigrant workers in America, the Haymarket anarchists were heroic martyrs, brave enough to die for the cause of working-class emancipation. Indeed, the anarchists' trial and execution became, in the hands of working-class preservationists, a passion play about the prophets who surrendered their lives in order to give birth to a worldwide workers' movement. No other event in American history has exerted such a hold on the imaginations of people in other lands, especially on the minds of working people in Europe and the Latin world, where the "martyrs of Chicago" were annually recalled in the iconography of May Day.

In retrospect, the Haymarket affair marked a juncture in our history when many Americans came to fear radicals and reformers as dangerous subversives and to view trade unionists as irresponsible troublemakers. The explosion erupted at a time—the mid-1880s—when popular radical movements were attracting millions of farmers and workers, but after the bombing these movements labored under a cloud of suspicion. For mainstream trade unionists struggling to survive in a hostile environment, Haymarket was a catastrophe they wished to forget. The whole affair gave hostile employers and government officials an opportunity to brand all labor activists violent subversives and to reject out of hand all ideas about cooperating with their workers. Still, even conventional union leaders like Samuel Gompers of the American Federation of Labor could not forget that the revolutionaries put to death in Chicago were union organizers and leaders of the crusade for the eight-hour day—the cause that mobilized America's first national labor movement in 1886.[16]

The consequences of this tragedy for immigrants were far-reaching. Europeans of all nations had been welcomed to American shores during the post–Civil War years, but after the bombing in Chicago even the much-admired Teutonic peoples of Germany became suspect. At a time when immigrants seemed to be overwhelming cities like Chicago, the Haymarket events provoked a new kind of paranoia among millions of native-born citizens, who grew much more fearful of aliens in their midst. The memory of Haymarket haunted the national consciousness for decades because nativists painted a terrifying picture of the alien anarchist as "a ragged, unwashed, long-haired, wild-eyed fiend, armed with a smoking revolver and a bomb." This reaction to the Haymarket bombing created a long-lasting popular impression of the immigrant as a dangerous figure, somehow more menacing than even the most violent American.[17]

Indeed, the explosion and the red scare that followed the event created an atmosphere of fear and hatred that prevailed for decades and influenced the fates of other immigrant radicals, particularly those of Sacco and Vanzetti. The ordeal of these two Italian anarchists, executed in 1927 after being convicted of conspiracy to commit murder, dramatically reprised the case of the Haymarket anarchists put to death forty years earlier. What Edmund Wilson said of the Sacco and Vanzetti case and its meaning for twentieth-century America applied to the Haymarket anarchists' case as well: "It revealed the whole anatomy of American life, with all its classes, professions, and points of view and all their relations, and it raised almost every fundamental question of our political and social system."[18]

The Haymarket case refuses to die because it involves so many troubling questions about the causes of violent conflict and the limits of free speech, about the justice of conspiracy trials and the fairness of the death penalty and about the treatment of immigrants, particularly foreign-born radicals, by the police, the newspapers and the courts. And perhaps most troubling of all, the Haymarket case challenged, like no other episode in the nineteenth century, the image of the United States as a classless society with liberty and justice for all.

Americans had been using various languages of class to describe social reality since the American Revolution, and in the years after the Civil War they began to express serious worries about the possibility that bloody battles between workers and employers would erupt, as indeed they did in the mid-1870s. But almost everyone, politicians and preachers, employers and trade union leaders alike, thought these episodes were simply the product of hard times or the result of agitation by a few rabble-rousers. After the Haymarket events, however, more and more commentators openly expressed their concern that class conflict in the United States was becoming irreconcilable. For years this extreme view had existed only on the radical margins of public opinion, but in 1886 it moved toward the center of American public discourse about what came to be known as "the social question."[19]

IN THE DAYS AFTER the bomb exploded on Desplaines Street, as most Americans concluded that crazed immigrants were alone responsible for the Haymarket calamity, a few prominent men privately worried that the violence might have been caused by other forces, forces that menaced the well-being of the democracy itself.

One of these thoughtful citizens was George Pullman. In 1883, three years before the tragedy, the industrialist had told a Senate committee that he was "deeply disturbed" that the conditions of life in industrial cities had become so "dangerous and deplorable." He had invested millions in building a model industrial town to avoid the dangers of Chicago's urban jungle, but in the process he had created a feudal domain that denied his employees the freedom they cherished. On the morning of May 5, 1886, as Pullman wrote letters in his Michigan Avenue office, he learned that his own loyal employees, most of them native-born Americans or assimilated immigrants, were ready to strike for an eight-hour day. Even these privileged employees whose loyalty to Pullman had been rewarded with high wages and good housing had not escaped infection by the strike fever that gripped Chicago that spring.

One of the letters Pullman wrote that day was to his friend Andrew Carnegie in Pittsburgh, to thank him for sending a copy of his popular new book. In *Triumphant Democracy* the richest man in the world praised republican government as the reason why Americans enjoyed such exceptional opportunity, prosperity and domestic tranquility. Carnegie predicted that a new "American race" would be created when immigrants were educated and fused with natives "into one, in language, in thought, in feeling and in patriotism." Pullman ended his letter by telling Carnegie that publication of his book was very timely, because "owing to the excesses of our turbulent population, so many are uttering doubts just now as to whether democracy has been a triumph in America."[20]

Many ambitious men like George Pullman had been attracted to Chicago in the mid nineteenth century, a time when the city embodied just the kind of triumphant democracy his friend Carnegie extolled. But after working-class discontent surged through the city on May Day of 1886 and spilled into Pullman town, the famous manufacturer and reformer beheld a democracy in crisis, a society divided by mistrust and class conflict.

The governor of Illinois, Richard J. Oglesby, shared some of Pullman's anxieties during those frightful days of early May 1886. He was appalled by the news he received from Chicago of "a vicious and riotous disturbance by the anarchists," but he resisted demands from leading businessmen to call out the state militia immediately after the bombing. The governor feared that inserting militia companies might turn a tense situation into an urban civil war, because he knew that the discontent among urban workers ran deep, so deep that Chicago seemed to him like a "social volcano" ready to blow.[21] Indeed, the city had become so divided that it was difficult for Oglesby to imagine how Chicagoans would come back together again as they once had been when he had arrived in the city on another May Day not so long before. That May 1 had been in 1865, when the governor entered Chicago and saw its people standing by the thousands in the rain, bonded together in grief. The slow train that Oglesby rode into the city that dismal morning was decked out in flags and black crepe, and it bore the remains of his old friend Abraham Lincoln, the rail-splitter he had helped to make president of the United States.

Chapter One

For Once in Common Front

THE FIRST OF MAY was by custom a day of hope that marked the coming of spring, a day when children danced and twirled streamers around a Maypole. But in 1865 it was the gloomiest day Chicago had ever seen. For on that occasion "the merry May pole gaily wreathed for the holiday festivities of exuberant life" yielded its place to the "funeral catafalque draped with Death's sad relics." So wrote Abraham Lincoln's friend and ally Joseph Medill in the *Chicago Tribune* that morning of the day when the multitudes would assemble "to do honor to the great and good King of men," severed from his people when he was "slain so ruthlessly."[1]

In the dark hours of the early morning, crowds gathered all along the Illinois Central tracks on the lakeside. A light rain fell as the funeral train entered Chicago that morning; it hissed to a stop at Michigan Avenue and 12th Street, where 36,000 citizens had gathered to meet it. An honor guard loaded the presidential coffin onto an elaborate horse-drawn hearse, and citizens formed in military rank behind it. A group of thirty-six "maidens dressed in white" surrounded the carriage as it passed through an imposing Gothic arch dedicated to the "Martyr for Justice." After each young woman placed a red rose on the president's coffin, the carriage pulled away, followed by the column of Chicagoans who marched four abreast up Michigan Avenue toward the courthouse, where their martyred president's remains would lie in state. The procession grew to 50,000 as it moved slowly up the lakeside. Along the way twice that many people lined the streets. From all over the Northwest they came—by train, in wagons and buggies and on horseback, all united in silent grief. "In the line of march and looking on, sharing something in common," Carl Sandburg wrote, were native-born Yankees and foreign-born Catholics, blacks and whites, German Lutherans and German Jews—all "for once in common front."[2]

Up Michigan Avenue they trod in rhythm to the sound of drums beating in solemn tribute to Lincoln's memory, expressing, as the *Tribune* put it, "the devotion with which all classes looked up to him." A military band led the funeral procession of five divisions: first came the Board of Education and 5,000 schoolchildren, and then military officers and enlisted men, the combat troops of the Grand Army of the Republic led by the Old Batteries of the Chicago Light Artillery, whose cannon had laid siege to Atlanta. The black-coated men of the Board of Trade headed the next division, which also featured groups from various ethnic lodges, including 200 of the Turner gymnasts dressed in white linen. Contingents of workingmen followed, paying their respects to a president who said he was not ashamed that he had once been "a hired laborer, mauling rails, on a flatboat—just what might happen to any poor man's son!" Nearly 300 members from the Journeymen Stonecutters' Association walked behind a banner with two sides, one reading IN UNION THERE IS STRENGTH and the other proclaiming WE UNITE TO PROTECT NOT TO INJURE.[3]

All through that night of May 1 and well into the next day, mourners stood in the mud and drizzle waiting to file through the courthouse for a last look at the man whose storied path to the White House had so often passed through their city. On May 2, after 125,000 people had gazed upon the face of their departed president, his coffin was escorted to St. Louis Depot on Canal Street by another elaborately organized procession led by a chorus of 250 Germans singing dirges. Lincoln's corpse was placed inside its specially built car, and at 9:30 a.m. the funeral train pulled out of the terminal carrying Illinois's "noblest son" to his final destination in Springfield, leaving behind a city whose people he had unified in life and, far more so, in death.[4]

After its journey through the cornfields and little prairie towns Lincoln had visited as a lawyer and campaigner, the funeral train arrived in Springfield. The president's body was buried the next day in Oak Ridge Cemetery, where the eulogist recalled the late Civil War as a momentous "contest for human freedom . . . not for this Republic merely, not for the Union simply, but to decide whether the people, as a people, were destined . . . to be subject to tyrants or aristocrats or class rule of any kind."[5]

Leading Illinois Republicans who gathered at Lincoln's grave on May 4, 1865, rejoiced that free labor had triumphed over the slave system in

President Lincoln's funeral hearse passing beneath the arch at 12th Street in Chicago, May 1, 1865

that great war now won. They believed a new nation had emerged from the bloody conflict, new because now all of its people were "wholly free." The "four million bondsmen the martyred emancipator had liberated" were, said the *Tribune,* a living epistle to Lincoln's immortality.[6] But were all the people now wholly free?

IN THE YEARS after Lincoln's death, emancipated slaves found many compelling reasons to question the meaning of their new freedom in the face of the reign of white terror that descended upon them. At the same time, for quite different reasons, workingmen, the very mechanics who benefited most from the free labor system Lincoln had extolled, began to doubt the nature of their liberty. A few months before the war ended, the nation's most influential trade union leader, William H. Sylvis, came to Chicago and sounded an alarm that echoed in many labor newspapers in

the closing months of the war. The president of the powerful Iron Molders' International Union excoriated employers who took advantage of
the war emergency to fatten their profits while keeping their employees
on lean wages. When union workers protested with strikes, politicians
called them traitors, soldiers drove them back to work, and many loyal
union men were fired and blacklisted by their bosses in retaliation. How,
Sylvis asked, could a republic at war with the principle of slavery make it
a felony for a workingman to exercise his right to protest, a right President Lincoln had once celebrated as the emblem of free labor? "What
would it profit us, as a nation," the labor leader wondered, if the Union
and its Constitution were preserved but essential republican principles
were violated? If the "greasy mechanics and horny-handed sons of toil"
who elected Abe Lincoln became slaves to work instead of self-educated
citizens and producers, what would become of the Republic?[7]

Sylvis told his iron molders that tyranny was based upon ignorance
compounded by "long hours, low wages and few privileges," while liberty
was founded on education and free association among workingmen. Only
when wage earners united could they achieve individual competence and
independence. Only then would they exercise a voice in determining
their share of the increased wealth and the expanded freedom that would
come to the nation after the war.[8]

America had never produced a labor leader as intelligent, articulate
and effective as William Sylvis. Born in western Pennsylvania to parents
in humble circumstances, young William was let out as a servant to a
wealthy neighbor who sent him to school and gave him the key to a good
library. Later, after helping in his father's wagon shop, Sylvis apprenticed
himself to a local iron foundry owner, a master craftsman who taught his
young helper the ancient arts of smelting and smithing and the methods of
making molten iron flow into wooden molds to shape the iron products he
had designed. After he married, the young molder moved to Philadelphia
to ply his trade, but he found it a struggle working long hours every day to
provide for his family and failing to rise above the level of manual laborer.[9]

William Sylvis found another way to raise himself up. He became secretary of his local union in 1859, and then two years later secretary of the
new National Union of Iron Molders. By this time Sylvis had decided that
mechanics were losing their independence and respectability because
certain owners monopolized branches of industry and used their power to
reduce wages. The rugged individualist was no match against these men
who used money and political clout to advance themselves at the expense

of their employees. "Single-handed, we can accomplish nothing," he wrote, "but united there is no power of wrong we may not openly defy."[10]

In these years before the Civil War, however, prospects for a united labor movement were bleak. Only a few unions, like those of printers, machinists and locomotive engineers, had created national organizations. Most trade unions functioned within local settings where they had been formed by craftsmen who still dreamed of being masters and proprietors of their own shops and employers of their own helpers. These artisans often used radical language to denounce the merchant capitalists, bankers and monopolists, the "purse proud aristocrats" and "blood sucking parasites" who lived off the honest producers. Yet antebellum labor unionists, even radicals, tended to be craft-conscious more than class-conscious, barring females and free blacks from their associations and turning their backs on the women, children and immigrant "wage slaves" who toiled in factories.[11]

Before 1860 common laborers and factory workers rarely formed lasting unions, and when they took concerted action, it was usually to resist wage cuts rather than to force employers to recognize their organizations. Their strikes were often ritualistic protests that rarely involved violent conflicts.[12] The one cause that brought diverse groups of workers together was the campaign to shorten the workday to ten hours. Initiated by journeymen carpenters and women textile workers in 1835, the crusade gained thousands of adherents in northern shops and factories and then faded in the 1850s. Middle-class reformers and politicians took up the cause and lobbied for ten-hour laws in legislative halls, but their moderate arguments for shorter hours failed to produce effective laws. At the onset of the Civil War the ten-hour movement was dead.

When northern artisans and mechanics left the shops to join the federal armed forces in 1861, trade unions all but disappeared. The largest group of Union soldiers consisted of farmers, but as more and more troops were conscripted, workingmen constituted a growing proportion of the northern armed forces, so that by the end of the war 421 of every 1,000 soldiers who served in the northern ranks were wage workers, as compared to 35 of every 1,000 who listed business and commercial occupations. With their sons, brothers, cousins and neighbors dying on southern battlefields, those mechanics who remained at work fashioning and feeding the Union war machine found themselves working shorthanded and toiling harder than ever for greenback wages that could not keep up with astounding increases in the cost of fuel, rent and foodstuffs.[13]

William Sylvis was well aware of these conditions when he became his union's national president in 1863. And so, as the War Between the States raged on, he decided it was time to bring the union back to the foundries, even if he had to do it single-handedly. He was thirty-six years old by then, "a medium-sized man, strongly built, of florid complexion, light beard and moustache, and a face and eyes beaming with intelligence," wrote one reporter. Still lean from his days at the forge, he drove himself mercilessly, giving speech after speech in a passionate style of oratory. That year he visited more than 100 foundries and organized many new locals. He wore the same suit until it became threadbare, and the scarf he wore was filled with little holes burned in it by the splashing of molten iron.[14]

With tenacity and boundless energy, William Sylvis rebuilt the Molders' Union into the strongest in the country, creating the first effectively administered national labor organization in history, with a dues-collection system, a real treasury and a strike fund. "From a mere pigmy, our union has grown in one short year to be a giant," he reported, "like a mighty oak with branches stretching out in every direction."[15]

By 1865, when Sylvis addressed his national convention in Chicago, he reported that nearly all the foundry owners in the nation had agreed to employ only molders who held a union card. One of the strongest local unions of iron molders flourished at Chicago's premier manufacturing plant, the farm reaper works owned and operated by Cyrus and Leander McCormick. Their employees struck four times for wage increases in 1863 and 1864, and won each time. Plant managers reported feeling powerless to resist the well-organized molders.[16] When the Civil War ended, Sylvis's molders constituted the vanguard of what promised to become the nation's first coordinated union movement, a new army of labor. Trade union officers like Sylvis were painfully aware, however, that powerful forces had already been mobilized to block their advance.

DURING THE WAR the iron molders and other trade unionists encountered new employers' associations formed to resist any union demands for wage increases or reduced hours; these groups usually succeeded in destroying the fledgling labor unions by imposing lockouts and breaking strikes. Once they gained the upper hand, united employers fired and blacklisted union men and demanded that those who returned to work sign "yellow-dog contracts" promising not to rejoin the union. This coordinated opposition from employers frightened Sylvis and convinced him that a violent collision between labor and capital was coming. He concluded that union workers needed a national labor federation "to protect the rights of mechanics from being trammeled throughout the length and breadth of the land."[17]

In charting a new course for the postbellum era, William Sylvis needed the help of a good navigator. He found one in Andrew C. Cameron of Chicago, the editor of a feisty labor newspaper called the *Workingman's Advocate.* Cameron had already been a combatant in early skirmishes with employers that broke out in Chicago while the Civil War still raged. He had come to America from Scotland as a young printer's apprentice, having learned the trade from his father in Berwick-on-Tweed, a historic center of Scottish resistance to English rule. He grew up during a time when the North Country was awash with a great mass movement for a People's Charter that would democratize the English Parliament and legalize universal manhood suffrage. The Chartist movement left a legacy that many English and Scottish workers carried to America: a tradition of questioning the new industrialism and of proposing checks on the free play of the market—all this based on an outlook with a "dangerous tenet: that production must be, not for profit, but for *use.*"[18]

After securing a position as a printer for the *Chicago Times* in 1860, Cameron emerged as the leader of a wartime strike against the paper's imperious publisher, Wilbur F. Storey, who had dismissed his union printers in order to hire cheaper hands.[19] Unable to state their case in the city's daily papers, the strikers formed their own opposition newspaper, the *Workingman's Advocate,* "devoted exclusively to the interests of the producing classes," and asked Andrew Cameron to be its editor. It was a task he performed with all the "vim and independence characteristic of a Scotch Covenanter who hated tyranny and oppression from what ever source."[20]

Cameron shared William Sylvis's concerns about the high-handed behavior of certain offensive employers during the Civil War.[21] As he saw it, greedy monopolists ignored worker sacrifices at home and on the field of battle while taking advantage of the war to freeze wages and pad their pockets with federal contracts as they cornered markets and fleeced their men. This behavior, he wrote in the *Workingman's Advocate,* had produced in Chicago and elsewhere a "general dissatisfaction with the existing state of affairs" and a yearning to expand the boundaries of freedom for the mechanic and the laborer. Sylvis and Cameron believed that Lin-

William H. Sylvis

coln's ideal notion of an equal partnership between labor and capital had died with the martyred president. They also thought that workingmen who depended on wages paid by an employer no longer believed they could raise themselves up and become self-made men, as the Illinois rail-splitter had done. The wage system itself had created two distinct and antagonistic classes now locked in what seemed like an "irrepressible conflict." And so, as peace finally came to a war-torn nation, Cameron believed that "another battle was announcing itself."[22]

There was a way to prevent the violent collision of labor and capital the labor leaders feared, a way for workers to gain more equally from "the privileges and blessings of those free institutions" they defended "by their manhood on many a bloody field of battle." The way forward could be paved by a powerful movement capable of winning a historic victory: legislation reducing the sunup-to-sundown workday to a humane length of eight hours. This achievement would be the first step toward what Sylvis called the "social emancipation" of working people.[23]

The inauguration of the eight-hour system would end the degradation of the endless workday. It would create new time for the kind of education workers needed to become more effective producers and more active citizens. Beyond this, self-education would allow workers to create a cooperative system of production that would eventually replace the current coercive system in which men were forced to sell their labor for wages.[24]

All these ideas had been articulated by the founder of the movement, a machinist from Massachusetts named Ira Steward. The self-taught Bay State mechanic had launched a wartime reform movement that infected masses of common people with a desire, a fever, for freedom and equality. Steward believed that the right of a free laborer to come and go as he pleased had been rendered "abstract" by a wage system that allowed employers to unilaterally set the terms of work, and then to collude among themselves to artificially limit wages and maintain long hours. Steward, an ardent abolitionist, rejoiced over the abolition of chattel slavery and then looked forward to the liberation of the wage earner, that "free" laborer who worked from sunup to sundown and instinctively felt that "something of slavery" still remained and that "something of freedom" was yet to come.[25]

In 1866, Steward's followers established eight-hour leagues across the land as workers organized huge public meetings and labor processions. That year workingmen celebrated the Fourth of July in Chicago and other northern cities by singing Civil War–era tunes like "John Brown's Body" with new words composed by eight-hour men.[26] This postwar insurgency impressed Karl Marx, who had followed Civil War events closely from England. In 1864 he helped create the International Workingmen's Association in London, whose founders hoped to make the eight-hour day a rallying cry around the world. The association and its program failed to draw a significant response from workers in Europe. Instead it was from the United States that the "tocsin" of revolutionary change could be heard. "Out of the death of slavery, a new and vigorous life at once arose," Marx wrote in *Capital.* "The first fruit of the Civil War was the eight hours agitation," which ran, he said, with the speed of an express train from the Atlantic to the Pacific.[27]

The evangelical work of the eight-hour leagues produced "a grand revival of the labor movement," as new organizations multiplied and isolated unions amalgamated, forming more than thirty new national trade unions and associations. In Chicago, a new Trades Assembly, led by Andrew Cameron, doubled in size to include twenty-four unions and 8,500 workers by the end of 1865. The city's Eight-Hour League established itself in various working-class wards and laid the groundwork for an aggressive legislative campaign to make eight hours a "legal day's work." On May 2, 1866, one year after the city paid its respects to its deceased president, Cameron announced with great fanfare the convening in Chicago of the first statewide convention of the Grand Eight-Hour League. The mechanics and workingmen who attended the gathering resolved to make Illinois the first state to legislate the eight-hour system.[28]

In August of 1866, Cameron joined forces with William Sylvis and other trade union chiefs to found the National Labor Union, the first organization of its kind. Cameron's *Advocate* became the union's official organ and, after the organization's second congress, he helped prepare a summary of its resolutions.[29] The elegantly worded manifesto Cameron and four other workingmen drafted insisted that the eight-hour system was essential to the health and well-being of wage earners and their families and that workers themselves must take united action to win it. Their concerted effort must allow no distinction by race or nationality and "no separation of Jew or Gentile, Christian or Infidel." The failure of earlier ten-hour laws demonstrated that well-meaning reformers could not exert the pressure needed to achieve this much-desired reform. Only workers themselves could hold state legislators accountable to their constituents.[30]

The vision of emancipation articulated by Cameron, Sylvis and the eight-hour men could be realized only if workers acted together as citizens to make the republican system of government work on their behalf. They would need to use the power of the national state to correct the abuses workingmen had suffered at the hands of judges who threw out shorter-hours laws and at the hands of employers who created "combinations" to limit their wages, set their hours and break their unions. Here was a bold, even audacious insistence that the Republic accede for the first time in history to a working-class demand. As a result, the call for the "eight-hour system" seemed to employers less like a proposal for reform and more like a demand for radical change in the political balance of power.

Before the Civil War, labor activists could not have imagined such a new order because they were for the most part disciples of Jefferson and Jackson, who feared government tyranny as much as overbearing monopoly. But after the emancipation and the beginnings of Reconstruction, they saw arising a new kind of national state, one powerful enough to eradicate slavery and construct a new democracy in its place.[31] As a result, organized workers now looked to Washington with hopes of gaining their own liberation.

In 1866, Andrew Cameron used his growing influence as editor of the *Advocate* and organizer of the Eight-Hour League to launch a nonpartisan lobbying campaign for a state law to reduce the length of the working day. While Democrats and Republicans fought bitterly in the state capitol over other issues, Eight-Hour League activists energetically worked the legislative halls in Springfield, seeking a legal limit to the workday. Cameron refused to pin his hopes on either the Republicans or the Democrats and directed his activists to work both sides of the aisle. His strategy worked, as bipartisan support for a shorter-hours bill materialized. On March 2, 1867, the Republican governor of Illinois, Richard J. Oglesby, signed the nation's first eight-hour law, to take effect on May 1.[32]

Chicago workers expressed their unbounded joy at a packed lakefront rally on March 30 that they had organized to "ratify" the law and to display their newfound power. Governor Oglesby spoke to them and invoked his days as a young carpenter and a friend of Abraham Lincoln, who, as president, had sympathized with the mechanics' plight during the Civil War. A popular personality in Illinois, "Uncle Dick" Oglesby had invented the "rail-splitter" image for Lincoln during his first presidential campaign. Four years later the two men ran on the same ticket in the fateful wartime election of 1864. Oglesby, a war hero with a Minié ball lodged in his chest, ran for governor that year and courageously stood by the president, defending his Emancipation Proclamation and facing down racist Democrats as he did. In April of 1865, Oglesby was at Lincoln's bedside as he lay dying, and on May 1 he was on the funeral train that carried his friend's body to Chicago. Now, just two years later, Oglesby stood before a Chicago crowd and declared that eight hours of work was enough to ask of workingmen and that eight hours of freedom during the day was "none too long for study and recreation."[33]

Oglesby then introduced the state's new attorney general, Robert Green Ingersoll, who was also a decorated colonel in the Union army and a devoted Lincoln man. Like the governor, the young lawyer was a Radical Republican who supported forceful measures to reconstruct and reform the Confederate states. Ingersoll was a rare character in American politics then, a freethinker who opposed the influence of religion in civic life. Like many Radical Republicans in 1867, he had warmly supported the eight-hour day, even though the party's business supporters opposed it. Indeed, Ingersoll outdid Governor Oglesby in his endorsement of the cause, evoking lusty cheers from the assembled workers when he proclaimed that the workday should be even less than eight hours so that wage earners could "educate themselves until they become the equals in all respects of any class."[34]

A Chicago labor activist who witnessed this occasion believed that it marked a new beginning for his city. "In this great emporium, to all outside appearances devoted to the interests of commerce and middle men, it was a sublime spectacle; this clasping of fraternal hands, between the laborer and the highest officers of the State, over the heads of defiant capitalists . . . ," the writer observed. "Our State is full of rail splitters turned statesmen, and they have proved . . . to be the strongest and toughest timber ever used in the construction of national councils."[35] Here was a pregnant moment in American political history, when the dream of universal freedom created a bond between Republicans like Richard Oglesby who were determined to reconstruct the South and labor reformers like Andrew Cameron, set to make the nation's wage workers truly free.

The advocates of the eight-hour system believed that the American economy was capable of expanding infinitely to benefit all productive citizens. Their own political economist, Ira Steward, rejected the prevailing theory, which held that at any given time there was a fund of fixed size from which each dollar a capitalist paid in wages meant a corresponding cut in profits. Few economists of the era thought of wages as elastic, able to rise with profits as productivity improved. Steward argued, however, that workers themselves cultivated tastes and desires that required a higher standard of living, whereas "men who labored incessantly" were "robbed of all ambition to ask for anything more than will satisfy their bodily necessities."[36] If the great Republic could guarantee a producer the free time required to become an educated citizen who expected a decent income, a worker could climb out of poverty to gain independence and self-respect.

The eight-hour day would benefit employer and worker alike by creating more leisure and stimulating the desire for more consumption, and thus the need for higher wages. And so, the advocates believed, this one reform would lift all boats on a swelling ocean of prosperity and calm the rough waves of class conflict. Some businessmen accused the eight-hour men of being "levelers" who wanted the state to confiscate private property. But this was a canard, Andrew Cameron replied. Why would the labor movement want to destroy capital, he asked, when labor was "the sole creator of capital" and when worker and employer shared a common interest in producing and marketing goods for their mutual benefit?[37]

Nowhere in America did the dream of mutual gains seem more possible than it did in Chicago after the Civil War, a place where the demand for labor seemed insatiable and where the prospects for prosperity seemed unlimited. It was the city of self-made men who started out wearing overalls and using tools and ended up wearing silk suits and high hats. It was a city that would, its promoters promised, become a paradise for workers *and* speculators.[38]

Chapter Two

A Paradise for Workers and Speculators

ON MAY 15, 1866, Chicago's leading men gathered ceremoniously to open a new city slaughterhouse on the South Branch of the Chicago River. All members of the Common Council were there in Bridgeport, according to the *Chicago Tribune,* together with the police and health commissioners, "a number of the city's butchers and a miscellaneous assemblage of persons who, for lack of a better classification, are set down as citizens." When the mayor cut the ribbon, the band burst into patriotic tunes, and among the dignitaries there was "lots of propulsive hand shaking and how-de-dos." Then, after the first ceremonial pig was cut, the river echoed with cheers.[1]

There was much to celebrate in Bridgeport that day. The city's slaughtering and packing industry had boomed during the Civil War because politicians had secured lucrative military contracts to supply rations. By 1864 the city's pork-processing operations consumed so many hogs that if they were placed in a line, one promoter boasted, it would stretch all the way from Chicago to New York.[2] And now, two years later, prospects for further growth seemed unlimited, not only for the pork producers, but for all the city's entrepreneurs.

With easy access to eastern markets via the Great Lakes and to the western states via the Illinois & Michigan Canal link to the Mississippi, Chicago's businessmen enjoyed decisive advantages over all regional competitors. By the end of the Civil War, their city was the western terminus of every major railroad east of the Mississippi. All the eastern railroads were built to Chicago, and the western roads were built from it. The Chicago, Burlington & Quincy made the crucial link to Omaha and a vast Nebraska territory of corn and hog production, a connection that would soon extend all the way to the Pacific.[3] As a result, the city became "the principal wholesale market for the entire mid-continent," serving "as the *entrepot*—the place in between—connecting eastern markets with vast western resource regions," according to historian William Cronon.[4]

As their iron rails reached out from Chicago, the railroads introduced modern capitalist business methods to the whole region, methods that had been perfected in the city on Lake Michigan. Chicago's grain business was so profitable that it generated "an orgy of hazardous undertakings" in spot trading and futures trading as the Board of Trade more than doubled its membership. The city's enormous trade on the Great Lakes also swelled during the war, and then exploded afterward. The lumber industry was served by its own fleet of boats, which brought hardwoods from the north country, and by the Illinois Central Railroad, which hauled cars filled with southern pine from Texas and Louisiana. All along the banks of the South Branch of the Chicago River stretched vast lumberyards where stacks of cut timber, some as high as 30 feet, spread out for acres. A large corps of immigrant lumber shovers and dockworkers moved the wood all day long to ships in fourteen water slips and to waiting flatcars on fourteen railroad spurs built by the Chicago, Burlington & Quincy Railroad. Its trains hauled scarce lumber all over the treeless expanses of the great West, where farmers and townspeople awaited shipments of prefabricated stores, houses, churches and schools—all made in Chicago. Along with cut and milled lumber, the westerners received a vast array of valued products from the booming metropolis: tables and upholstered chairs, men's overalls and women's dresses, church organs and parlor pianos, as well as cast-iron stoves and tools from the city's foundries, endless barrels of salted pork from the stockyards and lager beer from the German breweries, Bibles and dime novels from the shops on Printers Row, fancy notions from Marshall Field's dry-goods emporium and, most important of all, plowshares to break the prairies and mechanical harvesters to reap their bounty.[5]

The cornucopia of material goods that issued forth from hundreds of Chicago factories, mills, forges and shops required an ever-expanding army of willing wage workers. As a result, the city acted like an enormous magnet that dragged in farm boys from near and far, along with gamblers, Civil War veterans, tramping artisans and Canadian adventurers; from Europe came trainloads and boatloads of displaced peasants and farm laborers, as well as failed tradesmen, frustrated apprentices, political exiles and unwilling conscripts.[6] Chicago's population doubled during the 1860s mainly because so many Europeans arrived—37,000 from the German states, 20,000 from Ireland, along with roughly 9,000 from Norway and Sweden, 8,500 from England, Scotland and Wales, and 7,700 from the British provinces in Canada. Some of these newcomers became entrepreneurs, land speculators and merchants serving ethnic customers, but most of them entered a wage-earning workforce created by the city's explosive industrial growth. The number of Chicago workers employed in manufacturing multiplied five times during and after the Civil War, and most of these new workers were foreigners.[7]

The city fathers harbored no doubt that these newcomers to Chicago would succeed and become productive citizens and homeowners. Indeed, during the late 1860s, wages earned by skilled workers increased significantly in terms of daily rates and of purchasing power. Furthermore, low-cost housing became more available in Chicago than in most big cities because of the invention of the balloon-frame house, the oversupply of cheap lumber and the seemingly endless availability of housing lots stretching west and south from the business district. Thousands of pine-box shanties arose on the prairie along with poorly built business blocks. All this plus sidewalks covered with pine blocks and planks created what one historian called "long lines of well-laid kindling." Some Chicagoans realized the risks that lay in a city built of pine, but contractors ignored all warnings of danger and threw up new, cheap houses for workers as fast as they could.[8]

As the labor editor Andrew Cameron moved through the city in 1866, he observed a new "aristocracy" settled on a few islands of wealthy real estate in a vast sea of working people who trudged off to work in the dim morning light and returned to their pine-box homes in the dark. Like Dickens, the most popular English writer of the time, the Scottish reformer told a tale of two cities. He knew that thousands of ordinary people had achieved success in the city as real estate salesmen, contractors, saloonkeepers, store clerks, brokers and tradesmen of all kinds, but he worried about the others, the tens of thousands who feared that wage labor at long hours had become a life sentence.

Yet Cameron was an optimist. He believed that when the new Illinois eight-hour law took effect on May 1, 1867, wage earners would no longer have to endure "a protracted life of endless toil." Labor reform would rescue these floundering multitudes and help bring them to another shore, where they would enjoy the free time to better themselves and to work their way out of poverty.[9]

THE REALIZATION OF Andrew Cameron's vision required more than the goodwill of a governor and a state legislature; it required the assent of the city's employers. Chicago's hard-driving businessmen soon showed they had no such inclination when seventy manufacturers formed a united front to resist the new statute. These employers despised the eight-hour law, which seemed to them a foolish attempt to diminish the wealth of both workers and capitalists. After all, they asked, what employee would willingly sacrifice two or more hours' pay every day, and what employer would accept reduced output from employees? The eight-hour law's opponents simply rejected the theory that an employee who worked eight hours would produce more, earn more and then purchase more as a consumer. In any case, they insisted that such a statute violated a sacred principle: the right of each employee to make an individual contract with an employer. If eight hours became the legal workday, it would deny a worker the freedom to work for nine, ten, twelve or more hours. Businessmen also opposed laws of this kind because they extended the functions of republican government far beyond what they saw as their intended limits. Republican leaders like *Tribune* editor Joseph Medill believed federal legislation was required to guarantee universal manhood suffrage and equal rights, but the state had to stay out of the marketplace and avoid offering protection to certain groups.[10]

As Chicago employers mounted their resistance in the winter of 1867, a Boston labor newspaper warned its readers that capital had its back up.[11] Fearing the worst, Cameron and other labor leaders threatened a general strike if employers defied the law when it took effect on May 1. Hoping for the best, tens of thousands of workers gathered in Chicago that May Day for a march from the Union Stock Yards to celebrate the eight-hour law's inauguration. The *Times* described it as the "largest procession ever seen in the streets of Chicago." It included divisions from forty-four unions represented by workmen carrying banners inscribed with the symbols of their craft and the slogans of their cause, such as EIGHT HOURS AND NO CONCESSION and WE RESPECT THE LAWS OF THE STATE. The Stonecutters' Association sent a contingent of 259 men in white silk aprons marching with three horse-drawn wagons, including one with a large banner that read HAIL TO MAY 1, 1867, A DAY LONG TO BE REMEMBERED BY ALL WORKERS.[12]

The workers moved in an orderly fashion toward the lakefront, where they gathered to hear speeches in English and German from their leaders, who warned them that "capital" might undermine their victory. Anxiety rose in this massive crowd when the city's Republican mayor, J. B. Rice, appealed for compromise in case the employers refused to accept the law. Other Republican officials sent letters of support but did not appear. Governor Oglesby, who had spoken so boldly for eight hours in March, remained in Springfield on May 1 and sent no message.

On May 2 the largest Chicago employers refused to obey the new law and ordered their employees back to work for the customary ten or eleven hours. In response, worker protests and strikes closed railroad car shops, shipping depots, lumberyards and wood-planing mills. In the Irish section of Bridgeport, workers shut down all the packinghouses and rolling mills. The powerful Machinists' Union ordered members out of their shops, and the Iron Molders' Union banked the fires in all but eight of the city's foundries. The McCormicks opened the gate to their harvester factory on May 2, expecting the men to work ten hours as usual, and were surprised when the union workers left work after completing an eight-hour day. This action led Leander McCormick to complain bitterly to his brother Cyrus about his troubles with "the Eight-Hour men." He wanted a stronger man to boss the works, a replacement for the current foreman, a former molder who remained too close to the men. "The union is controlling our shop . . . ," Leander complained, "and we ought at whatever cost to hire men outside of it." This message presaged the outbreak of a nineteen-year war between the McCormicks and their union molders.[13]

On May 3 gangs of workingmen and boys roamed the city's factory and freight yard districts, brandishing sticks and fence posts and forcing many other laborers out of their factories. Rumors spread that the strikers had set fire to the Armour & Dole grain elevator and that scores of them had been shot dead by soldiers. On May 4 all Bridgeport seemed roused as a large body of strikers marched up Archer Avenue, its ranks swollen to 5,000 with boys and unemployed men who pulled more men out of factories, slashed drive belts on machines and released steam from boilers. Some of the Irish butchers, lumber shovers and iron rollers in the crowd had served in Colonel James Mulligan's Irish Brigade during the Appomattox campaign. The use of force seemed justifiable to these men who had so recently fought on southern battlefields where terrible violence and death had been constant realities. Some of these workers took up arms, telling reporters that if they were jailed for rioting, Governor Dick Oglesby, the former Union army colonel, would pardon them.[14] They were encouraged when the governor rejected Mayor Rice's appeal for the state militia and expressed his confidence that, despite the disturbances in Bridgeport, the labor movement's intentions remained peaceful. The governor did not, however, promise to enforce the state's eight-hour law.[15]

Mayor Rice soon took matters into his own hands, calling upon the Dearborn Light Artillery to support the Chicago police. He also issued an order making it a crime to take action against employees who wanted to work for ten or twelve hours a day. By May 5, police officers and troops had gained control of the city's troubled industrial zones and immigrant neighborhoods, and by May 8 the backbone of the protest strike had been broken. Despondent eight-hour men returned to shops and factories with the long workday still in effect. Union leaders bitterly denounced the politicians who had deserted the labor movement and desperately appealed for help from eight-hour leagues in other cities, but it was too late.[16]

The defeat that Chicago employers imposed on the strongest labor movement in the country during those first days of May in 1867 disheartened eight-hour activists across the land.[17] And in Illinois the experience of defeat carried a deeper meaning. The betrayal of the eight-hour law struck a blow at the labor reformers' belief that they could rely on enlightened legislation to free toilers from artificial restraints like long hours that kept them from joining the ranks of self-made men. Indeed, the repression of the May protests in Chicago nearly extinguished a vision of parity that labor reformers had kindled during the Civil War.

IN HIS BITTERNESS over the 1867 defeat, Andrew Cameron snapped at the men who returned to their ten-hour jobs, calling their retreat "craven." He also admitted that the May 1 strikes had been poorly organized and undisciplined and that the rioting on Halsted Street damaged the eight-hour movement's respectability. There must be no more "groping in the dark," Cameron declared, no more disunity of the kind that undermined the strike. He took a long view of the struggle for freedom, reminding his discouraged readers that "revolutions never go backwards." The strike of 1867 would be a stepping-stone on the path to future success, leading to the creation of a stronger organization and the enactment of national legislation that would benefit labor and capital.[18]

After state government failed them, the eight-hour men turned their energy toward Washington. Illinois officials had claimed the 1867 law, if enforced, would have put the state's businessmen at a disadvantage with regard to their out-of-state competitors. National legislation would render this objection moot. The eight-hour reformers had other reasons to feel optimistic. If Congress could amend the Constitution to prohibit involuntary servitude and pass a civil rights act that outlawed coercive labor contracts such as the Black Codes, then surely Congress could adopt the measures the eight-hour men proposed to end the tyranny of the endless workday.[19]

In 1868 delegates to a National Labor Union congress elected William Sylvis president, made A. C. Cameron's *Advocate* their official organ and dispatched representatives to Washington to lobby for an eight-hour law for government employees. Much to their delight, Congress enacted such a law on June 25, 1868, one that mandated an eight-hour day for mechanics and laborers employed by the federal government.[20]

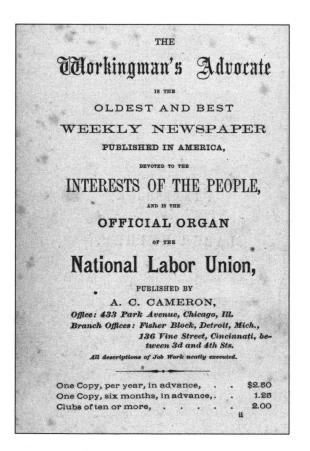

On the Fourth of July, Cameron trumpeted these glad tidings in his paper. He then reconvened the Eight-Hour Committee to plan a torchlight parade celebrating the first congressional victory that the labor movement had ever enjoyed. The procession that took place was, however, a pale reflection of the spectacular march to the lakeshore on May 1, 1867.[21]

The years that followed the defeat of the eight-hour strike were arduous ones for Chicago's workers, skilled and unskilled alike, as employers cut wages and hired newcomers, "green hands" willing to work for less pay. During the fall the ranks of unemployed people swelled and the lines of desperate people seeking charity lengthened. Of the forty trade unions that had marched in the grand procession on May Day a year before, only a few survived that grim winter.[22]

Everywhere he turned, it seemed, Cameron's efforts were repulsed, his hopes deflated. He even failed in his effort to put a legislative ban on convict labor. This new defeat was a painful coda to the betrayal of the 1867 law. Cameron's despair deepened when Washington officials refused to implement the eight-hour law for a few thousand mechanics employed by the federal government. Though President Ulysses S. Grant claimed to be in favor of the statute, his cabinet secretaries issued orders that negated the law by "virtually cheating workers" out of a portion of the pay they earned for eight hours' work.[23]

When William Sylvis died of stomach cancer in 1869 at the age of forty-one, the young labor movement he had inspired seemed to die with him. Sylvis's hopes for an emancipatory eight-hour law had been dashed by the realities of politics in Washington, and his dreams of a unified labor movement foundered on the rocks of race and ethnicity. Delegates to three National Labor Union congresses had listened respectfully to the celebrated reformer's appeal that "every union inculcate the grand ennobling idea that the interests of labor are one; that there should be no distinction of race or nationality," but each time they ignored him and refused to open their doors to black workers. The conventioneers had also listened to the president of the Colored Laborers' Union ask for their support for the reconstruction of the Old South, and they had heard his warning that the bloody struggle to grant the black man full citizenship would be "a complete failure" if he was barred from the nation's workshops, but they paid him no mind.[24]

Andrew Cameron delivered an eloquent eulogy to his friend Sylvis and returned to his desk at the *Advocate*, where he wrote renewed calls for racial equality in politics and industry. However, Cameron's hopes for a national labor movement based on egalitarianism were difficult to sustain after Sylvis's death. Indeed, the National Labor Union passed away soon after its leader died. Yet, something remained of William Sylvis's dream. The visionary iron molder left a legacy to future worker activists who would create the nation's first national labor movement. It was a legacy based on two powerful ideas: the idea of an eight-hour system that would allow the self-educated workman to rise out of wage dependency and the idea of one big labor movement that would unite working people, transcend their divisions and recapture the Republic for the great majority.[25]

In 1870, however, it seemed that even this intellectual inheritance would be lost forever. The year began with a hard and bitter winter for Chicago's working people. More than 20,000 "houseless wanderers" roamed the city by day and huddled in alleys and under bridges. The city's few existing unions shriveled up in the cold. It was then that Andrew Cameron sounded a bugle of retreat, announcing, without much emotion, that the Chicago Trades Assembly he had helped to create and lead through its glory days had died a natural death.

Gone was the spirit of solidarity that once infused the city's labor movement. German workers formed their own trades assembly and published their own newspaper, *Deutsche Arbeiter*, edited by a group of new exiles arrived from Germany who adhered to the socialist ideas of Ferdinand Lassalle and Karl Marx. But little came of their efforts, and these new arrivals soon disappeared from public view, submerged within the city's enormous population of German workers who were struggling to make their way in this workers' paradise.[26]

DURING THE LATE 1860s many of the European immigrants flooding into the city could not gain as much access to employment and housing as those who had arrived before the Civil War, according to an agent for the German Society of Chicago. The city's reputation for opportunity continued to draw a mass of people from overseas who came to Chicago expecting to find "a new El Dorado" but instead found a city filled with jobless and homeless immigrants suffering from hunger and misery.[27] An abundance of products was available for purchase in Chicago's many stores, but these goods were inaccessible to most of the newcomers. Houses were readily available to immigrants who could afford small down payments, but many newcomers did not have the cash or the income to make mortgage payments, so they flopped into rooming houses, crowded into the cramped quarters of relatives or camped outdoors. Those who could manage mortgages moved into houses in a vast district of pine shanties that spread west from the Chicago River's South Branch and farther south, to Bridgeport below the river, where open sewers and unpaved streets with pools of waste emitted a stench noxious enough to asphyxiate cats and dogs.[28]

During the Civil War era well-to-do merchants and lawyers had lived on the same streets as printers, tailors and brewers, and, in some cases, not far from the pine-box neighborhoods of factory hands and construction workers. But as the city's wealth in real and personal property grew (ninefold in the 1860s), the nouveaux riches moved uptown toward the new Lincoln Park and out of the West End to Union Park and to the town houses along tree-lined Washington Boulevard—far from the filthy, stinking streets of the old inner city.[29] In 1870 the median value of real estate properties owned by the upper classes averaged nearly ten times the valuation of homes owned by unskilled workers. Many clerks, managers and salesmen also bought more modest houses on the North and Far West sides. As a result, homeownership increased to 38 percent among business and professional men at a time when working-class homeownership declined.[30]

These social differences between the rich and the working poor were masked to Chicago's many wide-eyed visitors. Tourists invariably expressed amazement at the city's physical characteristics—the awesome distances it encompassed, the range of industries it incorporated, the huge volume of train traffic it handled, the stunning height of its grain elevators and office buildings, the unending passage of ships that came and went from its river and harbor every day. These observers were awed by the city's audacity in reversing the flow of the Chicago River so that its foul wastes would flow down a canal and into the Illinois and Mississippi rivers, and they were impressed by its ingenuity in creating a new water system to draw lake waters into its tunnels—a feat of engineering genius symbolized by a grand new water tower that rose 138 feet into the sky. They were taken, above all, with the city's sheer energy and vitality.[31]

A leading promoter of Chicago as the Empire City of the West was General Philip Sheridan, the Civil War hero who now commanded the U.S. Army's Division of the Missouri, with forces deployed as far south as Texas and as far west as Montana. Sheridan, knowing the city's centrality, had moved his divisional headquarters there from St. Louis. He rarely missed a chance to sing Chicago's praises, and he did so in 1870 when he traveled to France at the end of the Franco-Prussian War. When the general met with the German chancellor Otto von Bismarck after his forces defeated the army of Napoleon III, the two men reviewed the conquering troops and the "Iron Duke" told Sheridan: "I wish I could go to America, if only to see that Chicago."[32]

Chicago's entrepreneurs and promoters naturally basked in this kind of flattering attention, but some old settlers feared that the city's performance as a moneymaking machine would make it "a town of mere traders and money getters; crude, unlettered, sharp, and grasping." They feared that the civic virtue and sense of community they had cultivated would be lost amid the endless and ruthless competition for gain. The pioneers also worried that city government, fragile as it was, would simply become an arena for the buying and selling of influence.[33]

More than any other city in the nation, Chicago came to embody what Mark Twain and others would call the Gilded Age—an age of excess when businessmen accumulated huge fortunes, constructed lavish mansions, exploited the public domain and corrupted public officials. No one captured the spirit of the age better than Walt Whitman, who wrote in 1871 of cities that reeked with "robbery and scoundrelism."[34] The nation was like a ship sailing in a dangerous sea of seething currents without a first-class captain. Of all the "dark undercurrents" Whitman sensed beneath that sea, none was more dangerous "than having certain portions of the people set off from the rest like a line drawn—they not as privileged as others, but degraded, humiliated, made of no account."[35]

The famous poet put aside these fears, however, because he was seized with the hubris of Gilded Age nationalism. For all the danger that lay ahead as the "labor question" exposed "a yawning gulf" between the classes, it seemed to Whitman "as if the Almighty had spread before this nation charts of imperial destinies, as dazzling as the sun." That sun shone over a people "making a new history, a history of democracy," and that sun was moving west from Whitman's beloved Brooklyn toward Chicago and the vast Pacific. "In a few years," he predicted, "the dominion heart of America will be far inland toward the West." There in that region of "giant growth" Americans were fulfilling their destiny as a people. It was an epic era, one of those times, Whitman wrote, when "[a]ll goes upward and outward, nothing collapses."[36]

Chapter Three

We May Not Always Be So Secure

ALL DURING THE LATE SUMMER of 1870, as Chicago's economy roared on, readers of the city's dailies had intently followed news of the Franco-Prussian War: first the stunning news of the French army's defeat at Sedan, and then the capture of Napoleon III and the fall of his empire. Chicagoans pondered these events in the Old World with the assurance that their bloody war was behind them and that peace and prosperity now reigned.

In September all eyes turned to Paris, where citizens rushed to join a democratized National Guard and to defend their city when it fell under siege. When an armistice was signed in January of 1871, Parisians denounced it and crowds marched to the Bastille flying the tricolor and the red flag of the International. Within a month "a mysterious authority made itself felt in Paris" as vigilance committees appeared throughout the city. In March, just as the French army seemed ready to restore order, even more sensational news appeared in the dailies: the people of Paris were refusing to surrender their arms. Indeed, when French generals ordered the Parisian National Guard to disarm, the guardsmen turned their guns on their own army generals. Government forces withdrew to Versailles, now the seat of a new provisional government, and on March 28 the citizens of the former capital created an independent Commune of Paris. Americans were utterly fascinated by this news, and the press fed their hunger for information about the momentous event. As a result, the Commune became an even bigger story than the Franco-Prussian War had been.[1]

When the French army laid siege to Paris and hostilities began, the *Chicago Tribune*'s reporters covered the fighting much as they had during the American Civil War. Indeed, many Americans, notably Republican leaders like Senator Charles Sumner, identified with the citizens of Paris who were fighting to create their own republic against the forces of a corrupt regime whose leaders had surrendered abjectly to the Iron Duke and his Prussian forces.

As the crisis deepened, however, American newspapers increasingly portrayed the Parisians as communists who confiscated property and as atheists who closed churches.[2] The brave citizens of Paris, first described as rugged democrats and true republicans, now seemed more akin to the uncivilized elements that threatened America—the "savage tribes" of Indians on the plains and the "dangerous classes" of tramps and criminals in the cities. When the Commune's defenses broke down on May 21, 1871, the *Chicago Tribune* hailed the breach of the city walls. Comparing the Communards to the Comanches who raided the Texas frontier, its editors urged the "mowing down" of rebellious Parisians "without compunction or hesitation."[3]

La semaine sanglante—the week of blood—had begun as regular army troops took the city street by street, executing citizen soldiers of the Parisian National Guard as soon as they surrendered. In retaliation, the Communards killed scores of hostages and burned large sections of the city to the ground. By the time the killing ended, at least 25,000 Parisians, including many unarmed citizens, had been slaughtered by French army troops.[4]

These cataclysmic events in France struck Americans as amazing and distressing. The bloody disaster cried out for explanation. In response, a flood of interpretations appeared in the months following the civil war in France. Major illustrated weeklies published lurid drawings of Paris scenes, of buildings gutted by fire, monuments toppled, churches destroyed and citizens executed, including one showing the death of a *"petroleuse"*—a red-capped, bare-breasted woman accused of incendiary acts. Cartoonist Thomas Nast drew a picture of what the Commune would look like in an American city. Instant histories were produced, along with dime novels, short stories, poems and then, later in the fall, theatricals and artistic representations in the form of panoramas.[5]

News of the Commune seemed exotic to most Americans, but some commentators wondered if a phenomenon like this could appear in one of their great cities, such as New York or Chicago, where vast hordes of poor immigrants held mysterious views of America and harbored subversive elements in their midst.[6] One of these observers, Henry Ward Beecher, the most influential clergyman in the nation, preached a widely reported sermon in which he reviewed the wantonness of the destruction in Paris and likened it to the terrors of the French Revolution. He trusted that the religious faith of Americans would prevent such a godless outbreak in our cities. The nation would be spared the terror that afflicted Paris as long as America remained without an aristocracy, as long as it maintained a free press and offered free education, as long as it was blessed with cheap land for farming; but Beecher also warned his fellow citizens: "we may not always be so secure." He feared that an eruption like the one in Paris might someday occur here if the country stratified itself as European nations had, and if the upper classes did not show more concern for the poor.[7]

Andrew Cameron devoted a great deal of attention to the Commune and its meaning in his *Workingman's Advocate.*[8] Without comment, he ran in serial form sections of Karl Marx's *Civil War in France,* a fervid and favorable portrayal of the Communards.[9] Cameron did not endorse the revolutionary methods Marx espoused; nor did he excuse the incendiary acts of the Parisian street fighters. He did, however, tell his American readers that the people of the Commune "fought and fell for the rights you either enjoy or are striving for, *i.e.,* the right for self-government and the rights of the laborer to the fruits of his toil." He concluded by quoting Wendell Phillips, the abolitionist-turned-labor-reformer, who had declared: "Scratch the surface . . . in every city on the American continent and you will find the causes which created the Commune."[10]

BY THE TIME summer turned to fall in 1871, discussion of the Commune had disappeared from the press. The talk was all about business, because Chicagoans were enjoying another year of the sort of borrowing and investing, speculating and moneymaking that attracted hordes of newcomers each month. Banks recklessly lent money to entrepreneurs who were seriously depleting the cash reserves they held against liabilities, but business confidence kept rising, and still the city's economy seemed destined to grow relentlessly and to create enough wealth for all. Despite widening class divisions, Chicago's people shared a sense of pride in their thriving city. So many of the city's self-made men had risen from low estate that poor folks could believe that they too would be beneficiaries of Chicago's rapidly expanding wealth.[11]

In one night of horror, on October 8, 1871, all these dreams went up in smoke when most of the city burned to the ground in a fierce whirlwind of fire that reduced 17,450 buildings to ashes. The fire started in a miserable slum of wooden shacks around DeKoven Street on the West Side and quickly leapt the Chicago River, devastating the entire downtown business district and most of the North Side up to Lincoln Park. Humble workers' dwellings and marble mansions on the North Side, factories, lumberyards, banks, even City Hall and the *Tribune* building—all were incinerated by the holocaust. One hundred twenty corpses were found in the vast burned-over district, and many more bodies of missing persons were never recovered. Chicago, "unequalled before in enterprise and good fortune," said one newspaper, was now "unapproachable in calamity."[12]

An immense body of literature appeared as writers struggled to make sense of the tragedy. Many survivors said the Great Chicago Fire had created a communal sense of shared suffering in which personal suspicions and social distinctions disappeared and in which the virtues of Christianity and democracy prevailed. Few escaped the suffering, and for a few harrowing days the rich and the poor stood on common ground.[13]

Yet these inspiring stories of people coping together with a great disaster were overshadowed by horror stories of evil demons let loose in the chaos. The *Chicago Evening Post* said the blaze released "obscene birds of the night" from the city's worst districts: villainous men, "haggard with debauch . . . shameless white men, negroes with stolid faces" glided through the fleeing masses "like vultures in search of prey." Poor women with tattered dresses, hollow eyes and brazen faces "moved here and there, stealing . . . and laughing with one another at some particularly 'splendid' gush of flame." There were reports of riffraff actually fanning the flames and spreading the fire, and of aroused citizens lynching looters and arsonists. These accounts—all fabricated—fed nascent fears of the outcasts who dwelled deep in the city's bowels among the "dangerous classes."[14]

While some newspapers spread wild rumors about demon arsonists and avenging vigilantes, one editor turned boldly to the task ahead. The day after the fire, Joseph Medill headlined the *Tribune* with the words CHICAGO MUST RISE AGAIN. This command thrilled the nation and evoked the ethos that made the city great, a symbol of the age. But the bravado of confident city leaders like Medill masked a fear that their city remained vulnerable to another cataclysm.[15] Chicagoans could not bring them-

A drawing from Frank Leslie's Illustrated Newspaper *in which the artist imagines the chaos and social leveling that followed the Chicago fire*

selves to believe that the devastating holocaust was simply an act of God or a curse of Satan. They suspected that certain human beings within the city itself were responsible, people who refused to live by the Yankee values and Protestant ethics the city's leaders espoused. Unless the best men took action and removed the city's corrupt politicians from the scene, the catastrophe might be followed by thieving, rioting and, something worse, anarchy.[16]

While the fire's embers still smoldered, several downtown businessmen hired an ambitious Scottish immigrant named Allan Pinkerton to post armed men as guards around their property. Already well known for his Civil War activity protecting President Lincoln and sending spies behind enemy lines, Pinkerton ordered his guards to shoot any person stealing or attempting to steal. Two days after the event, a larger group of large property owners convinced the Republican mayor to place the city under martial law. The Civil War hero and Indian fighter General Philip Sheridan quickly took charge of militia and regular regiments. The elected police commissioner, an Irish Catholic with a labor constituency, protested this usurpation of his authority, as did the governor of Illinois, who said the mayor's order violated the state's rights, but to no avail.

Chicago's ruling elites meant to demonstrate their power and extend their control over the city in this critical period.[17]

As prominent Chicagoans acted to discourage any kind of disorder, they speculated endlessly on what caused the fire. The most popular story blamed a poor Irish woman, Mrs. O'Leary, for allowing her cow to kick over a lantern in her barn—a legendary account that placed responsibility on the shoulders of the lower-class immigrants. A. C. Cameron objected to these attempts to blame the main victims of the fire—the working people who were the largest element of the 64,000 people left homeless. Unlike well-connected merchant and professional families, these poor people usually had no friends or relatives to shelter them in the outlying neighborhoods and nearby. The dispossessed stood hunched over in soup lines and gathered around campfires where they boiled fetid water hoping to escape cholera and typhoid. At night they tried to sleep in tents on the charred prairie grounds as packs of dogs and rats hovered around them in the dark.[18]

Other commentators looked outside Chicago to find the cause of the disaster, which reminded them of the horrible blazes set by the desperate Communards in their last days; they wondered aloud if there was a connection. One imaginative writer suggested that a "firebird" had risen out of the Paris ashes and flown over the ocean to deliver a "scourge upon the queen city of the West." The *Chicago Times* even printed a "confession" of a "Communist incendiary" who had been sent from Paris by the Communist International to stir up strife between the mechanics of the city and their employers.[19]

Tribune editor Medill conceded that many people believed communists were "a secret power" working to undermine society, but he dismissed this confession as a phony. Furthermore, he explained, Marx's International had been nearly destroyed after the fall of the Commune. In any case, he added, he knew American members of the body, and they included more reformers than incendiaries. "The crowning evil of all times of tumult and disaster is suspicion," Medill opined. The Communist International had become the "great bugbear of modern times," but only timid men relied upon simple explanations for every calamity. Bold men assessed the real causes and set about eliminating them.[20]

Like other business leaders, the *Tribune* editor found more mundane but nonetheless troublesome explanations for the Great Fire. The much-despised ward politicians, the "bummers" who controlled the city's council of aldermen and its zoning practices, had allowed poor working

Joseph Medill

people to occupy a forest of pine dwellings that provided ample fuel to feed the holocaust.[21] Thus, even while he dismissed the rumor that a communist set the fire, Medill indicated that the irresponsible immigrants were to blame for the blaze having leapt across the river from a shantytown and laid waste to the business district.[22]

LESS THAN A MONTH after the fire Joseph Medill mounted a reform campaign for mayor, declaring he was "unalterably opposed from this time forward to the erection of a single wooden building within the limits of Chicago."[23] In November of 1871 he won an easy victory on the Union Fireproof Reform ticket. The new mayor promised that the poor would be fed and that the city would be rebuilt safely with fireproof construction.[24] Medill's plans to protect the city soon backfired, however. His attack on irresponsible home builders smacked of class prejudice in the minds of middle-class and working-class residents who said they could not afford to build brick homes that cost twice as much as wooden dwellings. As a result, they would be compelled to sell their land to "greedy land speculators" at "ruinous prices."[25] Their rhetorical response was soon followed, suddenly and unexpectedly, by mass action when a huge crowd composed largely of law-abiding Germans from the North and West sides stormed the Common Council chamber to protest the mayor's reform. The protesters were especially angry because they had worked hard and saved enough money to achieve the highest level of home ownership in the city, higher, in fact, than that of native-born Americans. Appealing to their immigrant aldermen, the foreign-born home owners easily created enough opposition in the Common Council to prevent Medill from banning all low-cost wooden housing.[26]

Before the furor over the housing ban died down, immigrant Chicago rose again, almost as one body, to stop another ill-fated reform. In 1873 a Committee of Seventy composed of leading citizens and clergymen convinced Mayor Medill to order the city's thousands of saloons to close on Sunday afternoon, a time when foreign-born workingmen loved to congregate in their favorite public drinking houses.[27] As a result, immigrant Chicago was thoroughly aroused. "Great, suffocating, mass meetings were held in every ward, every precinct," wrote one reporter, "and the Medill administration was everywhere denounced, lampooned, ridiculed, excoriated" by leaders of a new polyglot People's Party formed entirely for the purpose of removing the haughty Yankee mayor from City Hall.[28]

In the November 1873 city elections the new People's Party swept Joseph Medill from office, pulling thousands of new working-class voters to the polls.[29] The city's socialists, who emerged from the underground during the protests against City Hall, were suddenly encouraged, believing that they could form a labor party that might win an election in the future. A Swedish socialist said that the election had been a rude awakening for Medill and other people who came to Chicago from New England and had no idea that there was a "working class among them."[30]

Yet, after gaining office, People's Party officials refused to rock the boat. The Common Council not only refrained from raising taxes; the new populist mayor neglected to collect back taxes from delinquent property owners. In a city where property ruled, large landowners, bankers, speculators, merchants and manufacturers effectively blocked any civic measures they regarded as too costly.[31]

Even though they lost control of City Hall in 1873, Chicago's top businessmen remained confident that the laissez-faire policies they favored would prevail and would restore the city's economic power. Their confidence was rewarded when commercial and industrial activity rebounded, and businesses turned greater profits than they had before the Great Fire. Chicago had conquered disaster in a way that expressed to the London *Times* the "concentrated essence of Americanism."[32]

In this heady atmosphere the specter of the fire-breathing Communards faded. No commune could appear in this gifted city, opined the *Tribune*, because American workers had no inclination to turn against the rich and powerful. All the typical wage earner wanted or needed was a comfortable home and a larger wage; because these desires could be easily met, it would be impossible for a commune to arise in Chicago.[33]

THE CONFIDENCE OF Chicago's leading men held firm even after a financial panic struck in the East during the fall of 1873; and it prevailed when city bankers called in loans they had recklessly made to speculators and entrepreneurs. There was no way of escaping panic, however, when twenty big banks failed, along with nearly all of the city's savings institutions, sweeping away large fortunes and small accounts alike. The business palsy spread further when railroads and factories dismissed employees and slashed wages. New construction, which had raced ahead in the postfire years, slowed to a crawl. And it was clear that the city's miraculous reconstruction period had ended.[34]

As conditions worsened during the fall, Chicago's working people looked for food where they could find it, begging for it on the streets or crowding saloons for free lunches. When Thanksgiving arrived, the streets were crowded with tramps, and police station basements were filled every night with homeless wanderers. Still, not a ripple of unrest appeared in this river of dispossessed humanity.

Then, on December 21, 1873, an unexpected event disturbed the calm. On that cold evening more than 5,000 workers squeezed into Vorwärts Turner Hall on the West Side for a meeting to demand aid for the unemployed and their hungry families. Organized by German socialists who had formed a workers' association, the meeting featured speakers in English, German, Norwegian, French and Polish; all of them demanded that the city find work for those who were willing and able to labor. Furthermore, the protesters insisted that aid should be provided for the rest from the municipal treasury and that such aid should be distributed by a committee appointed by workers, not by the agents of businessmen who controlled the Chicago Relief and Aid Society, the private charitable association assigned to the task by the mayor when millions of dollars in aid money had poured into the city after the fire.

The society carefully investigated the lives of job applicants to make sure they were not pretending to be needy. The principle was that benevolence toward the poor should not derive from sympathy or pity, but from a well-considered strategy for reforming the indigent through work. The relief society abided by a simple rule: "He who does not work does not eat."[35] When the depression hit two years after the fire, the society, which still retained large sums of fire relief money, became a target of protest.

Those attending the Turner Hall protest meeting on December 21, 1873, demanded that the city recover funds still held by the Relief and Aid Society, whose directors they criticized for allowing rings of speculators to use the money for corrupt purposes while denying it to the distressed and impoverished. The protesters appointed a committee to deliver their demands to City Hall; and, to make a bigger impression, they called for a delegation of unemployed workingmen to accompany their spokesmen. The response to this plea startled all Chicago.

The next evening 20,000 workingmen of various nationalities assembled and then formed up behind the committee of eight, ready to march downtown. "The whole working-class population seemed magically to have drawn together," wrote the journalist Floyd Dell. "There appeared to be no leaders, but the men fell into orderly lines; and they marched, sometimes hand in hand, as a funeral procession to city hall." Many carried banners that read BREAD OR WORK. To astonished observers the solemn procession looked more like a well-drilled and disciplined military body than a crowd of protesters. This unprecedented march of the unemployed made a huge impression on the city councilmen, composed mostly of immigrant aldermen, and on the mayor, who had been elected as a candidate of the People's Party.[36]

The city was "entirely unprepared for anything of the kind," declared Horace White, the liberal Republican who succeeded Medill as editor of the *Tribune*. "The fraternization of immigrants of different nativities is not often observed in America," the editor explained. If they ever united, it would not be "for love of one another" but in "opposition to some common enemy" and in favor of some attainment that they all want "but which, divided, they are powerless to obtain."[37] Even more amazing was the protesters' demand for "bread or work," which struck the city "like lightning from a clear, blue sky." As far as White knew, nothing like this had ever been proposed by Americans. The new coalition of foreign nationalities obviously had some alien, un-American objective in mind, for it was led by men with ideas "wild and subversive of society itself."[38]

The unemployed movement's leaders pressed their case for days thereafter, and newspaper editors, previously unaware of the socialists' presence in the city, felt compelled to answer the demands and arguments of the so-called internationals. The *Tribune* called attention to a particularly dangerous new idea the socialists introduced—"the right to work." If the government provided work for the unemployed, these workingmen would lose any "inducement to take care of themselves." The socialists had been fooled by reading Karl Marx, whose writings had persuaded them to reject what the paper called the "immutable laws of our political economy." In so doing, they were acting like the Mohammedans who rejected Christianity.[39]

The city's businessmen refused to debate with the socialists; they were men of action, not men of words, and they were determined to prevent any more intimidating marches of the unemployed, or any repeat of the frightening general strike they experienced in May of 1867. With these concerns in mind, a group of important entrepreneurs gathered the following April to make plans to create their own militia company. These activists included many of the city's top hundred merchants, manufacturers, bankers and lawyers who had earlier formed a Citizens' Association; its leaders now began to raise the first funds needed to arm and outfit a businessmen's militia unit, called the First Regiment of the Illinois National Guard.

The new association's leaders also prepared to move against the incumbent People's Party, whose officials, including the city's Irish police commissioner, seemed far too sympathetic to the socialist-led demonstrators. The president, a wholesale merchant, declared that an excess of democracy had put "political power in the hands of the baser part of the community" and disenfranchised "the best part." The Citizens' Association would provide the organization these "best men" needed to take their city back from the bummers of the People's Party, who were branded by the *Chicago Times* as a bunch of "pimps, grogshop loafers, communist *lazzaroni* and other political deadbeats."[40]

The socialists nursed their own grievances against People's Party officials whose sympathy for the unemployed was not matched with any action. Therefore, socialist leaders decided to create an organization to sustain the movement for public relief and public works. In February of 1874 they founded the Workingmen's Party of Illinois, composed of ten German clubs as well as individual Bohemian, Polish, Irish and Scandinavian clubs. The party then established a German weekly newspaper, *Der Vorbote,* and put up socialist candidates to challenge the Republican machine in North Town during the spring elections.[41]

Chicago's German socialists maintained links with the International Workingmen's Association, which Karl Marx had directed from London until he and Friedrich Engels decided to move its headquarters to New York in 1872. The International's original stronghold in Paris had been destroyed along with the Commune, and in the aftermath Marx and Engels feared a takeover by anarchists loyal to their rival, the charismatic Russian insurrectionist Mikhail Bakunin.[42]

Ideological disputes among European Marxists and anarchists meant little in Chicago, however. Local socialists ignored commands from Marx's lieutenants in New York and charted their own course, plunging into electoral politics, opening their ranks to lawyers, saloonkeepers and tradesmen, and welcoming women who had been discouraged by the expulsion of the feminists Victoria Woodhull and Tennessee Claflin from the New York section. When a group of Chicagoans formed an English-speaking section of the International in the spring of 1874, they took on a new name, the International Working People's Association (IWPA), because there were plenty of women who wanted to join.[43]

The Internationals canvassed the city's immigrant wards in the spring elections of 1874, but Workingmen's Party candidates failed to loosen the grip the Republicans and Democrats held over different tribes of working-class voters. After the campaign, the German socialists in the party turned away from electoral competition and adopted Karl Marx's strategy of organizing workers: mobilizing the unemployed and building class-conscious trade unions as a basis for future political action.[44]

Marx's German followers in Chicago could hardly have chosen a worse time to implement such a grand strategy. As the panic deepened, employers laid off thousands of workers and locked out union members when they resisted wage cuts. For instance, the union iron molders at McCormick's Reaper Works struck to protest a drastic reduction in pay and held out for two months, but when the owners refused to negotiate, the strikers gave in and returned to work. The McCormicks, having demonstrated that resistance was futile, promptly slashed wages for workers in the rest of the plant. In the same year the Knights of St. Crispin, the only union to have organized factory workers, suffered a crushing defeat when shoe manufacturers locked them out and replaced them with "green hands." Even well-paid union craftsmen who enjoyed good relations with employers suddenly felt defensive. "No sooner does a depression in the trade set in than all expressions of friendship with the toiler are forgotten," remarked the conservative head of the iron puddlers' union, the Sons of Vulcan. Meanwhile, the editor of the industry journal *Iron Age* bluntly explained the situation as he saw it: if employers refused all concessions to unions and forced wages down to the lowest rates, simple workingmen would realize that they had been misled by demagogues and agitators who defied the "beneficent natural laws of progress and development."[45]

Newspaper editors also defended wage cuts, not just as economic necessities, but as moral instructions to misguided union workers. Employers could now take back everything they had conceded to union employees, said the *New York Times,* and then "bring wages down for all time." If workers resisted with some "insane imitations of the miserable class warfare" afflicting Europe, they should be replaced by men who understood the law of supply and demand. The results of the depression were not all evil, according to the *Chicago Evening Journal.* It would be good if the crisis taught workers "the folly and danger of trade organizations, strikes and combinations against . . . capital."[46]

Stern editorial prescriptions combined with the harsh medicine of layoffs and wage cuts were expected to cure workingmen of the delusions they acquired from socialists and trade unionists. If these remedies failed, more forceful measures should be taken. When the Workingmen's Party organized another march on the Relief and Aid Society, its organizers were intimidated by the appearance of a large armed force of policemen reinforced by the new First Regiment, a unit comprised of militiamen who were largely clerks, bookkeepers and managers of Chicago firms. Frightened by this show of force, unemployed workers stayed off the streets.[47] The call to arms issued by the Citizens' Association reassured Chicago's commercial and industrial leaders that the city would soon be back in the firm control of its "best men."

DURING THE SPRING of 1874, Chicagoans could look back on five years of terrible trouble when they had endured more fear and anxiety than other urban dwellers experienced in a lifetime. During that time social tensions had been ratcheted up again and again, creating hostile feelings among fellow citizens, common enough in "miserable" European cities, but previously unknown to Americans. The middle and upper classes had been frightened by the most violent general strike the nation had experienced, one that led to the worst riots a city had endured after the Civil War. Three years later Chicagoans survived the most catastrophic fire an American city had ever suffered—a disaster that leveled social distinctions and threatened the city with anarchy. After an exhilarating period of recovery and reconstruction, wealthy Chicagoans had been surprised when immigrants stormed City Hall in 1872 to protest the ban on wooden housing and public drinking on Sunday; this riotous behavior was followed late in 1873 by even more disturbing events, when the foreigners in the People's Party won control of city government and when the socialists appeared out of nowhere to mobilize the unemployed and to make unimaginable demands for work and relief. In May of 1874 it appeared the troubles might end: the socialists had been vanquished at the polls, strikers had been put back to work and the unemployed marchers had disappeared from the streets. The police and the militia seemed to be in firm control of the city, and yet, as they faced a second year of depression, few Chicago businessmen felt relaxed.

Chapter Four

A Liberty-Thirsty People

MAY 1874–MARCH 1876

WHILE COLD WEATHER lingered into the spring of 1874, unemployed people thronged the West Side. They looked for free lunches in saloons, surrounded the city's police stations seeking shelter in the night and prowled the factory districts hoping to find the odd job. And despite it all, trains and boats still arrived bringing more job seekers and fortune hunters to Chicago. Among the new arrivals were militant nationalists from Ireland and Poland and, in even greater numbers, socialists from Germany, Bohemia and Scandinavia. Many were admirers of the Paris Commune, and some were willing recruits for the International and its new Workingmen's Party. The *Tribune* expressed alarm over this influx of political exiles who swore loyalty not to their new nation, but to the Communist International formerly headquartered in London. Its leaders, the paper charged, were secretly manipulating the new socialist party and were "maturing plans to burn down Chicago and other large cities in the United States."[1]

Given these anxieties about the arrival of internationalists from European cities, no one noticed the small eddy of former Confederate rebels who made their way to Chicago, and no one would have guessed that one of them would become the most feared agitator in the city.[2] He came not from London, but from Waco, Texas, and his name was Albert R. Parsons.

Sometime in 1874, Parsons, accompanied by his wife, Lucy, arrived at the old St. Louis Depot wedged between Canal Street and the Chicago River. As they stepped out of the smoking station, the great pounding city would have assaulted their senses: steam engines hissing and clanging behind them in the depot, boat horns bleating on the river, horse-drawn trolleys careening down Canal Street, men shouting at each other to be heard above the unceasing din.

Albert was a slender young man with a sunburned face and the long mustaches favored by ex-soldiers. Though short in stature, he carried himself with a self-assured bearing. His young wife no doubt attracted the eyes of passersby: Lucy was a stunningly beautiful dark-skinned woman, with high cheekbones that accentuated her prominent brown eyes. She walked with an erect posture and seemed a well-fashioned lady, though she wore clothing of simple cotton she had made into a dress. An interracial couple was an odd sight on the Chicago streets. In the Levee District to the south on Harrison Street, white men consorted with black women in bordellos, but few respectable white men in Chicago were ever seen in public with a woman of color.[3]

Albert Parsons, who was twenty-six years old in 1874, had learned the printing trade in Texas, and possessed a set of valuable skills that made it possible for a typesetter to tramp around the country and find work with relative ease, even during a depression, because every small town had at least one newspaper and the big cities had far more. In 1874 eight dailies were published in Chicago, including the *Times,* where Parsons found permanent work setting hot type in a building that had survived the fire. He immediately became a member of Typographical Union No. 16, where some old-time union printers had followed Andrew Cameron in his crusade for the eight-hour day and still read his *Workingman's Advocate.*[4]

The legendary publisher and editor of the *Times,* Wilbur Storey, was a cranky, fiercely independent man who loved controversy. He became notorious during the Civil War as a "copperhead" Democrat who hated Lincoln and his draft, and who defiantly locked out Andy Cameron and his union printers in 1863. Storey was also a pioneer of modern big-city journalism, whose daily paper covered national and world politics in minute detail while featuring gruesome reports of murder, rape and mutilation. Public hangings created the most exciting news of all. For instance, in 1875, when four murderers repented their sins on the gallows, the *Times* headline read JERKED TO JESUS.[5]

Storey believed city people were on their own in a world where fear and disorder ruled. If workingmen were unemployed, they deserved nothing from the city, and if their demonstrations turned violent, they deserved to be put down with force such as the French army used against the communists in Paris. Rejecting all public solutions to the problems of the poor, Storey called instead for a "dismantling of city government."[6]

In his first months as a typesetter at the *Times,* Albert Parsons took a special interest in the heated public debate over the use of fire relief funds. He read the words of critics who charged the Relief and Aid Society with misusing its funds and denying them to the needy, and he read the furious editorials of Wilbur Storey, who dismissed the critics as "communists, robbers, loafers." Intrigued by the controversy, Parsons decided to investigate the matter. After studying the case, he concluded that the complaints against the Relief and Aid Society were "just and proper." Indeed, as the depression deepened during the hard winter of 1875, Parsons saw that the Chicago socialists were the only people who dared to protest on the behalf of the unemployed or to propose public remedies for their plight. The radicals' protests, and the abuse heaped upon the "communists" by the "organs of the rich," convinced him that "there was a great fundamental wrong at work in society."[7]

Albert Parsons had been born in Montgomery, Alabama, in 1848 to Yankee parents who died when he was a boy. He was cared for by a slave woman he called Aunt Ester until his older brother William brought him to Texas. There the youngster enjoyed an adventurous youth on a ranch in the Brazos River valley, where he learned to ride and to shoot from the saddle. His brother, a wealthy, influential landowner, sent Albert to

Socialist-led march on Relief and Aid Society headquarters on LaSalle Street, 1875

school in Waco and then to Galveston, where he served as an apprentice "printer's devil" in a newspaper office until the War for Southern Independence captured his soul.[8]

At age fifteen Albert talked his way into a famous company of cavalry scouts commanded by his brother. He saw action in battles along the Mississippi against federal troops and fought in one of the last skirmishes of the war, which occurred just before the news of Appomattox reached rebel units in the Southwest. After the fighting ended, Albert returned to his home county in East Texas and traded a mule he owned for 40 acres of corn in a field that was ready for harvest. He hired two freed slaves and paid them the first wages they had ever earned to bring in the crop. He used the rest of his earnings to enroll at a college in Waco and then found work practicing his trade as a printer in a local newspaper office.[9]

The columns Parsons set in type in the first years after the war carried news of stunning events in the Lone Star State. The first provisional governor found Texas in a state of anarchy, and in the worst condition of all the Confederate states because of the white population's unrelenting hostility to the federal government and its policies. Federal officials reported that "Union men and Negroes were fleeing for their lives and that murders and outrages on Negroes were on the rise, and that the criminals were always acquitted."[10]

In the midst of the white terror in Texas, Parsons started a little newspaper in Waco he called the *Spectator,* and, much to the amazement of his friends and neighbors, he used it to advocate for "the political rights of the colored people." The daring editor explained years later that he had been influenced in taking this step by the respect and love he had for the slave woman who raised him. In any case, Parsons became a Republican partisan and a supporter of federal reconstruction policies in Texas. It was an audacious stance for a Confederate veteran to take, and it earned him the hatred of his former army comrades, who stigmatized Parsons as a "scalawag"—a white southerner who betrayed his race. Displaying a boldness he had shown as a volunteer in the rebel army, the twenty-year-old veteran took to the campaign stump to vindicate his convictions. As a result, he was completely ostracized by his friends and associates and barred from shelter and lodging in white men's houses on the campaign trail.[11]

Parsons had picked a dangerous spot to start his political career. Waco was the county seat of McLennan County, the most violent place in Texas. When the county was protected by federal troops, several blacks were elected to the legislature, but soon Republican officeholders and Freedman's Bureau officials found themselves overwhelmed by the forces of terror.[12]

Nonetheless, during the fall of 1869 Parsons rode through East Texas campaigning for the interracial Republican Party. It was an unforgettable experience, "full of excitement and danger." Many years later Parsons wrote to a comrade of those days of bitterness and the hostility filled with attacks by the Ku Klux Klan and reprisals from blacks. "On horseback, over prairie, or through the swamps of the Brazos River, accompanied generally by one or two intelligent colored men, we traveled," he wrote in a memoir. "At noontime or nightfall our fare was only such as could be had in the rude and poverty stricken huts of the colored people." When night fell, former slaves from nearby plantations would gather in a field to hear young Mr. Parsons speak. There, amid the rows of slave huts, he would mount a wagon or a bale of cotton and, by the faint glow of a tallow tip, harangue the hundreds assembled around him.[13]

After the campaign, Parsons volunteered to become a militiaman, as his Connecticut Yankee grandfather, Samuel, had been in 1775. He saw plenty of action, including a standoff in one county seat, where he led twenty-five militiamen in defense of black men's right to vote, "a most warlike and dangerous undertaking." His career as a Radical Republican had begun in earnest.[14] However, he became so "odious" to the local whites that he had to shut down his unionist newspaper in Waco. Instead, Parsons found work as a traveling reporter and salesman for a Houston newspaper.

On one long trip for the paper, he returned to Johnson County, where he had spent his adventurous boyhood along the Brazos. He wrote later of stopping at a ranch on Buffalo Creek owned by a Mexican rancher named Gonzales and meeting the owner's beautiful niece, Lucy. He lingered and then left the ranch reluctantly, only to return and ask her to be his wife. She agreed, and they were wed at Austin in 1872.[15]

This was the story Albert and Lucy told of their union when they arrived in Chicago, but they invented some of it. Lucy identified herself as the daughter of John Waller, a "civilized" Creek Indian, and a Mexican woman named Marie del Gather, and denied any African ancestry, even though most people who met her assumed she was black. It is possible that Lucy did descend from Native American and Mexican people, but there is no direct evidence of this, or of a Hispanic uncle who raised her on a ranch. Lucy's biographer speculates that she was probably born a slave on the plantation of James and Philip Gathings, who owned more than sixty slaves, and that she may have been the daughter of one of the owners. Other evidence suggests that Lucy may have lived for a while with a slave from that plantation named Oliver Gathings (and this is perhaps why she might have invented the name "del Gather" for her mother). When newspapers began to pay attention to Lucy's activities, reporters described her as "colored" (or "bright colored"), indicating, as the *Chicago Tribune* suggested, that Lucy, despite her denials, had "at least one negro parent."[16]

Albert and Lucy probably met not on a Johnson County ranch, but in the contested terrain of nearby McLennan County, where Albert had become a hero to newly emancipated blacks and where a local newspaper later reported that Lucy was well known. There is no evidence to confirm young Lucy's whereabouts during slavery days or during the events of Reconstruction, but she later recalled knowing of the atrocities committed by white terrorists against emancipated blacks in Texas.[17] Lucy's family history and that of her earlier years will remain forever clouded; it is clear, however, that she chose to deny any African ancestry and to identify herself with what she saw as two proud peoples who had escaped slavery and resisted the European "invader."[18] In any case, Albert found in her the perfect mate, bold and beautiful, as fearless and righteous as he was. Friends and foes agreed that this man and woman of such different physical complexions and social backgrounds exuded a passion for each other rarely seen in married couples of their era.

By 1872, the year the Parsons said they were wed in Austin, Albert had not only won the trust of emancipated blacks in East Texas, he had earned the admiration of his fellow Republicans in Austin. These officials helped this fearless, articulate young southerner win a federal appointment as a revenue inspector. If Reconstruction had endured in Texas, Albert Parsons might have gone far in state politics. This was not to be, because in the summer of 1873 the Democratic Party, armed with the guns and the votes it needed, "redeemed" Texas from the black officials and their scalawag allies.[19]

After the Democrats returned to power in Texas and restored white rule by brute force, Parsons resigned as a federal revenue official and revived his career as a newspaperman. In that role he joined a group of editors on a trip through the Midwest sponsored by the Missouri, Kansas & Texas Railway, no doubt to promote trade and train travel between the regions. During the trip, the Texan saw Chicago for the first time. He was

impressed, as everyone was, by this booming city that had gloriously
risen from its ashes. When he returned to Texas, Albert persuaded Lucy
to come with him to start a new life in the big city up north.

Parsons's Republican Party career in Texas meant nothing in Chicago; there would be no federal appointment there. His skills as a typog-
rapher stood him in good stead, and so with modest prospects he and
Lucy began the search for lodgings all newcomers faced. They found a
small flat on Mohawk Street north of the downtown, where three-quarters
of the residents had been born in Germany. The young interracial couple
experienced some hostility, but they chose to remain on the North Side, a
place where almost everyone was from somewhere else.[20]

DURING THE 1870S, Chicago's overall population growth raced ahead of all
other large American cities because young men like Parsons flocked
there from the South as well as from the East, but mostly because 60,000
Europeans flooded the city, their numbers reaching a total of 204,859 by
1880. At that point, foreigners constituted 40 percent of the overall population and 56 percent of the workforce. By far the largest number of
these newcomers—163,482—came from the German Empire.[21]

Immigration from Germany to Chicago before 1860 originated mainly
from the southern provinces of Bavaria, Baden, Hesse and Württemberg.
Many of these newcomers were traditional Catholics from peasant and
small-town backgrounds who were drawn into the ranks of the Democratic Party. This influx also included many talented, educated people
who had been engaged in the skilled trades and professions, including a
few thousand German Jews and political exiles who had mounted the
barricades in the failed revolution of 1848. Many of these immigrants
broke with the Democrats in the 1850s and became active in the anti-
slavery movement and in the formation of the Republican Party. Chicago
German workers formed an Old World society (*Arbeiterverein*) during
these years to provide for their health and welfare; and, before long, they
deployed it in New World campaigns to elect Abraham Lincoln president
in 1860, to raise troops for his army, to agitate for the total emancipation
of slaves and to call for universal military conscription, because, as one
German put it, the "patricians of Michigan Avenue" thought their sons
could evade the hardships of military life, and that "only the sons of ple-
beians" were fit and "worthy to be slaughtered."[22]

After the Civil War, a new group of Germans migrated from the Prussian provinces that stretched east of Berlin beyond the Oder River as far as the Vistula: these were mainly peasants from large families whose incomes had been devastated when cheaper imported grain flooded the European markets. Soon after arriving in Chicago, they were sucked into the city's jobs machine—the men into the construction projects, factories, foundries and packinghouses and the young women into cigar shops, garment lofts and the servant quarters of well-to-do American families. During the 1870s the number of Germans in the city's labor force grew to 40,000. They congregated on the North Side close to the grain elevators, lumberyards and furniture shops along the river, the tanneries and rolling mills on Goose Island, and the breweries, bakeries and clothing shops that dotted the area.[23]

The new wave of German arrivals also carried with it a few highly literate young immigrants with idealistic beliefs and great aspirations. Augustus Vincent Theodore Spies was among them. A well-tutored youth of seventeen, Spies left his home in Landeck, Germany, in 1872. By the time he arrived in New York City, he had already read deeply in German history; it told the story of a people with a "rebellious spirit," a "liberty-thirsty people" who rejected the pessimistic religion of the Roman Catholic Church after Martin Luther set off "a mighty wave of Reformation" from the town of Wartburg, a place the young Spies could see from his mountain home.[24]

Once in New York, Spies quickly found a situation in a German-owned upholstery shop, where he learned the trade and then joined the wandering mass of young immigrants traveling the rails looking for their best chance. He tried farming but found it discouraging, and so he returned to shop work. Living in the mountains of Germany, Spies had little contact with wage earners, and he was puzzled by the ones he met on his American travels. They seemed to be slaves to work, powerless to resist the "arbitrary behavior of their bosses." Spies was dismayed by their "lack of manhood" and by their refusal to protest harsh treatment. He wondered why workers were "so servile," so willing to suffer silently from the "humiliating dictates" of their employers.[25]

Like so many wandering young Germans, Spies found himself pulled to Chicago, the vibrant capital of Teutonic life in America. His education, ambition, verbal facility and dashing good looks made it relatively easy for him to make a living in his new home, even during that grim first winter after the panic, when thousands of jobless men and homeless wanderers passed through Chicago looking for work, begging for bread and

searching for shelter from the brutal cold. Unlike the subservient laborers he met on the road, Spies remained an independent man and was, he
proudly recalled, never "put upon." His training as an upholsterer
allowed him to fit into an emerging sector of Chicago manufacturing: the
furniture business. Drawing on the vast hardwood forests of Michigan
and Wisconsin, craftsmen turned cherry, oak and maple planks into
chairs, tables, cabinets and church pews as well as pianos and organs
that filled thousands of homes, offices and hotels in the Midwest and the
great West beyond. When August Spies arrived in Chicago to ply his
trade, 150 furniture factories employed more than 4,000 workers, while
several hundred more skilled hands toiled in 19 upholstery shops like
the one in which the ambitious young German found employment.[26]

Spies joined a large community of Germans who settled on the North
Side, which they made into their own town, erecting Catholic and Luth-
eran churches, opening hundreds of saloons and stores and then naming streets, parks, clubs and businesses after renowned German poets,
composers and artists. To the west, Milwaukee Avenue ran out toward
Wicker Park, a settlement for prosperous Germans on the Northwest
Side—a thirty-minute ride on an omnibus of the Citizens' Line. Along
Milwaukee Avenue lived even more Germans, together with a large con-
centration of Swedes. There were scores of groceries, butcher shops, bakeries and tobacco stores as well as more than 100 saloons and beer
gardens where Germans congregated to sing and talk. Some of these
places, like Thalia Hall on Milwaukee Avenue, offered workingmen
free lunches with "union beer" and back rooms for their organizational
meetings.[27]

Chicago's Germans created a profusion of societies to satisfy their
desire to congregate, celebrate and help one another. Mutual-aid societies such as the German Society for the Protection of Immigrants and the
Friendless, and the Workers Association, meant that newcomers need not
rely upon American charities for relief.[28] The Turner Society (*Turnverein*)
erected numerous halls for gymnastic activities that also provided meeting places for all sorts of groups and served as venues for balls and con-
certs. The impressive Aurora Turner Hall on Milwaukee Avenue was the
most important German cultural center in the city.[29]

An enthusiastic gymnast, Spies reveled in activity at the Aurora. A
well-proportioned young man of twenty, Spies kept himself in excellent
shape, even though he drank several schooners of lager beer each day.
Blue-eyed, of light complexion, he had a high forehead and sharp fea-

Thalia Hall on Chicago's Milwaukee Avenue

tures. His hair, light auburn in color, was well coiffed, his long mustachios fashionably curved. He loved dancing at the Saturday balls and
was well known around North Town as an attractive bachelor and a
"ladies' man."[30] Everything about him indicated that August Spies was a
young man who would make good in Chicago just as so many of his gre-
garious and hardworking countrymen had done.

The Turners epitomized the rich tradition of associational life Germans brought from the old country to Chicago, where they created a
sphere of life outside the workaday world of established structures
and institutions. Unlike Americans, who thought the special nature of
women's feelings made the world of men's entertainment offensive, Germans welcomed women into the realm of festivity because they were seen
as having a special gift for expressing their feelings.[31] On Fridays and
Saturdays men and women flocked to music and concert halls where
brass bands and full orchestras played. On other nights they could be
found at numerous clubs devoted to song, band music and dramatics,
places where they performed for their own pleasure.[32]

Because all aspects of German working-class culture involved performance, many forms of theater flourished in immigrant neighborhoods,

where groups of amateurs enacted folk dramas, which offered up stories of the heroic common man, as well as comedies and farces, which provoked laughter. In some midwestern cities strict Protestants opposed the German theater with its libertine characters and profane Sunday performances, but it flourished in Chicago.[33] Like many of his country folk, August Spies adored the theater and yearned to display his own flair for the dramatic.

The city's large Scandinavian population came together in similar ways. By 1880 more immigrants from Denmark, Norway and Sweden lived in Chicago—nearly 26,000 people—than the combined total of Scandinavians in all other large American cities. Norwegians labored as lake sailors and shipbuilders, while the Danes and Swedes gravitated to trades such as house carpentry and cabinetmaking. Immigrants from the three Nordic nations created a vibrant cultural life for themselves, forming singing clubs, a Scandinavian Free Thinkers Society, Turner lodges and dramatic clubs.[34]

Scandinavians usually learned English readily, registered to vote, read American newspapers, sent their children to public schools and expressed a devotion to their new homeland. They appeared to be easily Americanized, but this perception deceived many casual observers. What is "this Americanization process we hear so much about?" asked the editor of the *Svenska Tribune.* "Did it mean shedding one's cultural identity like a snake skin?" No, he declared, it meant that in America "one could become more elastic" and "learn to view a matter from several angles."[35]

The Scandinavians, like the Germans, wanted to become Americans on their own terms, not those dictated by the city's native-born elites who thought their festivals overly expensive and ostentatious. Some Americans even suspected that immigrant parades on the Fourth of July were intended less to inspire loyalty to the United States than to re-create the joyful sociability common to the Old World.

Scandinavians from different lands and Germans from various states created new, broader ethnic identities for themselves in Chicago. One mass meeting at Aurora Turner Hall was held by all Scandinavian groups to "encourage greater cooperation and agreement among Nordic sister peoples in this place." On another occasion, these groups turned Norwegian Constitution Day into an all-Scandinavian event, decorating Milwaukee Avenue with Norwegian, Danish, Swedish and American flags. The Germans also forged new kinds of ethnic solidarity in Chicago, overcoming deep provincial and religious differences, especially when they celebrated Germany's victory over France in 1870.

During the two decades that followed, a time when the nationalist fervor aroused by the Civil War faded, immigrants in these huge Scandinavian and German domains expressed multiple ethnic and patriotic loyalties and began to work out their own versions of American nationalism at their own pace.[36] In any case, while effusive demonstrations of American nationalism took place principally on July 4, immigrant expressions of sociability, festivity and fraternity took place nearly every weekend in Chicago's Turner halls and saloons, and, from May to October, in the city's various groves and beer gardens—attracting Scandinavians of all nations as well as huge, passionate crowds of Germans from every part of their homeland.[37]

THE JOYOUS CONSUMPTION of beer and wine at these immigrant celebrations raised deep concerns among the city's Yankee elites, who were for the most part staunch advocates of temperance. The immigrant mob that intimidated the Common Council to protest the closing of saloons on

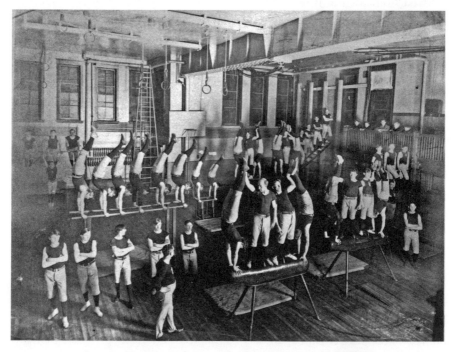

German Turner gymnasium in Chicago in the mid-1880s

Sunday afternoons steeled the city's moralists in their determination to recapture City Hall from the rebellious immigrant tribes who constituted the People's Party in 1873. Powerful businessmen and their temperance allies called for a referendum to hold a new election rather than allow the People's Party administration to serve a full term. Court challenges followed, a crisis ensued, and for a brief time the city had two mayors. Eventually the "best men" prevailed, and the People's Party disintegrated.[38]

Meanwhile, the city elites acted on their fear that the Chicago Police Department was undermanned, corrupted by saloonkeepers and gamblers, and filled with Irish immigrants who cared little about protecting wealthy Yankees and their property. They not only formed their own militia regiment, they also pressured City Hall to appoint a police superintendent who would ensure that the officers in his department faithfully performed their duties.[39]

This show of force confirmed the German socialists' fear that the city's top businessmen would stop at nothing to suppress protest and to protect their own interests, even if it meant forming private armed forces outside the boundaries of republican government. In reaction, German workers created their own militia company, the Lehr und Wehr Verein, aimed at mobilizing laboring men for the purpose of defending themselves and preparing to take on the militia created by the business elites.[40]

In the following months, energetic fund-raising in ethnic communities and in the ranks of the Workingmen's Party enabled officers of the Lehr und Wehr Verein to order rifles and the kind of colorful uniforms favored by volunteer militia in the Civil War. The soldiers were outfitted in blue blouses, white linen pants for the summer, red sashes and black Sheridan hats, made fashionable by the dashing Union general who now resided in Chicago. Volunteers sang while they drilled in order to spread *Gemütlichkeit* and to create a festive mood at the drills, which often included political rallies as well as band music, dancing and copious beer drinking.[41]

By the end of 1875 the city's small band of predominantly German socialists exerted a political presence in Chicago by stirring up a heated debate over public relief, organizing massive parades to demand bread or work and responding militantly when businessmen created their own militia. In the process the socialists attracted the attention of many newcomers searching to find their way in the great city.

August Spies, for example, made contact with the socialists about this time when his curiosity drew him to a lecture delivered by a young mechanic. While unimpressive from a theoretical standpoint, the socialist speaker nonetheless moved Spies with what he said about how wage earners experienced work under capitalism. A voracious reader since early childhood, Spies devoured every piece of literature he could find on the "social question." He had already studied the classic Greek poets, philosophers and historians, as well the modern German ones. He admired the "great thinkers," Schiller and Goethe, and he cherished the revolutionary ideas of liberty, equality and fraternity spread by Napoleon; but until he came to Chicago, Spies had not read the works of Karl Marx.[42]

Like Spies, Albert Parsons had been drawn into socialist meetings, which attracted larger and larger audiences as the depression lengthened. The young printer was impressed by the criticisms the internationalists made of the private relief effort, as well by their proposals to create public works; and he was appalled by attacks made upon them by his own employer, Wilbur Storey, who abused advocates of the poor in ways that reminded him of the attacks made by the southern slaveholders upon newly enfranchised blacks. Storey's Republican rival, Joseph Medill, was equally outrageous, in Parsons's view, when he falsely accused the socialists of planning to burn down the city and warned: "Every lamp post in Chicago will be decorated with a communist carcass, if necessary, to prevent whole sale incendiarism." When Medill predicted the return of vigilante justice, he reminded Parsons of how the Ku Klux Klan treated the Radical Republicans who sought to defend the rights of poor black citizens during Reconstruction. Years later, the young man who left Texas as a Republican would recall that his conversion to socialism was accelerated by the words of Chicago editors who recommended throwing hand grenades into the ranks of striking sailors and putting arsenic in the food distributed to tramps.[43]

The most decisive moment in Albert Parsons's political transformation came in March of 1876, when the charismatic socialist Peter J. McGuire came to speak in Chicago. Born of Irish parents in New York's Hell's Kitchen, McGuire was converted to a passionate brand of radicalism when police attacked a peaceful demonstration of the unemployed at Tompkins Square two years earlier. He then embarked on a career that would make him the most effective socialist agitator and union organizer of the late nineteenth century. McGuire, a captivating orator, told his

Chicago audience of the socialist program of the Workingmen's Party of America and how it would lead to the creation of a cooperative common-wealth to replace monopoly capitalism. When the speaker finished, Parsons sharply questioned him. Would such a communistic society, he asked, become a "loafer's paradise" in which the "parasite" would live "at the expense of the industrious worker"? McGuire responded that under the socialist system there would be true freedom of opportunity in which individual producers would receive the full product of their efforts, depending on time and energy expended. Parsons was satisfied. He signed up with McGuire's party, along with several other workers, including a cooper named George Schilling, who would become his friend and comrade in the struggles ahead.[44]

Schilling had arrived in the city shortly after Parsons, at a time when the depression was at its worst. He had been born in Germany to parents of peasant stock and was raised in Ohio. When he was still a teenager, Schilling began to wander, taking work on the railroad that lasted until he reached Chicago in 1875. Despite depressed conditions, Schilling found a job making barrels at a meatpacking company near the Union Stock Yards. An engaging, persuasive man with a jolly personality, the little cooper would become Parsons's best friend in the movement and would remain loyal to him even when they parted political company. Parsons and Schilling, bursting with confidence and conviction, traversed the city together speaking for Pete McGuire's new Social Democratic Working-men's Party in front of small crowds of workers on dusty street corners and in the noisy back rooms of beer halls whose rental sometimes cost them their last nickel.[45]

George Schilling, who played Boswell to Parsons's Johnson, was immediately struck by the Texan's gifts as an orator. Now in his late twen-ties, Parsons was already a practiced public speaker, well trained by his risky campaigns to defend the rights of emancipated blacks in Recon-struction Texas. He spoke in a sonorous voice with enough volume to carry in open-air meetings and enough energy to last for the length of one- and two-hour orations. He gesticulated, and articulated his words like an actor, stringing them together like musical notes. A witty man, he loved to poke fun at the rich and powerful, drawing instinctively on a southwestern brand of humor that could evoke subversive laughter.[46]

Parsons was the first socialist orator who attracted English-speaking audiences in Chicago and the first American speaker to appeal to Germans, Swedes and other immigrants. He also gained the attention of police detectives and newspaper editors, including one who denounced him as a Texas rebel, one of "a parcel of blatant Communist demagogues" doing the work of "the Commune." Parsons raged over these new assaults, but he was already accustomed to being notorious, and so he also found the hostile publicity energizing: he said it only added to his zeal for "the great work of social redemption."[47]

Chapter Five

The Inevitable Uprising

IN THE SPRING OF 1876, after Chicago's third punishing winter of depression, socialist agitators took to the streets all over the North and West sides. Every week they called workers to meetings to hear German and Czech speakers and their American spellbinder, Albert Parsons. Their activity was little more than an irritation to Chicago's men of power, who had vanquished the upstart People's Party and sent its immigrant leaders back to their neighborhoods. City government was once again in what they considered safe hands, and business activity was picking up. There was plenty of money on the streets of Chicago, and no one was paying much attention to socialist "calamity howlers."

One prominent Chicagoan felt uneasy, however. Former mayor Joseph Medill put his ear to the ground that summer and heard troubling rumbles of discontent. Back in charge of the *Tribune*, the publisher saw a city swarming with tramps and brimming with danger. As one journalist recalled a decade later, "The lumberyards, vacant buildings, sheds, railroad depots and all public places were thronged with idlers; crime of all kinds was on the increase; it was dangerous to venture out after dark; people were sandbagged, garroted or 'held up' on some of the leading streets." The Chicago police made more than 27,000 arrests in 1876, including many among what the police superintendent labeled a "dangerous class of vagrants called 'tramps' who would prefer to beg or steal than to work." However, these arrests did little to increase citizens' confidence in the police department, whose former superintendent had been jailed on corruption charges. Indeed, citizens looked upon "the average blue coat as a barnacle and nuisance" and only tolerated him because they could not figure out how to get on without him.[1]

In this atmosphere nervous businessmen hired private guards to protect their property and bought guns to protect themselves. The Western Gun Works offered a solution: a new lightweight, silver-plated pistol made of the best English steel with a rifled barrel. The .22-caliber weapon, with deadly accuracy and long range, could be purchased along with a month's supply of 100 cartridges for only $3. The gun was advertised as a "TRAMPS TERROR," valuable to bankers and policemen (who bought their own firearms), but also good for household use at a time when "Tramps, Burglars and Thieves Infest[ed] Every Part of the Country."[2]

Despite this "tramp menace," Chicago's prosperous citizens enjoyed themselves during the summer of 1876, promenading on the lakefront, spending a day at the races or a night at one of the opera houses and flocking downtown to celebrate the nation's centennial on streets the merchants had decked with American flags. Businessmen and working-men congregated in their clubs and saloons and talked of baseball and their White Stockings team led by the incomparable Albert G. Spalding, who had been wooed away from the Boston club and was now playing and managing a team of nine players destined to win the National League pennant.[3]

Amid all this hoopla, Medill cautioned the prosperous readers of his *Tribune* to avoid ostentatious displays of wealth during these mean times. The publisher, who cared deeply about the quality of life in his city, loathed Irish ward heelers and saloonkeepers, gamblers and socialist rabble-rousers, but he knew "honest poverty" when he saw it. Hardwork-ing men, unemployed through no fault of their own, deserved the respect and understanding of more fortunate Chicagoans, not their contempt. While the city enjoyed a lavish centennial celebration on July 4, Medill anguished over the future of the nation, "great in all the powers of a vast empire," but "weak and poor in social morality as compared with one hundred years ago."[4]

MEDILL'S FEARS WERE JUSTIFIED. Within the city's huge, largely invisible community of immigrant working people, embers of anger and frustration smoldered that summer. They flashed red-hot in one particular district on the Southwest Side, a dense settlement of pine shanties, saloons and lit-tle stores just above the South Branch of the Chicago River. This dismal-looking neighborhood called Pilsen contained a swelling population of Czechs; it was, in fact, the largest Bohemian community in America, greater in size than that of any city in Bohemia except Prague. Thousands of former Czech peasants toiled in nearby lumberyards, where they hauled and shoved lumber for $1.50 a day—a meager wage when contrasted with the earnings of the Irish dockworkers, who earned twice that, or locomotive engineers, who took home four times that amount.[5]

The massive Bohemian migration to Chicago also swept along a few artists, intellectuals and skilled workers from Prague. Among these literate Bohemians, a large sprinkling of "free thinkers" with socialist sympathies carried with them strong antipathies to the Roman Catholic Church. Dedicated nationalists, these young Czechs revered Jan Hus, who led his people in revolt against the domination of the church and helped make Bohemia the first Protestant nation in Europe.[6] These immigrants also clung to their cultural, social and linguistic heritage with "a tenacity that resisted easy Americanization." They created an array of benevolent societies based on similar institutions they had known in Bohemian cities and villages, and established Czech-language schools and publications as well as the first Czech socialist newspaper in the United States. Prokop Hudek, the most prominent of these Bohemian socialists, had come to Chicago before the Civil War, in which he fought as a Union army officer. After the war Hudek became commander of the Bohemian Sharpshooters, a local militia unit, and helped found the Workingmen's Party of Illinois in 1874.[7]

Freethinkers in Pilsen included socialists like Hudek, as well as atheists, agnostics and worshipers of Thomas Paine, the rationalist, and Thomas Jefferson, the deist, in addition to devotees of Illinois' famous freethinker Colonel Robert Ingersoll. Most were raised Protestant, but some were Catholics who did not attend mass regularly or accept the authority of the church hierarchy over parish affairs. Indeed, tension escalated in little Bohemia between the Catholic clergy and the members of free-thought societies because priests refused to wed freethinkers, baptize their children or bury their dead. Then, in 1876, a single event released the tension. When a Catholic priest denied a church burial to a Czech woman because she did not confess on her deathbed, a wave of anger swept the community, followed by an exodus from the church, as hundreds of people in Pilsen abandoned Catholicism and joined free-thought societies.[8]

Despite their poverty and their internal conflicts, the Czechs caused no trouble for the city's employers or public officials until the summer of 1875, when thousands of Bohemians toiling in the sizzling lumberyards struck to demand a living wage. Their protest ended quickly and peacefully, seeming to be little more than a brief outburst of frustration, but the following spring came the storm. When lumberyard owners cut the wages of common laborers from $1.50 to $1.25 a day, the Bohemians reacted to the blow as a community.[9] Thousands of lumber shovers left the yards en masse. When they were replaced by unemployed Irish workers from across the river, the strikers attacked the interlopers, and street warfare raged through the Southwest Side until wagonloads of police finally arrived and drove the Czechs off the streets.[10]

Medill's *Tribune* devoted three days of coverage to the "serious troubles in the Bohemian lumber district," but few of its readers would have paid any attention to the riots in a depressing river district no Americans visited other than salesmen, vessel men and policemen. A reporter for the *Chicago Daily News* looked back on this time a decade later and realized that the city's leading men had blinded themselves to the anger seething in the lumberyards and alleys of Pilsen, where workingmen had suffered intolerable wage cuts and feared more to come. When these men struck, they always failed and were forced to return to work for less pay

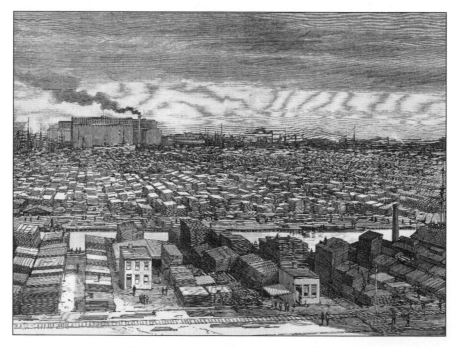

Chicago's lumberyard district near Pilsen

than they were getting before they went out. "There were ten pairs of hands ready and willing to take the place of every single pair of hands that quit," the reporter noted. With their families on the edge of starvation, the workingmen were being driven to desperation.[11]

If city leaders seemed unconcerned about the discontent seething in Pilsen, they were quite aware of the city's burgeoning radical movement, one that seemed to "grow luxuriantly in well-prepared soil." Socialist societies flourished in many poor quarters of the city, and their meetings filled Market Street, the Haymarket and a lakeshore park. Everyone in Chicago knew that it would take only one bolt of lightning to set off a thunderstorm of protest: "Everybody knew that," recalled the journalist John Flinn. "The businessman knew it, the 'Prominent Citizen' knew it, the mayor knew it. The superintendent of police knew it." And yet they did nothing to prepare for the coming storm.[12]

THE SOCIALISTS WERE indeed busy cultivating their party that spring. They nominated their best English-speaking activist, Albert Parsons, to run for City Council on the North Side. He and his wife, Lucy, had found larger quarters there, on Larrabee Street, thanks to his steady work in the *Times* composition room and her earnings as a dressmaker. It was during his run for office on the North Side in the spring of 1877 that Parsons met large numbers of German socialists, including the ambitious August Spies, who had by now worked his way out of wage labor as an upholsterer.[13]

Spies opened his own upholstery business in a little shop and brought over from Germany his mother, sister and three brothers. They lived together in a small town house near Wicker Park, some distance out on Milwaukee Avenue in a new development where well-to-do German businessmen and professionals were building comfortable but unpretentious brick homes. Acting on his growing interest in socialism, Spies agreed to take to the hustings for the new social democratic Workingmen's Party. During the campaign he frequented the scores of saloons and beer gardens along Milwaukee Avenue, talking with other German tradesmen and laborers about the political events of the day: the disputed Hayes-Tilden presidential contest, which Democrats called the "stolen election of 1876," and the compromise that gave the White House to the Republicans and ended military reconstruction in the South; the crisis in

Chicago's City Hall, where two mayors sat for a time; and the conviction of the city's top German Republican politicians in the sensational "whiskey ring" scandal.[14]

In this unsettled political climate, the socialists' most promising candidate was the party's eloquent American orator, Albert Parsons, who made speech after speech about the rotten state of affairs in the Republic. The cocky young Texan with a sharp tongue captivated his new German comrades, who worked like beavers for his campaign. When he polled 400 protest votes in his ward, even the North Side's Republican bosses were impressed with his political skills.[15]

Still, Chicago's top business and political leaders had no reason to notice a few hundred votes tallied by the socialists, because these elites were celebrating the reelection of a Republican mayor. With municipal government firmly in the control of the Yankee elites, the Citizens' Association turned to the state capital, where its leaders launched a concerted campaign to ban the workers' militia. In May, association members celebrated the first stage of militia reform, confident that under the state's new military code their own First Regiment would remain commissioned and that the German workers' militia, the Lehr und Wehr Verein, would be outlawed.[16] After facing four years of depression and travail, Chicago's business elites could relax and look forward to the restoration of order and the return of good times.

THEN, DURING THE HEAT of July, disturbing news ticked over the wires from the East, news with portents for the nation's railroad hub. Henry Demarest Lloyd, the *Tribune*'s brilliant young business columnist, was one of the first to notice the reports of workers blocking trains in West Virginia, strikers plundering an armory in Maryland, scores of "insurgent camp fires" surrounding freight houses in Pittsburgh.[17]

The uprising of 1877 began in the busy railyards of Martinsburg, West Virginia, on July 17, when engineers on the Baltimore & Ohio Railroad reacted to a wage cut by stopping trains. State militiamen tried to move a train and shooting began: a soldier and a striker fell dead. Train crews soon spread word of the confrontation all along the B&O line. The action quickly spread to Baltimore, where trainmen struck and closed Camden Yards. When militia units marched in to reopen the yards, a furious battle took place and ten people were killed by the troops.[18]

These spontaneous protests arose because of wage cuts imposed by the B&O's managers, who followed a trend initiated by the most influential businessman in America, Tom Scott of the Pennsylvania Railroad. Scott's managers compounded the resentment when they ordered engineers and train crews to haul "double headers"—dangerous trains with two engines and twice as many cars. Workers in Pittsburgh refused the order and surged into the yards, paralyzing rail traffic. The governor of Pennsylvania ordered out the National Guard, but many local militiamen from Pittsburgh refused to report for duty. In response to Scott's pleas, the governor then ordered militia units from Philadelphia to the scene.

The ensuing confrontation on July 22 between the soldiers and huge crowds resulted in a bloodbath when encircled militiamen fired on the protesters. Twenty people died, including a woman and a child. The immigrant neighborhoods erupted in fury. By the time the Battle of Pittsburgh ended, enraged crowds had killed several militiamen, driven the National Guard from the city, destroyed millions of dollars of railroad property, derailed trains, dismantled roundhouses and burned Union Depot to the ground.

The news of these events shocked Chicagoans, who read that "Pittsburgh was in the hands of a mob; that the property of the railroad companies was in flames; that blood had been spilled freely in the streets; that a reign of terror prevailed" and that "riot fever" was spreading west.[19] It seemed to one journalist looking back on these events that city leaders should have expected trouble in Chicago, given the palpable grievances of wage workers and aggravating protests organized by the socialists. Residents felt instinctively that the riots in the East would follow the iron rails directly to the hub of the nation's railroads, and "yet nothing was done to prepare for the impending, the inevitable uprising."[20]

The next day freight handlers on the Illinois Central Railroad struck and marched through other Chicago yards and shops calling others out to join them. The evening *Tribune* simply proclaimed: "It Is Here." That night the Workingmen's Party organized meetings in various halls, where workers shouted for resolutions of sympathy with the workers of Pittsburgh. Later on, runners circulated a leaflet calling for a "mass meeting" the next evening on Market Street. "Working men of Chicago!" it began: "Have you no rights?—No ambition?—No Manhood? Will you remain disunited while your masters rob you of your rights and the fruits of your labor? For the sake of our wives and children and our own self-respect, LET US WAIT NO LONGER! ORGANIZE AT ONCE!"[21]

The meeting on the night of July 23 was "a monster affair" with 30,000 people filling every foot of space on Market Street. Worn down by four years of depression, frustrated by one wage cut after another and enraged by the massacres of citizens in the East, Chicago workers gathered to hear news of the great uprising and to learn what it meant for them.[22] It was a thrilling moment for Albert Parsons, who delivered a memorable speech to the impassioned throng. George Schilling, who was there that night, marveled at his comrade's ability to capture the feelings of the workers.

Parsons told the crowd that railroad lords like Tom Scott had subverted democracy with money and reduced their own loyal employees to degrading poverty. But they could still be stopped by an aroused citizenry. "As long as we have a Republic, we have hope," he declared. Realizing that many Union army veterans stood among the assembled workmen, he invoked the name of the most prestigious body in postwar Chicago: the Grand Army of the Republic, the citizen soldiers who saved the Union. No longer honored veterans, Lincoln's soldiers were now being shot down like criminals by their own militia, and for what? For protesting yet another wage cut that meant less food for them and their hungry families.

"We are assembled here," Parsons exclaimed, "as a Grand Army of Starvation. We have come together to find the means by which the great gloom that now hangs over our Republic can be lifted," he shouted. "It rests with you to say whether we shall allow the capitalists to continue to exploit us. Will you organize?" When they cheered, he responded, "Then, enroll your names in the Grand Army of Labor." When Parsons finished, the enormous crowd chanted into the night air: "Pittsburgh, Pittsburgh, Pittsburgh!"[23]

On the morning of Tuesday, July 24, switchmen on the Michigan Central left their yards and marched through the city beseeching and cajoling other railroad men to join their ranks. Soon their parade swelled as gangs of rough-looking boys joined the men. By noon this small army poured through Burlington's yards and freight houses, gaining recruits in the process. Some bold railroad men even commandeered a freight train and moved it down to the Fort Wayne yards, where more switchmen left their jobs.[24]

Thoroughly alarmed, Mayor Monroe Heath closed the city's saloons and called upon citizens to organize armed patrols in their respective neighborhoods. When a prominent citizen offered to pay for extra police, the mayor accepted.[25] Several hundred civilian special deputies were sworn in, armed with clubs and sent to stations. That afternoon fire bells rang all over the city, calling the militia to their armories, and that evening Civil War veterans met to form volunteer companies under the command of former army generals, colonels and captains. Fearing the worst in Chicago, the United States secretary of war ordered the 22nd Infantry of General Phil Sheridan's Division of the Missouri to move into Rock Island, Illinois, and stand ready. No violence erupted that day, but a rolling tide of protest had swept out of the railyards and into the factories, lumberyards and brickyards of the South Side, where the Bohemians seemed to have been waiting for another chance to protest their lot.[26]

Leaders of the Workingmen's Party counseled peace that day and expressed concern that roughnecks in the crowds would provoke bloodshed. The party issued a flyer proposing a coordinated national strike for the eight-hour day without a reduction in pay. The circular called for a meeting that evening so a strike committee could be assembled to lead and coordinate the walkout and preserve the peace. By the end of the day, however, Workingmen's Party activists were laying low after being driven from the streets by the police.[27]

ON WEDNESDAY, JULY 25, Chicagoans awakened to suffocating heat and humidity, made worse by clouds of pollution. In the early-morning haze, strikers and young men from the shantytowns appeared again in the gloomy streets, roaming throughout the city, closing workshops and battling police. When strikers gathered to hold rallies and meetings, they were attacked by patrolmen, who made no distinction between the crowds hurling stones and groups of workers assembling peacefully. That night railroad men and gangs of Irish boys from Bridgeport again converged on the Burlington yards at 16th and Halsted, where they confronted a detail of police from the Hinman Street Station. The boys began stoning the railyards and an incoming passenger train; when they continued, the patrolmen opened fire. A Burlington switchman fell dead on the spot; a score of others were wounded, including two boys who later died.[28]

The next day, July 26, the city was an armed camp of soldiers, police officers and armed civilians, mainly clerks and managers, who had been made special deputies. Still, the day began with more violence as a large crowd returned to Halsted Street and began cutting telegraph lines and stoning streetcars that carried commuters to work. At the stockyards and the gasworks men forced officials to sign papers promising to raise wages. Meanwhile, other strikers patrolled the idled lumberyards, which had been abandoned by the Czech laborers, and a well-coordinated general strike spread to the North Side, closing all shops and factories as well as the tanneries and rolling mills on Goose Island. Workers who had been suffering from layoffs and wage cuts for nearly four years were suddenly aroused to mass action by the protests of the nation's railway workers.

The significance of the work stoppage was overshadowed, however, by warfare that resumed along Halsted Street. The flash point of the fighting was the viaduct where Halsted Street crossed 16th Street and the Burlington tracks. There, on the edge of Pilsen, officers confronted a huge crowd that included Bohemian lumber shovers lining the sidewalks. The blue coats attacked and drove people into the viaduct, firing their revolvers into the mass. After the officers emptied their guns, they ran for their lives.

The "battle of the viaduct" escalated when hundreds of striking butchers and meat cutters arrived from Bridgeport in a column flying the emerald and gold nationalist banner of the Fenian Brotherhood. They joined the Bohemians in a brawl with the police that raged all afternoon. Even mounted troops could not stop it. It was TERROR'S REIGN, according to the *Chicago Times*, and a sure sign of it was the presence of wild women in the crowd, "Bohemian Amazons" brandishing clubs in their "brawny arms."[29]

After the battle at the viaduct, the police forces drove men and boys up Halsted Street until they reached Vorwärts Turner Hall at 12th Street. Inside, several hundred members of the Harmonia Society, an assocation of cabinetmakers and their employers, were discussing the eight-hour-day question in German. Some of the members who were smoking cigars outside the hall shouted protests at the policemen, who wheeled toward them and chased them into the meeting hall with guns drawn.

When officers thundered into the meeting room, chaos ensued as police attacked the cabinetmakers with clubs. When the Germans defended themselves with chairs, some patrolmen opened fire. Charles Tessman, a twenty-eight-year-old union cabinetmaker, fell dead when a bullet ripped through his brain. Men clogged the stairs trying to escape the danger, and the police pounded them with clubs until they dropped in a heap at the bottom. Outside, witnesses saw a police sergeant firing his

Police attacking cabinetmakers' meeting at Vorwärts Turner Hall, 1877

pistol at bystanders, while his men beat cabinetmakers as they fled the hall in terror. Sent out to suppress rioters, the police became rioters themselves. Their attack on the Harmonia Society at Vorwärts Turner Hall aroused all of Chicago's Germania and provoked some immigrant workers, like the upholsterer August Spies, to join the armed organization of workingmen, the Lehr und Wehr Verein.[30]

That afternoon spirits rose in downtown Chicago as anxious residents saw sunburned regulars of the United States infantry marching down Madison Street with bayonets fixed, fresh from the Dakotas, where they had been fighting the Sioux. That evening, a forbidding moonless night, the shooting stopped and a few brave people ventured out of their homes to shop; some even rode out to the Exposition Hall on the lakefront for an evening concert of Wagnerian music. The program included selections like "Siegfried's Death" from *Götterdämmerung*, which matched the concertgoers' mood at the end of a violent day.

On Friday, July 27, an eerie calm enveloped the city. The great uprising had been put down. In working-class neighborhoods like Pilsen and Bridgeport, people gathered on street corners, in saloons and in meeting halls to ponder what had happened, while some made plans to bury their loved ones. Within a few days the body count had been tallied: 30 men and boys had died, most of them from the Irish and Bohemian wards around Halsted Street.[31] The police and the 5,000 specials they deputized suffered no casualties.

As the immigrants mourned their dead and the police girded for future confrontations, businessmen measured the costs of the uprising in dollars and cents: at least $6 million lost in shipping and manufacturing alone, not to mention the cost of property damage and extra pay for the special deputies. But these expenses paled at what would now be spent to make the city secure. Chicago's richest man, Marshall Field, would donate thousands to purchase arms and would insist the money be invested in constructing fortresslike armories. The Citizens' Association provided the police department with four 12-pound cannons with caissons, one ten-barrel Gatling gun, 296 Springfield breech-loading rifles and 60,000 rounds of ammunition. Police Superintendent Michael Hickey, designated a colonel by the mayor, infused the police force with a martial spirit, ordering patrolmen to drill regularly for street fighting and to receive instruction in handling their pistols and their new arsenal of heavy weapons.[32]

What could not be counted or measured, but only felt, was the hate and mistrust that now gripped Chicagoans of different social classes. The uprising of 1877 and its suppression left toxic fumes of animosity that would poison social relations in the city for years to come.[33] No one expressed these hard feelings more strongly than the editor of the *Tribune*, who drew some tough lessons from the episode for the police. On the first day of the strike patrolmen fired blank cartridges to no effect. On the second day they shot above the heads of the strikers and a few of the rioters were hurt, but on the third day of the riots the police began firing directly at the protesters, which "had a most admirable effect on the mobs." Had the police been ordered to fire low on the first day, the *Tribune* concluded, "fewer would have been hurt than were, and the city would have been saved the disgrace of three days' rule by the commune."[34]

WHILE THE MILLIONAIRE MERCHANT Marshall Field concluded that only a militarized city would be safe from another uprising, and while the editors of the *Tribune* decided the police now needed a shoot-to-kill strategy to suppress rioting, labor activists drew their own lesson from the conflict; it was not, however, the one conservatives feared, the one reached by the European anarchists who believed that state repression left workers with only one choice: to commit acts of violence that would spark an armed revolution. In the United States, socialists and labor reformers began a search for American solutions to the dilemma they faced, solutions that would allow hardworking citizens to peacefully capture the republic from the money lords who ruled it and make it a democracy by and for the people.[35] These radicals were encouraged not only by the militancy of the strikers but by the behavior of hundreds of city dwellers who joined the workers in a series of community uprisings that expressed long-standing grievances against the railroads and their destructive invasion of urban space.[36]

All those who spoke for laboring people agreed on the challenge before them. The actions of Tom Scott and the other railroad chiefs confirmed the widespread popular belief that these men had risen above the law and descended below any accepted standard of Christian morality. They could discharge employees without cause, withhold their pay without notice and cut their wages without compunction. Scott and the railroad barons forced their workers to make a choice: submit to industrial serfdom and sacrifice their manhood or take concerted action and become outlaws. This, wrote one labor reformer, was no way to treat hardworking citizens of the world's only democracy.[37]

Workingmen and their leaders had feared monopolists like Tom Scott for decades, but in 1877 they encountered a new threat: the massive use of the militia and the U.S. Army to suppress civil protest. For the first time, citizen strikers and their allies confronted a hostile array of forces deployed by their own cherished government. As if to exacerbate workers' fears and to reassure frightened property owners, the popular *Harper's Weekly* featured a frightful illustration of militiamen pouring rifle fire into a group of Chicago workers armed with sticks and stones. The scene, depicting the battle at the Halsted Street viaduct, was a vivid but misleading one; the police, not the militia, had fired all the fatal bullets in that assault. Nonetheless, National Guard units had killed scores of strikers and other citizens in Maryland and Pennsylvania, and these shootings were more than enough evidence to confirm the popular view that the railroad kings could influence governors, intimidate mayors, exploit the militia and in effect subvert the republican system of government. After the smoke had cleared in 1877, George McNeill, a leading labor intellectual, expressed a new fear, a fear that the "spirit of hate that

The Battle of the Viaduct at Halsted and 16th streets, 1877, in which National Guard troops are inaccurately depicted as firing on a crowd

now centers upon the great monopolies will soon extend to the government that acts as their protector."[38]

And yet the insurgency of 1877 offered a surprisingly affirmative message to labor leaders. Samuel Gompers of the Cigar Makers recalled that the strikes alerted discouraged union men to the enormous latent power of the wage-earning class. Made desperate by their accumulated miseries, the railway workers rebelled, but, lacking strong organizations, they were doomed to defeat. Still, their rebellion in the "name of American manhood" and in defense of their rights as citizens inspired labor activists like Gompers, who wrote later that the trainmen sounded "a tocsin" with "a ringing message of hope for us all."[39]

No one heard the alarm bell in July more clearly than Albert Parsons. Indeed, on the second day after the strike began in Chicago, he experienced a sequence of unforgettable events that shook him to the core.[40] That Tuesday morning after the printer said goodbye to his wife, Lucy, in their North Side flat, he took the Clark Street horsecar downtown, feeling excited about the great enthusiasm his speech had generated the night before. His mood changed quickly when he entered the *Times* building and learned that he had been removed from the rolls of working compositors. He had been fired because of his rousing speech. Feeling dejected,

Parsons walked a few blocks to the offices of his party's German newspaper, *Arbeiter-Zeitung*, hoping to find some consolation from his fellow union printers. As he was telling his story, two men entered the building and informed Parsons that Mayor Heath wanted to see him at City Hall. He readily joined them, thinking that perhaps city leaders might want to consult him about finding some way to calm the workers before another hideous riot exploded.

As they walked away, Parsons realized that his escorts were policemen in plain clothes, and soon he learned they were taking him not to the mayor's office, but into the bowels of an old wooden building called the Rookery, which had served as a temporary police headquarters since the fire. Assuming he was being arrested, Parsons was amazed when he was ushered into a large room filled with well-dressed businessmen he recognized as Board of Trade members. He was put in a chair and lectured by Police Superintendent Michael Hickey on the great trouble he had brought upon the city of Chicago. Hickey wanted to know: Did Parsons think he could come up from Texas and incite working people to insurrection without arousing suspicion?

Parsons tried to respond, but his voice sounded pathetically thin. He had a cold and was hoarse from speaking outdoors the night before. He was also weak from lack of sleep and shaken by his firing that morning. Yet he summoned his strength and explained that he had not called for an insurrection at the rally, but had addressed the causes of the uprising and outlined the program of the Workingmen's Party. Then, more boldly, he proclaimed that a strike would not have erupted "if working men had voted for their own party and elected good men to make good laws." This remark infuriated some businessmen in the room, who burst into jeers and shouts. A few screamed, "Hang him, lynch him!"

Parsons's ordeal lasted for two hours. When it ended, Hickey told him to leave the city because his life was in danger, that he could be assassinated at any moment on the street. The superintendent then opened a spring latch door, shoved Parsons into a dark hallway and whispered in his ear, "Take warning."

Lost in a dark labyrinth of the Rookery's empty corridors, Parsons walked aimlessly, not knowing where to go or what to do. He felt "absolutely alone, without a friend in the world." This, Parsons wrote later, was his first experience with "the powers that be" in Chicago, one that made him conscious that they were powerful enough to give or take a person's life.

Parsons wandered the nearly deserted streets that night and sensed "a hushed and expectant feeling" pervading the city. He picked up an evening newspaper reporting that the strikers had become more violent, that the Commune was about to rise and that he, Albert Parsons, was the ones who caused it all. Frightened now, he decided once again to look for support from his union brothers. He called upon the printers at the *Chicago Tribune* to see if he could get a night's work and, as he later wrote, to be near men of his own craft, whom he instinctively felt would sympathize with him. He entered the composing room and began talking with union typographers on the night shift about the great strike, but was soon seized from behind by two men who pushed him out of the room and down the stairs, ignoring the angry shouts from his fellow compositors. As the men dragged him down the stairs, Parsons protested at being treated like a dog, but he soon fell silent when one of them put a pistol to his head and threatened to blow his brains out.

In less than twenty-four hours Albert Parsons had been fired, removed from his trade, blacklisted, threatened with lynching, had a gun held to his head and been warned to leave the city. But he was not absolutely alone in the world; he had many friends in Chicago. Furthermore, he knew how to live with the burden of being a marked man. For five dangerous years he had defied the Ku Klux Klan and risked his life to defend the rights of black freedmen in Texas. He had held his ground then, and he would do so again. The Board of Trade was not going to drive Albert Parsons out of Chicago. Within a month after his ordeal, he would be back on the streets, campaigning for the Workingmen's Party.

Chapter Six

The Flame That Makes the Kettle Boil

IN SEPTEMBER OF 1877, Albert Parsons, running hard for county office as a socialist, harangued crowds in saloons and railyards, in Turner halls where German immigrants still seethed over the deadly police attacks of July and on street corners in riot-torn Pilsen. Everywhere he went he spoke of the great uprising of July and its bloody suppression.[1]

When Parsons topped the Workingmen's Party ticket, polling a total of 8,000 votes, his former employer at the *Times* simply dismissed his tally as "a riot vote" garnered by one of those "long-haired idiots and knaves" who denied the inexorable laws of political economy.[2] The socialists, however, were elated; they had gained favorable public attention and tapped into widespread popular indignation over the behavior of the railroad barons. Up to this point in his young but eventful political life, Albert Parsons had been a reformer, a socialist who believed that as long as workers lived in a republic, they had hope of gaining power through the democratic process. Over the next six years, however, a series of discouraging events would dash that hope and send him down a revolutionary road.

In December of 1877 the Chicago socialists sent a delegation to their party's national convention, where they agreed to merge their party with a new organization, the Socialistic Labor Party. The following spring the party ran a full slate of candidates in all the city's wards, calling for the circulation of paper currency (greenbacks) and for the enactment of an eight-hour day; the socialists also demanded the abolition of vagrancy laws used to punish the unemployed, conspiracy laws used to persecute unionists and convict-lease arrangements used to exploit forced labor and undermine free laborers.[3]

Albert Parsons, now residing in the 15th Ward, made another impressive showing in a race for a City Council seat, polling 744 votes, just 116 votes fewer than the winner. He believed, however, that he had actually won the election and that Republican election officials had counted him out.[4] Being cheated out of public office reminded Parsons of the blatant election fraud carried out by Democratic officials in Texas against his old Republican allies. It seemed to matter little which party was in power: the people's will was denied either way. Having served his time as a militia colonel defending freedmen's voting rights in Texas, Parsons was now prepared to take up arms to protect workingmen's voting rights in Chicago. Indeed, some of the German workers who had voted for him in Ward 15 had already done so.

That spring, units of the Lehr und Wehr Verein began drilling in public and deploying their militiamen in defense of socialist meetings and picnics. By the summer, the workers' militia could marshal four companies with several divisions (each with forty men). Its officers explained that the militiamen would act only if workers' constitutional rights were violated, as the police had done when they invaded the cabinetmakers' meeting at the Vorwärts Turner Hall that summer. These assurances failed to calm the nerves of worried city leaders, and when the Bohemian Sharpshooters were observed drilling on a prairie lot outside Pilsen, word spread that the socialists were preparing for an armed insurrection. The Sharpshooters' commander ridiculed the rumor. Albert Parsons, however, spoke in a different tone. "If people try to break up our meetings," he threatened, "as they did at Turner Hall, they will meet foes worthy of their steel."[5]

The Citizens' Association's leaders took this warning seriously and accelerated their efforts to raise money to arm their own regiment and to push legislators to ban public drilling by the worker units. One year after the great uprising, Chicagoans were hiving off into armed camps.

The city's businessmen, the *Tribune* reported, openly expressed their alarm at the possibility of "trouble with the Communists" that summer or fall. Perilous days lay ahead, warned the Chicago *Inter-Ocean*. Poor people were desperate for relief; they were listening to the socialists and questioning the conventional wisdom about economic laws. "There is distrust, dissatisfaction, discontent about us everywhere," the paper's editor declared. "Communism proper has little to do with it, but a common feeling of disgust, discouragement, and uncertainty feeds the flame that makes the communist kettle boil."[6]

Albert Parsons at about age thirty

BY NOW LUCY PARSONS had joined her husband, Albert, in fanning the flames of discontent. The couple immersed themselves in the city's lively socialist movement and in the cultural life it spawned. By the fall, the Socialistic Labor Party had established four German sections in various neighborhoods, as well as Scandinavian, Bohemian, French and English branches. The party's German newspaper, *Der Vorbote*, expanded its circulation and its members started a Danish paper, as well as an English paper, the *Socialist*, which Albert helped to edit. Lucy contributed as well with a mournful poem about poor people "wandering up and down the cheerless earth, aimless, homeless, helpless," as "the cries of their hungry children and the prayers of their despairing wives fell upon them like curses." Lucy also joined Albert in debates sponsored by socialist societies, plunging into the discussions, speaking with her own resonant voice and arguing with what one male observer called "spirit and animation."[7]

Propelled by young enthusiasts like Albert and Lucy Parsons, the Chicago socialists mounted an ambitious campaign aimed at the spring municipal elections of 1879. They nominated a popular and respected German physician, Dr. Ernest Schmidt, for mayor, and put candidates up for all major offices.[8] The campaign reached a climax in March at an ambitious rally and festival: a lavish celebration of the Paris Commune's eighth anniversary. The socialists rented the largest meeting hall in the city for the event—the enormous Exposition Building on the lakefront, constructed after the fire to showcase the commercial and industrial accomplishments of Chicago. The pageant featured ceremonial maneuvers by 500 armed men who formed units of the Lehr und Wehr Verein, Bohemian Sharpshooters, the Irish Labor Guard and the Scandinavian Jaegerverein. People flocked to the event, and so many of them packed the hall—more than 40,000—that it was impossible to carry out the full program of speaking, singing, dancing and drilling. Still, the event was a spectacular achievement for the socialists and a reminder that the memory of the Paris Commune had acquired mythical power in the minds of many immigrant workers.[9]

The next day a *Tribune* editorial asked who were the thousands who had jammed the Exposition Building that night. The answer oozed with contempt. "Skim the purlieus of the Fifth Ward," read the editorial, referring to Irish Bridgeport, "drain the Bohemian socialist slums of the Sixth and Seventh Wards, scour the Scandinavian dives of the Tenth and Fourteenth Wards, cull the choicest thieves from Halsted and Desplaines Street, pick out from Fourth Avenue, Jackson Street, Clark Street and State Street and other noted haunts the worst specimens of female depravity, scatter in all the red-headed, cross-eyed and frowsy servant girls in three divisions of the city and bunch all these together . . . [and] you have a pretty good idea of the crowd that made up last night's gathering."[10]

The socialists knew, however, that their pageant had attracted many respectable immigrants—merchants, builders, musicians, teachers, doctors, tradesmen and saloonkeepers who still resented the *Tribune* and its haughty editor. They remembered well that Medill, as mayor, had offended them, not only with his hostile words but with his attempts to close their saloons on Sundays and to stop them from rebuilding their wooden homes after the Great Fire.

City elections in Chicago were usually fought out over issues like tax rates, building codes, construction contracts and saloon regulations, but in 1879 the socialists addressed economic issues that concerned unemployed workers as well as consumers, saloonkeepers and home owners. Voters were startled by the socialists' dashing confidence and the boldness of their proposals, such as municipal ownership of the streetcar lines and utilities, which were owned and operated by high-handed monopolists.[11]

Dr. Schmidt finished third in the spring election of 1879, polling 12,000 votes. The socialist vote constituted only one-fifth of the total, but it was large enough to deny a victory to the Republicans, who, since 1860, had always prevailed in two-party races with the Democrats. Dr. Schmidt had attracted support from German and Scandinavian tradesmen and professionals who had traditionally supported the Republican Party, as well as from saloonkeepers and brewery owners angered by the Grand Old Party's zeal for temperance reform. As a result, Kentucky-born Carter Henry Harrison became the city's first Democratic mayor since the Civil War.[12]

The businessmen who led the city's Republican Party were furious about losing control of City Hall so soon after they had won it back from the immigrant People's Party, but socialists like Albert and Lucy Parsons were in high spirits, riding the waves of a surging political movement and anticipating the birth of their son, Albert, Jr., who was expected in September.

Lucy's pregnancy did not slow her down; indeed, she escalated her political efforts by joining the new Chicago Working Women's Union and helping to expose the plight of female domestic servants, who could be dismissed by their mistresses without notice if accused of "misconduct." Here she encountered a small but brilliant constellation of radical women that included Lizzie Swank, a frail young woman of Yankee stock. Swank could have joined the Daughters of the American Revolution, but instead she adopted her mother's libertarian beliefs and began writing for the provocative anarchist paper *Lucifer*. Attracted to Chicago from Iowa by the great uprising of 1877, Swank found work in a sewing shop and soon after joined the Working Women's Union. There she met Lucy Parsons, who persuaded her new friend to join the insurgent socialist movement. The two young women bonded immediately and plunged into radical activism with abandon. In the summer of 1879 they took part in a joyous three-day festival around the Fourth of July, riding on top of a float decorated with pink cloth and ribbons bearing banners praising STRENGTH OF UNION and promising world peace in these words: WHEN WOMAN IS ADMITTED TO THE COUNCIL OF NATIONS, WAR WILL COME TO AN END, FOR WOMAN KNOWS THE VALUE OF LIFE.[13]

The high hopes of summer did not last, however, for in the fall elections the socialists' vote plummeted. The German distillers, brewers, tavern owners and saloonkeepers who voted for Dr. Schmidt in the spring as a protest against the antisaloon elements in the Republican Party returned to the ranks of the Grand Old Party in 1880 after party leaders assured them their breweries and beer gardens would remain open. Democratic workers, who had favored the socialist program for public relief, found the demand less compelling when the long depression finally ended. The party's ward bosses soon shepherded most of these stray workingmen back into the fold. What is more, the newly elected Democratic mayor, the shrewd charmer Carter Harrison, offered city jobs to socialists, who eagerly joined the mass of job seekers flooding City Hall.

Socialistic Labor Party militants angrily branded the office seekers opportunists and accused some of their leaders of corruption. Faction fights raged among former comrades. The quarreling socialists patched up their differences and put a ticket in the field for the spring elections in 1881, but the party had lost its dash and its sense of common purpose. Socialist vote totals fell in all but one ward on the Northwest Side, where Frank Stauber won reelection to the council—only to be counted out by two election judges who brazenly stuffed the ballot boxes. For many socialists like Albert Parsons, already dejected by the fickle habits of Chicago voters, this blatant case of fraud crushed what little faith they retained in the efficacy of the ballot. "It was then," Parsons remembered, "that I began to realize the hopeless task of political reformation."[14]

AT THIS POINT, disillusioned radicals like Albert Parsons and August Spies bolted the Socialistic Labor Party. The rebel faction, which included most of the Chicago party's German members, believed that running candidates for office was futile without the thorough organization of workers into aggressive, unified trade unions. Incumbent party leaders, mostly English-speaking socialists, insisted that trade unions serve as auxiliaries to their party. There was another bone of contention. The dominant group objected to armed workers' organizations because they frightened potential socialist voters, while the militants maintained that their meetings and rallies would be attacked if left undefended, and that, even if their candidates gained public office, they would simply be removed without an armed force to defend them. These debates hardened hearts and closed minds, leading passionate young socialists like Parsons and Spies to reject electoral politics completely.[15]

The argument among socialists over the workers' militia became even more heated when the Citizens' Association succeeded in persuading the legislature to outlaw the activity of such militias. The Supreme Court of Illinois upheld this ban on armed marches of proletarian militiamen— a decision Parsons and Spies denounced as a clear violation of the Second Amendment of the U.S. Constitution, which protected citizens' rights to bear arms.[16]

This court decision seemed like a seismic political event to both young men. Parsons, grandson of a patriot militia commander in the American Revolution and a militia colonel in his own right, and Spies, who had drilled with the Lehr und Wehr Verein, would frequently refer to what they regarded as a monumental injustice in the court's decision: the businessmen's First Regiment would continue to arm itself and conduct drills on public streets, but the workers' self-defense groups would be banned. The decision provoked an enduring sense of anxiety and hostility among Chicago socialists, who now believed the Bill of Rights no longer protected them, but only their sworn enemies.[17]

In order to convince other workers that a crisis was at hand, the socialist militants took control of the party's daily German-language newspaper, *Arbeiter-Zeitung*, which was nearly bankrupt. The dissidents hired August Spies to manage this publication as well as the weekly *Vorbote* and the socialist Sunday paper *Die Fackel*. Reviving the socialist press was a discouraging venture, because the party was so weak and divided, but Spies leapt at the challenge. He found a capable assistant in Oscar Neebe, a well-traveled young man who had left his birthplace, New York City, and come to Chicago at the age of sixteen. He worked first in a German saloon near the McCormick Reaper Works, where he heard molders and blacksmiths talk bitterly about the 1867 eight-hour campaign and its betrayal. Then, after several stints as a cook on lake vessels, Neebe found work at good wages in a stove factory, where he labored until 1877, when he was fired and blacklisted for defending the rights of other workers. Neebe endured months of near starvation before he found work selling compressed yeast, a job that took him all over the city and into the company of August Spies.[18]

Spies, who owned his own shop, and Neebe, who had worked as a salesman, used their business skills to boost sales of all three socialist

August Spies (left) and Oscar Neebe

newspapers, and in just a few years they turned their Socialistic Publishing Company into a flourishing business. In the process, the daily *Arbeiter-Zeitung* became for thousands of German-speaking workingmen what the *Chicago Daily Tribune* was for native-born businessmen. Spies's mastery of German, his skill as a speaker and writer, his knowledge of world politics and his sense of outrage over injustice made his editorials and essays well known to thousands of immigrant workers in his adopted land. Indeed, in no American city did a radical journalist speak to an audience of the size August Spies reached in Chicago.[19]

Using his influence as an opinion shaper, Spies helped convene a meeting of militants who shared a sense of urgency about what they viewed as a vast conspiracy to deprive working people of their rights. The congress at a North Side Turner hall in October 1881 aimed at attracting all socialists "weary of compromise and desirous of accomplishing the social revolution by means other than political action."[20] Some delegates who came from New York City had already given up on electoral politics and taken up the revolutionary banner. Indeed, a few of them reported with high excitement on a meeting just concluded in London, where a band of revolutionaries had decided to revive the International Workingmen's Association, the organization Karl Marx had dissolved when he feared it would be captured by the anarchist followers of Mikhail Bakunin.

The London meeting had pulsated with talk about the Russian

nihilists who had recently stunned the western world by assassinating Czar Alexander II. The result of this act was not the rising of the peasants envisioned by the conspirators, however, but rather a wave of savage repression that shattered the revolutionary movement. Still, this reaction from the czar's forces did not discourage Bakunin's London followers; indeed, they made the Russian conspirators into martyrs and vowed to follow their example.[21]

The anarchists who formed the new International Working People's Association in London acted on their belief that socialist propaganda could not effectively reach workers through trade unions and political parties; nor would revolutionary change result from strikes, mass demonstrations and election campaigns. If the Reichstag of Germany could ban the most powerful socialist party in the world and if the imperial troops could crush any demonstration or strike, then revolutionaries must resort to a new method—"propaganda by deed." These revolutionaries believed that an *attentat,* a violent act planned by a secret conspiracy and committed by a dedicated militant, could impress the world with the evil of the despotic state and with the fearless determination of those who intended to destroy it. Many European anarchists believed such deeds would terrorize the authorities who were targeted, arouse the masses and trigger a popular insurrection.[22]

The new "Black International" formed in London would become a "fearful specter in the eyes of governments throughout the Western Hemisphere, which suspected it of being the directing power behind various acts of assassination and terror committed in the ensuing decades," according to the historian Paul Avrich. These suspicions were "utterly without foundation," however, because the International existed as little more than an information bureau that led a "phantom existence and soon faded into oblivion."[23] The one city where the Black International attracted an impressive following among workers was Chicago.

DURING THE 1880S Chicago's total population increased by 118 percent—a rate of growth five times faster than that of New York City. The city's foreign-born population doubled, reaching 450,000, a total that made immigrant Chicago larger than the total population of St. Louis or any other city in the Midwest, a total swollen by thousands of impoverished Polish Catholic peasants and Jewish refugees from the ghettos of Russia.[24] To many native-born Protestants, who constituted but one-fifth of the city's people, it seemed that Chicago had become "a foreign city," a place that now contained "more Germans than Anglo-Saxons."[25]

Political refugees from Germany formed a small but outstanding segment of this new immigrant population. For example, among the embittered German exiles who escaped Bismarck's police forces came the well-known socialist Paul Grottkau. Born in 1846 to a noble family of Brandenburg, he went to Berlin to study architecture but became a stonemason instead. Grottkau soon became a prominent socialist editor and organizer, and was forced to flee Germany when the antisocialist law took effect in 1878. The exile made his way to Chicago and immediately joined the Socialistic Labor Party, whose members already knew him by reputation. A compelling speaker and writer, Grottkau became editor of the *Arbeiter-Zeitung* and a role model for August Spies and other young Germans who joined him when he led the revolt of socialist militants against the party's leadership. Like Grottkau, these young Turks began calling themselves Social Revolutionaries.[26]

Another newcomer from Germany, Michael Schwab, would soon fall under Grottkau's influence as well. Schwab was born along the Main River in northern Bavaria and raised in a prosperous family of devout Catholic peasants until he was orphaned at the age of sixteen. Forced to support himself, the youth became apprenticed to a struggling bookbinder for whom he worked sixteen hours a day. During the rest of the time he devoured books as fast as he could lay his hands on them. Soon after he joined a bookbinders' union, its socialist leaders converted young Michael to the cause. Volunteering as an agitator in the weaving towns, Schwab was appalled by the condition of workers, who ate thin, brown bread and fat for dinner, and by the factory owners, who made young working girls their mistresses. After this disheartening life on the road as a traveling "trades fellow," Schwab left his fatherland behind forever, having learned that political liberty without economic freedom was "a mocking lie."[27]

The studious Schwab brought these views with him to America in 1879. When he first arrived in Chicago, the bookish Bavarian kept aloof from all organizations and spent his energy studying the English language and reading American history. Eventually he discovered that bookbinders were paid no better in his adopted city than they were in Hamburg and that, here too, thousands of children were "worked to perdition." In 1881, when Schwab could get no work as a bookbinder, he found a job translating an American romance into German for *Arbeiter-*

Zeitung. His skill impressed editor Grottkau, who hired him as a reporter for the daily. Before long, Schwab had resumed his life as a socialist agitator. He attended many meetings where German comrades delivered elaborate speeches and long denunciations of their rivals. But even a dedicated social revolutionary like Schwab was bored by all this talk. Yearning to be inspired, he joined a throng of German workers who packed into the North Side Turner Hall one night in October 1882 to hear a speech by the notorious firebrand Johann Most.[28]

Most, already well known to Chicago's German socialists as a revolutionary agitator and bold provocateur, was born an illegitimate child to poor parents at Augsburg, Germany, in 1846. He lost his mother to cholera when he was a little boy, and then endured a bitter childhood under the rule of a stepmother. At age thirteen his miserable life worsened when a botched operation on his jaw disfigured him and crushed his hopes for a career on the stage. His misery deepened after he apprenticed himself to a cruel master bookbinder.[29]

Ridiculed and ostracized because of his deformity, Most found solace in reading books after he finished a long day of binding them. Resentful and embittered, he left Germany when he was nineteen and wandered through Switzerland, where he lived in isolation until, in Zurich, he met some socialist workers who befriended him and shared their ideas with him. "From then on," he recalled, "I began to feel like a human being."[30]

Dedicating his life to "the cause of humanity," Most returned to Germany and threw himself into the burgeoning socialist movement. A tireless organizer, orator, songwriter, pamphleteer and popularizer of Marx's *Das Kapital,* he even won election to the Reichstag for two terms. But when Bismarck launched his assault on the socialists, Most was arrested and imprisoned. Upon release, he left Germany for London, where he published his own newspaper, *Freiheit,* and used it to attack all authority with boundless fervor.

When Most wrote an ecstatic response to the assassination of the czar in 1881, British authorities jailed him. After enduring sixteen months of hard labor, the agitator emerged from prison a hero and a martyr to German revolutionaries in exile around the world.

When Johann Most reached Chicago in 1882, 6,000 people came to hear him speak. The crowd spilled into the aisles and massed outside to hear his furious bombastic attacks on the capitalists and their government lackeys, who had already declared class war on the poor. Speaking in English with a heavy German accent and performing like a seasoned

Johann Most

actor, Most elicited thunderous applause from the huge immigrant audience, who found him shocking, entertaining and enthralling at the same time. Many immigrant workers who heard him speak were thrilled by his acidic diatribes against the rich and powerful and excited by his talk of manning the barricades and dynamiting police stations. Utterly contemptuous of election campaigns and legislative reforms, he insisted on direct action and revolutionary violence.[31]

Most galvanized young German socialists like August Spies and Michael Schwab, who felt mired in the tedium of their own propaganda. Though they were thrilled by Most's speeches, Chicago's social revolutionaries did not form conspiracies or launch violent assaults on the authorities. Most appealed to them more on visceral or emotional terms than on practical ones; indeed, the city's revolutionaries remained convinced by Marx and Engels that the road to socialism was a long one and that there were no shortcuts through individual acts of terror. And so, in 1883, Spies, Schwab and their comrades patiently set out to organize new clubs of Social Revolutionaries and to expand the circulation of their paper, the *Arbeiter-Zeitung.*

ALBERT PARSONS WAS ONE of the few Americans who played a prominent role in this activity because he shared the young Germans' belief that workers needed their own clubs and newspapers to absorb revolutionary ideas just as they needed their own militia to defend their rights; yet a truly powerful and radical workers' movement required something more as well: a unifying issue and a solidifying organization. Parsons found the issue in the old eight-hour demand, and he found the organization in a mysterious order called the Knights of Labor.

Founded in 1869, the Noble and Holy Order of the Knights of Labor existed secretly in a few eastern cities for several years and then emerged out of the shadows to hold its first national assembly a few months after the 1877 railroad strike.[32] Albert Parsons had joined the order on July 4, 1876, a time when the organization was little more than a fraternal order of craftsmen with elaborate rituals, mostly borrowed from the Masons. The mystic aura of the Knights attracted him, as did their moral code, one that glorified chivalrous manhood and generous fraternity. The young printer also believed that the Knights could create a genuine "brotherhood of toil" among men of different crafts, religions, races and nationalities, even among men who fought on opposing sides in the Civil War. Furthermore, he shared the conviction of the order's founders that the wage system created opposing classes and caused bloody conflicts, and that it should be replaced by a cooperative economy that would allow dependent wage workers to become independent producers. Soon after he joined the Noble and Holy Order, Parsons linked up with his comrade George Schilling and founded the first Chicago assembly of the Knights, later known as the "old 400."[33]

Meanwhile, Parsons tried, almost single-handedly, to revive the eight-hour crusade Chicago workers had abandoned after their devastating defeat in 1867. He invited the legendary founder of the Eight-Hour League, Ira Steward, to the city and then joined the old man in an effort to create a new movement that would "band together all workers" of all races and all nationalities into "one grand labor brotherhood." In 1882, Parsons's hopes for such a movement suddenly rose when union carpenters walked out to reduce their workweek and German bakers struck to reduce their long, hot workday, which averaged more than fifteen hours and often stretched to seventeen or eighteen. These job actions confirmed the view of Parsons and other socialists that the eight-hour system could be achieved only through direct action by workers, not by laws that could be subverted by judges, ignored by elected officials and defied by employers.[34]

Such a transformation would not occur without a new kind of labor movement that amalgamated the fractured trade unions into one solidified organization. The few existing trade unions, based largely on the power of craftsmen like carpenters, cigar makers and ironworkers, had formed a new national Federation of Organized Trades and Labor Unions in 1881, but no unified action had taken place as a result. The first sign of change came in March 1882, when a group of German tanners struck and demanded a wage equal to that of the more skilled English-speaking curriers. When employers refused the demand and the curriers struck in sympathy with the immigrant tanners, this action astounded the *Chicago Tribune,* because the curriers acted not on the basis "of any grievance of their own, but because of a sentimental and sympathetic feeling for another class of workmen." The sympathy strike even surprised the editor of the trades council newspaper, who said it was "something new and wonderful." The seventy-two-day exercise in solidarity was, according to the Illinois Bureau of Labor Statistics, "one of the most remarkable on record," an action "conducted on the principle of the Knights of Labor which proclaims that 'an injury to one is the concern of all.' "[35] Suddenly, a group of divided workers actually demonstrated the ideal of working-class solidarity espoused by dreamers like Albert Parsons.

A few weeks later the Knights of Labor found a new constituency among Irish brickyard workers on the Southwest Side who took a job action to restore wage rates cut during the long depression. The Knights advised the strikers to refrain from the violence that had characterized earlier protests in what police called the "terror district." After hearing these assurances, Mayor Carter Harrison ordered the police to stay out of the conflict. Unable to shield strikebreakers from running a gauntlet of verbal abuse by the strikers, their families and their neighbors, the brickyard owners conceded to their workers' demands and the Knights' prestige soared.[36]

During the spring of 1882 hundreds of immigrant workers in Chicago became Knights of Labor—butchers and packinghouse workers in the stockyards, brick makers and iron rollers on Goose Island, blacksmiths and brass finishers on the West Side, dry-goods clerks and telegraphers in the downtown business district. Besides trade assemblies for skilled workers, the Knights created mixed assemblies to reach out to unskilled workers of all kinds: female bookbinders, shoe stitchers and carpet weavers, even 7,000 "sewing girls" who toiled in clothing factories.[37]

In the summer of 1883 one assembly of the Knights felt confident enough to challenge one of the nation's most important monopolies, the Western Union Telegraph Company, controlled by railroad magnate Jay

Gould. The telegraphers formed an assembly of the Knights, and when Western Union's president refused to talk with them, the operators struck on July 19, 1883. Even the religious press, uniformly hostile to strikes and to unions, supported the walkout, because it was conducted peacefully, and above all because it was caused by a monopoly company under the control of the notorious speculator Gould. *Harper's Weekly* expressed amazement that several thousand men and women in the United States and Canada had quit work at precisely the same moment and had then managed their strike with "great skill and marvelous precision." The journal said that Western Union had displayed a "grasping and unscrupulous attitude" toward its operators, but its editor worried that the walkout would cause a disastrous breakdown of the nation's communication system.[38]

The telegraphers' unified action caused an enormous stir in Chicago, where Western Union was headquartered and where the nation's railroads and commodity markets were centered. No city depended more upon instant telegraph communications. Yet the strikers won widespread public support, despite the "universal inconvenience" caused by their actions. All trade unionists and many small businessmen avidly supported the telegraphers in their brave stand against the mighty Gould empire. To Albert Parsons and the socialists, the strike represented far more than a moral stand against monopoly power. At one packed meeting of strikers and their supporters, Parsons likened the union telegraphers to his own printers, referring to both groups as "brain workers" whose fingers controlled the composition and flow of information so essential to modern business and government. These highly skilled workers were quite capable of running the nation's communications industry without the likes of profiteers like Jay Gould in the way.[39]

Expressions of solidarity with the telegraphers, including Parsons's eloquent outburst, did not, however, arouse tangible support in the form of strike relief or sympathetic action. When the aid the strikers expected from the Knights of Labor did not arrive, the head of the telegraphers' union called off the strike and ordered the men back to work. Those who returned to Western Union were required to sign "an ironclad oath" pledging not to join any labor organization.[40]

The telegraphers' defeat added to the woes of the Chicago Knights, who, after the spectacular strikes of 1882 and the heady months of expansion that followed, now faced employers who refused to recognize the order or to arbitrate disputes with them. By the fall of 1883 the

Knights' hopes of organizing 50,000 workers in Chicago had faded and their ranks had dwindled to a mere 1,000 members.[41]

IT WAS UNDER these sobering circumstances in October 1883 that Albert Parsons and August Spies boarded a train for Pennsylvania, where they would meet with other social revolutionaries to create a new organization that would prepare workers for what they saw as the hard and bitter struggle ahead. The Chicago militants joined other trade union delegates in Pittsburgh, where they announced the creation of the International Working People's Association (IWPA), a militant body dedicated to "agitation for the purpose of organization [and] organization for the purpose of rebellion." The manifesto they addressed to the workingmen of America began by quoting Thomas Jefferson's "justification for armed resistance" in a situation "when a long train of abuses and usurpations" created an "absolute despotism."[42]

The Pittsburgh Manifesto, written in part by August Spies and Johann Most, rejected formal political institutions as agencies of a propertied class that was becoming richer every day by stealing the labor of others. This system of exploitation of the laborer by the capitalist would continue until "the misery of the wage-workers is forced to the extreme." There was no possibility of voluntary relief: "all attempts in the past to reform this monstrous system by peaceable means, such as the ballot, have been futile, and all such future efforts must necessarily be so."[43]

Spies and Parsons returned to Chicago, distributed copies of the Pittsburgh Manifesto and organized about a dozen little clubs for the IWPA. But with business booming, the Knights of Labor fading from view and the socialist movement reduced to two small camps of warring sects, there seemed little likelihood that workers would notice, let alone respond to, the bold declarations of a few frustrated union militants with revolution on their minds.

The socialists realized that most workers in Chicago maintained ancestral loyalties to their own kind and endured their hardships with surprisingly little complaint; this passivity seemed especially pronounced among devout Catholics of peasant origin. Most of these wage earners, especially immigrants, remained intimidated by the police and the businessmen's militia and indebted to their employers and local patronage bosses for their jobs. They yearned for lives of security and comfort, not for futures filled with struggle and strife. Even the best socialist propagandist in the city, August Spies, had not over-come his fear that most workingmen were "simply tools of custom"—"automatons incapable of thinking and reasoning for themselves." And even the best socialist agitator in the city, Albert Parsons, did not hide his fear that the new eight-hour movement was doomed to defeat by its enemies. "I know," he said, "that defenseless men, women and children must finally succumb to the power of the discharge, black-list and lockout . . . enforced by the militiaman's bayonet and the policeman's club."[44]

And yet, despite their doubts and fears, Spies and Parsons remained active in the Knights of Labor and the eight-hour campaign because they wanted to be part of a broader class movement and not stand aloof from the mass of workers. Moreover, they had convinced themselves, against all sorts of discouraging evidence, that workers would rise up again, as they had in 1877, that workers would be impelled by forces they felt but did not wholly understand to move unconsciously and irresistibly toward social revolution. This, they believed, was the natural order of things, the logical outcome of the events they had witnessed during the violent years that had passed since they came to Chicago as young tradesmen hoping to improve themselves.

Chapter Seven

A Brutal and Inventive Vitality

AT THE END OF 1883, Chicago's business was booming like never before. Every day 800 freight and passenger trains came and left the city's six busy terminals, hauling goods out and bringing people in. During the 1880s nearly 250,000 immigrants from Europe and Canada flooded the city looking for work in her roaring factories and mills. At this point, when labor was in high demand, the city contained forty foundries, fifty-six machine shops and five iron rolling mills, including the huge Union Steel Company on the edge of Bridgeport, where workers produced 180,000 tons of iron and steel rails each year during a decade of unprecedented railroad construction.[1]

Overall, Chicago's industrial production advanced at a breakneck pace, multiplying twenty-one times during the decade. The net value of goods produced by the city's leading manufacturers leapt from $28 million to a staggering total of $760 million in these halcyon years when Chicago's economic growth set a pace that amazed the nation and the world. A spontaneously exploding center of force, it embodied, as few other places could, "the brutal and inventive vitality of the nineteenth century."[2]

Nowhere was the creativity and brutality of "rough-and-tumble business Chicago" more obvious than in the slaughtering industry, where, as Saul Bellow wrote, progress was written "in the blood of the yards." The "revolutionary newness" that made the city famous was indeed evident at the huge Union Stock Yards, where spectacular new forms of production and discipline yielded unprecedented outputs and profits. The city's largest meatpackers, Gustavus Swift and Philip Armour, were true business revolutionaries whose innovations in industrial methods helped make Chicago "a world city."[3]

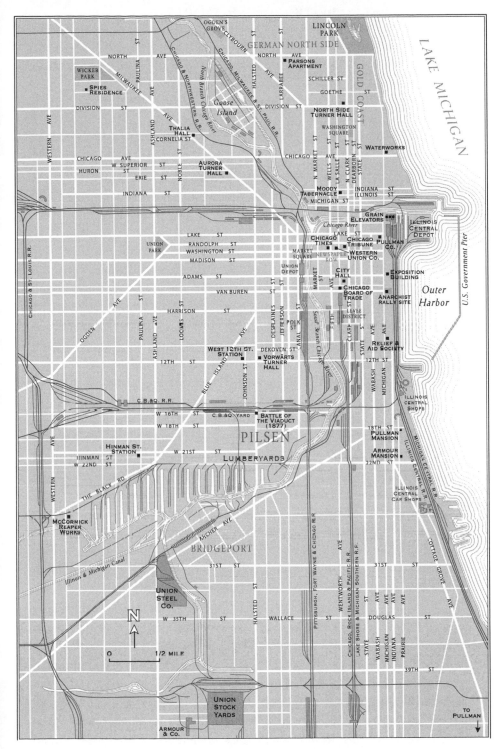

*Map of Chicago during the early 1880s, showing prominent
industries, railroads and other important sites*

Armour perfected the mechanized animal kill that became such a stunning spectacle to visitors, including writers like Rudyard Kipling, who later described the "pig men" who were "spattered with blood" and "the cow butchers" who "were bathed in it"—all working in a fearful stench with a furious intensity. Mechanization took command early and effectively in meatpacking, but soon other industrialists were following the packers' lead.[4]

The results of this creative activity were spectacular for Armour's company, which led the industry's consolidation and expansion over the next decade. The size of the firm's workforce doubled and the value of product grew by 344 percent, ten times faster than wages increased. In just nine years Armour's profits leapt from $200,000 to $5.5 million.[5]

When the depression ended, Armour's Irish and German butchers joined their fellow stockyard workers in demanding a larger share of the company's marvelous growth. Their leaders wanted the employers to agree to hire union members first and not to discharge them without just cause. Some small packers agreed to these terms, but Armour would have none of it.[6] He rejected the butchers' demands, locked out the union and reopened his plant with nonunion men. The strike leaders were blacklisted and never worked in the yards again.[7]

The city's skilled workers faced a vexing dilemma in 1883. Chicago employers paid higher wages than they could earn in other cities, but if they, the employees, demanded or even requested increases to compensate for the losses of the depression years or to keep up with the rising cost of fuel, food and housing, they met with stiff resistance. Employers like Philip Armour assumed that fixing wages, higher or lower, was a prerogative that came with ownership.

The union molders at McCormick Reaper Works had been more successful than most skilled workers in obtaining what they regarded as a living wage. Cyrus and Leander McCormick owned an extremely profitable business and paid relatively high wages; and, despite periodic strikes by union molders, the brothers retained the respect of their wage hands. Indeed, when the long depression ended, the McCormicks agreed to the union men's request to raise the wage rates they had reduced during the hard times.[8]

In 1880, Leander McCormick left the works after a feud with his brother Cyrus, who soon retired and put his twenty-one-year-old son Cyrus, Jr., in charge. Young McCormick immediately hired a new management team; but the men he entrusted with the direction of 1,200 restless factory workers lacked firsthand experience with a large industrial workforce. Hard feelings festered in the foundries and assembly shops. One employee wrote to the president and said the old hands were leaving because of harsh treatment: "We are treated as though we are dogs," he moaned.[9]

Cyrus, Jr., had attended Princeton, where he learned mathematics and economics. Applying this knowledge in 1881, he hired an accountant to calculate the firm's manufacturing costs per machine, along with the cost of labor per unit. The results appalled him so much that he established a new hard line on wages. When the union molders petitioned for a raise in 1882, McCormick's assistant superintendent told the men they were set on "a suicidal course." As the molders' union gathered its strength and prepared for a long struggle, McCormick's managers began to explore ways of using machines to replace the union men.[10]

CYRUS McCORMICK'S NEW SOLUTION to his problems with skilled union men was a strategy scores of other Chicago manufacturers had chosen by investing millions of dollars in new machinery to replace certain handworkers and to speed up the pace of work for the rest—all within a very short and decisive period from 1879 to 1884.[11]

McCormick Reaper Works on the Black Road in 1885, looking south

Some trades were devastated by the invasion of machines. In the slaughtering and packing industry, skilled butchers continued to give way to more advanced "disassembly lines" in larger and larger plants. Even small manufacturers mechanized their works, like one German sausage producer who let seventy-five of his workers go and replaced them with a single machine he claimed was more efficient than all of them combined. Owners of cooperages also installed new machines for making barrels that took the pride and joy out of the coopers' work, according to one craftsman. When English curriers struck in support of German tanners in 1882, the tannery owner imported whitening and fleshing machines that he planned to use to halve the workforce. After Irish brick makers waged a battle for higher wages that year, their employer introduced a machine that allowed an individual worker to make three times as many bricks in a day.[12] Fights over wage rates had been erupting in Chicago shops off and on for years; it was simply a fact of industrial life. But mechanization hit the skilled trades with such suddenness that it shocked craftsmen and filled them with dread.

New machinery made the greatest impact in the trades where German immigrants were concentrated, such as woodworking and cigar making. The city's enormous army of carpenters also found their trade imperiled by contractors who bought windows, doors and other standardized wooden pieces made by machine and hired unskilled "green hands" to install them. Working for piece-rate wages, these installers were paid half the money earned by an experienced, all-around carpenter.[13]

The men who rolled cigars faced a similar threat. Proprietors of two sizable Chicago cigar shops installed newly invented machines operated by teenaged boys and girls who earned 50 cents to $1 a day. The producer could now have 1,000 cigars of the best brand made for $8 compared to the $18 it cost to pay union craftsmen to make the same batch by hand. In an analysis of the cigar industry, an *Arbeiter-Zeitung* reporter calculated that the manufacturers' profits leapt 400 percent as a result of "plundering" their workers.[14]

The logic of capitalist enterprise made using machines instead of men an obvious choice for owners who could afford to mechanize. But among the craftsmen displaced by this logic a moral question remained: Would machines, driven by the endless hunger for profit, destroy a way of life that gave skilled workers a sense of pride in what they produced and gave the consumer a high-quality product as a result? Is this what progress meant? The German sausage makers insisted that machines could not do the work as well humans did, pointing out that bits of refuse remained inside the machine-made sausages. But such complaints seemed futile in the face of machinery's "merciless advance."[15] In story after story, *Arbeiter-Zeitung* reporters revealed how machines ran the workers and how employers used machinery to tighten their control.[16]

Even after craftsmen lost their autonomy and entered larger shops and factories, many retained a moral code that governed how they worked, how they treated one another and how they ensured the quality of their products. Cheaper "green hands" who could be pushed and rushed by the boss often botched jobs and turned out shoddy goods. During his travels, August Spies had seen common laborers accept this kind of abuse; it seemed to him nothing less than an intolerable affront to their manhood. No self-respecting craftsman would allow himself to be driven or intimidated at work.[17]

By the same token, proud American and European craftsmen viewed other forms of unskilled or menial labor as degrading. Some men and women worked side by side in bookbinding and tailoring shops, but male garment cutters could not imagine performing the women's work of sewing clothing. And no white workingman ever pictured himself doing the menial work assigned to "colored" men in service or to the despised "Chinamen" in the laundries. The corollary was that few of the white trades allowed access to women or men of color or to unskilled immigrants, except on a segregated basis. In the white world, however, self-reliant craftsmen often expressed "a defiant sense of egalitarianism" toward other men who acted as their superiors. Their code was based on a sense of self-worth gained through long apprenticeship and mature workmanship in an honorable trade. They believed their work was noble, even holy, and that they should be regarded romantically as "knights of labor." Thus, manly workers refused to be put upon by their bosses or to accept any affront to their dignity. They also opposed efforts to pit them against one another. An honorable, respectable workingman did not steal work from his fellows or seek to undermine their customs and standards by rushing to please the boss or simply to make more money. Such were the ingredients of the craftsmen's code, traits that young and inexperienced workers who entered a trade were taught to honor and obey.[18]

The habits that craftsmen cultivated were first expressed in the early benevolent societies based on the principle of mutual aid and then in the first craft unions their members called "brotherhoods." These "rituals of mutuality" fused readily with the practices of democratic citizenship that evolved during the nineteenth century among white mechanics and work-ingmen who came to see themselves as the backbone of the republic.[19]

Being a skilled tradesman, a competent craftsman and an intelligent citizen required, above all, enlightenment through self-edification. Many craftsmen took pride in the breadth and depth of their reading, and appreciated what they learned from each other on the job. Cigar rollers sometimes asked a literate one among them to read a book or a newspa-per aloud to them while they worked. Samuel Gompers, who heard pas-sages from Marx's work from such a reader, wrote of his particular cigar shop as a little educational forum where he learned to think and speak critically. "It was a world in itself, a cosmopolitan world," inhabited by shop mates from many strange lands, he recalled. Good cigar makers could roll the product carefully and effectively but more or less mechan-ically, which left them free to think, talk and listen to each other or to sing together. "I loved the freedom of that work," Gompers recalled, "for I had learned that mind freedom accompanied skill as a craftsman."[20]

Manufacturers exerted little control over the cigar makers, who worked by the piece, and some producers complained that many of their men would come into the shop in the morning, roll a few stogies and then go to a beer saloon and play cards for a few hours, willfully cutting the day's production and voluntarily limiting their own earnings. These irreg-ular work habits appeared in other trades as well, for instance, among German brewers, who clung to their Old World privilege of drinking free beer while they worked in the breweries.[21] Coopers would appear at work on Saturday morning, like all wage earners did in those years, and then, in some places, they would pool their pay and buy a "Goose Egg," a half barrel of beer. "Little groups of jolly fellows would often sit around upturned barrels playing poker . . . ," wrote a historian of cooperage, "until they received their pay and the 'Goose Egg' was dry." After a night out on Saturday and an afternoon of drinking on Sunday, the coopers were not in the best condition to settle down to a regular day's work. They would then spend a "blue Monday" sharpening tools, bringing in sup-plies and discussing the news of the day.[22]

Into this world, with its honored traditions, its irregular work habits and its rituals of mutuality came the machine. It rattled on relentlessly "never tiring, never resting," wrote Michael Schwab, dragging the worker along with it.[23] And behind the machine stood a man, an owner or a fore-man, who regarded the craftsmen's stubborn old habits and craft union rules as nothing more than ancient customs, relics of medieval times in a modern world governed by the need for industrial efficiency and the unforgiving laws of political economy.

THE *ARBEITER-ZEITUNG* offered detailed reports and analyses of these new developments in Chicago's workshops to its German readers. Many editorials simply pointed out how bosses were displacing good workers and "plundering" others because they were greedy capitalists; others were quite sophisticated. For example, in an 1883 article on "How Wages Are Depressed," the author explained that "big capital" in Chicago had taken the lead in "employing the latest technology and imposing the division of labor" that came with it. The craftsman's skill and intelligence were no longer as valued and rewarded, and in many places he was reduced to the status of a day laborer who tolerated his situation until he could move up to a higher-paying job. The classification of workers within the same trade into various subordinate groups was destroying "feelings of solidarity that existed within individual crafts." A new spirit reigned within the city's factories, the writer noted: "Each man for himself, and the Devil take the hindmost." Moreover, existing trade unions that called themselves brotherhoods had failed to counter this self-serving attitude among employees in Chicago's big industries.[24]

In 1884 the city's small number of organized workers belonged to trade union locals affiliated with the city's Trades and Labor Assembly and with the young national Federation of Organized Trades and Labor Unions. Composed largely of skilled craftsmen, not common laborers, these trade unions were led by pragmatists increasingly irritated by the visionary Knights and by the socialists in their own ranks. They regarded their unions as ends in themselves, not as means to an ond, not as a force for building solidarity among workers or for achieving a cooperative society such as the one envisioned by the social revolutionaries at the Pittsburgh Congress in 1883. "We have no immediate ends," testified the president of the Cigar Makers' International Union that year. "We are going from day to day. We fight only for immediate objects . . . that can be realized in a few years."[25]

This careful posture seemed suicidal to many craftsmen in Chicago, who saw themselves being replaced by machines and "green hands." By June of 1884 the German socialists in the Chicago Cigar Makers' Union had had enough of going from day to day; they broke with the national organization and formed a "progressive" cigar makers' local. For this act of rebellion, they were expelled from the city Trades Assembly. Within a few months the German renegades had inspired eight other breakaway unions to join them in creating a new Central Labor Union closely allied with the International Working People's Association and its objectives. The radical leaders of the new labor body accused the Trades Assembly of being "a bogus labor organization" led by businessmen, not by true union men; furthermore, its members were craft unionists who constituted an "aristocracy of labor" and who expressed concern only for their own welfare and not for the condition of the unskilled workers.[26]

Underlying these tensions over union politics were older religious and ethnic differences among Chicago's workers. Most leaders of craft unions tended to be English-speaking Protestants of American, Canadian and British origins, although some were Irish Catholics. Religious hostilities had cooled during the Civil War, and by the 1880s Christian workers of all denominations readily joined the same unions. The Knights of Labor even abandoned their secret rituals to avoid condemnation by Catholic cardinals and to open their order to once-despised "papists." The social revolutionaries in Chicago took an opposite tack, alienating devout Catholics and Protestants alike by criticizing their clergymen and their beliefs and by calling their followers to secular meetings on Sundays. One of the few things the city's many ministers, missionaries, priests and rabbis agreed on was that the red internationals sounded terribly like the evil children of the godless French Jacobins and Communards.[27]

As the International Working People's Association extended its activities into the city's immigrant neighborhoods, Catholic priests in the German and Czech parishes swung into action against the heathens in their midst. The bishops of the church could be fairly sure that priests in Chicago's Polish and Irish parishes would keep their flocks inoculated against the infectious ideas spread by socialist subversives. Catholic clergymen were more worried that German and Bohemian Catholics were being seduced by freethinkers and socialist agitators.[28]

Protestant ministers and missionaries expressed even more anxiety than Catholic priests about the spiritual lives of poor city dwellers. Even Chicago's famous soul saver, the greatest of all evangelists, Dwight L. Moody, despaired when his big revivals failed to attract the downtrodden.[29] In a best-selling book, *Our Country,* Josiah Strong, a Congregational minister with midwestern roots, expressed the growing fear among native-born Protestants that immigrant workers in the great industrial cities could no longer be contained within their slums, where "volcanic fires of deep discontent" smoldered. The dangerous classes seemed ready, at any moment, to sweep like a flood over the homes of respectable Christian people. The city churches were asleep, Strong charged, citing one section of Chicago where thousands of children lived "without the gospel of Jesus Christ," a "district of saloons and dago shops and other vile places," where many more children were arrested than attended Sunday School.[30]

As concerned clergymen like Josiah Strong fretted over losing souls to the inner city, working-class reformers and radicals suffused their speaking and writing with biblical parables and verses, which they used to chastise their oppressors and arouse the spirits of their followers. For example, George McNeill, a founder of the first eight-hour movement and an influential figure in the development of young Knights like Albert Parsons, believed that the workers' dream of an equitable life on earth was revealed in the gospels. The Bible foretold a time, McNeill wrote, when the "Golden Rule of Christ would govern the relations of men in all their duties toward their fellows, in factory and work-shop, in the mine, in the field, in commerce, everywhere."[31]

This strain of Protestant millennialism even appeared in the speeches of August Spies, who admired the Protestant martyr Thomas Munzer and believed the Bible "commanded equality and brotherhood among men on earth." Like most other nineteenth-century American radicals, the social revolutionaries felt compelled to illustrate their secular complaints with sacred texts and to connect their vision of a truly free society with the Christian image of a heaven on earth. Unlike the European anarchists, whose hostility to religion knew no bounds, the socialist internationals devoted little attention to the ministries of their clerical opponents. They had much larger quarry in their sights: the evil capitalists who lived, as they saw it, in a paradise of riches while they made life for Chicago's workers a hell on earth.[32]

WHILE NEW FORMS of mechanization and industrial discipline affected certain trades during the early 1880s, a massive calamity befell a far greater number of wage earners. Another depression enveloped Chicago late in 1883, and the hardships that followed proved far more severe than those experienced in the long depression that had ended just three years before.[33]

Once again social commentators appeared to analyze the causes and assign blame for the calamity, as they had a decade before, but now the criticisms came not only from voices of socialists and trade unionists but from the pens of journalists like the *Chicago Tribune*'s famous business writer Henry Demarest Lloyd. The journalist no longer blamed the market for economic distress, but pointed his finger at railroad barons like Jay Gould who hoarded land and wealth and refused to raise wages or reduce hours for their wage hands. Henry George, author of the enormously influential book *Progress and Poverty,* also accused railroad magnates like Gould of causing the nation's worst social problems. The wealth created by railroads allowed a few "American pashas" to count their income by the millions each month while their employees survived on $1.50 a day. Even in the wealthy state of Illinois, where the nation's railroads converged, workingmen could not earn enough for their daily bread and were forced to depend upon the labor of women and children to eke out an existence. "The people are largely conscious of this," George observed, "and there is among the masses much dissatisfaction."[34]

Nowhere in the nation were wage earners as conscious of the crisis as they were in Chicago; this had less to do with the sophisticated commentary of reformers like Lloyd and George than it did with the speeches of socialists like Albert and Lucy Parsons and the reports of journalists like August Spies and his new associate Michael Schwab.

When Spies became editor of the *Arbeiter-Zeitung* in 1884, he sent Schwab into the streets of Chicago. Already well read and well traveled, the former bookbinder proved to be a tireless investigator, who exposed the city's dark side to tens of thousands of German-speaking workers. After a day in the South Side slums, he wrote of "hovels where two, three and four families lived in one room with little ventilation and barely a stream of sunlight" and of people he saw "living from the ash barrels where they found half rotten vegetables and from offal they were given by local butchers." Pride kept the destitute from seeking aid, and so they were left "deep in the shadows." He told a shocking tale of two cities: one city of overcrowded tenement houses and fetid streets where a smallpox epidemic took 2,000 lives, and another city of spacious mansions and well-groomed avenues where pedestrians caught the lake breezes.[35]

Besides exposing extremes of wealth and poverty in Chicago, the socialists insisted on dramatizing the contrast and moralizing about what it meant. On Thanksgiving Day, 1884, the International Working People's

Association staged a "poor people's march" to expose the self-indulgence of wealthy people who gave thanks to God for their blessings and blamed the poor for their own sufferings. While grateful families ate turkey dinners that day, the International marched its cadre of workingmen and workingwomen through the cold streets carrying "the emblem of hunger," the black flag. They proceeded through the fashionable thoroughfares of the city, said one police observer, with two women as standard-bearers carrying red and black flags, stopping before the residences of the wealthy and "indulging in all sorts of noises, groans and cat calls."[36]

Then the procession marched downtown to Market Street, where their speakers held forth. Albert Parsons began by saying, "We assemble as representatives of the disinherited, to speak in the name of 40,000 unemployed working men in Chicago" who had nothing for which to be thankful. To those who supped in their comfortable homes, he offered jeremiads, quoting first from the Epistle of James, Chapter 5, on the miseries that would come upon rich men when the treasures they heaped together for their last days became rusted and cankered, and then from the Old Testament prophet Habakkuk, who warned, "Woe to him who buildeth a town by blood, and establisheth a city by iniquity."[37]

Hard times had returned to Chicago, but the consequent ordeal did not turn working people into socialists. In fact, unemployment depressed them and forced them to depend on local charities and patronage bosses, or to seek out saloonkeepers and police officers who might give them a place to sleep at night; and it often compelled them to beg for work and accept it on any terms the employer dictated. What roused many of the city's workers from a state of hopelessness was the incessant activity of the socialists, because they offered thousands of unemployed poor people a way to understand the crisis they experienced and to identify who was to blame.[38] Albert Parsons, for one, delivered many lectures about why periodic panics occurred and why they were growing more frequent and intense. The main cause of the current crisis, he said in 1884, was overproduction caused by the race for profit. In this competition among capitalists who wanted to corner the market, wage earners were the first to suffer because, during business panics, wage cuts and layoffs would always be made in order to preserve profits.[39]

And yet social revolutionaries like Parsons believed that beyond the current crisis there was hope for the future. Insufferable conditions were making workers more conscious of common class interests. As a result, despite the many differences that divided them and the many delusions that clouded their thinking, wage earners would come together. When they did, workers would feel their power and grasp the possibility of creating a new cooperative society to replace the old competitive order.[40]

IN THE EARLY 1880S, few American social commentators, other than the socialists, believed class consciousness could emerge in the United States, because of its open frontier, its endless opportunities for entrepreneurs and its vaunted democracy. Class hatred existed in Europe, but in America it existed only in the minds of deluded socialists. In 1883, however, some leading citizens remarked on an alarming deterioration of relations between a huge population of laborers and a tiny population of employers, investors, bankers and lawyers. Some even found themselves using the language of class to describe what they saw and felt in testimony before the United States Senate Committee Upon the Relations Between Labor and Capital.[41]

When asked by commissioners about the state of feeling between the laboring class and the employing class, the *Chicago Tribune*'s Joseph Medill said that a general feeling of distrust and dissatisfaction existed and was increasing fast enough to pose a serious threat to the country. "The trades unions of this country are feeling more and more dissatisfied with their position, and they are developing more and more of what might be called a communistic feeling—a tendency or desire to resort to what might be called revolutionary or chaotic methods for rectifying things. They are not satisfied with their division of the profits of business, and they look at the enormous and sudden acquirement of fortunes by a few speculators with feelings of anger."[42]

Medill blamed these hard feelings on strikes by "trades union people" who seemed in unanimous agreement that employers could afford to pay higher wages without increasing prices, and that the bosses refused out of "pure selfishness." Given this regrettable bias among union men, said Medill, it was no wonder that worker protests threatened "to rend the social fabric" and that every strike seemed like "a species of civil war."[43]

The situation Medill described seemed particularly acute in Chicago, where he expected trade union people to cause a good deal of trouble in the coming years. The first sign of the big trouble to come appeared at the McCormick Reaper Works, where the union iron molders angrily grumbled over a 10 percent wage cut young Cyrus had imposed even though the company had earned record profits the previous fall. When some of the workers struck on March 16, 1885, McCormick's general manager discharged men in the wood department to intimidate the rest of the workforce; he also ordered crews to build barracks inside the plant gates to house strikebreakers around the clock. Meanwhile, a call went out for nonunion molders, who were offered protection from the strikers by guards hired from the Pinkerton Detective Agency, headquartered in Chicago.

The agency's founder, Allan Pinkerton, had become renowned eight years earlier when he hired a spy, James McParlan, to infiltrate the Molly Maguires, a militant cadre of Irish coal miners who had been fighting a guerrilla war against mine operators and their hired gunmen in Pennsylvania. Pinkerton's famous informer testified against the Mollies in a murder trial that sent ten mineworkers to the gallows on June 21, 1877. The hangings provided a stunning demonstration of the state's power to impose the ultimate penalty on militant workers, and it left a haunting memory of "Molly after Molly walking to the gallows in the pale light of dawn, often holding a single rose sent by a wife or girl friend." This terrible day of retribution was known as Black Thursday not only in Irish mining patches but in urban ghettos across the land, places like Bridgeport in Chicago, where crowds of Irish iron molders and their supporters encountered the hated "Pinks" at the McCormick works in the winter of 1885.[44]

Young McCormick had made the decision to cut wages with no understanding of the possible consequences; nothing he had learned at Princeton or as an understudy to his father (who had died the previous year) had "given him any insight into the feelings or the temper of the 1,400 men who labored in his factory."[45] McCormick also failed to realize that hiring Pinkerton gunmen to protect strikebreakers would infuriate the Irish residents of Bridgeport. Indeed, confrontations between the strikers and the agents quickly turned violent. During one set-to, Pinkerton's men fired off a few rounds from their Winchesters, seriously wounding several people, including some bystanders. The police viewed this action as cowardly and arrested four of the private guards, who were later charged with manslaughter, but McCormick's general manager wrote in despair that, while most of the men wanted to keep working, a "fighting Irish element" was ready to knock down and beat anyone who wanted to work and not a policeman would stir a hand to offer protection.[46]

A climactic struggle erupted at the plant gates on April 28, 1885, when the Pinkertons failed to hold their ground after strikers attacked trolleys full of strikebreakers headed for the plant. The union forces then assaulted a busload of Pinkertons, beat them with fists and clubs, burned their vehicle and seized a case of rifles intended for use in guarding the factory. One of the agents reported back to the agency's downtown office that the attack on the guards was the work of Irishmen employed as molders and helpers, "nearly all members of the Ancient Order of Hibernians, who have the most bitter enmity against the Agency since the hanging of the Molly Maguires in Pennsylvania."[47]

In 1885 many of the Irish workers employed at McCormick's were members not only of the Hibernians but also of the radical Land League and the secret Clan-Na-Gael, whose nationalist cadre, led by Chicago's Alexander Sullivan, had begun bombing government buildings in London. Both organizations were condemned as communistic by Catholic clergy, just as the Mollies had been condemned; nonetheless, all three groups remained popular among Irish workingmen in Chicago. Although the anarchism of the International won very little support in the city's poor Irish parishes, Catholic laborers displayed passionate attraction to various forms of radicalism, including currency and land reform, as well as cooperation. All this developed alongside a growing nationalism spurred by the war for land in colonial Ireland.[48]

The Catholic Church governed the religious practices of the Irish, just as the Democratic Party determined their voting habits, but neither parish priests nor ward bosses were able to control working-class militants or radical nationalists (they were often one and the same) as their activities escalated in the mid 1880s. In 1885, German anarchist workers and Irish nationalist workers at McCormick's swam in different streams of radicalism, but early in the following year, the two streams would join at the big farm machinery plant on the South Branch of the Chicago River.

In the midst of the April crisis in 1885, McCormick appealed to Mayor Carter Harrison for more police so that the plant could run at full capacity. The mayor refused, and instead called for a settlement of the dispute. He also praised the union negotiating committee, even though it included labor leaders the company regarded as prime movers in the disturbance. McCormick still refused to meet with the men in a body and insisted that the wage cut was necessitated by the business depression. At this point Chicago industrialists became alarmed that the rising tide of union defiance would produce a general strike. Philip Armour firmly

Cyrus McCormick, Jr.

advised Cyrus, Jr., to give in to the men because the strike was becoming an "open war."[49]

At the risk of losing face in the business community, McCormick withdrew the wage cut he had imposed on his unionized craftsmen. The skilled molders refused to accept the offer, however, unless it was extended to the less skilled piece-rate men and unless all strikebreakers were removed from the works. McCormick again relented, but the harrowing experience convinced him that he must rid the works of the union molders by replacing them with machines.

After the settlement, Cyrus McCormick received a letter of rebuke from his mother, the estimable Nettie Fowler McCormick, who had run the works for a time after her husband retired. She had turned the company over to her son and then devoted her time to philanthropy, but from far away in Philadelphia she kept an eye on things at the reaper works. After the plant reopened, she wrote to Cyrus, Jr., with "a sore heart" that his actions were "all wrong" and that the violent strike had damaged the family's relations with its workmen. As a result, trouble had come to hundreds of families and in consequence "fierce passions" had been aroused.[50]

Emboldened by the union molders' triumph over McCormick and the

Pinkertons, iron-ore shovelers in the nearby docks struck, as did printers and rolling-mill workers, and even hospital nurses. As this surge of worker militancy gathered force, news came of a horrible tragedy in the quarries just south of the city near Lemont.

When quarry workers walked out to protest a wage cut and employers imported strikebreakers, large crowds arrived to block the replacement workers. Local authorities, overmatched by the strike force, called on the governor to send in the militia. Richard Oglesby, who had been elected to another term in 1884, reluctantly gave the order. Soon after the troops arrived in Lemont, the general in charge wired the governor to report that A. R. Parsons, the "Chicago communist," was there inciting the strikers and plotting to "organize a commune." The agitator had apparently failed in these efforts, but he remained in Lemont to cover the story for his anarchist newspaper.[51]

On May 4, Parsons saw a crowd of quarry workers confront the militiamen who were protecting strikebreakers. When the strikers cast stones at the troopers, the troopers fired their Winchesters into the assembly, killing two men instantly and wounding many others. Parsons described the scene in an enraged newspaper report. "The shrieks of wounded and dying men filled the air," he wrote, "the warm blood of the people bathed the flagstones of the sidewalks." The shootings at Lemont made an indelible impression on Parsons and confirmed his belief that "without arms and organization, the worker is left to the mercy of those who rob, murder and enslave him."[52]

On May 20 a group of social revolutionaries met in Chicago to condemn the militia for the killings at Lemont; they also vowed to organize themselves into an armed company to defend workers against the militia and to establish "a school on chemistry" where the manufacture and use of explosives would be taught. One speaker went far beyond this call for armed self-defense. A *Tribune* reporter reportedly heard "Citizeness" Lucy Parsons make threats "redolent with gore," which she directed at the militiamen and at the men whose interests they served. She even called for a "war of extermination" against the rich, saying, "Let us devastate the avenues where the wealthy live as Sheridan devastated the beautiful valley of the Shenandoah."[53]

The deaths at Lemont gave the anarchists fresh text for a storm of leaflets they dropped on the city. These circulars helped swell their meetings, but failed, one journalist noted, to create any great disturbance. In fact, when such a disturbance did erupt, the anarchists had little to do with it. It came on the city's West Side during the sweltering month of July, when streetcar drivers and conductors, who were predominantly Irish Catholic, quit work to protest the sacking of fifteen union leaders who had demanded a wage increase. The company was an unpopular monopoly, so the strikers easily won public sympathy as West Siders, male and female, young and old, walked to and from their homes boycotting the line, while fervently hoping the car men would win.[54]

Mayor Carter Harrison joined the Knights of Labor in urging arbitration, but the president of the company said there was nothing to arbitrate, because, if the union men were reinstated, it would imply that the company could not dictate who should be hired or fired. The mayor found himself pressured as never before, as businessmen protested that the city was threatened with anarchy and insisted that the police take forceful action against strikers who controlled the streets and made moving the cars impossible. On the second day of the confrontation, company and city officials held a war council and devised a systematic plan to break the back of the strike and reopen the West Side line. Mayor Carter Harrison attended the secret meeting and voiced his concerns about the planned police action, but at the end of the day, he consented to it.[55]

SERVING HIS FOURTH consecutive term as mayor of Chicago, Carter Henry Harrison was widely regarded as the most popular and effective big-city mayor of his era. A much-loved figure in the city's immigrant wards, saloons and trade union halls, he was personally responsible for keeping the city's warring tribes at bay.

Carter Harrison was an unlikely populist hero. A Kentucky gentleman who lived in a grand house on Ashland Avenue, he dressed in silk vests, smoked the best Havana cigars, read literature in German and French and quoted Shakespeare from memory. He was thoroughly at ease with members of the city's aristocracy of wealth, whose interests and concerns he readily understood. Towering above all other Democrats, he managed to keep the city's corrupt patronage system from destroying public trust in city government. He was not personally corrupt, but he accepted and tolerated the "bummer" councilmen, the gamblers, the saloonkeepers and the policemen who protected their interests. The city's big newspaper editors hated him for it and generally accused him of "being responsible for all the filth in the community."[56]

A few businessmen and bankers realized, however, that Mayor Harri-

Mayor Carter H. Harrison

son had exhibited rare political genius following his election in 1879. He had co-opted leading socialists into his administration. He then created a labor-friendly regime that helped cast the Socialistic Labor Party into oblivion. Moreover, he restored social peace after five harrowing years of civil strife.[57]

Carter Harrison was a naturally gifted politician who loved "pageantry and display of almost any kind"—marching bands and ethnic parades, Irish wakes and high masses, German folk festivals and socialist picnics. He attended them all, usually riding upon his white thoroughbred horse and wearing a black felt hat tilted rakishly to the side. He was extremely insensitive to criticism and could be tactless around influential men, but these traits, along with "bubbling geniality," his "sense of fair play" and his "social insight," put him "in touch with the desires and aspirations of the masses."[58]

Unlike his predecessors, Harrison recognized that Chicago was a foreign city, and he made the most of it. He spoke some German and a little Swedish, claimed Norwegian and Irish roots, and knew something about Bohemia from his European travels. He was a truly cosmopolitan man. "Harrison," the *Tribune* observed, "is American only through an accident of birth." He was also a crafty urban politico who earned and maintained the trust of Chicago's immigrants.[59]

Harrison presided over a city with a huge working class of people who had endured a terribly long depression and now faced a second one. He knew that many of these people resented the high-handed editors who chastised the poor, and despised the hard-driving employers who turned the Pinkertons and police loose on their own employees. It was not surprising to Carter Harrison that skilled agitators like Spies and Parsons found an audience in the city's working-class wards. The mayor was quite familiar with the socialists; he read their newspapers, observed their rallies and heard their speeches. They fancied themselves orators, he later recalled, and often "talked like damn fools," but they did not seem like dangerous men. Better to let them speak than to arouse popular wrath by closing their newspapers and banning them from the streets.[60]

Harrison had succeeded year after year, performing like a seasoned ringmaster in Chicago's human circus, but as he took office for a fourth term in May 1885, the mayor was a weakened leader. He had gained reelection by a razor-thin margin of 375 votes, and now he waited as the Republicans challenged the election results in court. In the meantime, the Citizens' Association issued a report that denounced the police for their "flagrant neglect of duty" during the strike at McCormick's and accused the mayor of being afraid to anger "any large body of rioters" for fear of losing their votes. In fact, the votes Harrison feared losing were those of businessmen and property owners, who helped provide him with the popular mandate he needed to keep the peace and attempt to govern an ungovernable city.[61]

HARRISON MAINTAINED HIS balancing act as usual during the first few months after his reelection, but then, on July 2, 1885, he lost control of the forces under his command. Before dawn that day 400 police officers reported to the Desplaines Street Station near the Haymarket to hear orders from their field commander, Captain John Bonfield, who was determined to break the strike of the streetcar drivers on the West Side line. City officials needed a hard man to head the strikebreaking force, and they found him in Bonfield, a failed businessman who had joined the force in 1877, just in time to see action in the great uprising that summer. He saw riot duty in Bridgeport, where he was humiliated after being disarmed and beaten by a gang of strikers. Following this traumatic incident, the ambitious Bonfield rose rapidly in the force. After being promoted to lieutenant, he was assigned to the West 12th Street Station, not far from where the Great Chicago Fire had started in 1871; this was a frontier police station in the midst of the sprawling Second Precinct, one that included Pilsen and the polyglot Southwest Side, home to more than 30,000 immigrant working people. Located in the heart of what the police called "the terror district," it was a command center during the violent summers of 1876 and 1877, when the lumber shovers' strike and the railroad workers' uprising "were so admirably repressed," in the words of the police department's historian. It was here that Lieutenant Bonfield won fame by putting the nation's first system of call boxes on street corners, so that patrol wagons could quickly be called into action when trouble began in a precinct where "scarcely a month passed without some kind of demonstration, strike or riot."[62]

Bonfield joined the Chicago Police Department in 1877, just before it emerged as the nation's first effective antistrike force, acting with a lethal effectiveness unmatched in any other city. But during the early 1880s the influence of Irish trade unionists and politicians on the mayor kept the police at bay during strikes. The force was so unreliable in the eyes of many large employers that they equipped small armies of militiamen as reserve forces or hired private guards to protect strikebreakers. In Captain John Bonfield, these employers found a man who would change all that.[63]

As morning light broke and the temperature rose on July 3, Bonfield's lead patrols found Madison Street lined with people looking as though they expected a great procession to pass. The captain ordered his men to keep people moving, but the crowds were too dense to budge. Many people on the streets, local residents and passengers as well as union workers of all sorts, came out to support the car men. Others in the throng appeared simply to witness what promised to be an especially exciting episode in the ongoing drama unfolding on Chicago's turbulent streets.

In spite of the crowds that grew as the morning passed, Bonfield moved ahead with his plan to open the line by sending in nine horsecars loaded with a huge body of 400 policemen he had gathered. Very soon after the convoy got under way from the Madison Street barn at the city's western limits, it halted before a barricade of lumber, gas pipe, cobblestones and beer kegs. "As fast as the police removed these obstructions others were raised," wrote one journalist. This method of street warfare

Captain John Bonfield

seemed "so decidedly Parisian and communistic in character" that the captain assumed anarchists were responsible.[64]

Bonfield, a "large, powerful, resolute, ruthless man," believed that unarmed crowds could be dispersed by a sizable, well-trained force of men ready and willing to club protesters into submission. The patrolmen could carry revolvers, but if they executed their captain's tactical instructions with disciplined brutality, they could prevail without using firearms.[65]

Enraged by the blockades, Bonfield ordered his men into action as the convoy moved slowly down Madison Street toward the city. Officers were seen wading into the crowds lining the street, their "clubs descending right and left like flails," said one observer, "and men falling before them, often frightfully injured." The captain led the assault, beating down an elderly man who did not respond to his order to fall back. When some construction workers pitched shovels of dirt in front of the cars, the captain ordered them arrested. Two of them questioned Bonfield, and he beat them until they lost consciousness (one worker suffered permanent brain damage). Using these tactics, policemen cleared the streets and opened the line by nightfall, after taking 150 prisoners.[66]

The next day, the Fourth of July, Chicagoans flocked to their picnics and baseball games, but West Siders still seethed with anger over the brutal assault they had witnessed the day before. Some of them even left the holiday celebrations and joined several thousand workers on the lakefront, where the International Working People's Association held its own Fourth of July celebration. Various speakers, including August Spies, denounced Bonfield's "vicious attack" on the citizenry and, according to one report, "advised streetcar men and all other working-men to buy guns and fight for their rights like men."[67]

Looking back on these events eight years later, and trying to explain why the Haymarket tragedy occurred, the governor of Illinois, John Peter Altgeld, offered a historical explanation. For a number of years prior to the bombing and the riot, there had been serious labor troubles, he wrote. There were strikes in which "some of the police not only took sides against the men, but, without any authority of law, invaded and broke up peaceable meetings." And in many cases, officers "brutally clubbed people who were guilty of no offense whatever." In the most notorious case, the invasion of a Harmonia Society meeting in 1877, one young man was shot through the back of the head; and in the streetcar strike on the West Side eight summers later, Governor Altgeld noted, "some of the police, under the leadership of Captain John Bonfield, indulged in a brutality never equaled before." After the police assault on the West Side, leading citizens prayed for the dismissal of Bonfield, but, "on account of his political influence, he was retained." (Indeed, a few months after the strike, Mayor Harrison had promoted the notorious captain to chief inspector, arousing the fury of organized labor.) In other cases, the governor continued, laboring people had been shot down in cold blood by Pinkerton men—some were even killed when they were running away—and yet none of the murderers were brought to justice. "The laboring people found the prisons always open to receive them," he concluded, "but the courts were practically closed to them."[68]

After reviewing the bloody history that preceded the violent clash in the Haymarket, Governor Altgeld drew what seemed to him an obvious lesson: "While some men may tamely submit to being clubbed and seeing their brothers shot down," he observed, "there are some who will resent it, and will nurture a spirit of hatred and seek revenge for themselves."[69]

DURING THE FALL of 1885 a cloud of class hatred hung over Chicago; it seemed as thick as the smoke that darkened its streets. Yet no one in the resentful ranks of the working class, not even the bombastic speakers of the socialist International, took revenge against the police and the Pinkertons. Instead, the social revolutionaries urged workers to join a mass movement for radical change and to arm themselves for the next confrontation with the forces of repression. The next time Bonfield's blue-coated "clubbers" and Pinkerton's "blackguards" moved against strikers, the workers of Chicago would be ready for them. They would be prepared to defeat the armed forces sent against them with the best weapons they could find. Moreover, they would be prepared to act against the powerful men who ordered the policemen around like hunters calling out their bloodhounds. Workers would be prepared, in other words, to carry out the "social revolution."

The social revolutionaries seemed to be everywhere in the city that troubled summer and fall —on the lakefront where they held "high carnival" every Sunday, in picnic groves where they delivered angry speeches, on the downtown streets where they led mass marches and demonstrations. They were, noted one alarmed observer, "free to come and go as they pleased, to hold meetings, parade in the streets, to expose their sentiments . . . to dispense their poisonous doctrines, to breed discontent."[70]

By the end of 1885, Chicago's working-class districts were seething with discontent, and the socialists were doing their utmost to incubate it, but they were not its only breeders.

Chapter Eight

The International

AS THE TUMULTUOUS MONTHS of 1885 drew to a close, the Chicago Internationals looked back on a year of astonishing progress. They had enrolled nearly 1,000 core members into fifteen groups or clubs in the poor neighborhoods of Chicago ranging from the North Side to the South Side areas of Bohemian Pilsen and Irish Bridgeport. The IWPA expanded in other cities as well, but by 1885 one-fifth of all its members lived in Chicago, where the association had attracted 5,000 to 6,000 sympathizers, most of whom were immigrant workers recruited to militant trade unions grouped together in the Central Labor Union, with a membership of 20,000 that rivaled that of the established Trades Assembly.[1]

Nearly all the workers who joined the International or supported it read the newspapers published by the Socialistic Publishing Company. A year after August Spies became editor of the *Arbeiter-Zeitung* in 1884, the German daily reached a circulation of 20,000, matching that of the Republican *Staats-Zeitung*. The society also printed an English paper, the *Alarm*, edited by Albert and Lucy Parsons, and unleashed a blizzard of literature in 1885, including speeches by Albert and Lucy Parsons, the writings of Marx and Engels, Bakunin and Johann Most, as well as thousands of copies of the Pittsburgh Manifesto translated into German, Czech and French.[2]

The blossoming of the International in Chicago owed something to serendipity. The severity of the depression and the rapidity of mechanization, the hostile activity of Cyrus McCormick, Jr., and his rifle-bearing Pinkertons, as well as the brutality of Captain John Bonfield and his club-wielding police divisions—all of these experiences generated potential recruits for the insurgent movement within Chicago's various immigrant working-class districts. But what transformed that discontent into social protest was the "intrusion of subversive propagandists."[3] The International's surprising growth in Chicago came about because socialist agitators, particularly Spies and Parsons, possessed the ability to articulate workers' grievances, as well as the unflagging energy it took to engage in relentless political activity. No other American city had ever witnessed anything like the agitation the Internationals created.

ON APRIL 28, 1885, the day strikers routed the Pinkertons at McCormick's, the IWPA conducted an audacious protest over the dedication of the palatial new Board of Trade Building. Elaborate and gorgeous ceremonies were planned that night to open this majestic monument to Chicago's economic power. The building dominated the financial district at the end of LaSalle Street with its 310-foot clock tower. Thick granite walls punctured by the austere stained-glass windows of the trading floor gave a churchlike look to this "temple of commerce." To critics like the journalist Henry Demarest Lloyd, however, the Board of Trade seemed like "a great gambling shop," where syndicates of traders cheated the market to keep commodities scarce and prices dear. The fixing of prices for essential commodities like bread invited big trouble, he feared. In a famous article, "Making Bread Dear," Lloyd warned that just such "crimes" had provoked the *sans-culottes* of Paris to take to the streets and ignite the French Revolution.[4]

Before marching to LaSalle Street, the Internationals rallied, as usual, in Market Street, where they heard Albert Parsons describe the Board of Trade as "a Board of Thieves" and a "robber's roost," and, according to a police reporter, declare that the new building ought to be blown up. When he finished, the band struck up "La Marseillaise," the anthem of the French Revolution, and then Parsons linked arms with August Spies to lead the march downtown. Lucy Parsons and Lizzie Swank joined them in the lead, holding their red flags on lofty poles. As they marched toward the Board of Trade Building, the band's music and the marchers' shouts bounced around in the canyons formed by the tall, dark stone buildings. Curious spectators lined the sidewalks, and some of them fell in line with the marchers. The Internationals had become the most engaging troupe performing in Chicago's colorful theater of urban life.

The protesters never reached their destination that afternoon, because they were stopped and turned away by a formidable squad of 200 policemen. Many of the marchers, expecting a police assault, had armed themselves, but thanks to a cool-headed police captain, William Ward, no conflict erupted because the captain kept his men in line and persuaded Spies to turn his followers around.[5]

Gaudy demonstrations and tense confrontations of this kind made exciting news and attracted enormous public attention, not only from downtown businessmen, but also from workingmen in the factory districts. But in the working-class precincts of the city, it took more than street-level theatrics to convert wage-earning people to socialism; it took hour after hour of serious political and philosophical discussion.[6]

IWPA club meetings were organized so that various members would present thirty-minute prepared talks on assigned topics, to be followed by comments and discussion. Thus, the socialist clubs served as arenas for group learning and for individual intellectual growth, as well as settings in which to recruit new members among workers who had enjoyed little schooling. Each group elected its own librarian and allocated funds to buy literature. Members could also borrow books from the central library located at the *Arbeiter-Zeitung* offices on Fifth Avenue.[7] Some of the more educated Internationals also volunteered to instruct children in socialist "Sunday Schools," partly in response to aggressive efforts made by Catholic priests in German and Bohemian parishes to recapture the souls of wayward immigrant children. The socialist instructors offered such children "reading, writing, natural history, geography, literature, general history and morality," and as much of "ethics as young minds are capable of receiving."[8] Of course, these instructors also taught their pupils about socialism and, more specifically, about what they called anarchism.

AT SOME POINT in 1884 the militant socialists of Chicago began identifying themselves as anarchists. This caused confusion among observers as well as among members of the International, because the movement's leader, August Spies, insisted he remained a follower of Marx, and not of Marx's anarchist enemy, Bakunin. It was true that Spies and his Chicago comrades had given up hope of finding a peaceful path to socialism via elections and legislative changes, that they had broken decisively with their former comrades in the Socialistic Labor Party. Yet the Internationals continued to label their publications socialist in 1885, because they adhered to Marx's belief that capitalism would be destroyed by its own

Arbeiter-Zeitung *building*

contradictions and by the inevitable emergence of a class-conscious movement of workers prepared to abolish private property along with the forms of government that sanctioned and protected it. The Chicago militants thought of themselves as socialists of the anarchist type—that is, as revolutionaries who believed in liberating society from all state control, whether capitalist or socialist. Anarchists proclaimed that true freedom in a socialist society could be gained in self-governing communities and workplaces where working people determined their rights and responsibilities democratically, without the domination of a powerful national state with its judges and laws, its police forces and armies. This was the freedom anarchy promised, said Albert Parsons, in contrast to the vision of his old socialist party comrades, who still embraced "State Socialism," which meant "the government controlled everything."[9]

Johann Most, the world's leading anarchist in 1885, exerted a strong hold on Parsons, Spies and the Chicago Internationals, but they did not fully embrace his view that individual acts of violence would provoke a revolution; indeed, they faithfully adhered to the lesson they had learned from Karl Marx: that socialism could be achieved only through the collective power of workers organized into aggressive trade unions—the "great lever by which the working class will be emancipated." The anarchists imagined militant workers' organizations as more than movement building blocks; these unions could be "the living germs of a new social order which would replace the bourgeois world," or, as Parsons put it, the "embryonic" groups of a future "free society."[10]

This concept of revolutionary unionism, later known as "the Chicago idea," appealed to European artisans like Michael Schwab who were familiar with the watchmakers and other artisans in Europe who embraced Pierre-Joseph Proudhon's anarchist ideas about free association and mutual aid. A few of them had even put these cooperative ideas into practice in their own shops and benefit societies. The notion of workshops controlled by intelligent craftsmen was not a utopian dream to them. Furthermore, the idea that artisans, shopkeepers and other ordinary citizens could govern a city was not simply a theoretical possibility, because this, they knew, was precisely what the people of Paris had done with some success during the days after they created the Commune in 1871.[11]

American craftsmen like Parsons were also quite familiar with practical experiments in cooperative production and exchange, because the Knights of Labor and, on a much larger scale, the Farmers' Alliance were busy creating them all over the country in 1885. Through these efforts, the popular movements of the time instilled a new kind of collective self-confidence in working people and a new kind of hope that they could reconstruct the economy on a democratic basis. Thus, the dream of a self-governing community of equal producers articulated by Parsons and the Chicago anarchists had something in common with the idea of a cooperative commonwealth embraced by labor reformers and agrarian populists in the 1880s.[12]

In any case, Parsons and his fellow agitators devoted themselves far more to practical activity—writing, speaking, agitating and organizing—than they did to creating coherent revolutionary theory. The Chicago anarchists applied Marx's axioms when they seemed to explain what was happening before their eyes, but they also salted their speeches and pamphlets with songs and mottoes from the French Revolution and the Declaration of the Rights of Man; from the writings of Proudhon, who believed property was theft; and from the anarchist pronouncements of Mikhail Bakunin and Johann Most.

The Chicago anarchists also drew inspiration from American revolutionaries: from Thomas Paine, the most influential of all propagandists; from Thomas Jefferson, who proclaimed the right and the duty to rebel against unjust authority; from Patrick Henry, whose words "Give me liberty or give me death" were often quoted; and from John Brown, the most heroic of all revolutionary martyrs. Albert Parsons, though raised in the slave South, considered himself an abolitionist at heart; that is why he devoted himself to winning political rights for emancipated blacks, why he never abandoned the language of Radical Republicanism he acquired in Texas and why he often cited John Brown and other abolitionists in his attacks on "wage slavery."[13] In the process of cooking this stew of radical ideas, the Internationals of Chicago invented a peculiar, in some ways American, brand of revolutionary socialism they called anarchism.

Parsons once wrote that the Chicago socialists initially accepted the anarchist label in defiance of their enemies who branded them with the name, but this bizarre explanation may have reflected his own pugnacious personality. In any case, adopting such a political identity seemed virtually self-defeating, because, to most Americans, anarchy simply meant chaos, violence and disorder. The word had been used, for example, to describe Paris in the last horrible days of the Commune and Pittsburgh in 1877, when enraged crowds surrounded the militia and set fire to the railyards. Anarchy was even thought to have appeared in the Arizona Territory, where, as one newspaper had it, the "savage" Apaches, "the Reds of America," fought to preserve their "communal system of government."[14]

The anarchists, however, regarded such outbreaks of violence as unnatural behavior provoked entirely by the oppressive actions of the state and the forces of private capital. They argued that anarchy, a society without a state, was natural to humanity, as compared to monarchy, the kind of rule that still prevailed in Europe, or as compared to democracy as it had evolved in the United States. Even with an elected government, they insisted, American citizens could be tyrannized by the police and the army just as they were in Europe. They lived in a society that called itself a democracy, but it was a sad state in which lords of industry behaved like monarchs who mocked democracy with their imperious actions.[15] In the midst of the "great barbecue" held by the robber barons and politicos of the Gilded Age, agitators could produce plenty of evidence that money and influence had polluted the great republic, if not poisoned it to death.[16]

STILL, IT WAS a daunting endeavor, this anarchist effort to create an alternative intellectual and moral world in a city devoted to the pursuit of private property and personal wealth, a place that thrived on speculation and competition of every kind, a city that epitomized American capitalism. At times, Parsons and other movement evangelicals saw themselves acting out roles played by the early apostles of Jesus Christ as they led a sect of true believers out of a wilderness of sin and corruption. In fact, the anarchists were atheists, or at least freethinkers, who regarded organized religion as little more than a drug clergymen gave workers in order to pacify them. Yet, for all their contempt for churchmen, Christian charity and Victorian decency, the anarchists of Chicago were men and women who believed in monogamous marriage and craved respectable home lives. No talk of free love was heard among them. But this did not mean the anarchists were joyless puritans. In fact, they indulged in endless entertainments and celebrations and made performing, singing and dancing essential ingredients of their social and cultural lives.[17]

Each year the anarchists' festive calendar began with the annual commemoration of the Paris Commune in March and continued until the Oktoberfest, when the dark beer arrived. By 1885, Die Commune Fieren had become too large to contain in a single hall, so the IWPA organized two memorials in Turner halls on the North and West sides that attracted international crowds. The Czechs sponsored their own "Paris Communal" at a new hall in Pilsen. The anarchists paid no attention to Easter and Passover, and instead eagerly waited for the spring Maifest, which came along with the bock beer. May 1 festivities inaugurated a high season of excursions, picnics, pageants, concert performances and poetry readings, as well as colorful demonstrations, parades and mass meetings on the lakefront, where city officials allowed the anarchists to congregate outdoors every Sunday. Come summertime, the IWPA groups and local unions picnicked together whenever possible—often at the conclusion of a rally and march to Ogden's Grove on the North Side, where there would be a great deal of sausage to eat and beer to drink along with a lot of dancing and singing to enjoy after the speeches ended.[18]

The Fourth of July, the one public holiday all Americans celebrated in the nineteenth century, was a grand occasion everywhere. The anarchists used the holiday to interpret the Declaration of Independence their own way and to honor their own red flag, not a star-spangled banner. "The flag of America" had "become the ensign of privilege," the banner of monopoly, Albert Parsons proclaimed in 1885. "Wage slaves of Chicago," he declared, "turn your eyes from that ensign of property and fix them upon the emblem of liberty, fraternity and equality—the red flag."[19]

Like his idols Tom Paine and Thomas Jefferson, Parsons believed in honoring two revolutions, the American and the French. And so when Chicago's colony of French immigrants celebrated Bastille Day in 1885, many of the anarchists joined them; but when the city's American families enjoyed the Yankee holiday of Thanksgiving that year, the Internationals arranged for "an indignation meeting" at Market Square, where Parsons asked sarcastically what in the world "plundered workers" and "hungry tramps" had to be thankful for.[20]

Given the anarchists' penchant for theatrical street performances, it was not surprising that they created their own dramatic societies and performed their own plays, such as a popular melodrama, *The Nihilists*, in which Spies and Neebe, the managers of the *Arbeiter-Zeitung*, played minor roles. This production, which re-created the scenes from the lives of Russian revolutionaries plotting to overthrow the hated czar, was so

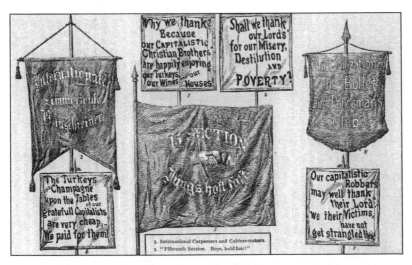

*Anarchist banners displayed in a Thanksgiving poor people's march
in 1885 and in other street demonstrations*

popular that it was later performed in a commercial theater; so too was *The Proletarian's Daughter,* the story of a working-class girl who falls in love with a factory owner's son, only to be spurned by her class-conscious father.[21]

During most of these demonstrations and festive occasions, the air was filled with music, often performed by German and Bohemian anarchists who created their own brass bands and singing clubs. IWPA club meetings and rallies usually opened and closed with songs that aroused a sense of collective confidence and martial spirit, most especially the much-loved "Marseillaise," a song that Parsons often sang solo at meetings and rallies in his lilting tenor voice.[22]

The International also sponsored dances in various halls every weekend, often to celebrate anniversaries and to raise money for the workers' militia or the socialist press, or to celebrate the club's founding date or an occasion like the Maifest or the birth of a movement hero like Tom Paine or Karl Marx. The German members usually chose the venue and the band, and the dances were frequented by various nationalities, such as the one described by a *Chicago Times* reporter who saw every couple at one anarchist ball enjoying a variety of European dance steps from waltzes to polkas.[23]

Friedrich Sorge, who had served as Marx's most trusted representative in the United States, described these festivities as "wonderful events" that drew enormous crowds, far more people than he had seen at similar socialist occasions in Europe. They highlighted what he called an "extraordinary and effective propaganda campaign carried on in public meetings held in halls and in the open"—a sustained effort "to shake up the people, the workers, and to frighten the philistines and the politicians."[24] Through it all, even through the endless club meetings, the threatening speeches and noisy street demonstrations, the anarchists seemed to be having fun.

In the early days of the IWPA's development, Albert and Lucy Parsons appeared an odd couple of Americans in a German cultural world of beer gardens and concert halls, singing societies and drama clubs. Then, in 1885, their speeches and articles in the *Alarm* began to attract some English-speaking workers to the American Group they had formed. By the end of the year the group had grown to 150 activists, including a broad-shouldered Englishman named Samuel Fielden, who would become the anarchists' most effective evangelist.[25]

Fielden joined the group in 1884 after spending fifteen years in the city digging ditches and hauling stone. He had learned about injustice from his father, a Lancashire handloom weaver who became an agitator for the ten-hour day, and had encountered it firsthand when at age seven he followed the children of other poor Lancashire folk into the cotton mills—an experience that left him with a memory of cruelty he called "satanic."

Young Fielden also received passionate religious instruction from his mother, a devoted Methodist, and before he turned twenty he had become a popular speaker at revival meetings in Lancashire. A restless youth who hated the cotton mills, Fielden left England in 1868. Landing in New York, he traveled far and wide, always working with his hands, and always reading and learning while listening to Americans. When he settled in Chicago, Fielden spent his days at hard labor and his free time in libraries and at meetings of the Liberal League, a group devoted to free thought and critical debate on social questions.[26]

When business improved in 1880, Fielden bought a team of horses and used them for hauling stone to Chicago construction sites. He joined a fledging teamsters' union and met George Schilling, the socialist labor activist, who became his mentor. Having gained a reputation at the Liberal League as a powerful speaker, Fielden was asked to address a labor meeting at the lakeshore in 1883, and there he met Parsons and Spies, who recognized his talent as an orator. By 1884 the stone hauler from Lancashire had become a devoted socialist and a popular speaker for the International.

In the American Group, Fielden encountered a bevy of restless, intellectually voracious men and women, as dedicated to anarchism as he had once been to Methodism. He participated in lively group meetings at Grief's Hall on Lake Street, where members delivered papers on political economy and anarchy followed by intense debate, and where they heard reports about ongoing strikes and assaults on workers. On occasion, he also listened to Albert Parsons and Lizzie Swank discuss the struggles of Indians, particularly the Métis, people of mixed French and native blood who rose up against British rule in the Northwest Territory of Canada, and the Apaches, who were making a last stand against the U.S. Army in the Arizona Territory.[27]

Meetings of the American Group were organized by Lucy Parsons's close friend Lizzie Swank Holmes, who usually closed gatherings at the piano and led the members in singing "La Marseillaise." She maintained a leading role in the group's political affairs, even after she moved out of the city to Geneva, Illinois, to live with her sickly new husband, William Holmes, who served as secretary of the group. A slender, pale young man who had been a woodworker in Wisconsin, Holmes chaired meetings, moderated debates, kept records and with Lizzie contributed much to the growth of the American Group. In the process, he came to know and admire Albert Parsons, and the two men grew as close as their wives had become.[28] The two couples joined a small inner group of devoted comrades who loved one another's company. Lizzie Holmes later wrote of many occasions she and William spent in lively communion with their friends. "I used to believe nothing could be more pleasant," she recalled, "than to gather with Mr. Parsons and his wife, Mr. Spies, Mr. Fielden, and others around a table, or in a small circle, and listen to conversation that flowed and sparkled on so smoothly."[29]

By now Albert Parsons had become a notorious figure in Chicago, a working-class hero admired for his courage as a bold character who suffered the blacklist for speaking out. His infamy among employers only added to his allure among workers. He cut a dashing figure in public appearances, taking the lead in huge street marches of people carrying crimson banners as they wended a long red line through the downtown streets. Sometimes he rode on horseback as a marshal, displaying the impressive riding form he acquired as a young cavalryman. On a podium Parsons struck reporters and critics as a vain character who dyed his hair black, coiffed his mustache and put on the airs of a gentleman; they also found him arrogant, insulting and audacious. Plebeian audiences, however, loved his dramatic persona, his blunt talk, his cutting sarcasm and his angry temper.

At the age of thirty-seven Parsons had reached the height of his growth as an orator. He displayed a scholarly command of history and demonstrated a remarkable memory for statistics. He often expressed his love for poetry and for the legacy of the French Revolution; these qualities appealed immensely to the German workers in his audience who were, in many cases, avid readers and "enlightened" thinkers themselves. Even those who did not share his passionate belief in anarchism often found Parsons impressive.[30]

In great demand as a speaker not only in local working-class venues but in other cities, the "famous labor agitator" even aroused curiosity among wealthy Chicagoans of a liberal bent. Early in 1885 he was invited to address a meeting of the West Side Philosophical Society. The hall was filled with well-to-do, respectable people. "I am the notorious Parsons, the fellow with long horns, as you know him from the daily press," he said with a smile. It was odd, he continued, for him to speak before an audience of gentlemen with nice white shirts and ladies wearing elegant and costly dresses. He usually spoke before meetings of people dressed in "coarse and common garments," people whose labor allowed these swells to wear fancy clothes and live in fine palaces. "Are not these charitable people—these *sans-culottes*—very generous to you?" he asked, as hissing resounded through the hall. Undaunted, he pressed on, telling them that 35,000 people in Chicago went hungry every day and that on such a cold winter night the Desplaines Street Police Station sheltered "as many as 400 homeless, destitute men." Then, his tone rising in anger, he exclaimed: "Listen now to the voice of hunger, when I tell you that unless you heed the cry of the people, unless you harken to the voice of reason, you will be awakened by the thunders of dynamite!" The hall exploded with angry cries and the speaker could not continue.[31] There would be no more invitations from respectable societies.

Lucy Parsons joined her husband in many of his Chicago activities, contributing articles to the *Alarm*, marching by his side in parades, engaging in debates at meetings of the American Group and speaking at lakefront rallies. She did this while keeping up her dress shop on the North Side to supplement her husband's meager earnings and caring for six-year-old Albert, Jr., and their daughter, Lulu Eda, who was born in 1881. Lucy's activities started attracting the attention of reporters, who were not used to seeing married ladies, let alone black women, making such angry public displays. An *Inter-Ocean* reporter who heard her give a furious speech at a Sunday rally described Lucy as "a very determined negress" who insisted on speaking even with her two "anarchist sucklings" at her side.[32] Albert and Lucy Parsons expected to be harshly treated by the press; if anything, the abuse made them more heroic in the eyes of the American Group, whose members treated them with special affection and admiration.

THE AMERICAN GROUP was an exceptional piece in the mosaic of Chicago's anarchist club life. Other groups consisted largely of Germans and Bohemian immigrants who were not for the most part recent arrivals or political refugees. The largest single element in the anarchist movement were workers from Germany who had become naturalized citizens after living in Chicago for five to ten years; in other words, they were foreigners who became radicalized after they arrived in America.[33]

Some of the Internationals made good as small proprietors, particularly the saloonkeepers—men like Charles Zepf, Moritz Neff and Thomas Grief, who advertised their taverns as meeting places for the city's socialists. These "red saloons" would become targets of police surveillance in 1886, when movement activity reached a fever pitch—places like Bohemian Hall in Pilsen, where the Czech workers' militia met; Neff's Hall on the North Side, where the Lehr und Wehr Verein gathered; and Thalia Hall on Milwaukee Avenue, where the largest North Side group of the IWPA congregated.[34] These socialist beer halls were some of the 5,000 drinking establishments that existed all over the city in the mid-1880s. The Chicago saloon exuded an atmosphere of freedom, serving as "the workingman's school," a discussion center, a free space

A group of worker militiamen of the
Lehr und Wehr Verein with the socialist
saloonkeeper Moritz Neff lying down

where the immigrant laborer learned the real rules in the game of city life.[35]

With the exception of the saloonkeepers and a few teachers, musicians and journalists, the Chicago anarchist movement was composed of immigrant wage earners like the lean young printer Adolph Fischer. Fischer had settled into the North Side with his wife and three children after arriving in Chicago during the spring of 1883. Already a well-assimilated immigrant, he had worked ten years as an apprentice in the print shop of his brother, who published a German paper in Little Rock, Arkansas. When he left Bremen, his birthplace, at the age of fifteen, the blond youngster had already enjoyed eight and half years of school, much more education than most immigrant workers received. As a boy, he had absorbed the doctrines of socialism from his father, so Fischer, like Spies and Schwab, arrived in Chicago a self-taught intellectual, exceedingly well read in philosophy, history, literature and political economy. Soon, the twenty-five-year-old newcomer joined their company, after hiring on as a compositor at the *Arbeiter-Zeitung*.[36]

A tall man with the body of a long-distance runner, Fischer appeared light in complexion and wore a wispy blond beard and mustache on his thin face. He sat silently at socialist meetings with a faraway look in his blue eyes, but the quiet young man was always ready to perform any task. "He kept himself and his little family nearly destitute because he gave the greater part of his wages to the cause," Lizzie Holmes recalled. "He did not think life worth living as things existed, and cared only for the time when all should have justice and equal opportunity." He was "in every fiber of his being, the man of action."[37]

Fischer joined the Lehr und Wehr Verein soon after he arrived in Chicago, in order to prepare for the armed struggle he believed to be inevitable. "Would a peaceable solution to the social question be possible, the anarchists would be the first ones to rejoice over it," he wrote later. But the fact was that, in almost every strike, militia, police, even federal troops, were dispatched to protect the interests of capital. So, it seemed unlikely to Fischer that big employers would give up their power and their property without going to war.[38]

Late in 1885, Fischer linked up with a group of ultramilitants who shared the same apocalyptical views. George Engel was their leader. Born in Kassel, Germany, Engel was the son of a mason who had died, leaving his wife a widow with four young children.[39] George suffered a hard and bitter youth. No one would take him in and give him training in his chosen trade, shoemaking, a situation that would have provided him with food and clothing. Without money, Engel wandered through northern Germany, working in various cities at different jobs until he married and settled in Rehna, where he started a toy business in 1868. Unable to make much of a living, he decided to leave for America in 1873. After several desperate years in Philadelphia, where he suffered from illness and his family endured constant hunger, Engel made his way to Chicago, where he found work in a wagon factory and met a German wheelwright who showed him a copy of *Der Vorbote*, the socialist weekly. The newspaper held "great truths" about the capitalist order, Engel wrote, truths that explained his own life of misfortune.[40] When he met the workers who supported the newspaper, he was astonished to see that men could work so eagerly without pay for the cause of humanity. Even during the depression, Engel worked steadily and saved enough money to open a little toy store on Milwaukee Avenue with his wife and daughter. Freed of handwork in the factory, Engel found much more time to read and to participate in socialist activity.[41]

Engel seemed like an old man among young followers like Adolph Fischer. At age forty, the anarchist toy maker was a stolid figure with a flat face and a mild, genial way; he looked more like an ingratiating waiter in a *Wursthaus* than a dedicated insurrectionist. George Engel had, however, moved a long way to the left since the time he canvassed the North Side wards for Albert Parsons and other socialist candidates. Indeed, in 1885, Engel had fallen out with his International comrades, Spies and Schwab, whose efforts to create a mass movement of organized workers now seemed like hopeless gestures; and by the time the new year dawned, Engel had decided it was time to prepare workers for "a violent revolution" that would begin when the capitalists declared war on working people.[42]

THE CALL FOR revolutionary action was gaining new converts in Chicago in early 1886, especially among hundreds of German anarchists who had read Johann Most's extremist views in his provocative newspaper *Freiheit* and in his notorious pamphlet *Revolutionary War Science: A Little Handbook of Instruction in the Use and Preparation of Nitroglycerine, Dynamite, Gun Cotton, Fulminating Mercury, Bombs, Fuses, etc. etc.* Most offered up various recipes in this cookbook of destruction, but he empha-

sized the special value of explosives because they would be the "proletariat's artillery" in a revolutionary war—and the surest means of gaining
a victory. Success would be assured if revolutionaries stocked adequate
quantities of dynamite bombs that could easily be concealed in their
clothing. Most even imagined that these explosive devices would allow
insurgents to defeat a fully equipped army.[43]

The Chicago anarchists fell in love with the idea of dynamite as the
great equalizer in class warfare. "One man with a dynamite bomb is
equal to one regiment," wrote one of the *Alarm*'s correspondents in a typ-
ically exaggerated claim. On several occasions in public speeches and
newspaper articles, Parsons and Spies advocated its use in revolutionary
warfare; they seemed enamored of its scientific mystique, but they also
valued dynamite because its potential power promised to instill a sense
of courageous manhood in workers intimidated by the police and the
militia. No one outdid Lucy Parsons in her fantastic claims for the impor-
tance of explosives: "The voice of dynamite is the voice of force, the only
voice which tyranny has ever been able to understand," she proclaimed.[44]

In January 1886, talk of bombs took a more dramatic turn when
August Spies showed a newspaper reporter a piece of tube he said could
be used as a casing for a dynamite bomb. "Take it to your boss," he said
with his usual bravado, "and tell him we have 9,000 more like it—only
loaded." He repeated this demonstration to other reporters later, to show
that the anarchists were deadly serious. Many years later, after these
reckless gestures helped tie a noose around Spies's neck, the writer
Floyd Dell suggested that the anarchists and the newshounds served
each other's purposes. Dell, who had been a Chicago reporter, knew how
much his fellow "bohemians" of the press loved a "lurid story," and
he knew how much the anarchists wanted to create the impression that
they were dangerous men. He doubted that Spies actually made any
bombs; what he needed most, Dell suggested, was the "symbolism of
dynamite."[45]

If anarchists like Spies and Albert and Lucy Parsons indulged in
"bomb talking" to frighten the authorities and to encourage their followers, there were, among their comrades, other men, men of few words,
frustrated militants who were prepared to make and use bombs in the
showdown they expected to come.[46] One of these men was a young carpenter named Louis Lingg. Born in Baden, Germany, to a father who
toiled in a lumberyard and a mother who kept a laundry, he suffered a
miserable childhood. His father almost died following his employer's

instructions to retrieve a heavy oak log from the surface of a frozen river. The ice broke and the lumber shover nearly drowned in the frigid water. Before Lingg's father could regain his health, he was discharged by his employer. By the time he reached the age of thirteen, Lingg had seen his father's health deteriorate while his former employer's wealth accumulated. These experiences, he recalled, left him with what he called "a bitter hatred of society" and all its injustices.[47]

As a teenager, Lingg entered an apprenticeship with a master carpenter, but before long he left Germany for the freer atmosphere of Switzerland. On this sojourn as a tramping artisan, the young carpenter became a freethinker and joined a workers' club, where he received food and companionship and benefited from what he called a kind of "practical communism." Lingg was supposed to return home to serve in the army, but he refused and became a wanted man. Now alienated from his fatherland, Lingg found a place in Zurich's community of exiled revolutionaries; and there he met the outcast leader of the German anarchists, August Reinsdorf, at the time Reinsdorf was planning to assassinate the king of Prussia. Lingg, still in his teens, was captivated by Reinsdorf and became his disciple.[48]

In 1885, at the age of twenty-one, Louis Lingg left his fugitive life behind and made straight for Chicago, where, he knew, there was a large community of German anarchists. The new arrival found work and immediately joined the new International Carpenters and Joiners' Union organized by revolutionaries. Despite his youth, Lingg quickly won the admiration of other German carpenters, who elected him as a delegate to the Central Labor Union. Soon afterward, he was hired as a full-time organizer for the burgeoning new union movement. Though he spoke little English, Lingg's ardor and stunning physical presence attracted attention among anarchists. William Holmes remembered Lingg as the handsomest man he had ever met. His well-shaped face, "crowned with a wealth of curly chestnut hair," his "fine blue eyes" and peach white complexion, his athletic body and his physical vigor all made Lingg seem like a Greek god to Holmes. When Spies and Schwab met this newcomer, they too were impressed by his charisma and physical courage, though they found Lingg's ideas so peculiar and puzzling that "they never knew how to take him."[49]

Although he worked as a union organizer of German and Bohemian carpenters, Louis Lingg harbored no illusions about the ultimate success of trade unionism or about the odds faced by unarmed strikers when confronted by the employers' armed forces. Talk of reviving the eight-hour movement did not impress him, but bomb talk did.

BY THE END OF 1885 the Chicago anarchists had frightened the city's philistines and politicians. The revolutionaries' public speeches and demonstrations seemed threatening enough, but when word leaked out of their private discussions, anxieties rose even higher.

The Internationals were aware that spies were infiltrating their meetings, and so they made halfhearted efforts to identify strangers. Nonetheless, Pinkerton agents hired by businessmen and plainclothes police detectives attended meetings of the International without being noticed. The private spies brought back lurid stories of bloody threats and plots to dynamite buildings like the Board of Trade. Many of these reports were wildly exaggerated, and some were fabricated to please the men who paid the detectives, but when these stories appeared in the press, they fed a growing fever of anxiety among middle- and upper-class Chicagoans that a vast anarchist conspiracy was in the works.[50]

At this point, the Chicago anarchists' threats remained rhetorical. No mansions had been bombed, no police stations had been attacked, no member of the workers' militia had fired a shot in anger. But Chicagoans had reason to fear that dynamite bombs would explode in their city, as they had in London that year—not ignited by German anarchists but by Irish-American nationalists.

Early in 1885 a cadre of the secret Clan-Na-Gael had bombed Westminster Hall, London Bridge, the Houses of Parliament and the Tower of London, wounding scores of people. The popular Irish republican paper *Irish World,* along with three other Chicago Irish papers, supported the bombing attacks. Indeed, the editors of the influential *World* "took great delight in every blast, declaring that dynamite was the only means of retaliation the Irish had against a tyrannical power." Europeans, however, were appalled by this new use of dynamite as an instrument of terror; they were painfully familiar with the actions of nihilists and other revolutionaries who assassinated imperial rulers and police officials. But the actions of the bomb-throwing anarchist seemed at least intelligible to the London *Times.* By comparison, the evil work of the "Irish-American 'dynamite fiend' " seemed incomprehensible because he chose to assault crowds of innocent civilians and ordinary travelers in order "to inspire terror."[51]

Despite all the talk of bomb throwing by revolutionaries in Chicago, no one had suffered from any anarchist attacks. Nonetheless, by the end of 1885, the city's businessmen had not only come to fear the Internationals in their midst, they had grown "to hate them and wish for their destruction." The anarchists' rhetorical threats were not the only reason for this antipathy. The city's most powerful men were less afraid of bomb talk than they were of the large working-class following the anarchist-led Central Labor Union had attracted in various immigrant districts. The Internationals embodied the worst fears native-born Americans harbored of aliens who refused to profess their loyalty to God, country and private property. The daily press, Republican and Democratic, magnified this hostility with dehumanizing descriptions of the immigrant revolutionaries, who were called "long-haired idiots and knaves." Their women, the papers said, acted like harlots and amazons, marching brazenly down the streets and cheering speeches by a "determined negress" who said she wanted to "devastate the avenues of the rich." The communists were bilious immigrants, libertines with no self-control, people who were drunk with beer and intoxicated by the fumes of revolutionary talk. They were heathens and homicidal maniacs, incendiaries and bloodthirsty worshipers of *La Commune*. They were not humans, but wolves from the darkest dens in Europe, beasts worthy of extinction.[52]

The anarchists played their own part in this degrading war of words, branding Board of Trade men as gamblers and thieves, and industrialists as bloodsucking "leeches." They castigated policemen as obedient "bloodhounds," militiamen as heartless mercenaries and the Pinkertons as common criminals paid to gun down innocent civilians. The Internationals also nursed their own conspiracy theory: that the city's wealthy men were plotting to turn all the armed forces at their disposal against workers in some imminent attack. Certain of this, the anarchists beseeched workers to arm for their own self-defense and prepare to meet force with force. In response, more immigrant workingmen joined the Lehr und Wehr Verein and began drilling in secret, and more began talking about making bombs, if not actually manufacturing the infernal devices. No wonder a Chicago police reporter recalled the last months of 1885 as a time when "everything pointed to a dreadful culmination."[53]

Chapter Nine

The Great Upheaval

THE DEEP WINTER of 1886 passed quietly as Chicagoans hunkered down and endured cold blasts of wind off the plains and the snowstorms they carried; it was no time for street warfare. That time would come after the harsh weather broke in March. Then, prosperous city residents feared, anarchist activity would resume at a much higher level of intensity. They were not disappointed.

As expected, the Internationals took to the streets again, and anxieties rose with the temperature. But then something happened that no one expected, neither the anarchists nor the capitalists, not the editors of the *Arbeiter-Zeitung* or of the *Chicago Tribune*. Historians would call it the Great Upheaval, but in 1886 no one knew how to describe the working-class unrest that welled up throughout industrial America.

Beginning in March of 1886, a strange enthusiasm took hold of wage-earning people in industrial centers across the nation as the dream of an eight-hour day suddenly seemed within their grasp. The agitation for shorter hours appeared to be everywhere by April, drawing thousands of unorganized workers into the swelling ranks of the Knights of Labor. Soon a strike fever gripped the nation's workforce; it peaked on May 1, when 350,000 laborers from coast to coast joined in a coordinated general strike for the eight-hour day.

The strike wave broke for a while and then returned in the fall with another surge of walkouts. By year's end 610,000 workers had struck, compared to 258,000 the year before. In 1885, 645 job actions affected 2,467 establishments; in 1886, however, more than 1,400 strikes hit 11,562 businesses.[1] Nothing like this had ever happened in America, or in Europe. These huge protests stunned observers like Friedrich Engels, who wrote from London, "History is on the move over there at last." The

Americans, he remarked, were "a people full of energy like no other," a people who astonished European socialists with "the vastness of their movement."[2]

When the Great Upheaval reached its climax on May 1, 1886, Chicago was its epicenter. At least 40,000 workers struck there, but after a while it was impossible to keep count. Perhaps as many as 60,000 laborers left their jobs. Unlike the strikes in other cities, where a few trades took the lead, the upheaval in Chicago reverberated through scores of shops and factories, construction sites and packinghouses; it emptied the huge lumberyards of workers, clogged the harbor with lake vessels and stranded trains in the huge railyards of the nation's transportation hub. The general strike even sucked in thousands of immigrant factory operatives and common laborers: nowhere was the unskilled proletariat mobilized the way it was in Chicago.

There were many reasons why the eight-hour strikes in Chicago were the largest, most aggressive and most successful in the nation; one important reason was that the anarchists had become so involved in organizing the unskilled, raising the stakes of the struggle and directing the flow of worker protest toward the general strike on May 1, or what they called "Emancipation Day."[3]

NO ONE DREAMED that such a massive strike movement was possible in the fall of 1885, when Chicago unionists were still reeling from the police assault that had broken the streetcar strike in July. Indeed, when George Schilling and a few other activists organized a new Eight-Hour Association, union members in the mainstream Trades and Labor Assembly paid no attention; they were still preoccupied with halting the use of labor-saving machines and ending the use of contract laborers, convict laborers and child laborers—all of whom displaced skilled journeymen. These union members seemed to have forgotten that two years earlier their national Federation of Organized Trades and Labor Unions had endorsed a bold call for the inauguration of the eight-hour system on May 1, 1886. Trade union delegates had adopted this resolution when they met at Chicago's Henry George Hall in 1884, but, as Schilling recalled, the conventioneers "returned home, after passing this resolution, and went to sleep."[4]

When fall 1885 turned to winter 1886 and the depression strengthened its hold on the city, trade unionists began to respond to Schilling's wake-up call. The patient efforts of the Eight-Hour Association now attracted a following among craftsmen who found themselves thrown out of work by the twin evils of overproduction and underconsumption, or else replaced by machines or by young women, farm boys and "botch men" willing to work by the piece. The eight-hour activists' arguments made sense to these proud but beleaguered craftsmen, who were persuaded that, if employers reduced hours, workers would demand higher wages to compensate for lost time; and, with more free time, they would also want more of the good things in life that the leisure classes enjoyed. As they attained a higher standard of living, workers would become a new mass of consumers whose purchases would alleviate overproduction—the curse of the American industrial system and the cause of depressions.[5]

The eight-hour reform also appealed to some leading citizens, including Mayor Harrison, who regarded it as a way to reduce unemployment and assuage discontented workers; it even elicited favorable remarks from some newspaper editors, like the *Tribune*'s Joe Medill.[6] The anarchists dismissed the revived eight-hour demand as a mere reform until early 1886, when Albert Parsons convinced Spies, Schwab and Neebe that the Internationals needed to join the new movement that was generating so much enthusiasm among the skilled and unskilled alike.[7]

Once again the anarchists found themselves working with former socialist comrades and fellow trade unionists. Serious differences remained, however. The leaders of the Eight-Hour Association hoped that employers would voluntarily accept the eight-hour system as a legitimate reform with mutual gains for labor and capital alike. The Internationals, on the other hand, predicted massive employer opposition and argued that success would only come as a result of an aggressive general strike on May 1.

During the next few months the excitement and anticipation of a showdown brought hundreds of fresh recruits into the Knights of Labor. They joined newly formed local assemblies, and like similar bodies across the nation, they resolved to take joint action on May 1, 1886. In doing so, these Knights defied the orders of Grand Master Workman Terence Powderly, who opposed a general strike because he feared it would generate destructive class conflict. He also complained about the "quality" of the new members rushing to join the Knights and even suspended organizing for forty days, but to no avail: his defiant organizers kept on recruiting.[8]

Propelled by the eight-hour movement's momentum, the Knights even penetrated two fortresses of antiunionism, the McCormick Reaper Works and the Pullman car shops. After conceding defeat in his battle with union molders the previous year, Cyrus McCormick, Jr., had regained the offensive, determined to win his war against the union.[9] In the summer his manager fired top union leaders, and in January 1886 the company terminated nearly all the skilled molders in the works, including the union members who had protested the wage cut the previous March. These skilled men were all replaced by common laborers who operated pneumatic molding machines. Moreover, when McCormick demanded police protection, he now received assurances from city officials that the department would take strong action to protect strikebreakers in any future labor dispute. Chief Inspector Bonfield assumed personal command of the area around the reaper works, replacing the popular Irish captain who had restrained his patrolmen during the last strike at the plant.

Despite all this, McCormick found his control of the works hotly contested by die-hard unionists, who organized a militant new District Assembly of the Knights on the Southwest Side. By February 1886 the union activists had organized nearly everyone in the harvester plant, strikebreakers and all, into two new divisions. The skilled machinists, blacksmiths and pattern makers were grouped together in the United Metal Workers, a militant union allied with the anarchist-led Central Labor Union, and McCormick's army of common laborers and machine operators were enrolled in the new Knights of Labor District Assembly.

On February 12, 1886, a joint committee of unions presented a list of demands that called for advanced wages in all departments, for an extension to the brief time allowed for toilet use, for the discharge of all scabs, for preferential hiring of old hands displaced by molding machines and for a pledge from management not to terminate any workers for union activity. McCormick accepted some of these proposals but refused the union's demand that he remove five nonunion men from the plant. In response, a mass meeting of all unions voted to strike in protest. Before the workers could act, however, McCormick declared a lockout and shut the factory down. The stage was set for the final showdown at the reaper works on the Black Road.

After organizing the common laborers at McCormick's in February, Knights from District Assembly 57 ranged throughout Cook County as far south as Kensington, the wide-open town where George Pullman's workers went to drink their beers and speak their minds. In April the agitators George Schilling and Albert Parsons addressed a packed meeting in the town's Turner hall and afterward recruited 400 of Pullman's skilled car builders for the Knights of Labor. The radical advance men of the Chicago movement had arrived at the gates of the model factory town.[10]

WITHIN A WEEK, the upsurge in organizing at the McCormick works and Pullman town became episodes in a much larger national manifestation of worker unrest, one triggered by a second titanic confrontation between the Knights of Labor and the managers of Jay Gould's immense southwestern railroad system.

The Knights of Labor had achieved a spectacular victory against Gould's railroads the previous July, but soon afterward they saw their members suffer from arbitrary wage cuts, layoffs, transfers and other abuses. When one Knight in Texas was summarily fired for attending a union meeting, he protested that he had been given permission, but to no avail. The company refused to take him back. In response, the order decided to act on its motto: "An injury to one is the concern of all." On March 6, 1886, the Knights announced the ultimate solidarity strike, calling out all the men on the Texas & Pacific line as a protest against arbitrary treatment of one union railway man. They demanded that management meet with union committees and arbitrate disputes, instead of relying on unilateral action.[11] Railroad company managers often dealt with individual craft unions of engineers, firemen and switchmen, but the Knights seemed far more menacing because they stood for all grades of workers and because they believed in cooperative enterprise.

The 1886 strike on the Gould system assumed an epic significance because it raised an essential question about American freedom: When a wage earner freely contracted with an employer, did the employee agree to sacrifice his liberty in return for compensation? The railroad owners believed so and stood firmly on the principle that "the right to hire men for what labor is offered in the market must be upheld against brute force," if necessary.[12] The Knights of Labor rejected this principle, insisting that men with empty stomachs made no free contracts, and that workers who sold their labor in order to live usually assented or submitted, but rarely consented, to the terms of an employment contract. With-

The Strike, *a graphic reproduction of a painting by Robert Kohler depicting the scene at a factory during the Great Upheaval*

out a union, the Knights argued, the railroad worker found himself in a kind of indenture, a form of "involuntary servitude" prohibited by the Thirteenth Amendment.[13]

The Knights not only posed fundamental questions about freedom; they raised the specter of two new kinds of concerted action by workers: the boycott and the sympathy strike. The unionists had been extremely effective in organizing boycotts to support fellow workers on strike in various cities, notably in Chicago, but they had never engaged in a sympathetic strike like the one the Knights called against Gould's railroads in 1886, initiating a trend that disturbed employers for years to come. During the first five years of the 1880s, only 33 sympathy strikes occurred; after 1886 came a five-year period when workers struck in support of fellow workers 397 times.[14]

Terence Powderly and other leading Knights warned their southwestern members not to take the risky job action against the nation's most powerful capitalist, but to no end. The walkout kept spreading along the rail lines of the 10,000-mile southwestern system, so that in a few days 14,000 railroad men had quit work. The strike soon became the most violent conflict the nation had suffered since the 1877 uprising, as strikers halted engines, intimidated strikebreakers and battled armed posses of railroad gunmen along the routes. In some places the conflict seemed like a "social war" as rank-and-file Knights of Labor demonstrated an extreme bitterness toward their employers.[15]

No strike seemed more like a "species of civil war" than the confrontation at the McCormick works in Chicago. After locking out striking molders, plant managers trolled the Midwest for replacement workers and issued revolvers to 82 loyal employees who were ready to work when the plant resumed operations; they also set up kitchens to serve food to a formidable detachment of 400 police sent to protect strikebreakers. When McCormick reopened with a nonunion workforce, Chief Inspector Bonfield commanded an all-out assault on the combined union picket lines and opened a cordon sanitaire for the strikebreakers.[16]

The locked-out workers immediately called a mass meeting near the plant, which was addressed by leading Knights as well as by Albert Parsons of the *Alarm* and Michael Schwab of the *Arbeiter-Zeitung*, who spoke in German. Despite the garrisoning of the works by Bonfield's men and Pinkerton's agents, the battle at McCormick's raged into April as strikers and their neighbors "waylaid the scabs on their way to the plant," in the words of one reporter, who added that police were kept jumping from one point to another in a vain attempt to protect the nonunion men.[17]

As the area around the big reaper works began to resemble a war zone, it became clear that the tension building between rival forces could no longer be relieved—not by McCormick, who vowed to destroy the union; not by the strikers, who refused to sacrifice their manhood by returning to work on McCormick's terms; not by the anarchists, who were preparing for street warfare; not by the mayor, who no longer controlled the police department; and certainly not by Inspector Bonfield, who intended to crush the workers' resistance.

Then, in the midst of this tense standoff, news arrived from downstate that heightened the strikers' worst fears of what might happen in Chicago. On April 9 the great southwest strike against the Gould rail system leapt across the Mississippi River into Illinois at East St. Louis, a bustling railroad town less than half a day away from Chicago by fast train. The Knights, led by determined switchmen, had disabled trains at this important western terminus of several major rail lines. That day, a sheriff's posse composed of railway employees opened fire with Winchester rifles on a picket line after one striker defied a warning and set foot on company property. The deputies, largely recruited from loyal Gould employees, killed seven strikers and wounded many more. Railway workers and their supporters, enraged by the massacre of unarmed men, reacted by burning railroad shops and destroying property in the yards. The news of the killings so alarmed Governor Oglesby that he placed the city under martial law and ordered seventeen companies of National Guard troops to East St. Louis. Reports of the massacre infuriated the anarchists in Chicago and became the cause célèbre of nightly protest meetings.[18]

It did not take long for the Great Upheaval to rumble into Chicago. The next day, April 10, 1,300 union switchmen paralyzed train traffic in the city's numerous railyards when they left work to demand that their brothers be hired instead of nonunion men. For a few days the specter of 1877 again hung over the city, until Philip Armour and other packing-house owners persuaded the railway company executives to accede to the strikers' demands rather than cause another "railroad war."[19]

THE EXCITEMENT GENERATED by the Knights' revival at the McCormick works and by the railroad workers' challenge to the mighty Jay Gould reverberated through all of Chicago's factories and shops. New Knights of Labor trade assemblies popped up all over the city as 10,000 workers poured into the resurgent order. The Knights also organized more mixed assemblies to accept common laborers and other immigrants, some of whom said they wanted to enlist in the grand army of labor so that they too could turn out on strike. New recruits included young women who toiled as domestic servants and the "sewing girls" in the city's huge clothing industry.[20]

After one garment-shop owner locked out his female employees, the union women formed "Our Girls Cooperative Clothing Manufacturing Company." Its objective was "to elevate the intellectual, social, and financial condition of its members, and the manufacturing of all classes of clothing, and the sewing of any cloth goods in use in wholesale or retail trade." Capitalized at $10,000, the cooperative was owned entirely by union members who bought shares of stock for $10 each. Net profits were divided equally among stockholders, workers and the cooperative fund of the order's General Assembly. Forty women were steadily employed in the worker-run shop, where they labored for only eight hours a day; it was one of twenty such cooperative initiatives launched by the Chicago Knights.[21]

The urge to organize and mobilize even seeped into the worst sweat-shops on the West Side, filled with the city's newest immigrants—Jews who had fled the horrendous pogroms in Russia a few years before. Abraham Bisno, a young cloak maker, remembered that these newcomers spoke no German or English and knew nothing about boycotts or the eight-hour strikes reported on so extensively in newspapers that reached other immigrants. Still, the eight-hour fever was so contagious it crossed into this isolated Jewish settlement. At one meeting August Spies addressed the cloak makers with the help of a Yiddish translator, and at another an American Knight struggled to explain the eight-hour cause in English. "There was great tumult," Bisno recalled, "everybody was talking and nobody quite knew what this thing was about." But even a Yiddish speaker like Bisno grasped the core message. "All I knew then of the principles of the Knights of Labor was that the motto . . . was 'One for All, and All for One.' "[22]

Whether their pay was high or low, Chicago workers flocked to the eight-hour cause because it constituted a freedom movement. Eight-hour visionaries looked forward to a new day when wage earners no longer lived just to work, and simultaneously looked backward to a time when people toiled together under the sky and close to the earth, passing the time of day without clocks and factory whistles, without machines or foremen to govern their pace.[23] The Knights opened and closed their meetings and rallies with songs that evoked this desire for freedom from the long arm of the job. Their anthem was the "Eight-Hour Song."

> We want to feel the sunshine;
> We want to smell the flowers;
> We're sure God has willed it.
> And we mean to have eight hours.
>
> We're summoning our forces from
> Shipyard, shop and mill;
> Eight hours for work, eight hours for rest,
> Eight hours for what we will.[24]

Chicago's workers, who were mostly newcomers from other places, usually small towns and rural districts, missed feeling the sun on their faces and smelling the flowers in warm months, for they lived and worked in a "city of smoke" where, as one traveler noted, "not even a ghost of the sun" shined.[25] Still, some found themselves tantalizingly close to nature at times. Those who toiled at the reaper works and in the lumberyards could see the prairie grasses fading into the western horizon, and, on some days they could even smell the crops when a dry prairie wind blew in from the northwest. On most days, however, a sickening odor drifted out of the stockyards and blanketed the immigrant neighborhoods of Pilsen and the West Side.[26] In a city where industry slaughtered millions of animals, blotted out the sky with smoke, poisoned the river with blood and guts and ground up fingers of factory hands like sausage stuffing, workers yearned to save part of themselves and to reclaim part of their day from the chaos of Chicago industry and from what Kipling called its "grotesque ferocity."[27]

AS MAY 1 approached, thousands of working people took heart from the radical notion that wage earners could unilaterally cut the length of the workday by making one unified show of solidarity instead of relying upon a frustrating legislative strategy. Many of the workers who flooded into the new assemblies formed by the Knights of Labor said they were joining the union so they could prepare to strike on the great day to come. The "mushroom growth" of the union worried its national leader, Terence Powderly, who strongly disapproved of strikes—the very actions that had brought about the order's great revival—arguing that if the eight-hour day was to be achieved, it must come through legislation, not through aggressive job actions or boycotts and not through the general refusal to work more than eight hours on May 1.[28]

Grand Master Workman Powderly found himself on the horns of a dilemma as May 1 approached. A small, slender man with magnificent mustachios, the Knights' leader looked to one Chicago labor writer "more like a college professor than a man who swung a hammer." Yet Powderly was a gifted orator, a charismatic personality who captivated his audiences and who won thousands of recruits to his order. A man of soaring ambition, he hoped that, as master of the order, he would become one of the leading men of his time. Under his guidance the Knights had begun to realize William Sylvis's dream of a unified national labor movement that extended itself to women, blacks, immigrants and other sympathetic members of the producing classes. A Catholic reformer who embraced a moralistic idea of socialism, Powderly sought to take the high road; that is, he hoped to create a reform movement and ultimately a new social

*Terence V. Powderly, Grand Master
Workman, Knights of Labor, 1886*

order in which class conflict would be replaced by cooperative enterprises and collaborative solutions to workplace conflicts. So, like many
union leaders of the day, he feared strikes and regarded such job actions
as desperate measures to be employed only as a last resort.[29]

However, the rank-and-file Knights, including many who had been
inspired by Powderly, were in a radically different mood, especially in
Chicago, where militant local leaders showed no qualms about striking
McCormick's and boycotting hundreds of "rat" employers. The unions
waged two effective boycott campaigns against prison-made shoes and
"rat made" boxes produced by the Maxwell company; both efforts promoted the growth of the Knights, according to the *Tribune*—so much so
that nearly every local assembly needed to find larger meeting halls to
accommodate new members, who now poured in at a rate of 1,000 per
week.[30]

The anarchists viewed the Knights' new power as "a very favorable
development" and hoped the eight-hour movement would lead union
members "in the right direction toward radicalism."[31] Like the Knights,
anarchist union organizers were using the eight-hour issue to recruit
thousands of new members in 1886. Albert Parsons, the most effective
labor agitator in the city, spoke at numerous venues and did everything in
his power for the eight-hour movement. Meanwhile, August Spies and

Oscar Neebe of the *Arbeiter-Zeitung* organized hundreds of butchers, bakers and brewers. All three groups won shorter hours at increased pay from their employers, mostly small-time German entrepreneurs.[32]

Anarchist organizers like Louis Lingg also succeeded in efforts to organize German and Bohemian carpenters into new unions, some with "armed sections." Other carpenters of various nationalities responded to the agitation for the eight-hour day by rushing into the Knights of Labor's five trade assemblies. The original craft union in the trade, the Brotherhood of Carpenters and Joiners, was riddled by defections to these two new bodies. In spite of their rivalries, all three union groups unified around the demand for shorter hours. They formed a tripartite United Carpenters' Committee, opened negotiations with the Contractors' Association for an eight-hour day and quickly achieved success. With prosperity around the corner and spring construction projects set to get under way, the contractors quickly acceded to the United Carpenters' demands.[33]

By the end of April more than 47,000 Chicago workers had gained a shorter workday, some of them without a corresponding reduction in wages. The City Council had approved an eight-hour day for public employees with Mayor Harrison's warm endorsement. It looked as though the movement was unstoppable.[34] Albert Parsons was so encouraged that he allowed himself to hope that the culmination of the eight-hour crusade on May 1 would not lead to violence. "The movement to reduce the work-hours" was not intended to provoke a social revolution, he informed the press, but to provide "a peaceful solution to the difficulties between capitalists and laborers."[35]

After establishing beachheads in the stockyards, the breweries and the bakeries, the anarchist-led Central Labor Union reached out to unorganized groups like tanners and saddlers, masons and wagonmakers, grocery clerks and sewing girls, Russian tailors and Bohemian lumber shovers. CLU organizers and IWPA agitators spoke at meetings almost every night in the city's industrial districts, addressing various groups of unskilled workers in German and Czech, as well as Danish and Norwegian; and, for the first time, Polish agitators appealed to their countrymen, the largest and lowest-paid group of unorganized workers in the city.[36]

One of the CLU's greatest accomplishments came in the fast-growing furniture-making industry, where a small organization of 800 mainly German craftsmen in smaller custom shops extended its benefits to men who operated woodworking machines in larger factories. In the third week of April these allied furniture workers walked out of two large firms, demanding eight-hour workdays and increased pay.[37]

These actions by unskilled workers marked a turning point in the eight-hour movement. It was now clear that common laborers would take disciplined action for a demand that had been initially conceived of by skilled workers. The craftsmen who launched the movement had proposed a simple bargain to their employers: if the men were granted a shorter working day, they would accept pay that was reduced accordingly. Even if they lost two or more hours of wages each day, the eight-hour men believed they would achieve their initial objective. The "eight-hour system" would serve as a first step toward reducing unemployment and inducing a desire for a higher standard of living among tradesmen with more leisure and more desire to consume. But as the eight-hour movement in Chicago broadened, this incremental strategy disintegrated. Low-paid butchers, bakers, brewers and lumber shovers were unwilling to accept a pay cut to achieve what they now regarded as a legitimate right. And so they rallied to the new demand raised by the anarchists in April: eight hours' work for *ten hours'* pay.[38]

The anarchists' cry of "eight for ten" appealed to the soldiers in Chicago's huge army of common laborers. These were people who had endured long hours and frozen wages, as well as pay cuts, for two years; now, with prosperity returning and city industry booming, they refused to accept another loss of income as the price of winning the eight-hour day. George Schilling and the leaders of the Eight-Hour Association objected to this radical demand, however, because they knew it would provoke outrage among their supporters in the press and among employers who were willing to consider shortening the workday as long as wages were reduced accordingly.

The militants' goal of winning shorter hours without losing pay also called for a more unified, more militant movement. While craft unionists could attack one employer or a few contractors at a time and use their skilled training as leverage, unskilled laborers needed to act together to wage mass, industry-wide strikes. And so, the logic of solidarity espoused by the Knights and the International made sense to them.[39] As common laborers and factory operatives joined the eight-hour movement, the anarchists took heart. This was the breakthrough Albert Parsons had dreamed of when he linked up with the old eight-hour philosopher Ira Steward six years earlier: the skilled and the unskilled mobilized together in a "class movement" ready to take militant action to achieve a common goal.[40]

ON APRIL 25, 1886, after Chicago's employers and their families attended Easter services in the city's Protestant churches, some of the churchgoers gathered along downtown streets to watch a spirited march of 15,000 workers to the lakefront organized by the Central Labor Union. The column extended for two miles and passed 50,000 people who lined the route to the lake.[41] The marchers started out from the West Side, where red banners floated over hundreds of buildings, and paraded slowly and merrily through the deserted streets of downtown until they reached the lakeshore. There, in a festive atmosphere, Parsons and Fielden spoke in English while Spies and Schwab spoke in German to what one reporter called "a multitude of discontented workingmen." Moved by the occasion, Schwab reverted to the imagery of Easter he recalled from his Catholic boyhood in Bavaria. He told the crowd that their ancestors had been celebrating this day as the springtime revival of nature since ancient times, just as their fathers and grandfathers had celebrated the Redeemer's resurrection. "Today, the workers of Chicago are also celebrating their resurrection," Schwab proclaimed. "They have risen from their long indolence and indifference; they have seen what they can accomplish walking hand in hand."[42]

The ebullient mood on the lakefront that Sunday contrasted with the impatient mood the business press expressed on Monday. Boycotts, lockouts, strikes and labor actions had interrupted the city's newfound prosperity, the *Chicago Journal* complained. Every form of business and industrial enterprise had been "attacked or threatened" by eight-hour strikers. Employers who were willing to accept shorter hours at reduced wages were now faced with more than 20,000 strikers demanding ten hours' pay for eight hours' work. The *Tribune* labeled this fresh demand a "simple impossibility" and blamed it on the "Communistic element fermenting among the laboring classes." There was no doubt now that the crisis lay ahead: Chicago businessmen had better prepare for the worst.[43]

Chief Inspector Bonfield agreed, telling the press he expected "a great deal of trouble" on May 1 and issuing an order that would place the entire force on duty come Saturday morning.[44] The First Cavalry Regiment of the Illinois National Guard had already conducted an impressive drill and full-dress parade at the request of the Commercial Club, a group that had been formed after the Great Uprising of 1877. After reviewing the cavalry, the club members, led by Philip Armour, raised funds to equip the First Infantry militia with better arms, including $2,000 to "furnish the regiment with a good machine gun, to be used by them in case of trouble."[45]

Editors focused their attention more than ever on the anarchists, who were, despite their denials, accused of plotting to use the May Day strike as an occasion to precipitate a riot. The *Chicago Mail* singled out Parsons and Spies as "two dangerous ruffians" who had been "at work fomenting disorder for the past ten years." They should have been driven out of the city long ago, said the editorial. Now they were taking advantage of the excitement generated by the eight-hour movement to instigate strikes and to cause injury to capital and honest labor in every possible way. Spies and Parsons did not have one honest aim in mind, said the *Mail*. They should be marked by the police and held personally responsible for any trouble that came to the city.[46]

Even under these circumstances, Spies and Parsons betrayed no fears; indeed, they wrote and spoke with more assertion and conviction than ever. Privately, however, they may have shared the anxiety of their comrade William Holmes, who feared that when this great test between the labor movement and the "money power" reached its climax on May 1, "desperate days" would follow very soon.[47]

Chapter Ten

A Storm of Strikes

ON THE EVE of May Day, Chicago throbbed with excitement as workers met and rallied all over the city. Leaders of the Upholsterers' Union, for example, organized what they claimed was the largest meeting of upholsterers ever held in the United States. The members voted to take Saturday off and to return to work Monday on the eight-hour system. Minute instructions were issued to members on how to act in case any shop refused to accede to the new system.[1] Freight handlers on the city's major railroads also gathered and rallied to support men who had already struck for eight hours. Their leaders called a "monster mass meeting" of all warehouse workers on the morning of May 1 at the Harrison Street viaduct. Chicago, the nation's freight handler, was on the brink of paralysis.

The *Tribune* feared the worst trouble would come in the lumber district, where 12,000 workers had demanded "reduced hours and advanced pay with no probability of getting them." The German section of the Lumber Workers' Union met at Goerke's Hall and decided to walk out if yard owners refused to accept their demand for eight hours' work for ten hours' pay and double pay for overtime. The Bohemian branch, which added 400 new members in one day, was expected to do the same. "The Lumber Workers Union is not a branch of the Knights of Labor but of the notorious Central Labor Union," the *Tribune* explained, adding that the majority of the men employed in the lumberyards followed the anarchists. The lumberyard owners called these demands "very impudent and imperative" and vowed to reject them. That meant that a strike by the lumber shovers, chiefly Germans and Bohemians, would completely paralyze the vital lumber trade. An unidentified anarchist told the paper that these two groups of immigrant workers were ready to do the aggressive work and to defend themselves with arms if necessary. But this leader did not expect serious trouble because he believed employers would give in rather than allow their competitors in other cities to steal their business.

ON THE MORNING OF Saturday, May 1, the *Arbeiter-Zeitung*'s headline shouted THE DIES ARE CAST! THE FIRST OF MAY, WHOSE HISTORICAL SIGNIFICANCE WILL BE UNDERSTOOD AND APPRECIATED ONLY IN LATER YEARS, IS HERE.[2] Even "the businessmen's newspaper" expressed excitement over the momentous events about to unfold. THE GREAT DAY IS HERE, announced the *Tribune*—LOUD CRY HEARD FROM WORKINGMEN ALL OVER LAND. The first five pages of the paper were crammed with detailed reports from hot spots all over the city. Telegraph messages poured in from other cities, where the general strike had begun, but by noon it was clear that Chicago was hardest hit. At least 30,000 laboring people were on holiday from work of their own accord. A "storm of strikes" affected almost every segment of the workforce, from the men who handled freight in the railroad warehouses to the girls who sewed uppers in the shoe factories. "The streets were thronged with people, the manufactories were silent, and business in general was almost at a standstill," recalled one reporter. For once, the dark, sooty sky over the city was clear. "No smoke curled from the tall chimneys of the factories, and things assumed a Sabbath-like appearance."[3]

The great refusal of May 1 quickly transcended boundaries that separated Chicago's polyglot working class. Craft workers, who had reached agreements with their bosses, took actions to support workers already on strike. More generally, workers and consumers boycotted sweatshops and bought eight-hour cigars and wore eight-hour shoes.[4] Meanwhile, certain groups of strikers revived an old ritual of solidarity prominent in the uprisings of 1867 and 1877—the strikers' march, "a moving torrent of men, women and children closing every workplace in its path."[5]

At one shop, sheet metal workers agreed to remain at work because the proprietors answered their demands with a proposal that the firm share a certain percentage of the profits with the men, who would set their own hours at eight or more. "The proposition, when presented to the men, was received with cheers and expressions of confidence which were very gratifying to the firm." Packinghouse owners decided to avoid a strike at the stockyards by letting the men "have their way in the matter of fixing hours."[6] Concessions like these emboldened other strikers. Spurred on by the anarchist leaders of the Central Labor Union, some workers, like a group of Bohemians on the lumber docks, began to act on the audacious demand of eight hours' work at ten hours' pay. In other places, laborers wanted not only more freedom *from* work, but more freedom *at* work. The German brewers and maltsters insisted on the eight-hour day achieved by other members of the Central Labor Union, but they also desired more free time to rest, eat their dinners, enjoy conversation and drink free beer. They proposed that two hours a day be set aside "for visiting the tap room and for meals," meaning that a brewery worker could take "the whole two hours for food and drink or divide up the time as he chooses." The *Tribune* was aghast at the demand and about the news that the owners might comply "with the terms and conditions of their thirsty Communistic hands."[7]

Amid these surprising events, the most amazing development of all unfolded at the McCormick works, where locked-out union molders continued to harass the employees who kept the foundries and molding machines running under the protection of a police garrison. The

Workers at Horn Brothers Furniture Company just prior to the May 1, 1886, strike

workers inside the plant could not be quarantined, however, and as eight-hour marchers swept through the factories on the South Side, even loyal McCormick employees were infected. Half of the newly recruited replacement workers suddenly joined the strike movement. Management, now desperate to hold the loyal employees at work, promised the strikebreakers an eight-hour day if they would return, but made no such concession to the strikers, who remained locked out of the plant.[8]

The Great Upheaval was frightening to employers for many reasons, and not simply because it aroused militancy among loyal workers or because it propelled anarchists into leadership roles. The insurgency was largely nonviolent, so it could not be branded a civil insurrection; indeed, it was planned, coordinated and mobilized by a new kind of labor movement. It was a movement that pulled in immigrants and common laborers, as well as artisans, merchants and even populist farmers in Texas, where the Farmers' Alliance was regarded as "the spinal column" of a great people's war against railroad king Jay Gould. What happened on May 1, 1886, was more than a general strike; it was a "populist moment" when working people believed they could destroy plutocracy, redeem democracy and then create a new "cooperative commonwealth."[9]

What is more, the upheaval arose during an era of great uncertainty. The 1880s were years when the enormous power of industrial and financial capitalists had become fully apparent, but millions of Americans questioned the moral and social legitimacy of large private companies and their owners; when the laws of the market operated freely without any public restraints, but millions of Americans rejected those laws as immoral and inhumane; when wage labor had completely replaced slavery as well as most forms of industrial self-employment, and yet nearly all leaders of the first American labor movement denied that wage labor was free labor and agreed that the wage system had to be abolished. The events of the 1880s revealed other paradoxes as well. More Europeans than ever were emigrating to the United States, hoping and searching for liberty, yet immigrants increasingly questioned whether America was the land of liberty. Urban police forces began modernizing and arming themselves, yet middle- and upper-class city dwellers felt insecure and more worried about working-class violence than ever before. Federal armies had defeated all but a few Indian tribes and had brought "civilization" to the frontier, but the United States government was unprepared to deal with large-scale worker insurgency in its most advanced cities.

ON SATURDAY May 1 the sun shone brilliantly over the city of Chicago as workers took a "holiday" from their normal duties, and eight-hour marchers trod their way through industrial districts. The mood was a festive one, and the marches were peaceful. The Knights and Federation members carried the Stars and Stripes and held signs bearing symbols of their trade and the mottoes of the movement, while the anarchists waved crimson banners, though the *Tribune* reported fewer red flags than were normally seen at Chicago street demonstrations.

It was a day the Internationals would never forget, and it was, as the *Arbeiter-Zeitung* predicted, a day of "historical significance" that would be appreciated in the future. Indeed, only four years later May Day gained symbolic power in the international labor movement as radical workers established a tradition of demonstrating their power by parading with red flags and wearing the crimson flowers of the season.[10]

As the sun sank over the prairie horizon that evening, the first day of the general strike ended peacefully. Saturday nights in Chicago were always filled with sounds of revelry that lasted long hours, but the evening of May 1, 1886, was an especially boisterous one. Striking workers joined their neighbors and shop mates dancing polkas and waltzes in music halls and drinking beer and whiskey in thousands of saloons uptown and downtown, from Swedish beer gardens on the North Side to the Irish pubs in Bridgeport. On Lake Street on the West Side, the gaslights in Grief's Hall and Zepf's Hall burned later than ever that night as German anarchists toasted each other and celebrated their "Emancipation Day."

The English-speaking Knights of Labor and the trade unions celebrated May Day in a more formal way with an "eight-hour ball" in an armory, where 1,000 dancers enjoyed an evening of speeches and lively music—all presided over by the movement's godfather and guest of honor, Andrew C. Cameron, the feisty printer and workingman's advocate who had initiated the city's first eight-hour movement in 1863, only to see it betrayed on another May Day, in 1867.

There was no dancing or merrymaking in store for Albert Parsons that night. While the city's workingmen drank to a new day, he rode a night train to Cincinnati, where 30,000 workers had struck that afternoon. The Internationals there wanted the famous Parsons to address a rally on Sunday and bring them news from the storm center of the great strike. The next morning Parsons took part in a second huge parade of eight-hour demonstrators led by 200 members of the Cincinnati Rifle Union bearing Winchester carbines. They marched behind a large red flag through downtown in a "jolly" mood, as one German striker recalled, because they were "dead certain" of victory. When they arrived at a park, Parsons addressed the throng and told them that their movement was not a "foreign" crusade, as their enemies charged. The desire for liberty and justice concerned all Americans, native and foreign-born.[11]

MEANWHILE, THAT SUNDAY began quietly in Chicago, so quietly that many hoped the excitement had died down and that on Monday workers and employers would resolve their differences. There were no demonstrations, no marches led by rifle-toting Internationals. In fact, there were hopeful signs that the crisis might indeed end on Monday. The city's powerful railroad company executives met and raised the expectation that they might accept the freight haulers' demands. This action, if taken, would influence other employers to follow suit and make the eight-hour day a reality. "Good feeling seemed to prevail in most quarters," according to one Sunday report, except in the old "terror district" around the lumberyards, where police detectives from the Hinman Street Station kept a close watch on Bohemian and Polish lumber shovers who had marched the day before with red flags and with American flags turned upside down.[12]

Tensions within the labor movement had not disappeared even amid this euphoria. George Schilling of the Eight-Hour Association was furious with his old comrade Parsons and other anarchists who raised the "impossible demand" of eight hours' work with no pay cut. A protracted session of the Trades and Labor Assembly led to a hot debate when the carpenters proposed making a closer alliance with the anarchist-led Central Labor Union because it had, according to some delegates, such "great influence among the workingmen." The venerable A. C. Cameron warned against closer cooperation between the two bodies, because he could not see how those who carried the "red flag of European socialism" could be truly joined with those who carried the banner of American "democratic republicanism."[13]

Scores of other eight-hour meetings took place in other venues, such as Ulrich's Hall, where 300 male and female dry-goods clerks met to plan concerted action for shorter hours. Their own organization, the United Dry-Goods Clerks' Union, had asked their employers to close stores every night at six o'clock, except on Saturdays, and to remain shut all day Sunday. This proposal infuriated Marshall Field, the city's richest, most influential capitalist, and the first merchant to electrify his dry-goods establishment so that shopping and selling could go on in his State Street emporium from morning to evening seven days a week. That Sunday, Field seethed with anger at the owners of dry-goods stores like City of Paris who had already conceded to their salesclerks' requests to close up shop on the Christian Sabbath.[14]

While Marshall Field fumed, railroad managers worried that the freight handlers' strike would expand and cripple midwestern commerce, and the owners of Great Lakes vessels feared that Bohemian strikers might set fire to their boats and to the nearby lumberyards. But most Chicagoans seemed to put their worst fears aside on that cool spring day of rest and enjoyed their normal Sunday activities. Families picnicked in the groves, couples strolled in Lincoln Park and derby-hatted men watched sandlot baseball games and talked with great anticipation about the opening of the professional season, when the city's heroic White Stockings were expected to take another pennant.

That morning, Protestant churches were full of worshipers listening to sermons titled "Jesus, the Peacemaker" and "Labor and Capital Viewed in the Light of Christ's Dictum" by ministers who felt compelled to address the burning question of the day. The city's most liberal clergy-man, Dr. Hiram W. Thomas, known as "the Emerson of our American pulpit," addressed the social question directly. Preaching in a taber-nacle attached to McVicker's Theater, Thomas sensed a queer uneasi-ness sweeping the land as workmen made unrealistic, immoderate demands. He wondered if there was something in the stars that caused working people to question the way of the world. There would always be men with property and men without, he explained. Workmen should realize that capitalists made their labor possible. "The laboring classes," he concluded, "are trying to wrestle from fate a thing that fate had made impossible."[15]

The city's famous revivalist, Dwight L. Moody, who rarely addressed political questions, departed from his usual form that day. The great Moody, who had returned from evangelistic labors in the South, spoke with his penetrating voice to 5,000 people at a Sunday-evening service at the Casino Rink. "What's all the unrest of this strike that's agitating the city?" he wondered. It seemed natural that workingmen were simply "in the pursuit of rest." But it was a vain pursuit, he warned, because there was no rest, not for the mechanic or even for the millionaire. "There is only one place where it can be found," Moody preached: "at the foot of the cross." This message reassured a nervous audience of middle-class Protestants who hoped that Moody's words would inspire the restless urban masses, whose refusal to work for more than eight hours seemed like a wild intoxication that would pass on Monday when business resumed as usual and employees came to their senses.[16]

AND INDEED, ON MAY 3, it seemed that the passive mood of Sunday might prevail. In the planing-mill section of the lumber district along 22nd Street, the day passed quietly, even though the side streets swarmed with strikers and locked-out men who enjoyed playing games and drinking bock beer on the streets.[17] Uptown, 400 girls and women left their sewing shops on Division Street in a joyous mood; they "shouted and sang and laughed in a whirlwind of exuberance that did not lessen with the distance traveled." Several hundred workingmen followed, offering their support. The whole carnival-like procession was headed by two tall Bohemians armed respectively with an ax and a mallet. When the strikers crossed the river and streamed into the downtown area, their chants and songs became more vociferous. A reporter described them as "shouting Amazons" infected "with a particularly malignant form of the eight-hour malady"—that is, they were demanding the same wages for less work.[18]

The anarchists were thrilled by the progress of the eight-hour strike. Many city employers had already given in and more would follow. The railroads would have to yield because, one socialist observed, they had too much at stake and could not afford to be idle. He expected further that the Knights would soon bring out the English-speaking workers, who had been holding back awaiting developments. This prediction seemed to be validated later that day, when two English-speaking crews of workers walked out of the Pullman wheel shops to win eight hours' work at ten hours' pay. More were expected to follow on the morrow. Even the residents of George Pullman's model town were stirring.[19]

The labor movement had much to celebrate on May 3. The brewery owners agreed to employ only union members, to reduce the use of apprentice boys, to limit Sunday work to three hours and to set five break periods each day when workers could drink beer in the taprooms. More important, when the pork and beef producers gathered at the Grand

Pacific Hotel to discuss an unexpected strike of 3,000 butchers and laborers in five packinghouses for increased wages and decreased hours, they agreed to an experimental settlement offering to pay their men at the ten-hour rate for a reduced workday. The labor movement was, it seemed, "having things pretty much its own way."[20]

Then, on the afternoon of May 3, came news of two calamitous events that shook the confidence of the ebullient strikers.

First came word that the Knights of Labor had been vanquished on Jay Gould's railroads. Their national leader, Terence Powderly, had unilaterally ended the southwestern strike because he believed it was doomed to failure. At the *Tribune,* Joseph Medill composed a stern editorial: "The Southwestern Knights have been starved into submission . . . ," he proclaimed. "The surrender is unconditional." Management would take back only such strikers as it saw fit, "leaving all the other instigators, agitators and perpetrators of violent acts permanently blacklisted." When this news arrived in railway offices, it galvanized the superintendents, who then organized an unprecedented meeting at the Burlington Building. The railroad managers announced the next morning that every man who did not appear for work would be discharged and his place filled by a new employee.[21]

The lumberyard owners also deliberated over their employees' demands that day. The stakes could not be higher, said a *Tribune* editorial; enormous amounts of skill and capital had been invested to keep the Chicago trade strong in the face of competition from many new lumber centers. Now the strike of "Communistic yard men and lumber-handlers" put the whole industry in jeopardy. "The suddenness of the blow has paralyzed this great business and there is no alternative left but to stop it," the editorial concluded.

Once again, Chicago capital had its back up, as it had when the eight-hour law was to take effect on May 1, 1867, and once again, city leaders had their armed forces at the ready. However, conditions had changed: the old-time police department had included only 250 patrolmen to protect an enormous city; by 1886 the force had grown to nearly 1,000 well-armed officers, including the nation's largest corps of battle-tested veterans, men experienced in suppressing demonstrations, controlling riots and breaking strikes. Chief Inspector Bonfield placed the regular force on round-the-clock alert and ordered training exercises for a reserve force of 75 men recruited from the banks, commercial houses and railroad companies to serve as specials. Militia commanders also prepared their troops for action. The area around the First Regiment Armory was abuzz with activity as National Guard companies drilled in the streets, while soldiers assembled their new Gatling gun.[22]

The second shocking event of May 3 occurred on the Black Road at the gates of the McCormick works, the scene of many violent clashes in the past. On this afternoon a fatal confrontation took place that set relentless forces in motion, forces that would propel striking workers and Chicago policemen toward the tragic climax of their struggle.

AUGUST SPIES SEEMED to be everywhere in the city on that tension-packed Monday, putting together a general strike edition of the *Arbeiter-Zeitung*, rallying the striking sewing girls and addressing groups of strikers all over the city. By Monday, he was exhausted from weeks of speaking in public and late nights spent putting out a daily newspaper, but he was elated by the breadth and depth of the general strike. Early in the afternoon a Czech leader of the lumber workers asked Spies to come down to the Southwest Side and speak to a meeting of German and Bohemian lumber shovers on the prairie along Blue Island Avenue. Spies was reluctant to make the trip and give yet another speech, but a committee of workers insisted that he was needed and persuaded him to go.

Arriving at the rally about three o'clock, Spies was impressed by the size of the crowd but dismayed that the speakers were so poor and that workers seemed uninterested. He mounted a boxcar on the Burlington tracks and began to speak in German to the lumber shovers gathered on the railbed and the prairie beyond. Behind him, a short distance away, the machinery of the McCormick Reaper Works ground away. At the rear of the crowd in front of him was a group of 200 restless workers who had been locked out of the plant and had endured weeks of combat with Pinkertons and policemen around what they called "Fort McCormick."[23]

Shortly after he began, Spies was heckled by some Catholic strikers, but he persisted. The speaker carried on for about twenty minutes, addressing the eight-hour question and telling the men "to hold together, to stand by their union, or they would not succeed." He referred mostly to the struggle in the lumberyards and did not mention the McCormick lockout. While he was still orating, the factory bell at McCormick's clanged behind him, signaling the end of the workday for the strikebreakers still toiling in the plant. Before Spies could grasp what was happening, someone cried out in an "unknown tongue" (probably Czech or

Polish) that the scabs were leaving the plant. The group of McCormick strikers wheeled away en masse and surged toward the factory gates. Spies continued to speak, urging the lumber shovers not to join the rush on the plant. Then he heard the crackle of gunfire from the factory yard. He was told the strikers had attacked the strikebreakers and that the police were firing on them. Again, he beseeched his audience to remain still. But it was no use. Most of the lumber shovers fled up the Black Road back to Pilsen.

Spies clambered down from the boxcar and ran toward the plant, where he saw a wild melee in progress. Roughly 200 police officers were attacking the strikers with clubs and firing at them with their pistols. Some men were hiding behind railroad cars on the Burlington spur, and others were running as the police fired pistols at them. The sight, Spies

Painting of August Spies speaking near the
McCormick Reaper Works on May 3, 1886

recalled, made his blood boil. A young Irishman peeked out from behind a car and told Spies that he had seen two men lying dead and that four others had been killed by police gunfire. After hearing this, Spies raced back to the lumber shovers' rally and urged those who remained to come to the aid of the men under attack, but few workers remained on the prairie, and none of them rallied to his call. He looked back down the Black Road to the reaper works and said to himself, "The battle is lost."

Spies returned to his newspaper office with the sound of Colt revolvers ringing in his ears and dashed off a circular denouncing the attack. "I was very indignant," he later testified. "I knew from experience of the past that this butchering of people was done for the express purpose of defeating the eight-hour movement." Spies sent his leaflet to a compositor, who boldly added his own single-word title at the top of the leaflet: REVENGE! The rest of the text read: "Workingmen, to Arms!!! Your masters sent out their bloodhounds—the police—they killed six of your brothers at McCormick's this afternoon."[24]

For days Spies had been speaking as a leader of a disciplined union campaign for the eight-hour demand. Now the voice of the revolutionary broke through: "You have for years endured the most abject humiliations; you have endured the pangs of hunger and want; you have worked yourself to death; your children you have sacrificed to the factory lords." Worse yet was what happened when the workers demanded relief: the master sent "his bloodhounds out to shoot you to kill you!" "If you are men," the circular concluded, "if you are the sons of grand sires who have shed their blood to free you, then you will rise in your might, Hercules, and destroy the hideous monster that seeks to destroy you. To arms, we call you. To arms!"[25]

THAT NIGHT, ANARCHISTS DISTRIBUTED hundreds of English and German copies of what came to be known as the "Revenge" circular. A horseman rode down Lake Street dropping leaflets at union halls and saloons, including Grief's Hall, where anarchists of the Northwest Side group were meeting in the basement. George Engel and Adolph Fischer attended the meeting, as did two commanders of the Lehr und Wehr Verein. These were hard men who had little faith in the eight-hour movement or in the leadership of union-oriented anarchists like Spies, Schwab, Parsons and Fielden.

This meeting would later take on enormous significance in the trial of the eight anarchists accused of the Haymarket bombing, even though only two of the defendants, Engel and Fischer, were present in Thomas Grief's saloon cellar that night. During the trial prosecutors would describe this gathering as the birthplace of the "Monday night conspiracy" to commit murder and mayhem at the rally the next evening. Two anarchists who turned state's evidence in return for cash and safe passage out of the country testified that this group endorsed a plan Engel had laid out the night before to organize an armed response in case the police attacked striking workers. In the event of a dire crisis, a signal would be given by the appearance of the word *Ruhe* (rest) in the letter column of the *Arbeiter-Zeitung*. Then, according to the witnesses, armed groups would form to take action, bringing down telegraph lines, storming arsenals, bombing police stations and shooting law officers—all tactics, said the state's attorney, prescribed in Johann Most's writings. However, Engel also made it clear, according to witnesses, that the plan would take effect "*only* in the event of a police attack"—that is, as an act of armed self-defense.[26]

This serious business had been transacted when news of the deaths at McCormick's arrived. Shouts and curses burst forth from the men in Grief's basement. They were determined to respond to the outrage, but they did not decide to put Engel's plan into action. Instead, the group agreed to organize a public protest rally the next day in the usual meeting place on Market Street. Fischer argued, however, that this enclosed block would serve as "a mouse trap" if the police assaulted the assembly; and so the group agreed to hold the event the next evening in a much larger space—at the Haymarket, west of the river, where Randolph Street widened after it crossed Desplaines Street.[27]

As the Northwest Side anarchists headed home from Grief's Hall, the city's newspaper editors prepared their reports on what happened on the Black Road that afternoon. The *Tribune* offered the news this way: "Wrought up by the inflammatory harangues of a lot of rabid Anarchists, a mob of nearly 10,000 men, most of them fighting drunk, attacked the employees of the McCormick Reaper Company as they came home from work yesterday afternoon." When reinforcements arrived, "a sharp battle between the police and the rabble followed" in which a number of men in the mob were shot and carried away by their friends. The newspaper blamed one man, August Spies, for this "barbarian attack" upon the reaper factory.[28]

That evening, after quiet descended on the Black Road, the police escorted the employees trapped in the McCormick works to their homes. As they did, the wives, daughters and mothers of strikers attacked the officers with stones and sticks while shouting curses at them in broken English. At one point, police charged on these angry women and drove them off the streets.[29] "A bitter and vindictive spirit" prevailed on the South Side toward the police, according to the *Tribune,* but the forces of law and order had triumphed in Chicago's worst trouble spot. Chief Inspector Bonfield announced that the city was secure. "I believe we are strong enough to suppress any uprising," he declared. The police were ready to take action in all potential trouble spots. There would be more rioting, Bonfield warned, with "some blood spilling perhaps," but he did not anticipate anything like the riots of 1877. "The police had finally grappled with the McCormick rioters in dead earnest," a reporter observed, and whenever the men in blue were aroused to that point, he added, "then peace was sure to come to the city."[30]

Chapter Eleven

A Night of Terror

MAY 4, 1886

"A FAIRER MORNING than that which smiled across the blue waters of Lake Michigan on the 4th day of May, 1886, never dawned upon the city of Chicago," wrote the journalist John J. Flinn. "The wounded, crippled, bruised and bleeding anarchists who looked out upon it must have been maddened by the perfect beauty of the new day, the clearness of the sky, the freshness of the atmosphere, and the glorious awakening of Nature from her long sleep, made manifest in every peeping blade of grass and swelling bud." The sun rose on a quiet city, and to those who attended to business that morning "it seemed as though the excitement occasioned by the eight-hour strikes and the troubles at McCormick's was about to subside at last."[1]

In fact, the bloody rout of strikers at the reaper works did not end the excitement; on May 4 the strikes resumed, and tension began to grow by the hour. That day the *Tribune* reported acts of rebellion all over the city as ordinary working people behaved in extraordinary ways. A dozen laundry girls employed at the Clifton House Hotel told their foreman they wanted to run things their own way; when he refused, they got together and quit work. Two hundred pupils in a Bridgeport school named for the city's military hero, General Phil Sheridan, engaged in a miniature riot and demanded a one-hour reduction in the school day. When the principal refused, the boys went out and began "to demolish the windows of the school house" and, in one journalist's view, to "deport themselves as full-fledged strikers," until a police patrol restored order in the school yard. Groups of young women from the clothing shops turned their protest for an eight-hour day into a general strike; at one shop strikers removed the belt from an engine and brought everything to a standstill, and then laughed at the owner's predicament.[2]

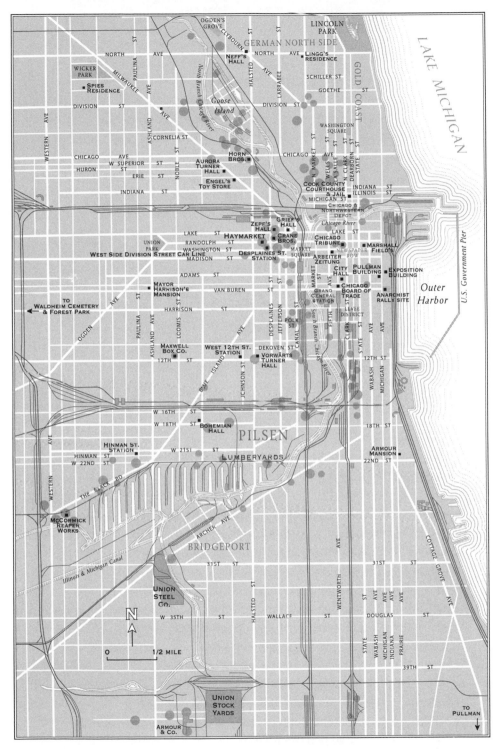

Map of Chicago showing locations of major strikes taking place during the Great Upheaval from April 25 to May 4, 1886

The *Tribune*'s leg men also saw more worrisome "specks of war" arising from the freight yards and lumberyards. The dreaded freight handlers' strike seemed about to become a general one, because the railroad managers had rejected their employees' proposal. Business came to a halt at the Rock Island freight house and several others as well. Office clerks and managers handled freight in some warehouses, but movement was very slow. Even the officials of the imperial Chicago, Burlington & Quincy were "rattled," the *Tribune* reported. They fretted even more when union switchmen on the Fort Wayne road left the yards clogged with trains on tracks shared by many other railroads using the busy Union Depot. Some railroad chiefs remained openly concerned about the reliability of the police department, and therefore called for the creation of a law-and-order league that would enlist all the businessmen of Chicago to aid the railroads and to "save the city from ruination."

Meanwhile, along the South Branch of the Chicago River scores of vessels rode at anchor in the docks and slips, their cargoes untouched, because the lumber shovers had decided to stop work until they received ten hours' pay for eight hours' work. The *Tribune* quoted an angry member of the union who said of the yard owners: "They want to starve us. We told them if we didn't cull the lumber, they could not sell it, and they said they'd cull it and sell it in spite of us. Well, I tell you, we are not going to starve." Before the bosses moved their lumber with scab labor, he warned, the strikers might burn it. The worker was promptly arrested and charged with disorderly conduct.

Farther south, in Pullman town, union workers sent a committee to the company's palatial offices on Michigan Avenue to present their demands to Mr. Pullman. The delegation included cabinetmakers, tinners, finishers, carpenters, wood turners, car builders, wheelwrights, upholsterers and even common laborers who demanded a larger wage increase than the others. Suddenly, Pullman's paternalistic world was turned upside down. His workers had never dared to speak up, but now these "dependent, servile" people had found their voices.[3]

Pullman refused the committee's demands, complaining that the company's profits were not sufficient to allow a wage increase or a reduction in hours. Disappointed and discontented, the committeemen returned by train to the model city, where at 7 p.m. they met with all of Pullman's 3,000 employees at the company baseball park. After hooting at their employer's response to their demands, the employees voted en masse to endorse their committee's strike recommendation.

Following Pullman's lead, other major employers stiffened their resolve. The Furniture Makers' Association gained scores of new members over the weekend; they met that Tuesday to declare their unanimous resolve against granting the union shorter hours at higher pay and against dealing with the union in any way. After the strike was defeated, declared the owners, they would take back strikers selectively, one man at a time. Meanwhile, the railroad managers formed a common front to put pressure on a few company executives who were inclined to yield to their workers' demands. In making their case, the militant managers had reportedly expressed the fear that "Communist blatherskates" would wrest leadership of the freight handlers' strike from the "cool headed leaders" and might incite the men to violence. The Metal Manufacturers' Association also decided on all-out resistance to the eight-hour movement. The owners of some machine shops and foundries had already agreed to reduce the workday to eight hours when their employees accepted a two-hour reduction in wages. But on May 4 the association forced those owners to renege on their agreements and take a hard line on any reduction of hours. A. C. Cameron, chair of the mainstream Eight-Hour Committee, despaired because the employers were no longer considering how to settle the eight-hour strike; instead, they were uniting to force their employees back to work.

Besides refusing all concessions to their employees, anxious employers demanded a call-up of the militia to intimidate the strikers and protect strikebreakers. At noon on May 4, Colonel E. B. Knox, commander of the First Infantry Regiment, received a call warning that a mob of 6,000 strikers had formed in the lumber district and was marching downtown. Knox issued a call to arms and, within an hour, the National Guard armory was bustling with military activity. The mob from the "terror district" never arrived downtown because its existence was a fabrication, concocted perhaps by a nervous employer or an imaginative reporter. In any case, the threat of a unified workers' movement focused on a common demand provoked an extremely well-cordinated response from the most powerful entrepreneurs in the Midwest, their financial backers in the East and their local allies. Businessmen who had been ruthless competitors now joined hands to battle a "common danger"—a mass strike by workers who challenged the laws of political economy and who risked provoking bloody civil strife. So, in Chicago, as in New York, the Great Upheaval marked a crucial moment in what one historian called "the consolidation of the American bourgeoisie."[4]

Business leaders were so alarmed by the working-class mobilization of May 1886 that they went far beyond invoking the laws of supply and demand in condemning collective efforts to raise wages and reduce hours. The field of forces had changed so radically that employers now threatened to employ the "whole machinery of government," including the military, to "enforce the laws of the market." However, the man in charge of state government in Illinois was not ready to crank up that machinery. A few hours after the National Guard was marshaled in Chicago, Governor Richard Oglesby, an experienced military officer, told the militia commander he had exceeded his authority and that he should disband his regiment until he received further orders. Oglesby was troubled by the vagueness of the Illinois statute applying to the use of state militia. He knew the pressure a governor could endure from agents of "incorporated wealth," who impatiently demanded the use of militia in cases of threatened violence, as well as from elements of the press, who were ready to "malign, misrepresent and intimidate" public officials who refused to do their bidding. Oglesby's decision to restrain the militia earned angry rebukes from his Republican backers in Chicago, but he resisted further pressure to call out the troops. The governor believed that Chicago was so explosive that putting militia in the streets might well cause a violent eruption.[5]

Meanwhile, downtown at the *Arbeiter-Zeitung* office, the editors put together an afternoon edition of the daily. Spies, still infuriated by the killings he had witnessed on the Black Road the day before, wrote a column denouncing the police as trained "bloodhounds" and admonishing the McCormick strikers for being caught unprepared. Spies had no idea that he was tightening a noose that would later wring his neck when he wrote that the workers at the harvester plant could have defended themselves had they carried guns, as the Internationals had suggested. If the strikers, pitifully armed with stones, had instead been equipped "with good weapons and one single dynamite bomb not one of the murderers would have escaped his well-deserved fate."[6]

Unbeknownst to Spies, two young anarchist carpenters, Louis Lingg and William Seliger, were busily making bombs that day at Seliger's home on the North Side. After he was later arrested and turned state's evidence, Seliger testified that Lingg had been doing so for several weeks, and that on May 4 both men had stayed home to work diligently at the task with three other comrades. Together, they manufactured thirty or forty explosive devices that afternoon but made no plans for where or when to use them. According to Seliger, Lingg simply told his fellow bomb makers that the infernal devices would be "good fodder" to feed the police when they attacked.[7]

If Spies had known about the bomb factory, he might have approved of it, because he was convinced that the massacre at McCormick's was a rehearsal for something worse to come, some awful attack strikers must be prepared to resist in order to defend themselves. Yet the publisher vacillated that day as he issued violent threats on the one hand and made cautionary warnings on the other. After finishing his angry editorial, Spies objected strenuously when he read a militant leaflet prepared to announce the protest meeting at the Haymarket that night. Spies's compositor, Adolph Fischer, had taken it upon himself to add the words

Flyer announcing the Haymarket meeting
on May 4, 1886

"Working men, arm yourselves and appear in full force," even though no one at the Grief's Hall planning meeting had suggested that workers bring guns to the rally. Spies reacted angrily, fearing these words would frighten people and reduce the crowd at the Haymarket, and that the call to arms would heighten the chances of a police assault. He then said he would refuse to speak at the meeting as requested unless Fischer's bellicose words were removed from the leaflet. The presses were held up and the provocative line was stricken from all but a few hundred of the flyers.[8]

Spies rode home to Wicker Park that afternoon to get some rest and eat a supper prepared by his doting mother. "I was very tired and ill humored," he recalled. His mind must have been spinning as he pondered some awful questions. Where would the next massacre occur—in the freight yards or in the lumberyards, on one of the viaducts or in a Turner hall, the places where unarmed workers had been slain by police in 1877? Would the workers be prepared this time? Would the next attack become the revolutionary moment he dreamed of, or would the people be slaughtered again as they were in Paris when the Commune was obliterated? And yet, maybe the next confrontation would have a different outcome. Maybe his own highly visible activity could somehow, even against long odds, turn an impending tragedy into a history-making victory.

AFTER SPIES ATE SUPPER in Wicker Park, he and his brother Henry set out for the Haymarket on foot. "We walked slowly down Milwaukee Avenue," he recalled, because it was warm. The revolver he usually carried was a bother, because he had changed clothes and the gun was too large for his pocket. So Spies stopped at a hardware store and left the pistol with the owner, Frank Stauber, the socialist councilman who had been unseated in 1880. Spies told his brother that he did not expect any violence at the market that night because he did not believe that the police would attack "an orderly meeting of citizens."[9]

What Spies did not know was that six companies of city police had already gathered half a block away from the Haymarket in the Desplaines Street Station under the command of Captain William Ward, who had been ordered to move all available men from his precinct—100 in all—to reinforce the detail at the station. By early evening a formidable force of 176 patrolmen had assembled.[10] Nor would Spies have known that a squad of detectives in plain clothing had been ordered to mix with the crowd when it assembled, or that Inspector Bonfield had insisted on assuming overall command of the force at the Desplaines Street Station, that the police were "arming for war" with Colt .50s and that ammunition was being sent to stations in different sections of the city along with the order "Don't spare your powder."[11]

What Spies did know was that Bonfield's men had fired pistols at unarmed men on the Black Road. They had abandoned the chief inspector's policy of using extremely brutal force with clubs in order to avoid the use of bullets. The Chicago Police Department had no official policy on bearing and using firearms, but all officers carried guns in their pants pockets or in specially tailored overcoat pockets and could use them at their discretion.[12]

As the Spies brothers approached the market district from the north, they walked past George Engel's toy store and Aurora Turner Hall on Milwaukee Avenue, then headed south on Desplaines Street. The two men arrived late at the site of the demonstration, which they expected to be in progress. It was about 8.15 p.m., but nothing had been done to start the meeting. Groups of men were standing in the Haymarket, smoking, murmuring, waiting for something to happen. August Spies had expected Albert Parsons to kick off the rally, but he was nowhere to be seen. After searching the area for his comrade, Spies returned to the market, and, seeing a smaller gathering than expected on Randolph Street, he moved the group out of the market around the corner onto Desplaines Street. Then he jumped up on a hay wagon sitting in front of an alley by the Crane Brothers' Foundry and called the meeting to order. Before he began speaking, Spies sent one of his newspaper employees back to the *Arbeiter-Zeitung* office, where he had heard that Parsons, Fielden and Schwab were attending a meeting with Lucy Parsons and Lizzie Holmes to discuss organizing more women in the clothing shops.

In fact, Albert Parsons did not know he was supposed to speak at the protest rally. He had returned from Cincinnati that morning fatigued from his long train trip but exhilarated by the massive eight-hour demonstrations he had witnessed. After a morning nap, Lucy awakened him to tell him her own exciting news of a mass meeting of "tailor girls" who, she now believed, could be organized to join the eight-hour movement en masse. Parsons then walked downtown to Grief's Hall to find a room for such a meeting. But since all the halls were occupied with eight-hour strike meetings, he had to settle for the little room in the *Arbeiter-Zeitung* office. While he was making these arrangements, Parsons was invited to speak at the Haymarket meeting; he declined because he had already made other plans and because, as he later revealed, he did not approve of holding an outdoor rally on May 4 since he feared the police would break it up and, as a result, more violence would ensue.[13]

Later that afternoon Parsons met two reporters on the West Side who asked him where he would speak that night. During the interview, one of the reporters later testified that "Mrs. Parsons and some children came up just then and Parsons stopped a car and slapped me familiarly on the back, and asked me if I was armed, and I said, 'No. Have you any dynamite?' " Parsons laughed at this, and Lucy said jokingly of her husband: "He is a very dangerous-looking man, isn't he?" Later that evening, after eating supper, Albert and Lucy left their home at 245 West Indiana with their two children and Lizzie Holmes and made their way downtown to meet with the "tailor girls."[14]

Meanwhile, across the river in Haymarket Square, workers had gathered in the dark, waiting for the protest rally to begin. Unable to locate Parsons, Spies returned to the market and began the rally. Nearly spent, he decided to speak briefly and simply in English. The small size of the crowd, far smaller than the rally organizers had expected, deflated him even more. It was already quite dark in the dreary street, which smelled of horse manure and rotting vegetables. A single gaslight on a lamppost had been lit, casting eerie shadows on the factory walls. By day, the market was a jumble of horse carts that streamed in from the German and Dutch truck farms outside the city, bringing in tons of hay and bushels of vegetables.[15] By night, this lively market scene disappeared and the district took on an ugly, forbidding aura. It was bounded by huge piles of dirt from railroad construction, a few rows of "pitiful, wretched houses" crowded together like huts, a "horrendous grey-black junk shop" and the large foundry on Desplaines Street owned by the Crane brothers. The only cheerful signs of life in the dark streets came from the gaslight showing through the smoky windows of Zepf's Hall on Lake Street and the bright electric lights on the marquee of the Lyceum Theater on Randolph Street.[16]

Spies began by saying that the meeting should be peaceable, that it was called not to raise a disturbance but to protest the killing of strikers and to rally workers to the eight-hour movement. For twenty years, he declared, workingmen had asked in vain for two hours less work a day, only to be betrayed by legislators and treated with contempt by their employers. He then spoke about his role in the battle at McCormick's, calling the factory's owner "an infamous liar" for saying that he, Spies, had caused the riot. The men who stormed the reaper works the previous day were not anarchists but "good, honest, law-abiding, church-going citizens," who had been goaded to madness by the lockout. Spies said that when he first tried to speak at the rally on the Black Road, some workers in the crowd objected that he was a socialist, and that when he tried to restrain the breakaway group, they ignored him and, "like ignorant children, they indulged in bombarding the plant with stones."

Then Spies caught sight of the man he was looking for making his way happily through the crowd. "I see Mr. Parsons is here," he said with relief, realizing that his comrade had changed his mind about attending the rally. "He is a much abler speaker in your tongue than I am," Spies remarked, "therefore I will conclude by introducing him."[17] Parsons parted company with his family, and then, as Lucy seated herself on a nearby cart with the two children and Lizzie Holmes, he climbed up on the wagon near Crane's Alley and looked out on a street that was now packed from sidewalk to sidewalk with 3,000 workers.

The speaker began by calling the audience's attention to the discontent of the working class, not only in Chicago but throughout the world, and he declared that all this distress meant there was "something radically wrong with the existing order." He referred to his travels to depressed cities and industrial valleys where he met thousands of workers clamoring for redress and relief. He also spoke of "compulsory idleness and starvation wages and how these things drove workingmen to desperation—to commit acts for which they ought not be held responsible."[18]

Parsons reminded his listeners of the newspaper editorials inciting violence against strikers and tramps. He quoted Tom Scott, the railroad baron, who said of the striking trainmen in 1877: "Give them a rifle diet and see how they like that bread." He indicted another robber baron, Jay Gould, who had hired thugs in East St. Louis to fire on unarmed workingmen. At the mention of Gould's name, someone in the crowd yelled, "Hang him!" Parsons paused and said that this conflict was not about individuals, that it was about changing a system and that socialists did not aim to take the life of a millionaire like Gould but rather to end the causes that created the pauper and the millionaire.

When Parsons resumed, he condemned the police for the outrage at the McCormick plant the previous day as well as the newspaper editor who falsely charged him with inciting trouble at a time when he was out of town. He concluded by saying that all citizens who loved liberty and independence should arm themselves or else they would see their rights trampled underfoot and see themselves shot in the streets like dogs.[19]

Mayor Carter Harrison stood on the street smoking his cigar and listening as Parsons spoke. Harrison had decided to attend the meeting because he wanted to make sure the assembly did not lead to another riot like the one at McCormick's. He thought that if the Haymarket meeting threatened violence, it would be better for the mayor to personally disperse the protesters than to order any policeman to do it. Harrison was a courageous man not afraid to confront public assemblies, as he had demonstrated earlier that day when he rode his white horse through town, visiting places where strikers congregated. Some of them hooted and jeered at him, but he was not physically assaulted.[20]

In the midst of Parsons's oration, Harrison walked a short distance to the Desplaines Street Police Station and told Inspector Bonfield that the speakers were "tame." He had heard no call for the use of force; he had seen no one in the street with weapons in their hands, and so, the mayor later testified, he told Bonfield that since "nothing had occurred yet or was likely to occur to require interference," he "thought the chief had better issue orders to his reserves at the other stations to go home." Bonfield replied that "he thought about the same way."[21]

When Harrison returned to the meeting from the police station, Samuel Fielden was addressing the crowd in a loud voice. Still dressed in his dusty work clothes, the speaker alluded to premonitions of danger everywhere.[22] After listening to Fielden for a few minutes, Mayor Harrison relit his cheroot so that it would illuminate his bearded face—the most familiar visage in Chicago. He wanted the men on the wagon and the men in the audience to see that he was there. He listened to Fielden shouting to the crowd but heard him say nothing to incite violence. Shortly after 10 p.m. Harrison mounted his horse and, with a tip of his black slouch hat to the crowd, trotted off down Randolph Street toward his mansion on Ashland Avenue, relieved that the day had passed without more bloodshed.[23]

WHILE THE HAYMARKET MEETING continued on the West Side, Louis Lingg and William Seliger busied themselves on the North Side, loading the bombs they had made into a trunk. According to Seliger's later testimony, they carried the trunk to Neff's Hall on Clybourn Avenue, where several men appeared and took some of the explosive devices away with them; Lingg and Seliger took some as well. After they left the hall, the two carpenters walked past the Larrabee Street Police Station, where Lingg reportedly said "it would be a beautiful thing if we could walk over and throw one or two bombs in the station." Then the two young men went to a nearby saloon and had a glass of beer.[24]

Meanwhile, at the rally, Fielden was bringing his speech to a close with angry words about the workingmen at McCormick's factory who had been shot down by the police in cold blood. This was a horrible example, he told the crowd, of how the law was framed and executed by their oppressors. "Keep your eye on the law," he cried. "Throttle it. Kill it. Stop it. Do everything you can to wound it—to impede its progress." After hearing this, one of Bonfield's detectives decided to report back to the chief inspector and tell him that the speaker was making incendiary remarks.[25]

At this point the weather changed. The moonlit sky suddenly darkened, and the crowd was chilled as a black cloud blew over the West Side. A storm seemed to be brewing. Albert Parsons, worried about his children getting cold, suggested adjournment to Zepf's Hall. Fielden said this was not necessary because he was about to conclude. Parsons left anyway with Lucy, Lizzie, and his children, and some people in the crowd who followed them to Zepf's Hall on Lake Street, less than a block away. Even Adolph Fischer, who wrote the militant call for the meeting, departed the rally for the warmth of the saloon.

At 10:20 p.m. only about 500 people remained on the dark street listening to Fielden speak as a light drizzle fell. The speaker concluded his remarks to a shivering audience by saying: "The Socialists are not going to declare war; but I tell you war has been declared upon us; and I ask you to get ahold of anything that will help you resist the onslaught of the enemy." Then Fielden noticed a disturbance to his left at the corner of Randolph Street.

A tremor passed through the crowd as people saw through the dim gaslight an advancing column of blue coats that stretched across the entire width of Desplaines Street. George Brown, a young Yorkshire-born shoemaker, observed what he described as "a great company of police with their revolvers drawn, rushing into the crowd which parted to make way for them."[26] The column covered the 180 feet from the station to the wagon in what seemed like a few heartbeats. The police commander, Captain William Ward, cried halt to his men and, with Inspector Bonfield at his side, exclaimed, "I command you in the name of the people of the state of Illinois to immediately and peaceably disperse." Fielden protested, saying, "But we are peaceable." A tense moment of silence followed, and Ward repeated his command. Then Fielden replied, "All right, we will go," and moved to climb down to the street.[27]

At that moment, when all was quiet, scores of heads turned to look into the dark sky, where many people heard a hissing sound and then looked to see a lighted object arching out of the distance toward the front ranks of the police. One man thought it was a lighted cigar, but Lieutenant J. P. Stanton knew better. A veteran of the Union navy who commanded the third division of police, he recognized what he saw passing over his head: he had had enough active service to know what a bombshell looked like. He shouted frantically to his men, "Look out. Boys, for God's sake, there is a shell." A few men looked up, but there was no time to react when an orange flash lit the night sky and a terrific detonation resounded in the street.[28]

August Spies had just jumped off the hay wagon when he heard the blast, but he could not see what had happened. His first thought was that the police had fired a cannon into the crowd. In the next instant Spies heard a fusillade erupt from police pistols. "Everybody was running, and people fell, struck by bullets, right and left." As he crossed in front of Crane's Alley, a number of officers rushed past Spies into the opening, some of them crying out that they had been hurt. "They had evidently been shot by their own comrades, and sought protection in the alley," Spies observed. Spies and his brother Henry found themselves in the midst of the fleeing patrolmen, ducking to avoid the bullets whistling past them.[29]

As gunfire rattled around Desplaines Street and men screamed out in agony, someone slipped up behind August Spies and stuck a six-shooter in his back. Before the assassin could pull the trigger, Henry Spies grabbed the gun. It discharged into his groin, and he fell down. The Spies brothers then became separated in the sea of humanity roiling around in the black street. "I lost my brother in the throng," Spies wrote, recreating the scene, "and was carried away to the north." He fell a few times over other men who had dropped to the street, but he made it safely to Zepf's Hall, where he learned for the first time that the explosion he survived had probably been caused by a bomb.[30]

Just after he ordered Fielden to disperse the meeting, Captain William Ward heard a cry and turned to see the "bomb or shell thrown from the east side of Desplaines Street about 15 feet from the alley where there were a lot of boxes." He saw it immediately, attracted by the light thrown off by its sizzling fuse. The grenade exploded almost as soon as it hit the ground, about eight or ten feet from where Ward stood, splintering the wooden blocks that lined the street and filling the night air with acrid smoke. "I think I heard a shot to the east of me," he recalled, "and then I heard the command of some officer to the police to charge" followed by "a terrific firing from the officers." After the gunfire abated, Ward hurried back toward the station. It was then that he saw lying on the southwest corner of Desplaines and Randolph, a half block from the bomb's point of impact, the body of Officer Mathias Degan. He was already near death from his wounds.[31]

Albert Parsons was holding a schooner of beer, looking out Zepf's window toward the remnants of the rally, when he saw what appeared to be "a white sheet of light at the place of the meeting, followed by a loud roar and then a hail storm of bullets that punctured the windows and thudded into the door frame." Within a few seconds, men came rushing into the saloon to escape the hail of lead shot from policemen's pistols. Parsons, who had been under fire on Civil War battlefields, remained calm, moving about the room telling the others not to be frightened.[32] When someone shut the door and cut off the gaslights, many people rose

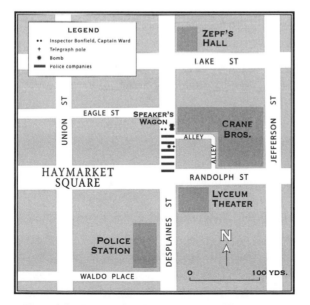

Map of the Haymarket Square area on May 4, 1886

from the floor and moved to the back room. There, Lizzie Holmes recalled, they all waited in an eerie quiet, "shut up in total darkness, ignorant of what had happened or what our danger was."[33]

THE MANY ACCOUNTS OF what happened that night in Chicago are in rough agreement up until the moment that Captain Ward gave the order to disperse; then the testimonies offered by witnesses diverge wildly. Some patrolmen thought they heard Fielden say, "We are peaceable," but others thought that he said, "Here come the bloodhounds. You do your duty and I'll do mine," and that he then fired a gun at Captain Ward. Some policemen also told reporters that the bomb came from Crane's Alley or from behind the speakers' wagon, not from the east side of the street as Captain Ward had said. The direction of the bomb flight would later become important, because prosecution witnesses charged that Spies had given the bomb to a man who threw it from the alley.[34]

Most of the officers testified that as soon as the blast erupted they took heavy pistol fire from the crowd along the sidewalks. Inspector Bonfield insisted that this proved the events that night were not a riot but a deliberate, rehearsed conspiracy, because, he argued, the anarchists had planned to open fire on the policemen as soon as the bomb exploded. Captain Ward said he heard gunshots immediately after the explosion, but could not be sure who fired first because the firing was indiscriminate. Otherwise, the officers' descriptions of the events that night were fairly consistent.[35] Their testimony would provide the main basis of press accounts of the bombing, the accounts that would shape public understanding of the tragedy.

The police version of the May 4 events would also serve as the foundation for the legal case state prosecutors would bring against the suspects accused of the bombing. Anarchists and supporters of the International, as well as other observers who were not connected with the unions or the radical movement, would, however, challenge this authoritative narrative of the Haymarket incident on nearly every crucial point. These witnesses did not hear Fielden say the bloodhounds were coming or see him fire a gun at the police. One of them, S. T. Ingram, a nineteen-year-old worker at the Crane Brothers' Foundry, read the Haymarket circular that day and returned to his workplace that evening to observe the meeting. Standing near the Crane building next to the wagon, he saw the police advance and Fielden jump from the wagon just before the blast echoed in the night air, but he saw no shots fired from the wagon. "After the explosion of the bomb," he testified, "I stepped back against the wall to keep from getting killed. There was a great deal of shooting going on then; most of it coming from the policemen, from the center of the street." He said his hearing and eyesight were very good, and he saw no citizen or person dressed in citizens' clothes use a revolver. "It was a very peaceable meeting."[36]

Three businessmen saw events in a similar way. None of them saw firing from the crowd; nor did Barton Simonson, a salesman who was an especially trustworthy eyewitness because he knew Captain Ward and Inspector Bonfield and other officers as a result of his prominence in charitable efforts to support soup kitchens for the destitute on the West Side. "The firing began from the police, right in the center of the street," Simonson testified. "I did not see a single shot fired from the crowd on either side of the street."[37]

There was no dispute about what happened after the police started shooting. One reporter described the scene as "wild carnage," and the *Tribune*'s observer went much further. "Goaded by madness," he wrote, "the police were in the condition of mind that permitted no resistance, and in a measure they were as dangerous as any mob of Communists, for they were blinded by passion and unable to distinguish between the peaceful citizen and Nihilist assassin."[38] What remained unreported was the likelihood that, as an anonymous police official later indicated, a very large number of the police were wounded by their own revolvers. In the riotous seconds after the concussion, "it was every man for himself" as many patrolmen, trapped in tight formation, "emptied their revolvers, mainly into each other."[39]

When the firing ceased on Desplaines Street, the stunned group huddled at the back of Zepf's Hall waited quietly in the dark for several minutes before they risked venturing out into the night. Lizzie Holmes, Albert and Lucy Parsons and their children headed north over the Desplaines Street viaduct, where they met Thomas Brown of the American Group, who told Parsons that he was a marked man. Since everyone knew him and knew his influence, it would be better if Albert fled the city. An urgent discussion ensued on the viaduct. At first, Parsons refused to flee the scene and leave his family members and friends to face the consequences without him. No one recorded Lucy's words to her husband that night, but her close friend Lizzie said she was able to convince Albert to run for his life. He had no money to buy a train ticket, so Brown gave him $5. And then, there on the viaduct, they decided to separate. Brown would go one way, Lucy, Lizzie and the children another, while Albert headed for the Northwestern Railroad Depot and a train that would take him to Geneva, Illinois, where William Holmes would be waiting to receive him. Before he turned to leave, Parsons looked at his wife and said in a sad voice, "Kiss me, Lucy. We do not know when we will meet again."[40]

At about the same time, Chicago Police Superintendent Frederick Ebersold was retiring for the night in his South Side home. He was terribly fatigued by his long hours at headquarters dispatching patrols throughout the strike-torn city and mobilizing divisions for the Haymarket protest. He had left his office at about 10 p.m. after hearing from Inspector Bonfield that no trouble had occurred at the Haymarket and that the policemen held in reserve at various stations could be dismissed. When the telephone rang at his home, Ebersold knew it meant serious trouble had occurred. He threw on his clothes and rushed his horse carriage uptown to the Desplaines Street Station. When he arrived, he told a reporter, "the building was illuminated from top to bottom, officers were carrying wounded men on litters, surgeons and police were working or praying." Ebersold, a combat veteran of the Union army and a survivor of the ghastly slaughter at Shiloh, had seen the gory aftermath of several Civil War battles. The scene of scores of wounded officers stretched on the Desplaines Street Station floor vividly recalled those pictures of battlefield carnage.[41]

Police officers told the superintendent that an unknown number of anarchists had been shot and killed, but the next day only one civilian death was reported in the *Tribune*. Carl Kiester, a laborer who lived near Albert and Lucy Parsons on West Indiana Street, had died after being shot just below the heart. Kiester was later described by the coroner as a "Bohemian Socialist." Nineteen other "Citizens or Anarchists" were listed as wounded, according to the paper. Six of them, reportedly in dangerous condition, gave names that suggested the national diversity of the Haymarket rally crowd: William Murphy, John Lepland, Joseph Koutchke, Robert Schultz, Peter Ley and Mathias Lewis, a shoemaker shot through the back. A few days later, police identified a comatose patient in Cook County Hospital as a man named Krueger, who lay with a bullet in his brain and with no hope whatever for a recovery. This was "Big Krueger," a militant in the IWPA. At least thirty more people at the rally and in the neighborhood were wounded by police gunfire, including

Henry Spies, who took a bullet for his brother, and Sam Fielden, who was shot in the leg as he ran up Randolph Street toward downtown.[42]

In the next days, the deaths of three civilians were recorded by the coroner, though more may have died in the hail of police gunfire without having their deaths and burials recorded by the city. In any case, these deaths seemed of no account to the press. What mattered to the public was that in the same span of time six more patrolmen followed Mathias Degan to the grave—seven brave men in all, men who marched with their fellow officers into the Haymarket that night faithfully performing their duties with no inkling of the fate that awaited them.[43]

Chapter Twelve

The Strangest Frenzy

AFTER HE LEFT the back room of Zepf's Hall, August Spies hurried up Milwaukee Avenue to his home in Wicker Park. When he returned that evening, his mother and sister told him that his brother Henry was alive and had received treatment for his wound. Spies's relief could hardly have displaced the anxiety he must have felt; in the previous thirty-two hours he had witnessed the massacre at McCormick's, found himself blamed for the bloodshed the next morning and then, the next night, had survived a bomb explosion, an assassination attempt and a hail of police gunfire in the Haymarket.

Spies left no account of how he slept that night or how he felt on the morning after the tragedy, but his actions were normal. He took the horsecar down Milwaukee Avenue and went to work at the *Arbeiter-Zeitung* as usual. There he joined Schwab in the urgent task of putting out the day's special edition on the sensational Haymarket events. Lizzie Holmes and Lucy Parsons also arrived at the newspaper building that morning after spending the night with Albert, Jr., and Lulu in a comrade's flat; they planned to compose a special edition of the *Alarm*, to denounce the police who had broken up a peaceful meeting and gunned down innocent workers. None of them had yet read the morning dailies with their accounts of police casualties and the "hellish deeds" in the Haymarket.

NOW IT IS BLOOD! proclaimed a typical headline. A BOMB THROWN INTO RANKS INAUGURATES THE WORK OF DEATH. Headlines screamed murder and zeroed in on the "Bloody Monsters" who committed it. City editors all adopted Inspector Bonfield's theory that the bombing was the work of an anarchist conspiracy rather than an act of an individual. Wilbur Storey's Democratic *Chicago Times* cried out for an immediate and remorseless repression. "Let us whip these slavic wolves back to the

European dens from which they issue, or in some way exterminate them."[1]

The owners of the Knights of Labor newspaper condemned the anarchists as harshly as the business press did. Like their leader, Terence Powderly, who immediately denounced the outrage on behalf of "honest labor," these men lashed out at the "band of cowardly murderers, cutthroats and robbers, known as anarchists, who sneak through the country like midnight assassins, stirring up the passions of ignorant foreigners, unfurling the red flag of anarchy and causing riot and bloodshed." Even though Albert Parsons was a founding member of the Knights, the two owners of the order's Chicago newspaper declared that he and his comrades "should be summarily dealt with," because they were "entitled to no more consideration than wild beasts."[2]

One report from the Board of Trade captured the mood of the city's businessmen: a broker said that if some in the financial quarter moved to hang the anarchists from lampposts, 500 men on the trading floor "would lend willing hands in the work." Even a highly regarded Chicago attorney said he believed that the nature of the crime was itself "a waiver of trial and a plea of guilty."[3]

Public antipathy toward the anarchists was naturally heightened by sympathy for the stricken police officers. When two more patrolmen, John Barrett and George Mueller, died on May 6, the *Tribune* headline tolled like a bell: TWO MORE DEAD HEROES.[4] Once despised by city elites and characterized as shakedown artists and bagmen, as the lackeys of saloonkeepers and "bummer" politicians from the Irish wards, the police were suddenly regarded as brave warriors who marched in "gallant platoons" to the Haymarket, never expecting resistance or the explosion of a bomb that devastated their ranks.[5]

However, the dead policemen were not buried with military honors. In fact, Mathias Degan, a widower and the first to die, was given a modest funeral at his humble residence on South Canal Street and was buried with only a few friends and police department representatives in attendance. John Barrett, age twenty-five, who had learned the trade of an iron molder before joining the force, was also put to rest in a humble funeral service conducted in a small room of his third-floor flat. The only police officers who attended the service were six patrolmen from the Desplaines Street Station who would serve as Barrett's pallbearers. The third deceased patrolman, twenty-eight-year-old George Mueller, who came to Chicago to work as a teamster, was not buried in the city but in his home-

Patrolman Mathias J. Degan

town of Oswego, New York. Mueller, said the *Tribune,* was one of the men "most horribly torn by the destructive bomb" thrown by the anarchists; he expired after suffering "such torture from his injuries that death came as a release to him."[6]

Unaware of the hurricane developing outside the *Arbeiter-Zeitung* office, the anarchists seemed unprepared for what happened next. As Spies and Schwab composed copy for their afternoon newspaper, a police detail arrived to arrest them. August Spies's youngest brother, Christian, a furniture worker who happened to be in the building, was also taken to jail. The police detective who led the raid later admitted that he searched the editors and their premises without a warrant.[7]

When Spies and Schwab arrived at the Central Police Station, they were confronted by Police Superintendent Frederick Ebersold, who was at his wit's end. He had placed 350 men at McCormick's disposal to keep the peace on the Black Road, but the result was a riot that left civilians dead. He had commanded Bonfield to assemble a large squad at Desplaines Street to keep order there, and now three policemen were dead and others lay dying at Cook County Hospital. He leapt at Schwab and at Spies, who recalled the scene this way: " 'You dirty Dutch sons of bitches, you dirty hounds, you rascals, we will choke you, we will kill you,' " Ebersold screamed, "forgetting in his rage that he was himself a German." Then the officers "jumped upon us, tore us from one end to the other, went through our pockets," Spies wrote. They took his money and everything he had, but he remained silent, fearing far worse abuse.[8]

After their German comrades were taken away from the *Arbeiter-Zeitung* office, Lucy Parsons and Lizzie Holmes nervously resumed work on the *Alarm*. In a short time, another detail of police burst up the stairs to their office and confronted the two women. When one of them grabbed Lizzie, she resisted. When Lucy protested, an officer pushed Lucy and called her "a black bitch." The police then marched the two anarchist women to the city jail for questioning. After the interrogation the officers released Lucy, hoping they could follow her to Albert, now the target of an intense dragnet. When she did not lead them to her husband, she was arrested and questioned two more times. The second time she was apprehended, the police arrested her in front of her children, who were staying in a friend's flat near Grief's Hall. They ransacked the place while Lucy kept up a running stream of protest. It was the beginning of a forty-year ordeal of episodic jailings for Mrs. Albert Parsons, whose activities would become an obsession with the Chicago Police Department.[9]

As soon as Albert Parsons and William Holmes learned of these arrests, they knew the Holmes house in Geneva would soon be searched. So Parsons disguised himself by shaving off his long mustache and washing out the shoe black that he normally used to dye his gray hair. He took off the waistcoat, shirt collar and necktie he always wore and dressed like a tramping worker before leaving on foot for the little city of Elgin, where he would catch a train to Waukesha, Wisconsin, and there take refuge in the home of a socialist comrade. Parsons decided to travel unarmed, hoping to avoid a shoot-out if lawmen tracked him down.[10]

When the police arrested Lucy and Lizzie, they also hauled off the entire staff of the *Arbeiter-Zeitung*. All twenty-two workers, including the compositor Adolph Fischer and several young printer's devils, were marched two by two to the police station past people on the streets who shouted angry words at them. Some cried out that the printers should be hanged immediately. The pressmen were charged with murder and held incommunicado for the night. Meanwhile, the police returned to systematically search the *Arbeiter-Zeitung* office, where they found 100 copies of the call for the Haymarket meeting, and in the room adjoining Spies's office they seized some material they believed was to be made into bombs.[11]

Oscar Neebe, assistant manager of the anarchist newspaper, went home that night distressed by the arrests that closed down the radical presses on a day when thousands of readers awaited news about the Haymarket affair. In the morning he was confronted by Captain Michael Schaack, who arrived at his house with a police detail. The officers found one Springfield rifle, one Colt .38-caliber pistol with five chambers fired out, one sword, a belt with a Lehr und Wehr Verein buckle and leaflets announcing the protest meeting at the Haymarket. On this basis, Schaack would go before a grand jury to ask that Neebe be indicted for conspiracy to commit murder.[12]

Captain Schaack, a close ally of Inspector Bonfield, knew the anarchists well. He commanded a police station on Chicago Avenue, where he kept up a steady surveillance on the radicals who lived and congregated in his district; he had promised to keep the Gold Coast a "safe haven" for the rich families who lived uncomfortably close to the immigrant masses down below Division Street. Described as "posturing, defiant, self-assured," a man full of "bluster and bravado," Schaack eagerly organized an anarchist-roundup that would soon make him the best-known police detective in America.[13]

The next day, May 6, Samuel Fielden awoke and found his leg wound superficial. His wife put a new bandage on it, and he felt strong enough to walk around the block. After doing this he came home and waited for the police. When they arrived, the officers ransacked Fielden's house without presenting a search warrant, but they discovered nothing incriminating. At the station, Fielden recalled, he was confronted by Superintendent Ebersold, who demanded to see his wound. When the prisoner pulled up his pants leg and Ebersold saw the wound from the bullet, he said, "Damn your soul, it ought to have gone here," as he pointed his finger at Fielden's forehead.[14]

Fielden was arraigned with Spies and Schwab, and then all three prisoners gave interviews to the press in which they explained their actions at the square the night before. The men "cast furtive glances downward," according to one reporter, because they "had undoubtedly heard the threats of lynching." Schwab, who was described as looking fifty years old and "thin almost to the point of emaciation," said he left the Haymarket before the rally and knew nothing of the bombing. "His eyes were covered with heavy, puffy lids," and he shielded them behind a pair of steel-framed spectacles. "His hair is black and tumbled, and his weedy, black beard falls down upon his breast and covers his upper lip. His hands are big and bony, and his thin body and legs are lost in his clothes.

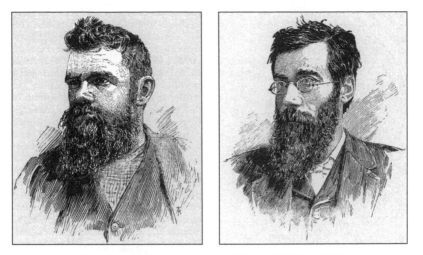

*Newspaper artists' drawings of Samuel Fielden (left)
and Michael Schwab from police photos*

His hands and legs writhe and intertwine, and his general appearance is that of a fanatic, half-insane."[15]

Fielden, who also protested his innocence, was depicted as being dressed in well-worn clothing of the poorest quality, wearing a "blue hickory shirt that gave him the appearance of a country man." He was heavyset and muscular, with swarthy features well covered with a thick growth of black hair and a beard. All these features seemed "repulsive" to one reporter, and Fielden's "low brow and catlike eyes" did not improve his appearance. When eight-hour leader George Schilling spoke up for Fielden, calling him "an old pupil" who had now gotten himself into very "deep water," the *Tribune* took this to mean that Schilling, "heretofore looked upon as a labor reformer acting for the benefit of working men," had actually been "a teacher in the school of anarchy." The conclusion was a harsh one: "The time has come . . . not only for suppressing the Spieses, Parsonses, and the Fieldens, but the Schillings also."[16]

In his interview August Spies called the bombing an impulsive and outrageous act, not a prearranged one. He said he knew nothing of the explosives the police said they took from his office; he thought they had been "placed there by the police in order to make a case" against him. He admitted that he kept two metal casings in his desk to show reporters but said they were "perfectly harmless."[17]

These expressions of innocence meant nothing to the coroner's jury when it convened that day. The inquest into Officer Degan's demise concluded not only that his death had been "caused by a piece of bomb, thrown by an unknown person," but that the perpetrator was "aided, abetted, and encouraged" by Spies, Schwab, Parsons and Fielden. An editorial in the *Tribune* that same day set the terms of prosecution in even more ominous specificity. It retold the story of Tuesday night's violence as a "murderous Communist conspiracy" and then explained that Illinois' criminal code regarding accessories to murder was broad enough to allow indictments against any offenders whose "seditious utterances" were followed by the commission of a crime. If it could be shown that anarchist leaders "advised and encouraged" the crime perpetrated on Desplaines Street, then, under state law, they would be subject to death on the gallows.[18]

While the searches, arrests and interrogations continued, the police kept busy raiding other places where militant workers and anarchists congregated. They closed Grief's and Zepf's halls on Lake Street because they were "headquarters of the foreign-speaking population which flaunts and marches under the red flag." The streets in the Haymarket district were usually crammed with farmers, workers and shoppers, but on May 6 all were deserted. The red flags that had flown from hundreds of buildings on the West Side during the previous week of tumult had all but disappeared.

Yet one spot in the district was filled with people that morning. Crowds of men and women were attracted to the scene of the tragedy. They stood in front of Crane's Alley talking in little groups and pointing at the houses and buildings in the area damaged by the shooting. On Desplaines Street as far north as Zepf's Hall, they could see shattered windows and doors pockmarked with bullets. Dr. James Taylor, a member of the International who had attended the rally, joined the curious bands of citizens on the street. He returned to look at a tall telegraph pole he had seen riddled by police bullets the night of the riot. Now he was surprised to see that the pole had been removed by someone who left telegraph wires strung along the street.[19]

Meanwhile, in Chicago's working-class neighborhoods, rumors flew as bloodied rallygoers returned home and sought treatment from local druggists and doctors. These witnesses carried with them lurid accounts of events in the Haymarket the night before, tales that caused excitement all over Pilsen. The next morning a crowd threw stones through the windows of a store owned by a man who had allowed police to use his telephone to report disturbances. When 500 strikers from the lumberyards gathered in another spot, three patrol wagons with 50 officers hurried to the area and found the street clogged with people. Brandishing their revolvers, the patrolmen forced the sullen crowd to disperse and then walked resolutely up the board sidewalks of Halsted Street, breaking up any and all gatherings. Bohemian women "acted like tigresses," and the police were "compelled at times to forget the sex of their assailants." The next day it was reported that the "backbone of Socialism" in the Bohemian district had been broken by the "bold front presented by the policemen and the readiness they showed in the use of revolvers."[20]

On May 7, the *Tribune* reassured readers that the socialists had been cowed by the aggressive measures of the authorities. No demonstrations of any note took place anywhere in the city. The area around the Haymarket was quiet, and so was the district along the Black Road that bordered the Bohemian district. Two days later the war was over in Chicago, according to the *New York Times*. "There is hardly an Anarchist in the city who does not tremble for fear of a domiciliary visit from the police. Search warrants are no longer necessary, and suspicious houses are being ransacked at all hours of the day and night." For nearly two more months Chicagoans would experience what a visiting economist, Richard Ely, called a "period of police terrorism"—a time when all civil liberties were suppressed in the name of public safety.[21]

However, reports of police action from the war zone did little to calm excited residents. People in suburban towns, unprotected by large armed police forces, feared acts of violence committed by marauding gangs from Chicago. In the city itself, where the police controlled the streets, middle-class residents were also petrified. Gun sales soared. High anxiety prevailed day after day throughout the month.[22]

Just when the last anarchist seemed to have been arrested, more were flushed out of their dens by detectives under the energetic direction of Captain Schaack. Almost every day detectives uncovered some dynamite plot or cache of weapons that they said indicated a dangerous anarchist conspiracy was still afoot. It was easy to persuade the terror-stricken population of the existence of a gigantic revolutionary conspiracy, recalled Chicago journalist Brand Whitlock. No rumor of a deadly plot seemed too fantastic to be believed by a hysterical public. It all produced, said Whitlock, "one of the strangest frenzies of fear that ever distracted a whole community."[23]

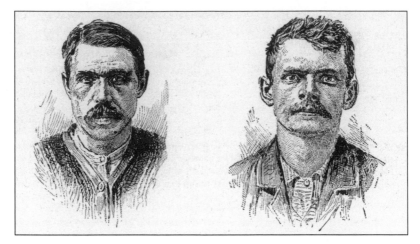

Drawings from police photos of Bohemian workers arrested
by police after disturbances in Pilsen, May 5, 1886

THE FEAR THAT GRIPPED Chicago that May did not arise simply from sensational police activities and newspaper stories. It fed on a fever of worry that had plagued the city ever since the Great Fire of 1871. The bomb, or something like it, had been forecast for years, but when it actually exploded, the fears it ignited were far worse than those produced by the holocaust fifteen years before. People's imaginations ran wild. Chicago was a city where citizens had been more fearful of the "dangerous classes" than in any other place; to them, the police, for all their corrupt qualities, represented the only means of preventing another inferno from which there would be no recovery.[24] If these trained law officers could be struck down by the black hand of anarchy, how could anyone be safe? There was simply no telling how many other bomb throwers had hidden themselves away in Chicago's "terror district."

On the Sunday after the explosion, an influential Protestant preacher, Professor David Swing, asked his huge congregation: "If men can pass their lives among us . . . and never be touched by one ray of religious, social or political truth, what can we say of America and what of Chicago?" Was their pride in the great Republic justified? "We need a careful definition of what freedom is," Swing continued. "If it means the license to proclaim the gospel of disorder, to preach destruction, and scatter the seeds of anarchy . . . the sooner we exchange the Republic for an iron-handed monarchy the better it will be for all of us."[25]

If Christian Chicagoans believed social order to be ordained by God, then disorder had to be the work of the devil and his agents, who lived on the dark side of life in this city of smoke. After all, there was no darker city in America than Chicago, even in the daytime. The anarchists often met at night, plotting conspiracies in saloon cellars and drilling their militia in basement rooms. The protest rally at the Haymarket took place at night. The bomb was thrown from an alley as dark clouds rolled in from the lake, and its explosion snuffed out the one gas lamp on the street so that the bomber, a creature of the night, could slip away unseen.[26]

The night of terror in the Haymarket challenged commentators to find words that could capture the horror of the event and the evil of the men who caused it. The urge to describe, label and signify went far beyond the white-hot editorials in Chicago papers. Every editor in the country had his say. Western newspapermen said frontier justice should be applied to the lawless city and the anarchists should be treated like horse thieves. Indeed, the citizens of Chicago, declared a Denver editor, could be excused if they formed vigilante committees and hanged "every man who was known to have advocated the throwing of dynamite bombs and the overturning of the law."[27]

Many editorialists relied on animal metaphors to describe the anarchists, whom they branded "ungrateful hyenas," "incendiary vermin" and "slavic wolves."[28] Some commentators conceded that the anarchists were human but were from the "lowest stratum," as the *Washington Post* put it. Following this kind of reasoning, the alien incendiaries were often compared to other hated groups like the menacing Apache Indians. The *St. Louis Globe-Democrat* applied an old frontier adage about "savage" tribes to the new menace. "There are no good anarchists except dead anarchists," it proclaimed.[29]

Other editorialists examined the particular European origins of the bomb throwers, and explained that the anarchists came from what the *Tribune* called "the worst elements of the Socialistic, atheistic, alcoholic European classes." The "enemy forces" that had invaded the city were the "scum and offal" of Europe, its "human and inhuman rubbish." "These aliens, driven out of Germany and Bohemia for treasonable teachings by Bismarck and the Emperor of Austria, have swarmed over into this country of extreme toleration and have flagrantly abused its hospitality," the paper declared. "After warming these frozen vipers on its breast and permitting them to become citizens," America had been bitten by these "serpents" who had been "warmed in the sunshine of tolera-tion." Thus, the *Tribune* concluded, all the death in the Haymarket resulted from the city's ill-conceived toleration of the anarchists.[30]

Standing up in the middle of this reactionary storm was Mayor Carter Harrison, whom the press and the business community held partially responsible for the attack on the police because he allowed the anar-chists to speak and assemble freely. The mayor temporarily banned all assemblies that might be dangerous and ordered the closing of the *Arbeiter-Zeitung*, but he also told reporters it was wrong for the newspa-pers to criticize elected officials while the city remained in a crisis caused by the eight-hour strikes. He also rejected the assumption that excessive free speech caused the tragedy. "If we had stopped them from speaking," he explained, "the same thing would have happened." Spies, Parsons and Fielden had aroused the anxiety of the crowd by warning of the array of policemen and soldiers surrounding them with loaded guns, but they had said nothing inflammatory, nothing to incite violence. Harri-son chose not to make the anarchists into martyrs by suppressing them and violating cherished principles. "Free speech is a jewel and the American people know it," he said.[31]

As he watched the nation's first red scare grip his city in the follow-ing days, the mayor told a neighbor what he did that Tuesday night on Desplaines Street, how he had listened to the speeches and heard noth-ing provocative and how he told Bonfield that the meeting was peaceful and that the crowd was dispersing. Harrison thought the bomb thrower was probably a lone lunatic and that the bombing was not a prelude to an insurrection or the result of an anarchist plot. He knew the anarchists were men who liked to hear themselves talk and who often talked like "damn fools," but, the mayor told his friend, they were not dynamite plotters.[32]

Now in his fourth term, Carter Harrison had been a brilliantly effec-tive mayor. He had won the affection of Chicago's many ethnic tribes by proclaiming fictive kinship with their elders, marching in their parades, honoring their traditions and rewarding immigrant supporters with jobs and favors. After he was first elected in 1879, Harrison brought Chi-cagoans together in the aftermath of the hard and bitter years when the fear of unemployment, strikes, lockouts and bloody riots pushed citi-zens into deep trenches full of animosity. Moreover, the mayor held the city together during the mid-1880s, when tensions between workers and bosses reached a breaking point—a time when his popularity was so wide it extended to all classes, races and nationalities.[33] But now, on May 5, 1886, he saw his beloved city breaking apart again.

No one uttered in public the views Mayor Harrison shared with his neighbor in private because no one expressed any doubt that an anarchist conspiracy had caused the deaths in the Haymarket. At first, the only editorial voice suggesting that the police were in some way responsible for the tragedy came from far away in New York City. There, the editor of a small but influential labor publication, *John Swinton's Paper,* pointed out that "[i]f the armed squad of policemen had not marched menacingly on the assemblage, if they had refrained from any attempt to break up the meeting as long as it was free from tumult, there is no reason to doubt that the diatribes of the speakers would have ended in silence and peace about the usual hour of ten o'clock."[34]

In John Swinton's view, the Chicago police had provoked the violence as a way of stopping the drive for an eight-hour day and the powerful strike movement that propelled it. The bomb, he wrote, was a "god send to the enemies of the labor movement," who would use it, he added provocatively, "as an explosive against all the objects working people are bent on accomplishing."[35]

As Swinton feared, during the next days responsibility for the crime of May 4 was extended beyond the "dynamite orators" to include thousands of eight-hour men who remained on strike. Some commentators blamed the whole movement for the bloodshed. Every drop, one editorial charged, could be "attributed to the malign influences, teachings, resolutions . . . of the Knights of Labor." The *Tribune* asked: "Why should the dynamite knights be allowed to exercise the rights of free citizens?" And then it warned that the strikers were deliberately injuring themselves and their employers by their "injudicious attempt to make Chicago an exception to the laws of political economy in a mistaken effort to improve their own condition." Protesters should return to work and reject the advice of miscreants who would lead them to common ruin.[36]

INSTEAD OF FOLLOWING the *Tribune*'s directions, thousands of workers stayed on strike on May 5; and the next day others joined them. By then, however, employers had been thoroughly mobilized, the police had been deployed all over the city and change was in the air as the eight-hour strike movement became a struggle mainly of skilled craft workers.[37]

The unskilled strikers were the workers most intimidated by the effects of Haymarket. For instance, the freight handlers, their backs to the wall, vowed to disown the socialists and keep the peace after being warned by Bonfield himself "to stay off the streets and to avoid every appearance of evil." Meanwhile, they were losing ground, as more and more business was being done at freight houses by strikebreakers without serious opposition from the union men.[38]

The Jewish tailors, latecomers to the labor movement, were utterly unprepared for the reaction that hit them on May 5. A small group of Yiddish-speaking workers, oblivious to the events that took place in the Haymarket the night before, marched from the West Side to downtown factories where manufacturers had hired nonunion laborers to perform their work. The strikers hoped, against great odds, to invade the open shops and pull out the workers inside, but when 600 of them crossed the Van Buren Street Bridge, they were surrounded by scores of policemen with billy clubs, who chased them back over the river and beat them as they ran for their lives. Limping back to their hall on DeKoven Street and nursing their wounds, the tailors conversed intensely in Yiddish, trying to find an explanation for what had happened. It was only then that one of the men who could read German told them what he had learned from a newspaper about Tuesday's Haymarket bombing: that the police were hunting the men who threw the bomb; and that one of them was the same August Spies who had lectured to them about the eight-hour strike. "After May 5th picketing became absolutely impossible," wrote Abraham Bisno, one of the Russian tailors the police beat on Van Buren Street. It was as though the city were under martial law.[39]

A prominent socialist summarized the situation for the *Tribune* on May 5. "A large number of trades that have compact organizations—the aristocracy of labor—will get ten hours' pay for eight hours' work," but, he added, an army of 50,000 male and female wage workers were in danger of losing out, and being left with ten and twelve hours for a day's work and wages of 50 cents to $1.50 a day. The anarchists were organizing with these people, he explained, encouraging them to make a stand. But now with the International's leadership behind bars, with Albert Parsons in hiding and with Lucy Parsons in and out of jail, they had no one to give them heart.[40]

By May 15 the eight-hour strikes had waned, and workers were returning to their jobs in Chicago and at Pullman town. The freight handlers and iron molders, whose strikes were most menacing, had been defeated. Employers in the planing mills, who had conceded eight hours

*Lucy Parsons in a drawing from a police photo
after one of her arrests in May 1886*

to their workers before May 2, now reneged on their agreement and returned to the ten-hour day. Master carpenters, plumbers, steamfitters and foundry workers all returned as ten-hour men, though some found that they had been replaced by nonunion hands. By May 18, the most tenacious group of strikers in the city, the lumber shovers, was all but defeated. When they too returned to work a few days later, the *Tribune* declared the eight-hour movement practically dead.[41]

Yet, even as the Great Upheaval subsided, the red scare gathered force. Every day the newspapers carried some sensational news. A bomb factory had been found at a house on Sedgwick Street, and the owner, William Seliger, had confessed to making explosive devices there with Louis Lingg. But Lingg, who was alleged to be the bomb thrower, was in hiding. Then, on May 14, came the thrilling news that Lingg had been captured after a furious fight with two policemen. After being subdued and disarmed (he had a knife strapped to his wrist), Lingg was hustled to the Chicago Avenue Station to be interrogated by Captain Schaack.[42]

While newspaper readers waited to learn more about Louis Lingg's interrogation, they were jolted by another report: an anarchist named Rudolph Schnaubelt was now being sought as the perpetrator after the police had mistakenly released him following his arrest on May 7. The suspect was identified as a large man, a machinist by trade, who was known to be an anarchist militant and who was seen standing near the speakers' wagon on the night of May 4. After he was arrested, Schnaubelt told detectives he had left the scene before the bomb exploded; when several witnesses corroborated his story, the suspect was released and promptly fled the city. The police and the press now agreed that Schnaubelt's flight made him the obvious suspect in the bombing.[43]

On May 18, Schaack's detectives entered George Engel's toy store on Milwaukee Avenue and took the shopkeeper in for questioning. Engel had been interrogated on May 6 but released as a result of an intervention by the coroner, a fellow German, who said he knew the shopkeeper well and that he was a "quiet and well behaved citizen." But twelve days later Engel was spirited away by the police, leaving his wife and daughter to believe that he had simply disappeared. In fact, Schaack was holding him incommunicado while his men gave Engel the third degree, hoping he would implicate his comrades in the bombing. Even though he was put in the sweatbox (a small, pitch-dark wooden container) for hours, the prisoner refused to tell the police what they wanted to hear. On the eighth day of his confinement, Engel's daughter finally managed to find her father and to persuade his jailers to allow him to see visitors.[44]

Even though most of the police work had concluded for the grand jury hearings, Schaack kept the pot boiling. He also told the jury that he had unearthed a gigantic plot to burn and sack a certain portion of the city and had the evidence to prove it. He needed only a few more days to complete the chain of evidence.[45]

Meanwhile, many rumors as to the whereabouts of Albert Parsons appeared in the dailies. The most-wanted fugitive was sighted in St. Louis, in Pittsburgh, in San Francisco and in Dallas, where he was reportedly recognized by people who knew him when he was a newspaperman. It was also rumored that he had either started out for Mexico on the Texas & Pacific Railway or was "hiding out among the negroes."[46]

Cartoons and drawings of the Haymarket events and the wicked-looking anarchists proliferated in the press that May. The most influential image appeared in *Harper's Weekly* on May 15 in an enormous two-page drawing of the bombing scene that would become, and remain until this day, the single most important visual representation of the incident. The artist's view is from street level just north of the speakers' wagon, where a white-haired figure, presumably Fielden, is gesturing at the police with one hand raised in the air. To the right in the rear, the flash of an exploding bomb illuminates policemen falling and writhing in agony. Nearby two policemen fire their pistols at the crowd, while in the foreground, a man in a bowler hat shoots at the officers as his comrades flee for their lives. Thure de Thulstrup's famous drawing elided a series of events that occurred over a few minutes' time into one dramatic moment of simultaneous action in which the violence seems clearly to have resulted from the speaker's effort to incite the crowd. This indelible image reflected and magnified a popular perception that the city streets had finally become domestic battlefields in a growing class war.[47]

During these wild days a grand jury listened as witnesses were called to testify that an anarchist plot had existed to annihilate the police at the Haymarket. On May 27 the jury returned murder indictments against ten anarchists, despite the objections of one troublemaker among them who argued that, before they indicted the men for conspiring to commit murder, they ought to know who threw the bomb.[48]

By this time, ten labor meeting halls, seventeen saloons and several newspaper offices had been raided; numerous houses had been searched, often without warrants; and 200 arrests had been made. Some prisoners were held without benefit of counsel, and some were pressured for hours in Schaack's sweatbox. Scores of witnesses were questioned, including

Thure de Thulstrup's imaginative depiction of events at the Haymarket, covering two pages of Harper's Weekly, *May 15, 1886*

forty-five people who were promised financial support in return for their testimonies. The state's attorney, Julius Sprague Grinnell, had gathered a mountain of evidence against the eight defendants who would finally stand trial for what was generally regarded as the worst crime committed in the United States since the assassination of Lincoln.[49] Grinnell wanted the trial to begin immediately, but the defense lawyers objected given the enormity of the task before them—one that seemed almost hopeless at this point, when many newspaper editors and city leaders demanded the speedy trial and execution of the men they held responsible for the shocking deaths of six policemen.[50]

Wilbur Storey's *Chicago Times* insisted that all the indicted anarchists in custody should be tried and hanged for murder, along with every leader of the Central Labor Union. Furthermore, justice also demanded the arrest, trial and execution of Albert Parsons and "the negro woman who passes as the wife of the assassin Parsons." Finally, the paper insisted that every organization, society or combination calling itself socialist or anarchist should be "absolutely and permanently suppressed."[51] Even a respected law journal expressed the opinion that "the long-haired, wild-eyed, bad smelling, atheistic reckless foreign wretches" who thought they could "level society and its distinctions with a few bombs" ought to be crushed like snakes. According to the *Albany Law Journal*, the anarchists' evil deeds almost justified resorting to "the vigilance committee and lynch law." At the least, Illinois courts should treat all these godless fiends as murderers and extirpate them from the face of the earth.[52] It was in this climate that the trial of the Chicago anarchists opened in the Cook County Courthouse on June 21, 1886.

Chapter Thirteen

Every Man on the Jury Was an American

MAY 28, 1886–AUGUST 21, 1886

WHEN TWO WELL-KNOWN Chicago socialists formed a defense committee for the eight accused anarchists during the heat of the red scare, they seemed to be embarking on a perilous journey. Yet Dr. Ernest Schmidt, the respected physician who ran as a socialist candidate for mayor in 1879, and George Schilling, the influential labor leader and eight-hour advocate, decided to swim against the roaring stream of public condemnation. Both men had vociferously criticized the anarchists for their violent words and ultramilitant demands, but they knew some of the accused men well enough to believe in their innocence. Schilling and Schmidt began quietly by raising funds in the immigrant union halls to pay for the legal services of two young lawyers from the Jewish community who had represented the Central Labor Union and many of its members after they were arrested in the police roundup that began on the day after the bombing.[1]

Moses Salomon, a twenty-eight-year-old bachelor, lived with his parents on the West Side. Raised in Peoria, Illinois, he attended public schools there and then went to Chicago to work in his father's grocery business. He clerked in a law office, and entered the city's Union Law School, where he prepared to pass the bar. Sigmund Zeisler, a year younger than Salomon, was born in Austria of German parents and resided on the North Side with his wife, a pianist. He had lived in the United States for just four years but had learned English quickly while in law school, where he won a prize for the best thesis. Salomon and Zeisler, who formed a partnership in 1885, were considered excellent "book lawyers" but novice defense attorneys. Leaders of the city's German-Jewish community had kept a distance from the labor wars that afflicted the city during the previous decade, but with Salomon and Zeisler on the anarchist case, the city's Jews may have felt themselves being pulled much closer to the fray.[2]

Because the two young lawyers were so inexperienced, Schmidt tried to persuade a pair of leading criminal lawyers to take the case; they refused, fearing the consequences for their practices. Eventually, the doctor found a way to convince a corporate lawyer named William Perkins Black to lead the team. A native of Kentucky and a descendant of Scotch-Irish from Ulster, Black had studied in Indiana, where he lived at the outbreak of the Civil War. He volunteered for the army and served under Union general Lew Wallace, then moved to Illinois, where he helped recruit an infantry company with which he saw combat as a captain. Black's battlefield heroics earned him the Congressional Medal of Honor before he turned twenty. After the war, the captain entered a profitable law practice in Chicago. Like his friend Carter Harrison, the lawyer engaged in Democratic Party politics and, with his wife, Hortensia, enjoyed the social life that flourished in the city's West Side Kentucky colony. An open-minded man, Black had once expressed sympathy for the Russian populists on trial for killing the czar, and had shown an interest in socialism, which he called the "cry of the people." He had heard Schilling speak on the subject, and he had been introduced to Spies and Parsons, though he had not studied their ideas.[3]

The captain's surprising decision to lead the defense team meant that the Blacks would be ostracized, excluded from polite society. Black also knew that his action would entail "an almost total sacrifice of business." But he made his decision and stuck to it, and Hortensia backed him up. Black's "act of heroism"—Attorney Zeisler's words—gave the defense a brilliant and respected lead counsel.

William Black was not a criminal defense attorney, however, so he set out to find a partner who could play that role. It took him three days to locate a trial lawyer who would join him—a criminal defense attorney named William A. Foster, who had arrived in the city from Iowa a few months before.[4]

On June 5, 1886, the grand jury presented its report to the court. It read: "We find that the attack on the police of May 4 was the result of a deliberate conspiracy, the full details of which are now in the possession of the officers of the law."[5] Five days later Captain Black asked the sitting judge to recuse himself because of prejudicial statements he had made. The new judge, Joseph Eaton Gary, was a sixty-five-year-old native New

Yorker, first elected to the Cook County Superior Court in 1863. Highly regarded as a lawyer and an impartial judge, he seemed to Black as good a choice as any, at least until Gary rebuffed Black's request for a delay in the trial. The proceedings would begin, as planned, on June 21.[6]

In the meantime, Black had entered into secret discussions with Lucy Parsons concerning the whereabouts of her husband. "Never had a fugitive from justice been more systematically hunted," wrote one chronicler of the trial, but, though police forces far and wide had been on Parsons's trail, they had not run him down.[7] Black argued that, rather than maintaining the appearance of guilt by hiding, Parsons ought to turn himself in and stand trial. After all, there was no evidence to link him to the bombing. It took some time for the captain to persuade Lucy on this point, but she finally agreed and sent out word to Albert that there were good reasons for him to return to Chicago.

For the previous six weeks Parsons had lived in secrecy and safety in Wisconsin, but all the while he endured the agony of being separated from his family and comrades, escaping the wrath they all endured in the city. He believed, as he later told a friend, that if he surrendered he "could never expect to be a free man again." Nonetheless, he left Waukesha on June 20 to meet his fate in Chicago. Still disguised, he jumped off the train on the North Side and made his way to a friend's house, where he met Lucy and the children for a joyful, tearful reunion.

On June 21, just six weeks after the bombing, the trial began, with scores of reporters in attendance. After the courtroom filled, the prisoners took their seats near the defense team. Black moved to quash the indictments and to hold separate trials for each defendant, but both motions were denied. Then, after the lunch recess, the proceedings resumed, and at about half past two that afternoon Albert Parsons calmly walked into the courtroom. Well dressed, his face tanned, his hair once again jet black, he made a dramatic entrance prepared to give a speech to the judge proclaiming his innocence and his willingness to face trial. One of the prosecutors immediately recognized him, however, and the state's lead attorney, Julius Grinnell, rose and said: "Your honor, I see Albert R. Parsons in the courtroom. I move that he be placed in the custody of the sheriff." Black strenuously objected that Parsons was there to surrender himself and that Grinnell's action was "gratuitous and cruel."[8] Judge Gary would not allow Parsons to address the court, however, and so, as the buzz of excitement wound down, the prisoner silently took a seat with the other defendants, who were surprised and excited by the appearance of their leader. These unexpected developments sent reporters rushing for the door to telegraph the story of the infamous fugitive's return. The stage was now set. The characters had taken their places, and the courtroom throbbed with excitement as the highly anticipated proceedings got under way.[9]

After Parsons's stage entrance, the courtroom calmed down and jury selection began. Because the normal, random process of selecting jurors had broken down, a special bailiff was charged to find jurors. The process went on for three weeks, and it went badly for the defendants, because the jurors who were seated seemed utterly biased against them.[10] Black objected over and over to jurors who seemed clearly prejudiced against his clients, but, again and again Judge Gary refused to accept Black's challenges for cause, even in the case of a juror who admitted kinship with one of the slain policemen. Nearly every juror called by the special bailiff stated that he had read and talked about the case and believed what he had heard or read about the defendants. Some even stated frankly that they thought the defendants were guilty. When these men admitted as much during the jury selection process, the defense attorneys rejected them one after another until they had exhausted their quota of challenges for cause.

In some cases, Judge Gary worked hard to convince jurors who admitted to bias against the anarchists that they could, nonetheless, be fair. In one instance Gary nearly browbeat a potential juror into saying he believed he could render a fair judgment in the case, even after the man insisted he felt handicapped. Several of the twelve jurors finally selected were men who had candidly admitted they were prejudiced, but each, when examined by Judge Gary, was persuaded to say that he believed he could hear the case fairly nonetheless.[11] To Black and the defense team, Gary's procedure in the lengthy jury selection process seemed blatantly unfair, but the press praised all of the judge's rulings and blamed the defense for needlessly delaying the start of the trial. When the twelfth juror was finally chosen, the newspapers cheered.[12]

The dozen men seated in the jury box came from similar walks of life and held similar views of the anarchists. H. T. Sandford, who lived in the town of Oak Park and worked for the Chicago & Northwestern Railroad, admitted to having an opinion as to the throwing of the bomb and the necessity of convicting the defendants and was in that sense prejudiced, but he still thought he could hear the case fairly. Sandford was one of five clerks seated in the jury box along with five salesmen, including the fore-man, an employee of Marshall Field. One juryman was a hardware dealer and another was a school principal.[13]

These dozen men did not constitute a group of the defendants' peers. Not one of them was an immigrant, a manual laborer or a trade union member, and, of course, none was a radical. Indeed, very few workers even appeared in the jury pool created by the bailiff, who had hand-picked many men in a stunning departure from the normal, random selection process.[14] Approximately 980 jurymen were placed in the pool and examined; most of them listed their occupations as traders, buyers, shopkeepers, cashiers, real estate agents, foremen or salesclerks, includ-ing many who said they had been identified by their employers as good candidates. Only 14 potential jurors identified themselves as wage earn-ers doing hand labor in the city's factories and yards or on its docks and construction sites.[15]

DURING THE TEDIOUS WEEKS of jury selection, everything seemed to work against the defense. The only encouraging sign was an item in the *Tri-bune* that hinted at weaknesses in the prosecution's case. On June 27 an anonymous police official criticized Inspector Bonfield's leadership, say-ing that no one on the force but Bonfield had wanted to disrupt the Hay-market meeting, that it should not have been disrupted and that, as a result, the chief inspector was responsible for the injuries and deaths. The unidentified police official also indicated that many of the wounds the police sustained came from bullets fired by other policemen.[16]

The unidentified source may have been Superintendent Frederick Ebersold, who resented Bonfield and Schaack for basking in the sun-shine of public acclaim. The Bavarian-born superintendent had been at odds with the two captains ever since Mayor Harrison appointed him, passing over Bonfield, a favorite of the Irish officer corps. Ebersold, who harbored self-doubts about his own conduct during the Haymarket affair, had reason to fear that Bonfield and Schaack would continue to under-mine his authority by questioning his competence and blaming him for mistakes made in the investigation, such as ordering the release of Schnaubelt, the suspected bomb hurler.[17]

On July 15, State's Attorney Julius Grinnell opened the prosecution case by indicating that this would be no ordinary murder trial. "Gentlemen," he began, "for the first time in the history of our country people are on trial for endeavoring to make Anarchy the rule," and "to ruthlessly and awfully destroy human life" to achieve that end. "I hope that while the youngest of us lives, this will be the last time in our country when such a trial shall take place," he declared. Grinnell then outlined the case in brief. He charged that Spies was the ringleader of a dynamite plot—a man who had frequently declared that only force could be used to achieve justice for workers, a provocateur who believed that the eight-hour movement could be used to further anarchy. The prosecutor declared that Spies had conspired with others for several months to start an uprising during the May strikes at a gathering like the one at the Haymarket and that he told this to a newspaper reporter and even showed him a bomb made of dynamite.[18]

Furthermore, Grinnell argued, the riot at McCormick's was deliberately provoked by Spies, who issued the "Revenge" circular in order to trigger the beginning of a large revolt when bombs were to be thrown in all parts of the city.[19] The conspiracy to destroy Chicago, he explained, had been hatched on Monday, May 3, when George Engel and the other plotters met in Grief's Hall. Engel was in contact with Lingg, who was making the bombs, including the one used on May 4. The bombs were supposed to be left in Neff's Hall, where the anarchists would take them to various targets. Finally, Grinnell claimed that the Haymarket meeting was to be the starting event in the uprising and that only the timely intervention ordered by Bonfield prevented a revolutionary plot from being carried out.

After this litany, the state's attorney remarked: "It is not necessary for me to go into any more details of that conspiracy. It was carried out to the letter." The indictment in this case was for murder, he concluded, adding that "it is not necessary in this kind of case . . . that the individual who commits the particular offense—for instance, the man who threw the bomb—to be in court at all. He need not even be indicted. The question for you to determine is, having ascertained that a murder was committed, not only who did it, but who is responsible for it, who abetted it, assisted it, or encouraged it?"[20]

Grinnell's remarks deeply troubled the defense team. The prosecutor had asked the jury to determine who murdered Officer Degan, yet the state had not charged any one of the defendants with actually throwing the bomb that killed the patrolman. It was later revealed that Grinnell

Julius S. Grinnell

had been reluctant to try the defendants for homicide without charging someone with actually committing the murder. However, the newspaper publisher Melville E. Stone met privately with the state's attorney and convinced him to take the case to trial anyway, because the anarchists "had advocated over and over again the use of violence against the police and had urged the manufacture and throwing of bombs," and therefore, Stone thought, "their culpability was clear."[21]

Here was an extraordinary turn of events. Chicago's newspaper editors had already prejudged the defendants and recommended capital punishment as the only just outcome of the case, but this was not unusual. Pretrial publicity often influenced juries in murder cases, but it was a rare instance when a newspaper publisher shaped the legal strategy of a state's attorney the way Melville Stone did in the Haymarket case.

The next day Judge Gary outlined the state's position in his charge to the jury. The prosecution would prove "the existence of a general conspiracy to annihilate the police force and destroy property" and show that the "defendants who were the instigators of it" were therefore liable for the act, "even if committed without their specific sanction at that particular time and place." This ruling surprised and further disturbed the defense team. After court adjourned that day, defense counsel Salomon told reporters that the state had tricked them by saying the eight men were being tried for murder when instead they were being tried for being anarchists before a jury whose members had, for the most part, admitted their bias against anarchists.

On the second day the prosecution called its first witness. Chief Inspector Bonfield reiterated his version of the events of May 4, emphasizing that men in the crowd opened fire on the police as soon as the bomb went off. Next, the IWPA leader Gottfried Waller took the stand. Arrested for presiding over the Monday-night conspiracy meeting, Waller had been persuaded to turn state's evidence by Captain Schaack, who agreed to give money to Waller's family and to find him safe passage to Europe. Born in Switzerland, a cabinetmaker by trade and a member of the workers' militia, Waller was a star witness for the prosecution, though his account of the events leading up to the bombing fell short of incriminating the defendants.[22]

Waller described chairing the May 3 meeting in Grief's Hall, where it was decided to hold the protest rally the next night. But he testified that nothing was said about preparing for the Haymarket event because no one expected the police to intervene. No one at the meeting said anything about using dynamite. At one point in examining Waller, Assistant State's Attorney George C. Ingham asked the witness if he possessed any bombs. Defense lawyer Foster routinely objected that Waller was not on trial, and then asked what he thought was a rhetorical question: "If you show that some man threw one of these bombs without the knowledge, authority or approval of one of these defendants, is that murder?" Ingham replied immediately: "Under the law of the state of Illinois, it *is* murder." Therefore, he added ominously, "the law is strong enough to hang every one of these men."[23]

DURING THE NEXT WEEK, the state called nine police officers and three private citizens to the stand. Reporters quoted Grinnell as being thrilled at how well the trial proceedings had started and described the anarchists as being alternately "nervous and frightened." For example, Fielden, who had been accused of firing a pistol at the police, hid his facial expressions when officers referred to him. However, the mastermind Spies listened imperturbably and smiled encouragingly when witnesses identified him.[24]

On July 22, before the afternoon session opened, George Engel's daughter Mary, a young woman of sixteen years, pinned geranium boutonnieres on the defendants' coat lapels as the anarchists' family members offered encouraging looks to the men in the dock. The court reporters became fascinated with the defendants and their entourage. Drawings of the characters in the courtroom opera appeared in the newspapers frequently. Some were quite unflattering to the defendants, but most depicted the anarchists as ordinary human beings. August Spies, whose family was described as seeming "modest and respectable," was "not by any means an evil-looking person either." To one journalist, Lizzie Swank Holmes appeared a wan young woman with a scrawny neck and a large lower lip. "From her meek appearance one would never guess she was a fire eater and a blood drinker, a member of the American Group, a blatherskite orator and a writer of inflammatory slush for anarchic publications."[25] Lucy Parsons attracted special attention from reporters, who described her homemade, yet stylish and colorful, attire. Albert, Jr., and Lulu were portrayed as shy, attractive little children whose fair hair and sallow complexions belied any sign of "colored descent." The reporter did not stop with this observation. Mrs. Parsons, one reporter noted, objected to being called a "colored" woman and claimed she was born to Mexican and Indian parents. "But she is decidedly colored, just the same," he wrote, "and any ordinary observer would conclude that at least one of her parents was a Negro."[26]

Every day there was a scramble to gain admission to the most sensational trial anyone could recall. Spectators entered and left constantly to satisfy their curiosity, and the courtroom doors flapped open and closed frequently, allowing a few breaths of air to enter the ovenlike chamber. Judge Gary, described as a "horse-sense individual" who would "stand no non-sense," nonetheless contributed to the theatricality of the event by filling the seats behind his chair with well-dressed young ladies who clearly enjoyed the spectacle. Mrs. Hortensia Black, the captain's wife, displayed a different demeanor as she leaned into the defense box and whispered encouragement to her fellow Texan, Albert Parsons, and the other defendants. When Mrs. Black's unexpected displays of sympathy toward the anarchists were reported in the press, she immediately placed herself beyond the pale of respectable Chicago.[27]

A large corps of reporters filed stories every day, highlighting some exciting aspect of the state's case or quoting at length one of the prosecutors' soliloquies. The defense lawyers were given their due, but at times Salomon and Zeisler were described like vaudeville performers.[28] On July 25 the press was aroused by the appearance of a Pinkerton agent

Captain William Black and his wife, Hortensia

who had infiltrated IWPA meetings, one of several spies assigned to the task after businessmen, including Philip Armour and Marshall Field, hired the agency to report on the actions of the International. The anarchists trembled, one headline claimed, when they learned that detectives had been placed in their midst. The secret agent spoke mainly about various speeches he claimed to have heard, including remarks by Fielden and Parsons, who said a few explosions in Chicago would help the cause. He also quoted Spies speaking hypothetically about the "green" soldiers in the National Guard, who could be easily scattered by a few bombs.

The prosecution made little use of this detective's testimony, even though the agent supported Grinnell's claim that the anarchists believed that May 1 would provide a good opportunity to start the revolution. Pinkertons were controversial figures in Chicago and had been strongly criticized by the mayor for causing trouble at McCormick's. At one point Captain Black threw up his hands in despair when the secret agent made what sounded like disclosures concocted to please his Pinkerton bosses and their powerful clients. Nonetheless, the spy's revelations seemed sensational to the press, because the agent exposed what appeared to be the sinister inner life of anarchist cells.[29]

The next day the prosecution produced two witnesses who claimed that Schwab and Spies were directly involved in the bombing. M. M. Thompson testified that he stood next to the two men during the rally and overheard them talking about the police. He thought the word "pistol" was spoken and that a man he thought was Spies asked his friend (presumed to be Schwab), "Do you think one is enough or hadn't we better get more?" Thompson took this as a reference to bombs. The witness said he tailed the two Germans until they met another much larger man. When shown a photo of the anarchist Rudolph Schnaubelt, Thompson identified him as the third man.[30]

Even more damning testimony came from a second witness, who said he saw August Spies light a fuse on a bomb that a man matching Schnaubelt's description threw from the street. However, the witness, H. L. Gilmer, seemed far from credible to a *Tribune* reporter who described him as an odd-looking eccentric claiming to be a painter by trade. Standing 6 feet 3 inches, he looked so lean and cadaverous that he could have been an escaped giant from one of P. T. Barnum's freak shows. "Dressed in a seedy black suit, and with his long, curling hair, sanctimonious visage, and great stretch of scraggy throat," Gilmer resembled a well-worn Methodist circuit rider. His long legs stuck out of the small witness chair, and one foot revealed the tattered sole of an enormous No. 14 shoe. When the defense lawyer Foster posed a question that puzzled him, Harry Gilmer would squint his eyes, purse up his lower lip and roll his head until he answered. "Sometimes he would place the tips of his fingers together, throw back his head until one would see about two feet of ropy neck, gaze up at the ceiling a moment, and presently come back to earth with the expected reply." He patronizingly referred to Mr. Foster as "my learned friend" and acted oddly enough to provoke his interrogator to ask if he was "an opium-eater or practiced the morphine habit."

Then came a moment of high drama. Asked whether he could identify the man who lit the match to the bomb, Gilmer "stretched out his long, bony, claw-like left hand, and, shaking it directly at Spies, said 'There is the man.'" The courtroom burst with excited exclamations. Spies jumped to his feet and laughed derisively, as the other prisoners shouted out protests in German and English. Judge Gary banged his gavel furiously for several minutes until the courtroom quieted.[31]

Gilmer's testimony seemed so absurd and so filled with inconsisten- cies and contradictions that the defendants returned the next day in a rather relaxed mood. Their lawyers were certain they could impugn the testimony of the state's witnesses with their own witnesses. Oscar Neebe was cheerful because no one had connected him with the incident. Par- sons casually read a newspaper, while Louis Lingg, who understood very little English, acted nonchalant and Michael Schwab seemed "philo- sophical." The dashing Spies divided his attention between his women friends and admirers and the witnesses who happened to be testifying. The anarchists were also buoyed by the news that the Central Labor Union had organized a meeting of 800 workers to protest press coverage of the trial, to show sympathy for the defendants and to raise money for their cause.[32] On July 30 the *Tribune* described the prisoners as "bearing up wonderfully well," whereas, "in fact, the strain of the trial is more telling on the lawyers on both sides than on the Anarchists." The jury- men seemed to be wilting in the hot air of the unventilated courtroom, as were the reporters, who complained that the judge insisted on keep- ing the windows closed to prevent street noise from drowning out any testimony.[33]

Gary tried to maintain an iron grip on the proceedings, yet he presided over a courtroom that began to seem more and more like a cir- cus ring. After Captain Schaack took the stand and introduced a truck- load of physical evidence, the center of the room looked a bit like a dynamite arsenal or a newspaper office. Files and baskets of anarchist papers were spread across tables and spilled onto the floor next to Lingg's trunk, which was surrounded by fragments of iron and splintered wood— the results of Captain Schaack's experiments in setting off several bombs the police had seized. While the captain described this evidence in grave tones, spectators cast nervous glances at various cigar boxes filled with dynamite, fuses and bombshells. Lingg, however, ignored the proceed- ings and kept reading a German newspaper, while Spies and his female friends found amusement in the bizarre display.[34]

On August 1, Attorney Salomon opened the defense case by arguing that none of the defendants had been charged with perpetrating the act of murder and that there could not be a trial of accessories without a principal. If none of the defendants threw the bomb, they could not be found guilty of committing murder. The *Tribune* dismissed Salomon's argument out of hand and described its maker's unlimited self-assurance as galling.[35]

Two days later the defense team called its star witness, Mayor Carter

Harrison. The courtroom was besieged by larger crowds than ever that morning, all eager to hear the testimony of the flamboyant mayor. When he took the stand, to one reporter the mayor seemed a changed man, aged by the events of the past two years. Harrison was bareheaded, his white hair thinned; his looks contrasted with the well-known impression he made as a man "swaggering along the street with his black slouch hat cocked jauntily on his right ear or trotting down a boulevard on his Kentucky thoroughbred." The mayor testified that he had carefully observed the crowd at the Haymarket meeting and saw no weapons at all upon any person. He also testified that after listening to the speakers he told Chief Inspector Bonfield nothing dangerous seemed likely to occur and that he should send the police reserves home.[36]

The defense team then called a large number of eyewitnesses; some were socialists or trade unionists, and some were unaligned bystanders. They all contradicted the prosecution witnesses. None of them heard Fielden's call to give the police bloodhounds their due, and none saw him shoot a pistol at the officers. No one saw Schwab at the rally where he was supposed to have been. No one saw Spies on the ground where he could have given the lighted bomb to Schnaubelt, the alleged hurler. No one saw the bomb come from the area around the wagon or from the alley behind it. And no one heard any firing from the crowd before or after the explosion. One witness, Dr. James Taylor, testified that he did not see Sam Fielden shoot at the police with a revolver, nor did he see the bomb fly out of the alley behind the speakers' wagon, nor did he see people in the crowd shoot at the police after the bomb exploded. Dr. Taylor said shooting erupted from the street where the police were standing.[37]

Here was a remarkable situation. The eyewitnesses called by the defense contradicted nearly every piece of incriminating testimony by the police and the state's witnesses. It was as though the two groups of people in Haymarket Square that night had seen completely different events unfold before their eyes.[38]

The young lawyers, Salomon and Zeisler, thought their witnesses had demolished the prosecution's case, but Black and Foster were not so sure and said nothing to the press. The older lawyers had perhaps anticipated the response to their arguments from the newspapers. On August 5 the *Tribune* reported all evidence produced by the defense to be of trifling significance to the jurymen, who seemed too weary to keep tabs on this new testimony; they had been much more alert when the prosecution was at work.[39]

"The Great Trial"

ON AUGUST 7 the accused anarchists began to take the stand to speak in their own defense. The courtroom quieted as Sam Fielden lumbered up to the stand. Nervous at first, he gradually gained confidence and, as he repeated his Haymarket speech, he seemed to be haranguing the jury. One reporter was so impressed that he said Fielden, if acquitted, could make a fortune on the lecture circuit. On August 9, August Spies, the accused ringleader of the anarchist conspiracy, addressed the court. Attired in a trim navy blue suit and a vest that sported a gold chain and tie pin, he looked to one reporter like a well-dressed salesman.[40] Speaking fluently with a strong German accent, Spies gave his account of the events at McCormick's and of his attempts to halt the men who charged the plant. He admitted that he approved the circular calling for the Haymarket protest but explained that he had ordered the words "Workingmen! To Arms!" removed from the leaflet. He denied receiving a bomb from Michael Schwab at the rally, repeating the point that Schwab was not even present in the square as prosecution witnesses charged. He also explained that he could not have given a bomb to a bomb thrower on the street, as some witnesses said, because he had remained on the wagon the entire time. Finally, Spies said that he had asked the people in the square to hold a peaceful protest.[41]

The climax in the anarchist trial approached when the state began to present its summation on August 12. State's Attorney Francis W. Walker started portentously: "We stand in the temple of justice to exercise the law, where all men stand equal," he proclaimed. One of the few native Chicagoans on the scene, the prosecutor was a corpulent young man of thirty years who shouted his words vehemently like a politico on the stump. His voice was so loud, it could be heard outside the courthouse on Clark Street.[42] Walker began by arguing that the defendants conspired to precipitate a social revolution, one that cost Mathias Degan his life, but then, carried away by the moment, he strayed far beyond the indictment, alleging that 3,000 men had participated in the conspiracy and that every one of them was equally guilty of the murder of Officer Degan, including all the members of the Lehr und Wehr Verein.[43]

After Walker finished, Sigmund Zeisler opened for the defense. He impressed one reporter as a good-looking young man with a mellifluous foreign accent and an excellent grasp of English, though his gestures seemed superfluously dramatic. Zeisler went after his opponent, Walker, like an archer shooting arrows at a straw target. He said the prosecutor's argument depended not on evidence but on stirring the prejudice of the jury. Showing no respect for the police, he dismissed their credibility as witnesses. "And before we get through," Zeisler declared, "we will show that these men were not heroes, but knaves, led on by the most cowardly knave who ever held a public position." Why, everyone wondered, did the police descend to disperse a peaceful meeting? Even detectives testified that the rally was breaking up when, Zeisler asserted, "this army of 180 policemen arrived armed with clubs and revolvers, headed by this hero, Bonfield, the savior of his country, to break up this meeting of peaceable and unarmed citizens. Was this courageous or cowardly?"

Zeisler also attacked the prosecution's claim that the defendants planned to start a social revolution on May 1. He said that anyone who had studied history knew, as the anarchists certainly did, that a revolution could not be called up at any given moment. A revolution was a thing that developed of its own accord, and no single man, or even a dozen men, could simply inaugurate a revolution on a certain day. "Has ever a ridiculous statement like this been made to an intelligent jury?" he wondered.[44]

Zeisler concluded by accusing State's Attorney Grinnell of being "blinded by malice and prejudice." He charged that the lead prosecutor had eagerly joined in a conspiracy with the police to send these men to the gallows, even if it meant relying upon the testimony of eccentrics like Harry Gilmer.[45] The young lawyer acted as though he were speaking before a public forum on the West Side, where citizens hated Bonfield and his blue-coated patrolmen, instead of before a jury who regarded the police as heroes.

George Ingham, the third state's attorney, followed Zeisler's polemic with an appeal by telling the jurymen that their verdict would make history. "For, if I appreciate this case correctly . . . the very question itself is whether organized government shall perish from the earth; whether the day of civilization shall go down into the night of barbarism; whether the wheels of history shall be rolled back, and all that has been gained by thousands of years of progress be lost."[46]

Defense lawyer Foster followed with his own passionate speech, one that lasted the rest of the day. A droll man with a shock of red curly hair and a mustache and complexion to match, Foster played every card he had used as a defense attorney in previous murder cases. He made it clear that he had no sympathy for the anarchists or their political beliefs. He was a defender of the law, but he wanted the law to be just. Foster then attacked the entire chain of evidence the state had tried to forge and found broken links everywhere. He said that Spies had no idea of the significance of the word *Ruhe* when it went into the letter box of his newspaper, a key item in linking Spies to the alleged conspiracy and the actual bombing. Turning to Parsons, the defense lawyer noted that no evidence had been produced that he was part of any alleged conspiracy. If Parsons had expected violence at the meeting on May 4, the attorney asked, why would he have brought his wife and children to the rally?

Foster also analyzed the prosecution's case against Louis Lingg. The defense attorney conceded that Lingg made some bombs and that one of the bombs he manufactured might have been thrown onto Desplaines Street. But even if the prosecution's chemical experts were correct in identifying the lethal bomb as one Lingg that had made, this evidence did not prove that Lingg was party to any conspiracy or that he deliberately gave one of his bombs to the man who threw it. The state's whole case against Lingg was based on guesses, suppositions and inferences.[47]

Foster next turned to the case against Oscar Neebe, who was on trial for his life because he left a few copies of the Haymarket circular on the bar of a saloon, and because police found a shotgun, an old revolver and a knife in his house. He asked the jurymen if they were going to hang Neebe on the basis of such evidence, or hang any of the defendants based on circumstantial evidence. "Are you going to be driven by passion, influenced by prejudice to do that which you will regret the longest days of your lives?" he inquired. "Are you going to do something which will haunt you to the grave?" Then Foster ended for the day by saying: "If these men are to be tried on general principles for advocating doctrines opposed to our ideas of propriety, there is no use for me to argue the case. Let the Sheriff go and erect the scaffold; let him bring eight ropes with dangling nooses at the ends; let him pass them around the necks of these men; and let us stop this farce now."[48]

The next day William Black presented his closing to a courtroom packed with 1,000 people. The captain impressed journalists, including one who described him as a tall, handsome, military-looking man with a graceful, gentlemanly manner, a large vocabulary and a powerful voice softened by a pleasing Kentucky accent. Black argued that the testimony of the prosecution's star witnesses, Thompson and Gilmer, had been utterly discredited and that the state's case was based entirely on circumstantial evidence. He said the whole story of Spies stirring up trouble was contradicted by testimony showing he went to the Haymarket to counsel peace. The prosecution had not proven that Spies knew anything about the May 3 meeting where the alleged conspiracy was planned, or that he had any contact with the bomb maker or the bomb thrower.[49]

Moreover, Black thought he had all the testimony he needed to show that six of the men charged with murder were not at the scene when the bomb exploded. The only ones present were Spies and Fielden, who were clearly visible on the hay wagon just before the explosion occurred. As a result, the state relied upon testimony that Fielden threatened the police and fired a gun at them—testimony contradicted by many witnesses. In the end, the prosecution stopped trying to show any direct connection between the defendants and the bomb thrower. Grinnell even admitted the defendants may not have known the bomber. The whole case rested on the contention that each of the indicted anarchists "abetted, encouraged, and advised" the throwing of a bomb and were therefore as guilty of murder as the one who threw it.[50]

This allegation was based on the existence of a plot hatched on May 3 to launch an armed struggle the next night at the Haymarket; the conspiracy supposedly involved Lingg, who volunteered to make the bombs, including the one that killed Officer Degan. However, Lingg was not present at the meeting, nor were any of the other defendants except Engel and Fischer. These two men did propose the Haymarket protest rally but, according to police witnesses, said nothing about taking any kind of action there. Even the testimony of two anarchists who turned state's evidence failed to show that any plot was formed on May 3 that led to the explosion on May 4. In any case, the prosecution had not proven that the unidentified bomber was part of that alleged conspiracy and that the defendants were therefore accessories who helped plan a criminal act.

Captain Black insisted that since the state charged the defendants with murder, the sole question before the jury was the matter of who threw the bomb. It would not be fair to convict the defendants by showing that they favored violent deeds. He appealed to the "twelve good men" who sat before him to put aside their prejudices against the defendants and judge them solely upon the evidence. "Gentlemen," he said, "these eight lives are in your hands" and "you are answerable to no power but God and history." The captain finished his closing with a testimony to the virtue of his clients and their beliefs, proclaiming that "Jesus, the great Socialist of Judea, first preached the socialism taught by Spies and his modern disciples." In this light, he could only close with the words of the "Divine Socialist": "As ye would that others should do to you, do even so to them."[51]

Julius Grinnell responded with a powerful closing of the state's case that displayed all of his eloquence and determination. He began by scolding Captain Black for descending so far that he compared "some low murderers to the Savior of mankind." He also objected to comparing the anarchists to martyrs like John Brown. Then he lectured the jury on government and republican politics. Not all governments ultimately resulted in despotism, as Captain Black had stated in his closing. In fact, in the United States republicanism had triumphed in the American Revolution and then in the Civil War, said Grinnell, and, as a result, freedom was extended to all, even former slaves and those "driven here by oppression abroad." But now that America was so free, it might be in danger, for "in this country, above all countries in the world, anarchy is possible." Indeed, the state's attorney warned, "there is but one step from republicanism to anarchy." Freeing the anarchists would mean taking that step. And that was why, he explained, "there never was in the history of this country . . . a case that has attracted such interest as this." If the jurymen unjustly acquitted the anarchists, their followers would "flock out again like a lot of rats and vermin." And so the jurors would be making history when they rendered their verdict. "The law which has made us strong today and which you have sworn today demands of you a punishment of these men. Don't do it because I ask you. Do it because the law demands it."[52]

After this grave discourse, Grinnell added an appealing personal note. "We may never meet again, Gentlemen. In this case I have been pleased to make your acquaintance. I hope I have done nothing to offend you, either as to propriety, decency, good sense, or anything else. If we part here, we part as friends." After these pleasantries, he ended by telling the jurymen: "You stand between the living and the dead. You stand between law and violated law. Do your duty courageously, even if that duty is an unpleasant and a severe one."[53]

After Grinnell finished, Judge Gary brought the long trial proceedings to a close, instructing the jurymen they could find the eight men guilty of murder even if the crime was committed by someone who was not charged. According to one observer, even the contemptuous Louis Lingg, "the tiger anarchist," finally seemed to realize the danger of his situation.[54]

On August 19 the jury retired at 2:50 p.m. to the nearby Revere House Hotel. Crowds watched them through the windows that evening and saw men in their shirtsleeves resting in easy positions, smoking and apparently enjoying themselves. Clearly, they had speedily reached a verdict.[55]

Judge Joseph E. Gary

More than 1,000 people gathered around the courthouse at ten the next morning, anxiously waiting to hear the jury's decision. A small army of bailiffs and policemen guarded the doors and held back the surging masses of people by sheer force. The well-dressed ladies who had been attending the trial as spectators were barred from entry this day; the only persons admitted were lawyers, police officers, relatives, reporters and a few favored members of the bar.

When the jurymen entered at 9:55 a.m., the defendants displayed their customary calm. Parsons, sitting near a window, took out his red handkerchief and waved to the crowd below. Schwab said to him, "I wish I could go down there and make a speech to those people." No longer side by side with the defendants, Captain Black sat down with his wife, who asked him, "Are they prepared for the worst?" "Prepared!" he said. "Yes, fully prepared to laugh at death." They talked about their end, Black added, much more coolly than he could.[56]

Then, in the perfectly still room, the jury foreman read the verdict. He said the jury had found seven of the defendants guilty of murder as charged and had fixed the penalty as death. Oscar Neebe was also found guilty of murder but was sentenced to imprisonment for fifteen years. At first the room remained silent, as though a thousand people had sucked the air out of it. Then the eerie quiet was broken by the hysterical screams of Michael Schwab's wife, Maria.[57]

Captain Black was shocked by the sentence; he had expected conviction from a jury he thought was prejudiced, but he never expected the death sentence to be pronounced on all but one of the eight men. The attorney hid his emotions in the moments after the verdict was announced and simply moved for a new trial. Among the prisoners sitting in the dock, only two men reacted. Oscar Neebe, who had been assured of acquittal by his lawyers, was visibly disturbed; and Albert Parsons, ever theatrical, was curiously affected: he stood, smiled and bowed to the audience and then turned to the window and tied the string on the shade into the form of a noose to let the crowd outside know the result. As the news leaked out into the street, cheerful shouts of relief erupted from the huge crowd.[58]

The bailiffs then led the prisoners back to their jail cells. Spies and Fischer looked pale, said one reporter, but not visibly disturbed, nor did Engel or Lingg. Neebe, however, walked like a stricken man, Fielden shuffled out with support from his comrades, and the frail Schwab tottered behind Parsons, who, it was reported, had "lost none of his Texas nerve."[59]

Outside, courthouse reporters elbowed each other to interview the attorneys and the jurors. One juror said he disliked lawyer Zeisler and was offended by Parsons's "impudence." Another commented, "Every man on the jury was an American," and, therefore, he explained, no one showed any "toleration for imported preachers of assassination."[60]

The evening papers featured high praise for these jurymen and reported that wealthy businessmen would raise a large sum to pay them as a sign of gratitude. The *Tribune* reported "universal satisfaction with the verdict" because "the law had been vindicated." The *Inter-Ocean* said, "The long strain of suspense and anxiety is over," adding that no trial in living memory had generated such widespread interest in a verdict. "Anarchism has been on trial ever since May 4; and it now has got its verdict. Death is the only fitting penalty." All editorialists declared that the defendants had been fairly prosecuted and ably defended; and some expressed dismay that the anarchists had exercised their right to appeal the decision, because it might delay their date with the hangman.[61]

DURING THE MID NINETEENTH century, murder trials became enormously attractive to the nation's newspapers, and then during the Gilded Age, when big-city dailies mushroomed and competed ruthlessly for readers, some courtroom dramas became national events and certain defendants became celebrities. The breadth and depth of coverage devoted to the Haymarket case exceeded all others in the post–Civil War years, because, except for the presidential assassins John Wilkes Booth and Charles Guiteau, no civilians had ever been tried for anything like the crime the eight anarchists were accused of committing; nor had any defendants in a local criminal court ever been prosecuted in such an overtly political trial. The defendants were not only held accountable for the unimaginable crime of murdering seven policemen; they were also being tried for attempting "to make anarchy the rule" in America.[62]

As a result, newspapers across the nation sounded a chorus of approval at the verdict and the sentences. Many editorials reflected the conviction, or at least the hope, that the impending executions would kill anarchism in America and rid the nation of the high anxiety that had existed since May 4, 1886.⁶³ For example, a New Orleans newspaper editor wrote that "all the chapters in the dramatic and horrible Haymarket tragedy have been written save one; all the acts finished but the last." When the curtain rolled up again, with a nation watching, the final tableau would reveal "a row of gibbeted felons, with haltered throats and fettered hands and feet, swinging slowly to and fro, in the air," said the *New Orleans Times-Democrat*. And then, to wild applause, the curtain would drop as the people exhaled in unison, knowing that anarchism was "forever dead in America!"⁶⁴

No one in the mainstream press would have noticed the few dissenting views on the trial contained in the radical press, such as the one voiced by the editor of the *Workmen's Advocate*. "Look at the case in the light of Truth and Reason," he urged his readers: a large squad of police raided a peaceful meeting, and were struck by a bomb thrown by an unknown assailant—as likely as not a Pinkerton agent provocateur. The next day a reign of terror began not only for the anarchists but for others who expressed similar criticisms of business and government. During the so-called trial, the prosecution called to the stand various "professional perjurers" but could not show that any of the defendants had any hand in the bomb throwing or had fired any shots at the police. The whole tragic performance, said the editor, concluded with the sentencing of the anarchists to death, not "for breaking any law, but for daring to denounce the usurpations of the robber rulers of our Satanic society."⁶⁵

For a week following the verdict, no one in Chicago except the anarchists and their supporters expressed anything but jubilation over the verdict. Then, in the next days and weeks expressions of consternation began to rise from the city's working-class neighborhoods, saloons and meeting halls. A small Chicago newspaper friendly to unions even reported that a vast majority of laborers in the city believed the bomb throwing was not the work of the anarchists but of some other party intent on deflating the eight-hour movement. This belief was rapidly spreading through all the ranks of labor, said the editor, but the city's businessmen still had no conception of the reaction the verdict would eventually produce among workers in Chicago or in other cities across the nation and around the world.⁶⁶

Chapter Fourteen

You Are Being Weighed in the Balance

THE DAY AFTER the verdict came down, a large group of discontented workingmen gathered at Greenbaum Hall on Chicago's West Side. The assembly represented all the divisions of the city's tattered army of labor—the skilled and the unskilled, the native and the foreign-born. There were Bavarian Catholics and Swedish Lutherans along with Irish-American Knights and British socialists, as well as German and Bohemian anarchists. Most of these men had voted for Mayor Carter Harrison and the Democrats in the last election; some had voted Republican, and some, the militants, had not voted at all. Now, after the tumultuous spring of strikes and a tense summer of trial news, they had had enough of politics as usual. They were assembled that day to found their own united labor party and run their own candidates for office. Before the proceedings began, the delegates all rose to give a standing ovation, not to a labor leader, but to a middle-aged woman in a dark matronly dress. The woman they cheered that day was Mrs. Hortensia Black, who spoke for her husband, Captain Black, the corporation lawyer whose exhaustive defense of the Haymarket defendants had made him a working-class hero in Chicago and beyond.

When the jury had rendered its verdict and its death sentences on August 20, few trade unionists commented in the press. Still, the news that came from Judge Gary's courtroom alarmed many workers, who now feared losing their rights to protest and speak out in anger. A dangerous precedent had been set that day: if some kind of lethal violence occurred after the trade unionists freely assembled and expressed themselves, then their leaders could be indicted and tried as accessories to murder.[1]

After hearing Mrs. Black's critical remarks on the Haymarket trial and verdict, the meeting at Greenbaum's voted to field a full independent ticket in the November elections, despite the opposition of some top union officials. On August 28, the *Chicago Express*, whose editor supported the Knights and the eight-hour movement, branded Inspector Bonfield the "real author of the Haymarket slaughter." And on Labor Day various Chicago union members met to denounce the verdict and the role of the newspapers in whipping up hatred and fear.[2]

Expressions of protest grew in volume during the fall, when Captain Black and his team harshly criticized the summer's trial proceedings and made the case for a new trial.[3] Judge Gary, who had received huge accolades from the fourth estate, gave the critics no satisfaction. After a week of hearings during the first week of October, he denied the defendants' plea with a blunt statement insisting that the anarchists had received a fair trial during which the people had shown unprecedented patience toward the accused.[4]

When the judge finished reading his ruling on October 7, the convicts were allowed to speak on their own behalf before the sentence was passed. Normally, this judicial ritual permitted defendants to offer a belated confession or to express sorrow over their victims' fate. What happened next in the Chicago courthouse was anything but normal, as the eight anarchists recited a litany of injustices perpetrated against them by the police, the press, the prosecutors, the judge and the jury. For three days the anarchists took the floor and held it while they addressed a higher court of popular opinion, a court constituted, in their minds, by the worldwide community of workers. The anarchists believed they were being tried for the words they had spoken in the past, and now they aimed to be remembered in the future for the last words they uttered.

On October 8, as August Spies rose to speak before the court, Judge Gary repeated his caution to the audience to refrain from any demonstration. He then ordered all to be seated, even though some had to sit on the floor. After some moving and shuffling, everyone quieted as the so-called ringleader of the Chicago anarchists looked out over the room and began to give the speech of his life. It lasted for several hours as Spies rebutted Grinnell's charges one by one, impeached the testimony of paid witnesses and took exception to the state's attorney's appeal to patriotism, "the last refuge of the scoundrel." "I have been a citizen of this city as long as Mr. Grinnell," he declared, "and am probably as good a citizen as Grinnell." Indeed, Spies asserted, he was a principled man, not a common murderer with no principles as the attorney charged. He was indeed

August Spies

a man of ideas and he would not allow the state to deny this. Spies said he would not divest himself of his ideas, even if he could, because they constituted part of himself.[5]

When Spies stopped defending himself, he took the offensive, challenging those who believed that killing the anarchists would bring an end to the nation's labor troubles. "If you think you can stamp out the labor movement, then hang us!" But, he added, "Here you will tread upon a spark, but here, and there, and behind you and in front of you, and everywhere, flames will blaze up. It is a subterranean fire. You cannot put it out. The ground is on fire upon which you stand." Spies concluded by declaring that if the state thought people should suffer capital punishment because they "dared to tell the truth," then he would "proudly and defiantly pay the costly price." "Call your hangman!" he said to Judge Gary. He was prepared to die like others before him—from Socrates to Christ to Galileo—who had been "crucified" for telling the truth.[6]

Like their leader, August Spies, the other defendants who addressed the court refused to beg for mercy. Michael Schwab offered a defense of anarchy, saying it was the antithesis of violence. Violence was used on all sides, he argued, and the anarchists only advocated "violence against violence"—as a "necessary means of self defense." Louis Lingg took a very different tack. His speech was emphatic and angry. He said he would die gladly on the gallows knowing that hundreds of people he knew would now make use of dynamite. Then he denounced the entire process as a sham. When his concluding remarks were translated from German to English, gasps arose in the courtroom. "I despise you and I despise your laws," Lingg shouted. "Hang me for it!"[7]

Oscar Neebe described his dilemma with biting irony, saying that he had been accused of the "crimes" of organizing workers, publishing a workers' newspaper, marshaling a parade of anarchist union members. No evidence had been introduced to show that Neebe was connected to the alleged conspiracy in any way, but for crimes like being the marshal of a demonstration, he was to be confined to prison for fifteen years. He alone would escape the gallows, but at this reprieve he expressed only despair. "Your honor," he concluded, to the dismay of his lawyers, "I am sorry I am not to be hung with the rest of them." Neebe said it would be more honorable to die suddenly next to his comrades "than be killed by inches" in prison.[8]

At the end of the day on October 8, Albert Parsons took his turn to speak. He had made many speeches in tense settings—at gatherings before freed slaves on Texas plantations and at rallies before vast throngs in Chicago's raucous market squares—but now he spoke in a court of law before a captive audience of a thousand of his fellow citizens and scores of reporters. He wanted to give a speech not only for the moment but for the ages, a speech that might not save his life but that would preserve his voice for posterity.

Looking sallow and wasted from his confinement, Parsons stood before the courtroom in a black suit with a red flower in his lapel and a necktie to match. He placed an enormous folder of papers on the table in front of him and then began speaking in his remarkably clear voice. At first, he assumed the role of a petitioner.

> Your Honor, if there is one distinguishing characteristic which has made itself prominent in the conduct of this trial it has been the passion, the heat, the anger, the violence of everything connected with this case. . . . You ask me why a sentence of death should not be pronounced upon me. You ask me why you should give me a new trial that I might establish my innocence and the ends of justice be served. I answer, your Honor, and say that this verdict is a verdict of passion, born of passion, nurtured in passion, and is the sum total of the organized passion of the city of Chicago. For this reason I ask your suspension of the sentence and a new trial.[9]

Then Parsons altered his tone, shifting from the part of petitioner to the role of denouncer. He first attacked those who claimed to represent public sentiment, "that vile and infamous monopoly of hired liars—the capitalist press." Addressing Gary, he proclaimed, "this trial was conducted by a mob, prosecuted by a mob . . . an organized and powerful mob." At this moment, the convict uttered the words that would be quoted over and over again by those who looked back in anger at the trial. "Now, your Honor, I hold that our execution, as the matter stands now, would be judicial murder." He kept on speaking through the afternoon and then, as evening approached and gaslights popped on, Parsons calmly turned to the judge and said: "Your Honor, if you will permit it, I would like to stop now and resume tomorrow morning."[10]

At 10 a.m. the next day, seemingly refreshed and composed, Parsons carried on with his discourse. He would hold forth for the rest of the day. Once again, he began in a solicitous way. "Well, possibly I have said some foolish things," he granted. "Who has not?" He explained that the plight of the workers and the assaults made upon them by policemen and militiamen overwhelmed him with feelings of pity and indignation, and so he had said some things he might not have said in a cooler frame of mind. The angry words he had uttered did not, however, mean that he was an assassin. "I am called a dynamiter by the prosecution here. Why? Did I ever use dynamite? No. Did I ever have any? No." Then why was he called a dynamiter? Simply because he told workers that dynamite would, like the invention of gunpowder, serve to equalize social power.

Then he was off again, speaking without apology. "So today," he declared, "dynamite comes as the emancipator of man from the domination . . . of his fellow man." Judge Gary grew visibly impatient, but Parsons refused to change direction. "Bear with me now," he said. "Dynamite is the diffusion of power. It is democratic; it makes everybody equal." After infuriating most of his listeners with this lecture, the speaker returned to the legal question of free speech. "It is proposed by the prosecution here to take me by force and strangle me on the gallows for these things I have said, for these expressions," he remarked, but did it follow that he was a dynamiter because he held these views and expressed them in angry speeches?[11]

Parsons continued in a less provocative way, assuming new speaking roles as he proceeded into the late morning. He spoke as a historian, narrating the development of the labor movement and the history of bloody lockouts and massacres suffered by workers, devoting special attention

Albert Parsons

to the Pinkerton Agency, "a private army" employers hired to terrorize workers and suppress their protests. He spoke as a political philosopher, defining the meaning of socialism and explaining that it took two forms—anarchism, an egalitarian society without a controlling authority, and state socialism, which meant governmental control of everything. He spoke as an economist, examining the wage question, the eight-hour reform movement and the relations of capital and labor. And he spoke as a journalist about the "real facts of the Haymarket tragedy," quoting the testimony of Mayor Harrison, who said that the meeting was peaceful and that none of the speakers had incited the crowd.[12]

Parsons even assumed the role of a prosecutor, turning the tables on the representatives of the state; they were the ones who had violated the defendants' rights to free speech, to a free press, to free assembly and the right to self-defense. Flipping the prosecution's script, the speaker claimed that the bombing itself was "the deliberate work of monopoly—the act of those who themselves charge us with this deed," and insisted that the accused were the real victims—victims of a conspiracy hatched by the city's millionaires to deprive them of their lives and liberties.[13]

As the day wore on, the audience shifted uneasily, and Judge Gary became increasingly agitated, expressing his irritation with hard looks and gestures. But there were still more voices of Albert Parsons to be heard. He even lectured the jury as a scientist on—of all things—the chemistry of dynamite. Parsons argued that the missile thrown on May 4 was not made of dynamite; it was instead "what was known in the Civil War as an infernal bomb composed of gunpowder, not nitroglycerin." The proof lay in the testimony of the surgeons who described wounds in the policemen's bodies that were far less serious than if dynamite had been used. Dynamite would have blown them into "unrecognizable fragments."[14]

Then, shifting abruptly to the high ground, Parsons identified himself as an American citizen, one whose ancestors fought at Bunker Hill and Valley Forge. He and Oscar Neebe were the only defendants who "had the fortune, or the misfortune—as some people look at it—of being born in this country," he said. The rest of his comrades were charged with being foreigners, "as though it was a crime to be born in some other country." Then, rallying his strength, the speaker declared himself "an Internationalist," one whose patriotism extended "beyond the boundary lines of a single state." Opening his arms wide, he declared, "The world is my country, all mankind my countrymen."[15]

At about 1 p.m. Parsons, clearly exhausted, asked the judge for a short lunch recess, explaining that he had been weakened physically by his confinement in a gloomy cell without his customary outdoor exercise. Judge Gary cut Parsons off and denied his plea for a recess.[16] Angry now, the speaker turned on the judge and addressed him directly in a thin but insistent voice. "I am here standing in the spot awaiting your sentence, because I hate authority in every form," he rasped. "I am doomed by you to suffer an ignominious death because I am an outspoken enemy of coercion, of privilege, of force, of authority." He was nearing the end. "Think you, the people are blind, are asleep, are indifferent?" Parsons asked, addressing all those in authority. "You deceive yourselves. I tell you, as a man of the people, and I speak for them, that your every word and act . . . are recorded. You are being weighed in the balance. The people are conscious of your power—your stolen power. I, a working man, stand here and to your face, in your stronghold of oppression, denounce . . . your crimes against humanity. It is for this I die, but my death will not have been in vain." Near collapse, he said in a low tone: "I guess I have finished. I don't know as I have anything more to say."[17] Not a single voice cheered, not a pair of hands clapped for this speech, the last one Albert Parsons would ever deliver.

In a heartbeat, the judge pronounced the sentence. Oscar Neebe was to be imprisoned in the Joliet State Penitentiary, to serve a fifteen-year sentence at hard labor. Each of the other seven defendants would, at the appointed time and in the manner prescribed by state statute, be "hanged by the neck until he is dead." Then Gary ordered the bailiff to remove the prisoners.

And so it ended, one of the most remarkable criminal trials that ever occurred in this country; remarkable for its sheer drama and for the passionate interest it aroused among people all over America; remarkable for the prosecution's unprecedented application of conspiracy law; remarkable for the quality of evidence used to convict seven men of murder; and remarkable for the way the proceedings and the verdict divided Americans along fault lines of class and nationality.[18]

JUDGE GARY HAD ORDERED the execution of the condemned men to take place on or before December 3, 1886, but Captain Black held out hope for a reprieve until the case could be reviewed by the state supreme court. In the meantime, the anarchists' supporters began to mount a defense campaign. Lucy Parsons took to the road and spoke to union audiences in several cities, where she raised money and aroused sympathy.[19] Support for the defendants surfaced in the anarchist-led unions as well as in various assemblies of the Knights of Labor, where Parsons and the other Chicago anarchists were known as organizers and leaders of the eight-hour movement.

During and after the red scare in May of 1886, the powerful movement for shorter hours had all but expired, as employers regained the offensive and restored traditional workdays of ten or more hours. On October 11, 1887, the big meat companies in the Chicago stockyards announced a return to ten hours a day after negotiations broke down over the Knights of Labor's demands to maintain an eight-hour day. A huge strike then erupted in the yards, where the Knights had recruited more than 20,000 members. The packers employed the Pinkerton Agency, which provided 800 armed guards to protect strikebreakers. The workers held out for three weeks, against the orders of national leaders, but they eventually gave up their struggle to save the eight-hour day, and trudged back into the yards in early November thoroughly defeated.[20] This was the beginning of the end of the Noble and Holy Order in Chicago and in other cities, where the Knights suffered from crippling internal conflicts and from other devastating defeats at the hands of unified groups of employers who abandoned their competitive ways to form a solid coalition against their unionized employees.[21]

The national leader of the troubled order, Terence Powderly, who had called an end to the stockyards strike, was denounced as a Benedict Arnold by his embittered followers in Chicago. He also faced growing sentiment among his members that the anarchists there had been unfairly tried and cruelly sentenced. At the union's national convention that October, Powderly's forces beat back a resolution declaring the anarchists innocent, but the delegates did issue a plea for mercy on behalf of the condemned.[22] After this meeting, the Knights in Chicago endorsed a much stronger resolution branding the verdict "an outrage upon common justice" and a result of a "capitalistic and judicial conspiracy."[23] As recriminations mounted within the order, the imprisoned anarchists were left with the cold comfort that they had long before warned the labor movement about the Grand Master Workman's cowardice.

A few weeks later the editors of the Chicago Knights of Labor newspaper, who had said on May 5 that the anarchists should be treated like wild beasts, gave up ownership of the newspaper as a result of rising anger over the trial and verdict within the ranks. These editors, Powderly loyalists, were replaced by Ethelbert Stewart, a radical, who had been mentored by the journalist Henry Demarest Lloyd when the young Stewart was working in a coffin factory. As editor of the Chicago *Knights of Labor,* Stewart published several editorials calling the anarchists' prosecution a blatant attack against workers' civil liberties.[24] Powderly soon demanded that all Knights stop supporting the anarchists, but Bert Stewart defied the edict and wrote another editorial insisting that the right to a "fair trial" was far more important than any order on earth.[25]

ON NOVEMBER 23, the anarchists' lawyer, Captain Black, argued for a writ of error before the Illinois Supreme Court in Springfield, and a few days later, for a stay of execution, which the justices granted, until a hearing on the appeal could take place.[26] It was Thanksgiving when Black brought the good news to the cold, dark confines of the Cook County Jail. There was much rejoicing as the anarchists ate and celebrated their reprieve with family and friends.

With this vital challenge met, Captain Black and George Schilling searched for another associate to aid in preparing the appeal. They called first upon Colonel Robert Green Ingersoll, who had championed the eight-hour law when he was Richard Oglesby's attorney general. The colonel had already consulted with the defense committee, expressing his view that Judge Gary had erred when he instructed the jury that they could convict the defendants of murder if they had spoken with criminal intent. Ingersoll also thought the men had been tried unfairly because the jury was dominated by clerks who were there to do the bidding of their employers.[27] The colonel believed that the anarchists had made terrible mistakes in word and deed, but he thought they were motivated by humanitarian considerations. As the nation's most prominent atheist, though, Ingersoll feared that he would harm, if not doom, the anarchists' case if he was associated with it.[28]

Captain Black and George Schilling then searched further and found the kind of attorney Ingersoll thought the appellants needed when they secured the services of a famous Illinois criminal lawyer. Leonard Swett, then sixty-one years of age, had become Lincoln's close friend when they rode the Eighth Circuit of Southern Illinois as young lawyers. Swett had worked with Richard Oglesby to help their friend win the Republican presidential nomination at the 1860 convention. During the Civil War, while he practiced criminal law, Swett had served as a trusted adviser to Lincoln. After the assassination in 1865, Swett moved his practice to Chicago, where he helped to found the city bar association and became renowned for winning acquittals in numerous murder cases.[29]

DURING THE NEXT MONTHS the anarchists gained something close to celebrity status as they received constant attention in the press and entertained a steady flow of visitors. Joseph R. Buchanan, a prominent organizer and editor for the Knights of Labor, arrived from Denver to bring good tidings from western workers; he then called regularly to see "the boys" after he moved to Chicago to work for the defense. Leading European socialists also visited the jail, including the German party leader, Wilhelm Liebknecht, along with Karl Marx's daughter Eleanor and her husband, Edward Aveling. Parsons enjoyed many visits from old friends such as the anarchist Dyer D. Lum, who would play a prominent role in the anarchists' story. Born and raised in Massachusetts, Lum had become an abolitionist and a devoted admirer of John Brown. He enlisted in the Union army to liberate the slaves and after the war joined Wendell Phillips in the reform movement. Lum met Parsons in 1879, when they were lobbying for a national eight-hour law, and drew closer to the Texan as both men moved toward anarchism. A brilliant writer and a sophisticated intellectual, Dyer Lum was utterly devoted to the revolutionary cause and as committed to the use of force as his hero John Brown had been. Lum was also deeply committed to the Haymarket defendants, so much so that he sold his business in New York after their arrest and moved to Chicago to aid in their defense and to reopen Albert Parsons's newspaper, the *Alarm*.[30]

In addition, the defendants were interviewed by scores of reporters from the very newspapers whose editors had already tried them and condemned them to death. One of them was Charles Edward Russell, who filed daily reports from Chicago for Joseph Pulitzer's *New York World*. The journalist spoke at length with them all, save Lingg. At first, they regarded Russell as their natural enemy and part of the capitalist press machinery that had convicted them in the public eye, but, eventually, the inmates became approachable, even cordial. The impressions the convicts made on this reporter and other journalists began to seep into news stories, which often described the anarchists as ordinary men visiting affectionately with family and friends. Russell, for example, found Spies attractive, "well educated, magnificently set up, fluent and plausible in English as well as German, a blue-eyed Saxon, emotional, sentimental and rash." Fielden seemed an affable, almost comic figure, a likable, awkward "galoot." Schwab looked the part of a German university professor, "a thin, angular, sallow person, spectacled, long-haired, black-bearded, unkempt"—a man with "the best mental equipment" but a "dreamy" way about him. Fischer, on the other hand, seemed to Russell a hotheaded youth, "a half baked student of German philosophical anarchism." Engel's beliefs, however, were the genuine product of his hard experience as an orphan who had been kicked from pillar to post. "He had a chubby, good-natured face, looked like an elderly German bar tender, seemed to cherish no resentments," and he "talked freely and entertainingly" with anyone who approached him.[31]

Albert Parsons was the special one to Russell, who confessed that he took a strong liking to the prisoner. The reporter found the Texan an immensely engaging conversationalist and a picturesque storyteller with good taste in poetry and an excellent singing voice. The reporter regarded Parsons's political thinking as incomplete and confused, but still found it impossible not to like him.[32] Thus the anarchists, once demonized as beasts, began, now that they were caged on death row, to be humanized by the newspapermen who had helped put them behind bars.

George Engel (left) and Adolph Fischer

Art Young, a twenty-year-old artist from Wisconsin, depicted the condemned men in their cells for the *Chicago Daily News* as they assumed casual poses. In one drawing Parsons is seated looking like a lawyer relaxing in a businessman's club, one leg thrown over the other, a newspaper dangling loosely from one hand, a cigarillo held elegantly in the other. Another less artful drawing by a different illustrator showed Albert embracing his daughter, Lulu, while Lucy is seen looking in at them from behind the bars. Young also drew Maria Schwab dressed in a shirtwaist and wearing a large hat, sitting in a chair and talking to her husband, Michael, as he leaned against the bars to be close to her.[33]

Lingg played a special part in this jailhouse mise-en-scène. His hostile looks, his defiance in court, his threatening words and his reckless attitude made the others seem less menacing. Art Young, who was the same age as the prisoner, drew him with his arms crossed and a faint smile on his lips. "My memory of Louis Lingg is distinct," Young wrote later, "because the sun was shining in his cell as I sketched him. He was a handsome boy, sitting proudly and looking directly toward me as much as to say, 'Go ahead, nothing matters.' " But to other reporters, Lingg seemed a horrifying character, the embodiment of evil. Russell found him a terrifying young man with a malignant stare. Indeed, Lingg seemed the only really dangerous man among the eight; so it struck the reporter as odd that this "tiger anarchist" had a sweetheart who visited him—a tall, statuesque brunette, who came frequently from the West Side and talked intimately with the prisoner through the steel bars and wire mesh of his cell.[34]

The most sensational visitor of all was Nina Van Zandt, a well-bred young woman who had become closely attached to August Spies. "She was about twenty-four, slenderly-fashioned, handsome, always exquisitely gowned," Russell recalled, and she conducted herself with the "deportment of a refined educated woman." She came to see Spies every day and spoke quietly to him for her allotted hour. It was impossible for the reporter to imagine a figure more incongruous in such a grim place. Other journalists were fascinated by Spies's lady friend as well, and they eagerly reported her appearances and speculated as to her motives.[35]

The only child of a wealthy Chicago medicine manufacturer, Nina Van Zandt was a graduate of Vassar and the heiress to a small fortune. Like many other ladies, she had been a curious spectator at the trial of the century, but unlike the others, she had gradually become convinced of the defendants' innocence. Driven by a feeling of horror that these men would die on the gallows, she plunged into defense work. After visiting all the prisoners, she turned her attentions mainly to Spies, and by December she had fallen in love with him. Though they spoke through iron bars and wire mesh, it was clear to observers that the couple had romantic feelings for each other. The jailers made no attempt to interfere, but after the installation of a new sheriff named Canute Matson, a tough disciplinarian of Norwegian origin, Nina's visits were drastically curtailed.[36]

In their next conversation the couple devised a bold plan. Because wives were allowed more visiting time than friends, Spies and Van Zandt decided they should be married. When their plans for a wedding on death row leaked out, the newspaper editors went wild with rage. Nina was suddenly the subject of unending abuse and ridicule. There would have been little comment, Van Zandt recalled, if she had been some "obscure, foreign girl," but she was regarded as an American lady of privilege and standing, so lowering herself by agreeing to marry a condemned criminal seemed to the press like something akin to prostitution.[37]

The defense attorneys, Black and Swett, were beside themselves with distress over Spies's romantic intentions, which they feared would damage their chances for appeal; but they could not persuade him to alter his course. The lawyers were relieved when the sheriff refused to allow the marriage to take place in the jail. Yet the sensational affair did not fade from the news; it reappeared on January 29, 1887, when Henry Spies repeated the marriage vows on his brother's behalf and Nina Van Zandt

Nina Van Zandt

responded for herself, promising to love, honor and obey the most notorious man in America. A few days later a gang attacked the Van Zandt home, and the sheriff barred Nina from visiting her newlywed husband at all.[38]

While the newspapers still buzzed with talk of the jailhouse love affair, Black and Swett began their arguments before the Illinois Supreme Court. The captain was confident of a reversal of the judgment because, even though the press remained adamantly supportive of the verdict, public opinion seemed to be shifting. At about this time, Black learned from Eleanor Marx and her husband that most of the working-class people the English socialists met on a multicity tour that winter believed the anarchists' trial to be a miscarriage of justice. Lucy Parsons reported similar responses while on the road for many weeks following the October sentencing. By March she had addressed fifty audiences in sixteen states, generating sympathy for the defendants and raising money for their defense. She was arrested in Columbus and Akron but pressed on with her solo campaign to seek support from various segments of the population.[39]

Captain Black's assurance of winning a new trial was based not on public opinion, however, but on his certainty that the appeal he drafted revealed that a legal travesty had occurred in Judge Gary's courtroom. When he appeared before the supreme court justices, a half-dozen elderly men, the attorney argued that no conspiracy to commit murder had been proven and that the anarchists had been convicted entirely for their beliefs.[40]

Attorney Swett chose a different approach. Speaking as a pioneer Illinois Republican and a close associate of Lincoln, the counselor appealed to those experiences he shared with the justices. He recalled the history of the party's formation, when its radical leaders denounced the Constitution, established the Underground Railroad and conspired to act against the laws of the United States by aiding and abetting the escape of slaves. The storm finally peaked, he added, when John Brown violated the laws of Virginia. Swett then applied this history lesson to the anarchist case, arguing that all the Republicans who gave such subversive antislavery speeches and "believed in the utopian idea of a change in society for the benefit of a class" were criminal conspirators with John Brown and, therefore, by this logic ought to have been hanged as well.[41]

After the plea had been argued before the supreme court, the city turned its attention away from the case to the exciting municipal elections taking place in April. Electoral politics, like most aspects of public life in Chicago, had been deeply affected by the anarchist trial. The new United Labor Party had made a surprising showing in the November elections, winning 26 percent of the vote across the city and much more in immigrant working-class wards. In the town of Lake, where eight-hour strikers in the stockyards had faced an occupying army of Pinkertons, sheriff's deputies and National Guard troops, the insurgent vote was even higher. From his cell in the county jail, Albert Parsons had claimed that every vote cast for the labor ticket in Chicago was a protest against the verdict in his trial.[42]

As the spring election neared, the socialists, anarchists and other labor activists cheered when Mayor Harrison refused to accept a fifth nomination as a Democratic candidate for mayor of Chicago; instead, he endorsed the Labor Party ticket headed by a socialist worker and supported by various factions of the union movement, including the anarchist-led organizations. Harrison's action was quickly forgotten when panic-stricken Democratic Party leaders endorsed the Republican mayoral candidate and joined forces with their old rivals against the threat posed by a third party with radical leadership. The United Labor Party candidates campaigned against "Black Jack" Bonfield and promised to remove him as police inspector if they won. The Republicans responded by charging that the new party was a stalking horse for the anarchists, who wanted to abolish the police department and create a state of anarchy. On election day, April 5, the *Tribune* told its readers: "Ballots should be cast for law and order as against anarchy and incompetency."[43]

The law-and-order coalition played effectively on the public's fear of urban disorder, a feeling that remained palpable nearly a year after Haymarket. As a result, the Republican mayoral candidate, John A. Roche, swept to victory and the Labor Party failed to increase its vote. Inspector Bonfield told the press there "wasn't a prouder man in Chicago" that night than he, for the election represented a vindication of his course of action and a rejection of those who wanted to drive him from the city. When Albert Parsons heard the news in Cell 29, the *Tribune*'s reporter wrote that he raged over the results like a lunatic and let loose "a string of oaths that would have captured a Democratic convention." From the day of his surrender, Parsons was sure the state was going to kill him, but he hoped that his trial and ordeal would at least revive the radical workers' movement he had led for a decade; now he felt frustrated enough to bark at a reporter, "The fools are as plentiful as ever."[44]

Spies, Schwab and Neebe were also visibly upset, but they made no comment to the press. Sam Fielden chose to speak to reporters and told them he was downcast after the election. "I feel very bad about it," he told one newsman. "Prejudice has been worked up by the press to such an extent during the campaign that popular feeling is now almost as bad as it was after the 4th of May, and this cannot but have a bad effect on the Judges of the Supreme Court." He no longer held out much hope that he would receive a new trial. "We were convicted in consequence of public clamor," Fielden said with his usual bluntness, "and we may hang from the same cause."[45]

Chapter Fifteen

The Law Is Vindicated

SAM FIELDEN READ the signs of the time correctly. His fate and that of his comrades was linked to that of the labor movement, as it had been since he arrived in Chicago. The United Labor Party disintegrated over the summer months of 1007, and the once-powerful Knights lost most of their remaining members. Chicago union members who had gained shorter hours in May 1886 now faced employers determined to stretch them out again. The building trades unions beat back contractors attempting to return to the ten-hour day in the spring, but the strikers were isolated now, no longer involved in a mass mobilization like the Great Upheaval that shook the city a year before. The Haymarket bomb, the *Tribune* reported with relief, had shattered the Internationals' attempt to build a unified movement of the skilled and unskilled through a general strike.[1]

Equally distressing to the anarchists, and to other trade unionists, was the news that, on the first anniversary of Haymarket, the Illinois House of Representatives had enacted a statute providing that anyone who spoke to any assembly in public or private or who wrote, printed or published any words that "incited local revolution" or the "destruction of the existing order" could be found guilty of criminal conspiracy; and that, further, if a life was taken as a result of such speeches and writings, the person accused should be considered a principal in the perpetration of said murder.[2] In other words, the unprecedented interpretation of conspiracy doctrine in the anarchist case had now been written into state law. This meant that the six state supreme court justices now reviewing the case would, if they ordered a new trial, not only have to discredit a prosecutor, a judge and a jury regarded as heroes in Illinois; they would also have to contradict the state's new conspiracy law.

Nonetheless, Captain Black remained hopeful that the errors in the

Haymarket murder trial would compel the justices to agree with his objections. Other Chicago lawyers agreed, men like Samuel P. McConnell and his father-in-law, John G. Rogers, the chief justice of the circuit court. Both men were critical of Judge Gary's conduct and of his rulings. McConnell thought the presiding judge had treated the whole Haymarket trial like a holiday event, as had the well-dressed women he invited to sit on the bench with him. Judge Rogers believed Gary had made new law and ignored established rules about jury selection that were intended to assure fair trials. As a result, the two men were as shocked as Captain Black was when, after six months of deliberation, the Illinois Supreme Court rejected the writ of appeal and affirmed the August verdict of the Chicago court. On September 13 the chief justice read the court's ruling to an expectant throng. Before he had even finished, reporters raced each other to telegraph offices to transmit the news that the death sentence would be carried out on November 11, 1887.[3] For the next two months the fate of the anarchists in the Cook County Jail captured the attention of the daily newspapers and the nation's leading magazines.

When Sheriff Canute Matson received the execution order, he doubled the guard around the Cook County Jail and ordered his deputies to escort Oscar Neebe to Joliet State Prison, where he would serve his fifteen-year sentence at hard labor. The prisoner was spirited away in the dead of night with no chance to bid his comrades farewell, but somehow he talked to a reporter during his passage. Neebe repeated that his only crimes were organizing brewers and salesclerks and publishing a workers' paper. "What I have done, I would do again," he told the *Daily News*, "and the time will come when the blood of the martyrs about to be sacrificed will cry aloud for vengeance, and that cry will be heard . . . before many years elapse."[4]

Organized labor responded immediately to the news from Illinois as union groups met in many cities to decry the supreme court justices' decision. In New York City prominent leaders of the Central Labor Union, led by Samuel Gompers, declared that the convicted workingmen were victims of "the misguiding and corrupting influence of prejudice and class hatred" and had been condemned to death without any conclusive evidence. The execution of the death sentence would, the labor chiefs declared, be nothing less than a "judicial murder prompted by the basest and most un-American motives."[5]

Captain Black denounced the supreme court's ruling as infamous, because it meant that nothing now prevented a citizen from being

FRANK LESLIE'S ILLUSTRATED NEWSPAPER

Entered according to Act of Congress, in the year 1887, by Mrs. Frank Leslie, in the Office of the Librarian of Congress at Washington.—Entered at the Post Office, New York, N. Y., as second-class Matter.

1,672.—Vol. LXV.]   NEW YORK—FOR THE WEEK ENDING OCTOBER 1, 1887.   [PRICE, 10 CENTS.

Magazine cover of Cook County Jail cells at visiting time, with inset portraits of
Nina Van Zandt and August Spies

arrested, tried, convicted and executed for simply speaking as an anarchist. While the lawyers prepared to make a new appeal to the U.S. Supreme Court, George Schilling and others on the defense committee created the Amnesty Association that they hoped would enlist a wide range of citizens in a petition drive asking Governor Oglesby to grant clemency. Robert Ingersoll signed on, saying there was hope because the governor was a courageous man with a good heart and noble instincts, even though he might be swayed by the general feeling among the upper classes in favor of the death penalty.[6]

Albert Parsons took his own case directly to fellow citizens in a public letter written on September 21. Commenting on the effort to prevent his "judicial murder" by seeking a commutation of the sentence to life imprisonment, he wrote: "Knowing myself innocent of crime I came forward and gave myself up for trial. I felt it was my duty to take my chances with the rest of my comrades," rather than "being hunted like a felon." Since surrendering, he continued, "I have been locked up in close confinement for twenty-one hours out of every twenty four . . . in a noisome cell, without a ray of sunlight or breath of pure air." He did not want to bear this for even a few more years and said he was prepared to die rather than plead for a life behind bars. And then with a flourish, he wrote: "No. I am not guilty. I have not been proven guilty. I cannot, therefore, accept a commutation to imprisonment. I appeal—not for mercy, but for justice." He ended by quoting his favorite revolutionary, Patrick Henry: "I know not what course others may take, but, as for me, give me liberty or give me death."[7]

Parsons's letter was reprinted in many labor newspapers whose editors regarded it as a heroic demonstration of courageous manhood; it even appeared in some mainstream dailies. The bold declaration enhanced Parsons's celebrity and convinced many readers of his innocence, but it caused dismay among leaders of the Amnesty Association. The clemency campaign proceeded, nonetheless, under the determined leadership of Parsons's old friend George Schilling, who held out hope he could change the convict's mind about pleading for his life. The tireless labor activist was assisted in this effort by Dr. William Salter and Henry Demarest Lloyd, two of the city's leading intellectuals, men who dared to risk public condemnation as a result.

William Salter had been educated in the best divinity schools, but he then turned to secular free thought and became a lecturer for the Ethical Culture Society. An open-minded person, he even accepted invitations from the International's American Group to debates about socialism. He had been one of the first citizens outside the International who came to the defense of the accused anarchists during the frightening days after May 4, 1886. When the verdict was rendered that August, Salter threw himself into defense work. After bravely venturing out to lecture against the death sentence at the Opera House, he endured a steady stream of condemnation, even from members of his own society.[8]

Henry Demarest Lloyd, who joined Salter in speaking for the defense effort, suffered even more tangibly. When he condemned the trial in a public forum, his powerful father-in-law, William "Deacon" Bross, an owner of the *Chicago Tribune*, denounced Lloyd and removed him as an heir to his fortune. Henry and his wife, Jessie Bross Lloyd, were drummed out of polite society and shunned in public arenas. Even an old friend gave him a "look of the most intense hatred possible from one human being to another." Yet Lloyd did not shrink from the commitment he made to advocate for the men he believed were unfairly tried and unjustly condemned. Indeed, the writer seethed over the conduct of the trial in which Judge Gary acted like a prosecuting attorney, over the behavior of the police who set a precedent of arresting citizens without warrant and over the conduct of a jury that condemned men to death for being outspoken protest leaders.[9]

Lloyd also knew that the anarchists were deeply involved in the eight-hour movement, a cause in which he placed great hope, and that his old enemies, Chicago's barons of banking, trading and manufacturing, were using the bombing to discredit the entire labor movement. The Haymarket tragedy was a transforming event in Henry Lloyd's life, propelling him into an alliance with the American labor movement and into a brilliant phase of his career as the most influential worker advocate and business critic of the early progressive era.[10]

Under his leadership, the Amnesty Association hoped to attract more support from the middle-class public, but at first the responses came mainly in the form of resolutions from labor unions and cash contributions from workers in many cities across the country, particularly from immigrant unionists in Chicago who were kept constantly informed by a revived radical press comprised of the *Arbeiter-Zeitung*, which had reopened under new management, Bert Stewart's *Knights of Labor* and Joseph Buchanan's *Labor Enquirer*, a popular radical newspaper the editor had produced in Denver until the Haymarket trial compelled him to move to Chicago and publish there. Buchanan was a major player in the national affairs of the Knights of Labor and one of Powderly's main adversaries. A legendary organizer with anarchist sympathies of his own and an editorial voice that had national resonance, Buchanan led the way in making the anarchist case a cause célèbre in the national labor movement during the summer of 1887.

Meanwhile, in New York City, John Swinton, the most influential labor journalist in the land, attacked the death sentence as a judicial murder intended to "gratify the frightened bourgeoisie." He then joined with fourteen union leaders representing various wings of the city's union movement to condemn the verdict and to call for a mass protest on October 20. That night, a large crowd jammed into the Great Hall of Cooper Union in New York City to hear Samuel Gompers, the new president of the American Federation of Labor, denounce the proceedings in Chicago. Unlike Powderly of the Knights, who refused to endorse the campaign for clemency, Gompers joined the venerable Swinton and other trade union leaders in making an appeal for liberty, free speech and justice, expressing their belief that the impending execution would be "a disgrace to the honor of this country."[11]

That same month, trade unionists and reformers in London spoke out against the executions; they were primed by the editorials that appeared in *Commonweal,* the socialist publication edited by William Morris, the noted poet and designer who worried that, after rioting by unemployed

Samuel Gompers (left) and John Swinton

marchers, Scotland Yard would adopt the repressive tactics of the Chicago police, who "hunted socialists like wolves."[12] Other European socialist newspapers also devoted an enormous amount of coverage to the Haymarket affair, far more than to any other news story in the post–Civil War era.

Although socialist leaders in Europe regarded anarchists as dangerous provocateurs at best, they embraced the Haymarket defendants as heroic social revolutionaries and gave their hard-hitting attacks on American freedom wide circulation. At a time when most Europeans regarded the United States as a promised land, a "new Caanan," the repressive red scare in May of 1886, along with the Chicago trial and the shocking death sentences that followed, proved, at least in the minds of radicals, that the same class struggle they observed on their continent was going on across the Atlantic. Coming in the same year as the French government's gift of the Statue of Liberty to the United States, the Haymarket events gave European radicals an unprecedented opportunity to challenge the popular view that the United States was an exceptional country, open, free and democratic.[13]

Coverage of the trial and the appeal hearings was especially extensive in Paris, a city with an active anarchist movement (though it was tiny compared to the International in Chicago). When word of the failed appeal to the Illinois Supreme Court reached France, the socialist newspaper *Le Cri du Peuple* announced a protest against what would be the most atrocious political crime since the hanging of John Brown. Public concern reached all the way to the municipal council of the Seine, whose deputies issued a plea for mercy to the U.S. legation, recalling the clemency that had been extended to the "vanquished leaders of the Southern rebellion." Many of the same deputies also signed a clemency petition to Governor Oglesby. In October radicals called Haymarket protest meetings in London, The Hague and Rotterdam, in Vienna, Brussels, Lyon, Marseilles and Toulon. It was no wonder, then, that the *Tribune* observed on October 11 that "[t]he eyes of the world seem to be on the Chicago anarchists."[14]

ON OCTOBER 27 the U.S. Supreme Court heard the appeal prepared by Captain Black with the assistance of three nationally known attorneys, including former army general Benjamin F. Butler, loved by workingmen in the North for his labor radicalism and hated in the white South for his ruthless military rule of New Orleans during and after the Civil War. The attorneys argued that the police and prosecution had violated constitutional amendments that protected citizens from unlawful searches (the Fourth), against self-incrimination (the Fifth) and against being tried by a biased jury (the Sixth).[15]

Defense lawyers also argued that the trial violated the due process clause of the Fourteenth Amendment. General Ben Butler proposed to the Supreme Court justices that the Bill of Rights and other constitutional amendments should govern state court cases, because they were the law of the land. "Any other meaning given to 'due process law' " would, he declared, make the Fourteenth Amendment "simply ridiculous and frivolous." But the old radical seemed resigned to defeat, concluding his Supreme Court presentation with the kind of histrionic remark that made him famous. "If men's lives can be taken in this way," Butler declared, referring to the Chicago trial and verdict, "better anarchy, better to be without law, than with any such law."[16]

On November 2, 1887, Chief Justice Morrison R. Waite read a unanimous decision of the court. The justices concluded that the constitutional violations cited by the appellants were relevant only in federal cases and, therefore, that the Supreme Court lacked jurisdiction because the case touched upon no federal law or national issue. In any case, the judges noted, "the defendants had not been deprived of a trial by a fair and impartial jury and had not been denied due process of law."[17]

At this point, the defense movement directed all its efforts to the governor's office in Springfield, hoping Richard Oglesby would commute the sentences of the seven condemned men to life imprisonment. Knowing the law required the convicts to write statements of contrition, defense lawyers, family members and other supporters persuaded Fielden, Schwab and Spies to write to the governor conveying their regret over the violence of May 4 and repudiating their own statements calling for the use of force. Spies was very reluctant to write such a letter, and when he did, he insisted on adding a statement that he deplored all violence, not only the loss of life in the Haymarket but also the violence suffered by strikers in East St. Louis, at McCormick's and in the Chicago stockyards. All three prisoners wrote that they had never advocated the use of force, except in the case of self-defense, and had "never consciously broken any laws." However, urgent efforts failed to move Engel, Fischer and Lingg to write letters of appeal. The three intransigents did write to Oglesby, but to demand liberation, not a commutation of their death sentences. Captain Black said of their letters, "They are manly and coura-geous, but I regret the men felt called upon to write them."[18]

Albert Parsons also refused to change his mind and beg for clemency, even in the face of imploring visits from close friends and luminaries such as Henry D. Lloyd. Melville E. Stone, the publisher of the *Chicago Daily News,* also made a plea. Stone talked with the condemned man for two hours, but to no avail. As he prepared to leave, Parsons said that he told the publisher, who had initially taken the lead in urging State's Attorney Grinnell to try the eight anarchists for murder, even though no bomb thrower could be brought to trial: "You are responsible for my fate. Your venomous attacks condemned us in advance. I shall die with less fear and less regret than you will feel in living, for my blood is upon your head."[19]

Even longtime friend and admirer George Schilling could not sway Parsons from his stance; nor could a letter from his revered older brother, General William Parsons; nor could passionate pleas and compelling arguments from Captain Black, who explained to his stubborn client that leading men in Illinois now wanted his sentence commuted. Because of Parsons's courageous surrender, many now believed the governor would grant him a reprieve if he would only comply with the state law that required a written petition for clemency from the condemned prisoner. Parsons heard him out but refused to renounce his beliefs. "I am an inno-cent man," he told Black, "and the world knows I am innocent. If I am to be executed at all it is because I am an Anarchist not because I am a murderer; it is because of what I have taught and spoken and written in the past, and not because of the throwing of the Haymarket bomb."[20] Having accepted and then embraced his fate as a martyr, Albert Parsons was now staking out his place in history.

While these intense conversations took place in Cell 29, the flow of petitions that poured into the Amnesty Association included more and more signatures from prominent citizens, including the banker and civic leader Lyman Gage and the head of the Chicago bar, William C. Goudy. Attorney Samuel P. McConnell then took the petitions to judges and lawyers, and several of them added their names; this reportedly left Judge Gary "very much aggrieved." When McConnell approached the esteemed Lyman Trumbull, a former U.S. senator and state supreme court justice, the old man carefully read the petition, then buried his face in his hands and said, "I will sign. Those men did not have a fair trial." Trum-bull was the most prominent political figure to lend his name to the plea.

George Schilling (left) and Henry Demarest Lloyd

Some pleas came from entire companies, such as one endorsed by 125 editors and reporters of the *Boston Globe*. Chicago druggists drafted their own appeal, as did two Jewish leaders, Rabbi Emil Hirsch and the attorney Julius Rosenthal. The Amnesty Association also set up tables outside City Hall where pedestrians could stop and affix their names to its petition for commutation; nearly 7,000 citizens did so on the weekend of November 5 and 6.[21]

Much of this public support for clemency was generated by the critical literature on the case produced to counter the uniform praise the prosecution had received in the daily press. General Matthew M. Trumbull wrote a widely distributed pamphlet called *Was It a Fair Trial?* The author, unrelated to the famous Republican senator with the same surname, had earned a distinguished reputation as a Union army officer and a respected Chicago attorney. The general had been a Chartist in England and an abolitionist in America, but he could not be accused of sympathy with the anarchists. Even so, after reviewing the case, the attorney bluntly stated that "the trial was unfair, the rulings of the court illegal, and the sentence unjust."[22] Far more influential inside and outside the city was Dyer D. Lum's *Concise History of the Great Trial of the Chicago Anarchists*, in which the author, a highly skilled writer, dissected the trial proceedings after studying the court transcript and highlighted what he saw as the inconsistencies and contradictions in the prosecution's case. Lum's pamphlet helped convince the nation's most prominent writer to join the movement for clemency.

William Dean Howells, the son of an abolitionist printer and an admirer of Abraham Lincoln, had reached literary heights by 1886, when he earned a princely sum of $13,000 a year as a columnist for *Harper's Weekly*. The former editor of the prestigious *Atlantic Monthly*, Howells was the "high priest of the genteel tradition" in literature and the author of popular novels like *The Rise of Silas Lapham*, a highly praised satire of the *nouveaux riches*. The nation's most noted author became deeply concerned with the case as it went up to the U.S. Supreme Court. When the justices rejected the appeal, Howells sent a letter to the *New York Tribune* explaining why he had joined in the appeal for clemency. The High Court had dismissed the case on formalities, he explained, but it had not ruled on "the propriety of trying for murder men fairly indictable for conspiracy alone"; it had not "approved the principle of punishing men for their frantic opinions, for a crime they were not shown to have committed," and it had not even considered the justice of the death sentence imposed on the men. This last question, wrote Howells, remained for history to judge, and he had no doubt about what the judgment of history would be.[23]

Howells's letter startled people who respected him as the dean of American letters. For speaking out on the Haymarket case, for what his biographer called a "lonely act of courage," the writer would endure a heavy stream of abuse. It was a time, Howells recalled in a letter to Mark Twain, that the public was betrayed by its press, and "no man could safely make himself heard" on behalf of strikers, let alone condemned anarchists.[24]

No other American of comparable stature came forward to appeal for clemency. Indeed, during the whole appeal campaign, an even stronger wave of reaction set in so that Governor Oglesby received more death-to-the-anarchists letters than he did clemency appeals. Even the most influential radical writer and political leader of the time, Henry George, turned down a request to join the clemency effort. Reversing his earlier position as a critic of the trial, George now proclaimed that the conspiracy case had been proved beyond a doubt and that an appeal for clemency was groundless.[25] This turnabout was probably motivated by George's political ambitions. He had nearly been elected mayor of New York City as a radical in the spring of 1886, when he spoiled the chances of an ambitious young Republican office-seeker named Theodore Roo-

Portrait of William Dean Howells on the cover of
Harper's Weekly, *June 19, 1886*

sevelt. The following summer, while George campaigned for state office in New York, Roosevelt attacked his old rival for favoring clemency and insisted that it was in the interest of all Americans that the "Chicago dynamiters" be hanged. Henry George not only lost the election in November 1887; he also lost his reputation as a champion of workers when labor leaders branded him a turncoat.[26]

BY NOVEMBER 7 an estimated 100,000 American citizens had signed the clemency petition. In addition, Oglesby had received numerous messages from Europeans who had reacted with indignation and horror when the Supreme Court refused to overturn the convictions, notably a telegram from London including the names of renowned artists and writers such as William Morris, Annie Besant, Oscar Wilde, George Bernard Shaw, Walter Crane, William Rossetti, Eleanor Marx and Friedrich Engels. The gloom that came over the amnesty movement after the U.S. Supreme Court decision was dispelled by this response and by the support of prominent Chicago citizens such as Lyman Gage.[27]

When Gage learned from Springfield that the governor would commute the sentences of at least four defendants if the most influential men in Chicago asked him to do so, the banker quickly organized a gathering of fifty of the city's most powerful financiers, merchants and industrialists. Henry Demarest Lloyd was asked to represent the Amnesty Association. Gage opened the meeting by bluntly stating the question at hand to his fellow businessmen: Should they see the convicts "choked" or should they ask the governor to show leniency? He then made a well-prepared case for clemency, arguing that the law had been vindicated by the highest courts and need not be reaffirmed by executing the men. In any case, the anarchists were more dangerous as martyrs than as "hostages" the state could hold against further anarchist threats. Even Joe Medill, whose *Tribune* had tried and sentenced the anarchists the day after the bomb exploded, now wrote to the governor that commutation was the best course, so that "no martyrs will be made." Finally, Gage drew upon his unusual understanding of the city's labor movement, explaining that since working people generally believed the capitalists wanted the anarchists executed, a request for clemency would be seen as a generous act that would relieve some of the class hatred poisoning city life.

Gage's arguments seemed to be well received by the businessmen gathered at his bank, particularly by some of the industrialists in the room who would have welcomed a relaxation of the tense relations they endured with their workers. But before a decision was reached, the most powerful businessman in the city, Marshall Field, intervened. He made his own opposition to clemency clear and then, unexpectedly, turned the floor over to a guest he had invited to the meeting. State's Attorney Julius Grinnell rose and held forth at great length. He reiterated his closing arguments to the jury in the Haymarket case and concluded by saying that, since law and order hung in the balance in this case, the death penalty must be imposed.[28] Grinnell's powerful speech won hearty applause and the mood of the meeting shifted. No clemency appeal would be made by the city's leading men. The anarchists would choke.

Henry Lloyd left the meeting dismayed but not devastated. After all, the leaders of the amnesty movement expected no mercy from men like Marshall Field, Philip Armour and Cyrus McCormick, Jr. They were counting instead upon increasing the tide of popular sentiment in favor of saving the anarchists' lives. And that tide was running stronger than ever as petitions of all kinds continued to pour into the Amnesty Association offices. Chief Inspector Bonfield told the press he was disgusted that so many cowardly citizens signed these appeals, and he now feared that none of the men would hang.[29]

The organizers of the mercy campaign held out the hope that Governor Richard Oglesby would find a way to stay the executions of the unrepentant anarchists. These expectations were not unreasonable, said Medill of the *Tribune,* because the governor was a "humane and sympathetic man averse to the shedding of blood," a man who had shown himself more than once to be "the warm friend of the working class." Oglesby was also one of the last Lincoln men in public life, one of the last Radical Republicans holding major office. Moreover, it was rumored that Oglesby was troubled by the conspiracy case made against the anarchists. When he came to Chicago to dedicate Augustus Saint-Gaudens's impressive statue of the martyred president in Lincoln Park, the governor told one amnesty supporter, "If that had been the law during the anti-slavery agitation all of us abolitionists would have been hanged a long time ago."[30]

As all eyes turned to Oglesby, a stunning incident occurred that dashed the petitioners' hopes: four bombs were discovered in Louis Lingg's jail cell. The news of this shocking discovery spread far and wide on November 7, when Sheriff Matson shouted to reporters, "Merciful God! We have been on the brink of a volcano!" The bombs were quite small, but their sheer presence inside a county jail was what counted. "What a revolution in public opinion this will produce," the sheriff exclaimed. Indeed, the discovery immediately put the clemency campaign in jeopardy. Everyone sympathetic to the anarchists assumed the police had placed the bombs under Lingg's bed, but no proof could be found that they were planted there or that they had been sneaked in with the food and gifts prisoners received through the bars. In any case, the shocking news discouraged the leaders of the defense. The *Tribune*'s headline on November 8 said it all: COMMUTATION UNLIKELY. FINDING BOMBS IN LINGG'S CELL CHANGES CASE.[31]

Nevertheless, a large party of Chicagoans assembled at Union Depot the next evening to head for Springfield to plead the anarchists' case before the governor. "It was a heterogeneous committee," according to one reporter, consisting of men and women of many backgrounds. Captain and Mrs. Black were present, along with Attorney Salomon and General Trumbull and Amnesty Association leaders Dr. Salter and Samuel McConnell. A large labor delegation led by George Schilling included many Knights and Federation leaders who opposed the anarchists, as well as Germans of the Central Labor Union who called them brothers. The senior member of the trade union contingent, the battle-worn A. C. Cameron, was also there. The Scotsman had seen the whole pageant unfold, beginning in the years after the Civil War, when he inspired the first eight-hour movement and engineered the first eight-hour law in the land, only to see it defied by employers on May 1, 1867. Now, after the hopes of a second May Day movement had been crushed, it had come to this—a desperate plea for the lives of four workers driven to extremes by two decades of struggle and defeat. Several wives of the defendants, as well as Spies's mother, sister and two brothers, also boarded the train. Even Chicago's famous spiritualist, Cora Richmond, joined the traveling party. In the same article that reported the delegation's departure, the *Tribune* pointed out that the carpenters would begin work on the scaffold outside the jail that night.[32]

Governor Oglesby was overwhelmed by his task of reviewing the

Governor Richard J. Oglesby

8,000-page record of the trial as well as the hundreds of letters and telegrams that arrived every day from all points. On November 9 alone he received 500 messages, half of them for commutation and half of them for execution. For example, the Republican editor of Chicago's leading German daily, *Staats-Zeitung,* wrote a letter that concluded with the comment that the only good anarchist was a dead one. The *Tribune* editorialized sympathetically on Oglesby's dilemma, saying no other amnesty campaign had ever subjected a governor to such an ordeal.[33]

On November 9, the delegation of appellants had swollen to nearly 300 with the arrival of a large contingent from New York City and smaller ones from Detroit and Quincy, Illinois. At 9:30 a.m., with everyone seated in the statehouse and the press gallery filled, Captain Black opened with a legal address. The governor listened judiciously, giving no sign of his feelings. General Trumbull spoke next and appealed to Oglesby "as an old soldier, who has fought with you on the battlefields of the Republic." Then Cora Richmond, speaking for the Amnesty Association, invoked the forgiving spirit of the "martyred Abraham Lincoln." Both petitioners knew, of course, that the governor had been at Lincoln's bedside as he lay dying, that he had been on the funeral train that brought the president's body home to Illinois and that Oglesby was considered "a high priest *ex-officio* in the cult of Lincoln" that flourished in the mid-1880s when several of the late president's associates published affectionate reminiscences. The governor was then presented with an additional petition from the Amnesty Association with 41,000 names of Chicagoans who had signed during the past week, and others from groups in Cleveland, Kansas City and New York City, where 150,000 people signed.[34]

After a short recess, a much larger gathering convened at a nearby hotel, where George Schilling organized a cavalcade of speakers, none more impressive, in the *Tribune*'s view, than Samuel Gompers of New York City's Central Labor Union and the new American Federation of Labor. A Jewish immigrant of small stature, this cigar maker had in less than two decades mastered English in the American idiom and acquired a sophisticated understanding of U.S. history and politics. Although he differed with the condemned men in theory and in practice, Gompers told the governor that they had nevertheless been "fighting for labor from different sides of the house." These condemned men had been done an injustice and should be saved from the gallows as a matter of principle, but, as usual, Gompers assessed the real politics of the situation as well. "If these men are executed it would simply be an impetus to this so-called revolutionary movement which no other on earth can give," he explained. "These men would . . . be looked upon as martyrs. Thousands and thousands of labor men all over the world would consider that these men had been executed because they were standing for free speech and free press." Therefore, Gompers pleaded with Oglesby to use his power to avoid such a calamity. He concluded by saying that if this country could be great and magnanimous enough to grant amnesty to Jefferson Davis, who had committed treason and led a rebellion against the government that cost countless lives, then surely the State of Illinois could do as much for the anarchists.[35]

The governor listened to many other speakers that afternoon and met privately with the overwrought wives and siblings of the defendants; then, after all this, Oglesby responded to a request from the radical editor Joseph Buchanan, who asked for a private meeting. The labor leader requested permission to read letters he carried that had been written by Spies and Parsons. The governor agreed, and behind closed doors Buchanan opened and read Spies's letter first. Spies explained that Engel, Parsons, Fischer and Lingg had not asked for clemency because they could not, in their innocence, accept commutation to a life sentence; and so, they would now die for their stand. Spies hoped to save them with a heroic act of self-sacrifice, saying he was ready to die in their place if it would allow the governor to spare the others. Buchanan, who found the letter difficult to get through, finished by reading these words from Spies: "In the name of the traditions of this country I beg you to prevent a sevenfold murder upon men whose only crime is that they are idealists. If legal murder there must be, let mine suffice." After he finished reading Spies's letter, Buchanan noticed "a deep look of sorrow" on the governor's face and "his eyes were full of tears."[36]

Buchanan then read a letter to the governor from Parsons, which he may have hoped would contain the legally required plea for clemency that Fischer and Fielden had made. Instead, the letter offered a parting shot, an ironic comment on the whole affair. Parsons wrote sarcastically that since his wife and children were also present at the Haymarket the night of the bombing, his own execution should be delayed so that they too could be arrested, tried and executed with him. Hearing this, Oglesby brought his hands to his face and cried, "Oh my God, this is terrible!"

Buchanan, who knew how bitter Parsons had become, was nonetheless thunderstruck and nearly burst into tears.[37]

After this long emotional day, unprecedented in appeals process history, the delegations headed home, and Oglesby retired to ponder his decision. On the afternoon of November 10, while he deliberated over the case, the governor received the stunning news from Chicago that Louis Lingg had exploded a dynamite cap in his mouth that morning and lay dying in the county jail. Wild speculation circulated through the city that the police had assassinated Lingg. After all, the prisoner had been removed from the others after the jailers discovered bombs in his cell. Who knew what really happened to Lingg? With his face blown apart, the victim could not utter a word of explanation in his last hours. Since the police were certain that one of Lingg's bombs slaughtered their fellow officers on May 4, they certainly had motive to seek revenge against the "anarchist tiger."

However, most people, including many anarchists, believed that Lingg desperately wanted to take his own life before the state he hated could do it. But if the police did not assassinate Lingg, how did he kill himself? The mystery of how the prisoner got hold of a cigar with a fulminating cap inside remained unsolved. Later on, a story circulated indicating that the explosive had been passed to him by a comrade, the anarchist Dyer Lum, who said so in a letter that became known after his death. Lum had expressed a deep admiration for his young German comrade as a devoted and fearless anarchist who never allowed himself the false hope of salvation from the death that awaited him. And so Lum would have endorsed the *Tribune*'s comment that Louis Lingg had "eluded the disgrace of the hangman's noose and the ignominy of a public execution." Fischer, Engel and Parsons told reporters they envied him.[38]

Two hours after receiving the shocking news of the explosion in Lingg's cell, Oglesby announced his decision. The governor commuted to life imprisonment the sentences of Fielden and Schwab, who had requested this in writing, and he upheld the death sentences for Parsons, Spies, Fischer and Engel, who had not begged for mercy. After he received the news from the governor, Captain Black sent a doleful telegraph message back to his office in Chicago, where the anarchists' loved ones had gathered together to share their desperate hopes and their worst fears.

Louis Lingg

THE FOUR CONDEMNED MEN on death row in Chicago were not surprised by the governor's decision; they had long expected it and prepared for it. Parsons even chose poems to recite for the occasion, one being John Greenleaf Whittier's "The Reformer," in which the writer proclaimed that whether a man died "on the gallows high" or on the battlefield, the noblest place a man could die was a place where he died for his fellow man.[39]

A few women were allowed to visit the jail on the afternoon of November 10: Engel's daughter Mary, Nina Van Zandt Spies and Adolph Fischer's "delicate little wife," Johanna, now evoked pity from onlookers, according to one reporter. But Lucy Parsons was denied entry to see Albert because she had reportedly acted deranged. Unable to see his loved ones for the last time, Parsons wrote Albert, Jr., and Lulu a letter to be read on the first anniversary of his death. In it, he implored them to love, honor and obey their mother, "the grandest noblest of women," and to read his message each recurring year in "remembrance of he who dies not alone for you but for the children yet unborn."[40]

After the night shift arrived for the death watch, Lingg's body was packed in ice and placed in a coffin. A clergyman made the rounds. The Protestant minister heard no confessions, although Spies freely talked with him about life and death. Then the lamps went down and death row was dark and silent. All remained quiet until midnight, when Parsons began to sing one of his favorite songs, "Annie Laurie." The jailers reported "there was in his tone a lonesome melancholy" as he sang the first stanza with the Scottish inflection:

> *Max Welton's braes are bonnie,*
> *Where early fa's the dew,*
> *And 'twas there that Annie Laurie*
> *Gave me her promise true,*
> *Gave me her promise true,*
> *That ne'er forgot shall be:*
> *And for Bonnie Annie Laurie*
> *I'd lay me doon and dee.*[41]

In the second verse, Albert Parsons's voice wavered and broke, the jailers said, and he seemed "cast down." After regaining his composure, he talked with them through the midnight hour. He told them how affected he felt about Spies leaving his new wife a widow and how worried Fischer was about the fate of his young and feeble wife. Parsons told his guards that he rejoiced that the wife he left behind was lionhearted and that his children were too young to "keenly feel bereavement." And then, at about one o'clock, he said to his guards, "I will sing you a song, one born as a battle cry in France and now accepted as the hymn of revolution the world over." As if to give them some encouragement, he sang in a low voice the English words of "La Marseillaise," "which the guards commended as both inspiring and well performed." Parsons slept little the rest of the night. Instead, "he chatted with the guards on the death watch and furnished them each with his autograph."[42]

The next morning at eight o'clock Parsons penned a letter to his friend Dyer Lum. "The guard has just awakened me. I have washed my face and drank a cup of coffee. The doctor asked me if I wanted stimulants. I said no. The dear boys, Engel, Fischer and Spies, saluted me with firm voices. Well, my dear old comrade, the hour draws near. Caesar kept me awake last night with the noise, the music of the hammer and saw erecting his throne—my scaffold." Yet Parsons had learned one good thing from the sheriff: the state would not dispose of his body secretly. Sheriff Matson had assured him that his remains would be sent to Lucy at the home address he gave to his jailers.[43]

On the eve of hanging day "an unbearable anxiety gripped Chicago," because citizens believed the execution would provoke an all-out anarchist attack on the courthouse and other targets. Newspaper men poured into the city from far and wide to file reports from the tension-packed city. When November 11 dawned, hundreds of reporters shivered in the dim morning air waiting to enter the courthouse. "To the spectacle that on the morning of that 11th of November Chicago presented, there has been no parallel in any American city in the time of peace," wrote *New York World* reporter Charles Edward Russell as he re-created the scene many years later. Ropes extended for one block around the courthouse and all traffic was blocked. "The jail itself was guarded like a precarious outpost in a critical battle. Around it lines of policemen were drawn; from every window policemen looked forth, rifles in hand; the roof was black with policemen. The display of force was overpowering."[44]

At six o'clock in the morning the reporters were admitted. They stood in one room, all 200 of them, cooped up while disturbing rumors played on their nerves. One morning extra edition was passed around reporting that the jail had been mined by the anarchists, who had buried great stores of dynamite beneath it, and that, at the moment of the hanging, the whole building would explode. The nervous tension rose to such a pitch that two of the reporters, tried and experienced men, turned sick and faint and had to be assisted to leave the room. "In all my experience this was the only occasion on which a reporter flinched from duty, however trying; but it is hard now," Russell wrote in 1914, "to understand the tremendous infectional panic that had seized upon the city and had its storm center at that jail."[45]

None of the relatives or friends of the four anarchists were allowed to witness the execution that day, so they had bid them goodbye the evening before. Because Lucy Parsons had been denied access to the jail, she set out the morning of the hanging day determined to see Albert one last time. After rising early, she put on a handmade dress of dark cloth and wound a long black veil of crepe around her face and over her hat; and then she hurried downtown with Albert, Jr., and Lulu. At the Amnesty Association office, she met Lizzie Holmes, who accompanied her to the fortified courthouse. Never afraid to confront the police, the women approached the line and asked to be admitted to the jail, but at every point the women and children were told to move on. Boiling with anger and frustration, Lucy screamed, "Oh, you murderous villains! You forbid me to see my husband, whom you are about to kill and not let him take a last look at his children, whom you are about to make orphans." In a rage she told the officers she had no bombs with her but that she could get them and use them if she wanted to. At this she was arrested along with Lizzie and the two children; they were put in a patrol wagon and driven off to Captain Schaack's Chicago Avenue Station, where a matron strip-searched the women and children, looking for weapons and bombs.[46]

AT THE COURTHOUSE and all around it, huge crowds filled the streets. At 10:55 a.m., 250 newspapermen, the 12 jurymen and other selected wit-

"The Execution"

nesses filed quickly through a dark passage under the gallows and into a corridor behind the courthouse. The bailiff begged the reporters not to make a rush out of the corridor when the drop fell, but to wait decently and in order. There they sat for the next hour and waited. As noon approached, their conversations turned to whispers. The witnesses fell silent when, according to one observer, "the tramp, tramp of men's footsteps was heard resounding from the central corridor, and the crowd in front of the gallows knew the condemned men had begun the march of death." Then all eyes turned toward the screen at the edge of the gallows platform that hid the four anarchists.[47]

At this point the news reporters, all seasoned witnesses of public hangings, made notes that would become nearly rhapsodic descriptions of the scene that unfolded after the first man stepped from behind the screen. "With a steady, unfaltering step a white robed figure stepped out . . . and stood upon the drop. It was August Spies. It was evident that his hands were firmly bound behind him beneath his snowy shroud." He walked across the platform to the left side, where he stood under the dangling noose that reached down to his breast. His face, said a *Daily News* reporter, was very pale, his looks solemn, his expression melancholy, yet "at the same time dignified." He glanced quickly at the noose and then gazed out on the hundreds of faces turned up to him. Fischer and Engel followed him and took their places on the line. Last came Parsons, who straightened himself before the fourth noose and, "as he did so, turned his big gray eyes upon the crowd below with such a look of awful reproach and sadness as it would not fail to strike the innermost chord of the hardest-heart there," wrote one observer. "It was a look never to be forgotten."[48]

The bailiff then fastened leather straps around the ankles of the four men, who all stood straight and remained quiet. Guards first placed a noose around Spies's neck, and when the rope caught on his right ear, he deftly shook his head so that it fell down around his neck. When the bailiff approached Adolph Fischer, "he threw back his head and bared his long muscular neck by the movement." Then he laughingly whispered some words in Spies's ear while Engel "smiled down at the crowd" and said something to his guard, "evidently some word of peace" that seemed to affect the officer. Parsons, however, looked angrily down at the witnesses.

The anarchists seemed to be choreographing their own final scene on the stage of life. They certainly planned to make the most of the ritual

moment when they could speak their last words from the gallows platform. But the bailiff, perhaps unnerved by their behavior, broke with tradition and immediately started putting shrouds over their heads as if to
block their words. In a few moments all four men stood upon the scaffold
clad from head to toe in pure white robes. The executioner took up his ax
and was poised to cut the cords that would trip all four trapdoors and
send the men to their doom. As the hangman paused, awaiting the order,
a "mournful solemn voice sounded" from the platform. It was Spies
speaking from behind his muslin shroud. His words would become his
epitaph. "The time will come," he said, "when our silence will be more
powerful than the voices you strangle today." Emboldened by this declaration, George Engel shouted in German, "Hurrah for anarchy!" and
Adolph Fischer proclaimed, "This is the happiest day of my life."

Then Parsons spoke from behind his mask, sounding sadder than the
others: "May I be allowed to speak?" he beseeched the sheriff. "Oh, men
of America! May I be allowed the privilege of speech even at the last
moment? Harken to the voice of the people," he was saying when the executioner cut the cord and the trapdoors snapped open with a crash, leaving four men dangling at the ends of ropes.[49]

The *Tribune*'s man on the scene spared nothing in his account of what
he saw when the floorboards shot open and the bodies fell 4 feet down.
"The light form of Parsons' body seemed to bound upward" much more
than those of the heavier men and, after a few minutes, his shrouded figure "settled into almost perfect quiet," as did that of Engel. Then, "all
eyes were directed to that of Spies, which was writhing horribly" as his
shoulders twisted, his chest heaved and his legs "drew up to his chest
and straightened out again and again" as he strangled to death. This
scene continued for several minutes as physicians kept checking the
pulse of each man. Seven and a half minutes after the bodies fell, the last
man alive, Adolph Fischer, was declared dead.

None of the four men died from a broken neck, the form of death that
was supposed to result from a state hanging. Instead, the convicts all
strangled to death during what seemed to those present like a terribly
long period of agony.[50] "The spectators of the hanging, many of whom
were visibly affected by the scene, remained seated even after life had
been declared extinct in each dangling figure," the *Daily News* remarked. "As the white forms hung in startling relief against the dark
background of the wall behind the scaffold the sight was more ghastly
than at any previous stage of the grim proceedings." The spectators

remained seated for some time, and the sheriff twice had to tell them to leave. Among the witnesses, the *Tribune* reported, the general mood seemed to be "one of pity and regret rather than exultation."[51]

While the coroners placed each body in a pine coffin, Lucy and her children remained behind bars in the Chicago Avenue Station, what she called "Captain Schaack's Bastille." Two hours after the execution, Lucy Parsons was told that her husband was dead and she could leave and take her children home.[52]

BY THIS TIME, runners had carried word of the deaths to the Western Union telegraph office and to newspaper row. The news was posted on billboards that had been placed all over the city. At the luxurious Palmer House Hotel the city's wealthiest citizens gathered after lunch to read this notice: "Trap fell. Spies, Parsons, Fischer, and Engle [*sic*] expiate their crime and the law is vindicated." One reporter described a palpable feeling of relief among downtown people, because the execution had occurred without a single hand being raised in violent protest.[53]

That afternoon the attorney Moses Salomon arrived at the jail with three union representatives to claim the bodies and carry the remains of the men to the undertakers. Barred from witnessing the execution, comrades and friends gathered to escort the five coffins back to the North Side. A large throng of mourners followed the remains of Engel and Lingg to an undertaker's parlor, where a crowd of 1,000 formed waiting to view the bodies. At the home of August Spies's mother a crowd of women and children lined the walk in front, many of them in tears, while at the Parsonses' flat nearby, Lucy was being attended to by other women after she fainted. One observer said that "the fearless wife of Parsons had been absolutely prostrated by the violence of her emotions" and that, when she regained consciousness, "she raved and moaned in a most pitiable manner." One of her comrades, Frank Stauber, told the journalist he had seen grief-stricken people before, "but never in my life have I seen such grief. I am actually afraid the woman is dying."[54]

Friends and relatives, advocates and supporters of the defendants had been preparing themselves for the deaths of the condemned men, but on the afternoon of November 11 they still found themselves uncontrollably distraught over the news. Even those in faraway cities were deeply affected.

From Boston, William Dean Howells wrote of his "helpless feeling of grief and rage" over the "civic murder" committed in Chicago. "[T]his Republic has killed five men for their opinions," he told his father. Howells believed the executions dishonored the nation and the memory of Abraham Lincoln, whose campaign biography Howells had written in 1860. After years of optimistic contentment with the progress of American civilization and belief in "its ability to come out all right in the end," the writer now felt the nation's story was "coming out all wrong in the end." The death of the anarchists in Chicago shattered his faith in the triumph of Lincoln's ideal republic, with malice toward none and charity for all.[55]

In New York City many Jewish working people in the tenement houses and clothing shops of the Lower East Side were palpably disturbed by the news that four innocent men, three of them immigrants, had died on the gallows in a land to which these foreigners had come seeking freedom and justice. "Heartbroken, we walked for days like mourners," the Jewish socialist Abraham Cahan recalled. The distress of these immigrant workers deepened, he reported, when they realized how many Americans applauded the verdict and its execution.[56]

In Chicago the defenders were too devastated to speak in public or to put their feelings on paper. Joseph Buchanan later described seeking a quiet refuge from the immense throng that crowded the downtown streets, and waiting in a hotel lobby where a clerk read minute-by-minute accounts from a ticker tape of the death walk, the hoods and nooses being adjusted, the last words uttered. Buchanan watched the long hand on a clock as it moved to the fateful hour of noon; when it struck twelve, he broke down sobbing over an event that would haunt him for the rest of his life. After passing "a night of horrors" as he agonized over the impending executions, Sam Gompers spent the afternoon of November 11 meandering through Chicago's streets, utterly depressed by the hangings and his failed efforts to win clemency for those now deceased. Captain William Black's rage over the executions was mixed with a gnawing sense of guilt over Parsons's fate. If he had not called the fugitive to return from Wisconsin and stand trial with the others, he might still be alive. Henry Demarest Lloyd, who was as disturbed as anyone on the defense team, wrote a poem dedicated to Spies and Parsons. That night, as tears flowed, his wife, Jessie, and his children joined Lloyd in singing his elegiac words to the tune of "Annie Laurie."[57]

No one was closer to Parsons than George Schilling, who spoke with him in Market Square the night the great uprising began in 1877, campaigned with him as a socialist candidate and joined him in founding the "old 400" assembly of the Knights. Schilling quarreled with Parsons over the anarchists' militant demands and violent words, but he loved and admired the charismatic Texan, and no one cared more about saving him and his comrades than Schilling did; no one, outside the families of the condemned men, bore a greater emotional strain during the long ordeal. As a result, Schilling was deeply shaken and thoroughly embittered by the hangings. Two years passed before he could gain some perspective on the event the anarchists would call Black Friday. "This 11th of November, 1887, has passed into history, and marks the chief tragedy of the closing years of the 19th century," he wrote. "The trial of Parsons, Spies, *et al* is over and the verdict of the jury executed, but the trial of judgment is still going on."[58]

Chapter Sixteen

The Judgment of History

NOVEMBER 12, 1887–NOVEMBER 11, 1899

SOON AFTER THE EXECUTION order arrived in Chicago, comrades of the condemned men began preparing for a funeral march and burial to take place on Sunday, November 13. Family members and friends planned simple wakes on Saturday for the deceased anarchists at three locations along Milwaukee Avenue; they were unprepared for the public response that came on that morning. At eight o'clock hundreds of people lined up along the street in front of the flat Lucy Parsons had rented on Milwaukee Avenue. All day people filed through the little living room to gaze on Albert Parsons's colorless face with the faint smile the undertaker had put on his lips. At times Lucy burst out of her room, weeping uncontrollably and clinging to Lizzie Holmes for support. By the time William Holmes finally closed the Parsonses' door at 11:30 p.m., 10,000 people had filed through the parlor to pay their last respects.[1]

A similar scene unfolded upstairs in the toy shop on Milwaukee Avenue where George Engel's body lay in a parlor next to Louis Lingg's corpse, with its poorly repaired face. During the day and evening 6,000 people viewed the remains. Even larger crowds pressed into Aurora Turner Hall, where August Spies lay in state surrounded by an edgy-looking honor guard of German trade unionists and militiamen.

The next morning, a clear, cold Sunday, elaborate funeral plans were put in motion, but within the strict limits set by Mayor John A. Roche, who prohibited speeches, songs and banners or "any demonstration of a public character." The bands accompanying the funeral march could play only dirges.

The procession began at the home of August Spies's mother. His coffin was loaded onto a carriage, which then proceeded down Milwaukee Avenue, stopping at the homes of the other anarchists, where other carriages were loaded with their remains. Then the cortege, carrying five red-draped coffins, rolled away to the sound of several brass bands playing somber tunes; the carriages were followed by a long line of 6,000 people who moved slowly down Milwaukee Avenue to the measured beat of muffled drums.

Along the parade route the streets and sidewalks were thronged with thousands of men, women and children; others looked out of windows or stood on barrels. Some of them wore red and black ribbons as an expression of sympathy. The funeral procession grew even larger as it left the immigrant North Side and headed downtown to the railroad depot, where mourners would board a long funeral train bound for Waldheim Cemetery, a nondenominational graveyard in the German town of Forest Park. Along the way even thicker crowds, estimated at 200,000 overall, packed the sidewalks to observe the cortege.[2]

After the procession turned off Milwaukee Avenue and headed down Desplaines Street, it passed within a block of the deadly spot where so many had fallen on May 4 of the previous year; it then proceeded east on Lake Street past Zepf's Hall and Grief's Hall, where portraits of the dead anarchists draped in mourning hung on the walls. At this point one of the bands broke the mayor's rule and burst into the melody of "Annie Laurie" in Parsons's honor. Another band struck up "La Marseillaise" as it passed Grief's Hall. More than two decades later, the reporter Charles Edward Russell vividly recalled the somber scenes of that Sunday funeral procession. The black hearses, the marching thousands and the miles and miles of streets packed with silent mourners—all left him with the impression that death had finally conferred amnesty on the anarchists.[3]

Chicagoans had never witnessed such a massive public funeral. The crowds exceeded even those that had gathered to march behind Lincoln's coffin on May 1, 1865. Then, however, Chicago's citizens had walked together in common front, unified in their grief. Now, on November 13, 1887, one class of people grieved while another gave thanks for the moral judgment rendered on the gallows, as Chicagoans divided into separate spheres of sentiment determined largely by where they lived and worked and by how well they spoke English.

The sun was low by the time the procession wended its way into Waldheim Cemetery. After the five caskets had been lowered into the ground, Captain William Black offered a traditional eulogy—one that would be fondly remembered by the dead men's sympathizers and bitterly denounced by their prosecutors. "They were called Anarchists," said

Black. "They were painted and presented to the world as men loving violence, riot and bloodshed for their own sake. Nothing could be further from the truth. They were men who loved peace, men of gentle instincts, men of gracious tenderness of heart, loved by those who knew them, trusted by those who came to know the loyalty and purity of their lives." They had lived for a revolution that would create a new society based on cooperation instead of coercion. Black said he did not know if such a society was possible in America, but he did know that through the ages poets, philosophers and Christian believers had lived for the day when righteousness would reign on the earth, and when sin and selfishness would come to an end.[4]

AS THE NEWS of the executions spread around the world in the weekend newspapers, those who had followed the trial reacted with extreme emotions, even though they had suspected for weeks that the anarchists would die. The defendants had gained widespread admiration in the eyes of European workers and radical intellectuals by maintaining their innocence and refusing to renounce their beliefs, even to save their lives. Their highly publicized hangings seemed to many Europeans to be nothing more than a ferocious attempt by the state to silence the strongest voices of dissent in America.[5]

In cities all over the United States and in other nations, workers expressed their rage at what seemed to them a historic atrocity. At a gathering of laborers in Havana, speakers condemned the executioners, and organizers collected $955 to aid the anarchists' family members. In Barcelona, artisans and sailors met in their little *centros* and lit candles around the images of *los mártiri*.[6] In Boston a large crowd gathered in New Era Hall to hear a mournful address by the secretary of the Knights of Labor, the esteemed George McNeill, who had helped found the first eight-hour movement in 1863. The white-haired philosopher of labor reform told his depressed followers that the hanging of the anarchists in Chicago was the act of desperate, unthinking men and that it would not remedy the evil of social inequity or wash out the stain of anarchy from the nation's political fabric. In Newark, New Jersey, Reverend Hugh O. Pentecost, one of the few clergymen to speak out against the execution, told his congregation that it was "one of the most unjust and cruel acts ever perpetrated by organized government—immoral and illegal."[7] And in Rochester, New York, a young Russian clothing worker named Emma

Goldman nearly became deranged when she heard news of "the terrible thing everyone feared, yet hoped would not happen." She had learned about the Knights of Labor, the eight-hour day and the Haymarket anarchists from other Russian Jews during her first year in America, 1886. After sewing garments in a factory for ten hours a day, she devoured every word on anarchism she could find and closely followed news of the Haymarket defendants during and after the trial.[8]

Devastated by the news at first, the seventeen-year-old immigrant found that the "martyrs' ordeal" implanted "something new and wonderful" in her soul, "a determination to dedicate myself to the memory of my martyred comrades, to make known to the world their beautiful lives and heroic death." From then on, she would honor November 11, 1887, as the day of her "spiritual birth." After she plunged into the anarchist and labor movements in the next years, Emma Goldman met hundreds of other people whose lives were also changed by the executions on Black Friday.[9] For example, there was Abraham Bisno, a cloak maker living in Chicago's Russian-Jewish colony, who knew nothing about the anarchists until he and his fellow strikers were beaten by the police on May 5, the day of the first arrests. In the next days and months he frequently discussed the case with other workers, while studying all the evidence he could find and learning in the process to lecture on social questions and to lead in organizing unions among his people.[10]

Mary Harris Jones, another Chicago resident, also followed the trial closely and attended the funeral. The widowed dressmaker heard the anarchists speak at Knights of Labor assemblies and at lakefront rallies, where she listened to what Parsons and Spies, "those teachers of the new order, had to say to workers." And though she was opposed to their violent message, Jones was deeply affected by their execution and by their immense funeral procession with thousands of wage earners marching behind their hearses, not because they were anarchists but because they were regarded as soldiers who sacrificed their lives in the workers' struggle. Many years later, after Mother Jones gained renown, she recalled that time in Chicago. "Those were the days of sacrifice for the cause of labor," she wrote. "Those were the days of the martyrs and the saints."[11]

Far away, in a mining camp at Rebel Creek, Nevada, high in the mountains, young Bill Haywood read about the hangings in a Knights of Labor paper. He called it a turning point in his life, a moment when he became entranced with the lives and speeches of Albert Parsons and August Spies. In the years that followed, no one did more to translate the words of Parsons and Spies into action than William D. Haywood did when he became the founder and notorious leader of the Industrial Workers of the World, a twentieth-century manifestation of the "Chicago idea."[12]

While some young workers like Emma Goldman and Bill Haywood were inspired by the Haymarket martyrs, most trade union leaders, even those who had fought to win clemency for the anarchists, were utterly dismayed by how much damage the anarchist case had caused. Samuel Gompers said the bomb thrown in the Haymarket not only killed policemen, it killed the eight-hour movement and struck at the foundations of the new house of labor he was constructing as head of the new American Federation of Labor. A decade later Gompers and his followers found ways to revive unionism and re-create a more moderate eight-hour campaign, but for Terence Powderly and the Knights of Labor there would be no recovery. Indeed, for visionary workers and labor reformers inspired by the Knights and the Great Upheaval, Haymarket was an unmitigated disaster; it sounded a death knell for the great hopes they shared in the spring of 1886 when they imagined their movement to be on the brink of achieving a new cooperative social order that would replace the wage system.[13]

A few American intellectuals were radicalized by the events and found themselves pulled closer to the labor movement, though the process was a painful one. H. C. Adams, a young economics professor at Cornell University, was one of the few academics who criticized the Chicago trial. The professor denounced the anarchists as vile madmen who had no understanding of how democracy worked, but he also insisted that even their incendiary speeches needed protection. If freedom of expression was denied to dissenters, he reasoned, even law-abiding protesters might turn to violence. Adams did not stop at this: he even charged that industrialists were using the anarchist hysteria to stigmatize the socially constructive proposals made by the Knights of Labor. The New York newspapers printed sensational accounts of Adams's remarks, and a Cornell benefactor, the wealthy lumber king Henry Sage, demanded the professor's ouster. The university trustees met in secret and agreed that the offensive professor Adams had to go. In the aftermath of Haymarket, even defense of the First Amendment seemed threatening. Dr. Adams took his medicine and decided economists had better not speak out against social injustice.[14]

Adams's case was one of several indicating that the Haymarket bomb marked a decisive event in the history of American free speech. After the Civil War, freedom of expression was denied to black citizens in the South, but other Americans were often able to express extreme opinions in speeches and writings without interference. This had been the case in Chicago, where Mayor Harrison had allowed the anarchists to make violent speeches on a regular basis. While some latitude prevailed for free speech during the Gilded Age, no one seriously examined the philosophical and political principles that underlay constitutional guarantees of liberty. As a result, legal precedent and tradition counted for little when the Haymarket affair precipitated a sharp turn against toleration for citizens expressing extreme opinions and for those, like Professor H. C. Adams, who defended their right to do so.[15]

Henry Demarest Lloyd was one of the only prominent journalists to denounce the prosecution of the Haymarket case, and he paid a price for it. Disinherited by his father-in-law, *Tribune* co-owner William Bross, shut out of the paper for good and ostracized by his friends, Lloyd did not begin writing and speaking again until 1890, when he turned his formidable talents to producing a series of moral attacks on the "cannibals of competition, tyrants of monopoly, devourers of men, women and children," culminating in the publication of his *Wealth Against Commonwealth*, an exposé of John D. Rockefeller's Standard Oil Company, the first influential muckraking effort of the progressive era.[16]

Lloyd's ostracism came at a repressive time in Chicago life. As a result of the red scare, the trial and the hangings, said the Illinois writer Edgar Lee Masters, the city's spiritual and civic life was "fouled" as "Hate and Fear and Revenge stalked about." Outspoken journalists and public figures like Lloyd had been silenced; the editors of the big newspapers who celebrated the anarchists' executions had won, but they too were fearful, and walked around the city with armed guards.[17]

Only a few clergymen, like Hugh Pentecost in Newark, responded to the events of 1886 and 1887 by criticizing the use of capital punishment and by urging acts of Christian charity and moral reform to address the social evils that bred anarchism. The Great Upheaval of 1886, the bombing and the red scare that followed traumatized many clergymen and churchgoers, especially native Protestants, who saw these events not as a crisis that called for moral reform, but as the opening scene in a doomsday scenario for the American city. The Haymarket affair exacerbated the hostility to organized labor that already existed in Protestant churches, while it also helped to push many middle-class people and their ministers out of the cities and into streetcar suburbs, where they could escape the lava of a social volcano that seemed ready to blow again at any time.[18]

UNDER THESE CIRCUMSTANCES, Chicago's dissenting voices remained quiet, and public discourse was dominated by those who celebrated the executions of the anarchists and venerated the memory of the police who died in the bombing and the shooting. A lavish history of the Chicago police appeared in 1887, supported by contributions from scores of businesses. The book, written in a vivid style by a *Daily News* reporter, John J. Flinn, featured heroic sketches of Inspector Bonfield, Captain Schaack and their brave men, along with a narrative of the strikes and riots that culminated in the Haymarket bombing, when the department "attracted the attention of all Christendom."[19] George McLean's *The Rise and Fall of Anarchy,* published in 1888, another handsome volume with lifelike drawings of all the Haymarket participants, offered a comprehensive account of events leading to the bombing and of the trial and executions that followed. The author left no doubt about the moral of the story. After saluting the courageous policemen who fell in defense of American freedom, McLean turned his pen to the "hideous cruel monsters" responsible for their "cold blooded massacre"—an act of treachery unparalleled in history.[20]

A year later came the publication of Captain Michael Schaack's enormous book *Anarchy and Anarchists: A History of the Red Terror and the Social Revolution in America and Europe.* Composed largely by two professional writers, the volume offered a sweeping history of revolutionary activity in Europe beginning with the French Revolution, all of which is seen as prologue to the events in Chicago. The title page, faced by a heroic portrait of Schaack, is followed by extensive documentation of the "Haymarket conspiracy" and sensational reports of Schaack's undercover men, along with vivid police photos of bombs, fuses, guns, cartoon-like drawings of anarchists and a moving group portrait of the slain policemen. The seven official "Haymarket martyrs" were pictured with an eighth officer who was thought to have died later of wounds he sustained on May 4, 1886. Although the funerals of the dead patrolmen were barely noticed in the press at the time, Schaack's book reminded Americans that these men were "as worthy as the heroes of a hundred military battles."[21]

Soon after the riot, Joseph Medill, publisher of the *Chicago Tribune*, started a fund drive to erect a statue in the Haymarket to honor the fallen police officers. Donations came slowly at first, but eventually businessmen's clubs raised enough funds to pay for a statue—a bronze figure of a policeman holding his right hand high. The model was Officer Thomas Birmingham, a statuesque Irish patrolman who had marched into the square that night. The monument was dedicated in somber ceremonies on Memorial Day of 1889, when speakers likened the slain officers to the Civil War heroes who defended the nation against the southern rebels.[22]

The police statue in Haymarket Square symbolized more than heroic sacrifice, however. The bronzed officer mounted on its stone base also stood for a victory of the forces of law and order, not simply over anar-

Police statue in Haymarket Square, 1892

chists who used public spaces so freely and spoke so defiantly of government, but also over the larger forces of disorder generated by the pitch and roll of an immigrant sea that had flooded urban America. A rough-and-tumble democracy had flourished in many cities since the age of Jackson, and had brought immigrant workingmen, and even some workingwomen, into the streets on various ceremonious and sometimes riotous occasions. Now, after the Great Upheaval and the Haymarket affair, the courts and the police would severely restrict urban workers' use of public spaces as arenas for self-expression and organization.[23]

Yet, for all the accolades Chicago's policemen received, they still seemed inadequate to the task of defending the city against what business elites feared would be the next mass insurgency. Marshall Field convinced members of the elite Commercial Club that they needed a U.S. Army fort close to the city, instead of a thousand miles away. While the anarchists awaited their fate in the jailhouse, the club raised money to buy 632 acres of land just thirty miles north of the city; its leaders then persuaded the secretary of the army to construct such a fort on this site. In addition, Field and his associates hired the famous architects Daniel H. Burnham and John W. Root to design and build a massive armory in the city to guard their neighborhoods and businesses. Within a few years the imposing First Regiment Armory at 16th Street and Michigan Avenue rose like a stone monster with a huge open mouth, poised between the downtown business district and the insurgent Southwest Side.[24]

While initiatives by the forces of law and order reassured an anxious bourgeoisie, they also heated up feelings of resentment that bubbled under the surface of plebeian life in Chicago. Labor leaders worried about the construction of military armories and criticized the use of militiamen to break strikes; some even urged their members not to join the National Guard. A gnawing fear spread among trade unionists that the nation's armed forces would be used to protect employers' interests, not to defend workers' liberties.[25]

Simmering working-class antipathy to the police also began to reach a boiling point. That sentiment spilled out when Chicago's *Knights of Labor* newspaper denounced the newly dedicated police statue in the Haymarket for honoring a police department its editor branded "the most vicious and corrupt the country has ever known." The paper was referring not only to the police conduct in the Haymarket affair, but to a scandal that broke in 1889 when Captain Schaack was removed from the Chicago police force as a result of wrongdoing. The case also involved Inspector

John Bonfield and two other commanders of the divisions that marched into the Haymarket on May 4. The *Chicago Times* revealed that the officers had been taking money from saloonkeepers and prostitutes, and had been selling items taken from arrested citizens, including some jewelry Louis Lingg had left to his sweetheart. When Bonfield reacted by arresting the *Times*'s editors and attempting to shut down the newspaper, the public outcry was enormous. As a result, the mayor was compelled to remove the heroes of Haymarket Square from the police force. A short time later, former superintendent Ebersold revealed that Schaack had "tried to keep things stirred up" in May of 1886 and "wanted to find bombs everywhere." He even sent out men to organize fake anarchist groups to keep the pot boiling. It is not clear how Schaack's demise affected the sales of his sensational book, *Anarchy and Anarchists*, but he retained many admirers in Chicago, including one editor who called his firing a triumph for the anarchists.[26]

Even though working-class demonstrators lost much of the freedom they had enjoyed to gather in streets and public places after 1886, freedom of the press was suspended only for a brief time. Issues of the anarchist *Alarm* reappeared during the trial, and the *Arbeiter-Zeitung* resumed publication, although the German daily never regained the mass circulation it had achieved in August Spies's day. In addition, anarchists produced and disseminated printed works memorializing the martyrs, including *The Autobiographies of the Haymarket Martyrs* and *The Famous Speeches of the Eight Haymarket Anarchists*, first published in 1886. The following year, Lucy Parsons issued a collection of Albert's prison writings on anarchism, and then in 1889 she edited *The Life of Albert R. Parsons*, which became a sacred text for the party of remembrance and a conversion experience for many readers unfamiliar with the case. Introduced by George Schilling, the volume was filled with Parsons's speeches and articles, an autobiographical essay and ephemera, most memorably the letters he wrote to his children just before his death and to Schilling recalling his thrilling days as a militant in the battle for black equality in bloody Texas.[27] *The Life of Albert R. Parsons*, along with the anarchists' autobiographies, typified the sort of personal narratives that had exerted a hold on the popular mind throughout the nineteenth century. Such heartfelt stories of tramps and beggars, former slaves and former prisoners and other lost souls, offered truthful, "unvarnished" accounts that presented compelling alternatives to official accounts and descriptions of reality.[28]

This literature was reproduced and translated to keep the anarchists' memory alive in the minds of workers around the world, but it was also aimed at countering, indeed subverting, the official accounts of the Haymarket story that enjoyed much wider circulation. In these texts the condemned men appeared as martyrs who died for freedom and democracy, while their state prosecutors are seen as relying not upon truth and virtue, but upon deception and intimidation.[29] The autobiographies and speeches of the Chicago anarchists were translated into several languages and reprinted numerous times over the next few decades, when they were interpreted by many readers here and in other lands as stories that confirmed their suspicions that the United States was not a truly free country.[30]

Lucy Parsons and the small company of anarchists who kept this literature in circulation did not, however, rely on the printed word alone. Lucy, for one, took to the road as often as she could in her own relentless and exhausting campaign to exonerate the anarchists and to venerate the life of her husband. She even embarked on a trip after she lost her daughter, Lulu, who died of lymphoma and whose body was placed in an unmarked grave near her father's tomb. She pressed on with her work even though she was criticized by socialists, excoriated by the mainstream press and harassed by the police, especially in Chicago, where the authorities seemed obsessed with the activities of this "determined negress."[31]

A pariah in her own land, Lucy was treated as a celebrity when she traveled to the British Isles on a speaking tour in 1888. "The heroic widow" of Albert Parsons was described by one English socialist as a "woman of American Indian origin, of striking beauty." Having invented a purely native identity for herself, she spoke to a London meeting as "a genuine American," one whose ancestors were indigenous people waiting to repel the invaders when they arrived from Spain. Lucy's violent speeches alienated some socialists, but her tour excited others and created an upsurge of support for anarchism in England.[32]

WILLIAM MORRIS'S SOCIALIST LEAGUE had prepared the way for the famous Mrs. Parsons by distributing a pamphlet on the anarchist case and printing an edition of *The Autobiographies of the Haymarket Martyrs*. In his London publication *Commonweal*, Morris had previously reported on the entire trial and appeal process, which he described as a travesty of justice. When news of the executions reached England, he wrote that the Haymarket case exhibited "the spirit of cold cruelty, heartless and careless at once, which is one of the most noticeable characteristics of American commercialism." By contrast, the editors of the London *Times* had praised the Chicago police and their use of armed force on the streets and suggested British police might well follow their example, and then cheered the death sentence when it was announced.[33]

On November 13, 1887, two days after Black Friday, the London city police had attacked a peaceful demonstration of the unemployed in Trafalgar Square with extreme brutality. Two hundred people were treated in the hospital and three of them died. Working-class London was outraged. The trauma of London's "Bloody Sunday," following so closely on Chicago's Black Friday, galvanized British radicals and reformers and gave rise to a British anarchist movement.[34]

The news of Haymarket exerted its greatest influence on Spanish workers, who had organized a powerful federation with anarchist leaders in the early 1880s. When their open trade unions were destroyed, anarchists formed hundreds of resistance societies that existed side by side with workers' circles, café clubs and choirs; the Spanish anarchists also supported newspapers that published talented writers and presented an enormous volume of information in accessible forms like serials and novellas. As a result, the story of the Chicago anarchists became so well known that the first anniversary of the executions in 1888 was widely observed by workers and radical intellectuals all over Spain, usually at evening festivities. Halls were transformed into shrines to the martyrs of Chicago as their *retratos* (portraits) were hung along with those of anarchist fathers like Mikhail Bakunin. Indeed, as the anarchist Peter Kropotkin reported, there was not a city in Spain worth mentioning where "the bloody anniversary" was not commemorated by enthusiastic crowds of workers.[35]

When Samuel Gompers appealed to Governor Oglesby to commute the sentences of the anarchists on death row, he predicted that executing them would cause thousands and thousands of workingmen all over the world to look upon the anarchists as martyrs. This is precisely what happened as workers created a ritualized memory of their heroes. When Gompers visited European cities in 1895, he noticed that in nearly every union hall there were pictures of Parsons, Lingg, Spies and the others, with the inscription: LABOR'S MARTYRS TO AMERICAN CAPITALISM. On later visits, he saw that the same pictures were still there.[36]

The memory of the Haymarket victims was further perpetuated when it became associated with the celebration of May Day as the International Workers' Day beginning in 1890. In cities all over Europe, the icons of the Chicago martyrs appeared in the First of May processions along with red flags and crimson flowers: in Barcelona, for example, where a militant strike for an eight-hour workday swept the city, and in Italian towns and cities from Piemonte to Calabria, where socialists and anarchists celebrated Primo Maggio with marches, festivals and strikes. Rank-and-file workers quickly transformed May Day into a potent ritual event to demonstrate for the eight-hour day, to assert a new working-class presence in society and, particularly in the Latin world, to commemorate the lives of the Chicago martyrs.[37]

Events took a different turn in Chicago on May Day 1890, when trade union members paraded in a dignified way that pleased the *Tribune*. There was no general strike like the one that paralyzed the city in 1886. By contrast, union carpenters struck for eight hours on their own four years later and then led other workers in an orderly march through the downtown. The marchers were mostly British, American, Scandinavian, Canadian and German craftsmen. There were no Bohemian lumber shovers or Russian clothing workers in the line of march, and no one carried red flags or black-bordered images of dead anarchists.[38]

THE RESPECTABLE DEMONSTRATION the Chicago carpenters led on May 1, 1890, indicated to the *Tribune*'s editor that the city had entered a new era of peace and quiet. To Jane Addams, who had recently arrived in the city to open her Hull House settlement for the West Side poor, it seemed clear that the repressive measures imposed after Haymarket were being lifted. But, she recalled, the riot and all that followed had had a "profound influence on the social outlook of thousands of people," especially of the city's reform community. Led by the financier Lyman Gage, the labor activist George Schilling and other liberal-minded individuals, citizens participated in regular public discussions of social problems in which, Addams recalled, "every shade of opinion was freely expressed." It seemed to her that many citizens of Chicago had decided that "the only cure for anarchy was free speech and open discussion of the ills of which opponents of government complained."[39]

During the early 1890s, as the eight-hour campaign resumed, the voice of labor made itself heard again in industrial America, especially in Chicago, where trade unionists of various political persuasions joined middle-class reformers in creating a new form of urban liberalism. What disappeared was the energetic working-class radicalism that had erupted during the Great Upheaval of 1886, along with the massive national labor movement the Knights of Labor had begun to mobilize. In the aftermath of Haymarket, the International Working People's Association was obliterated, while the Knights were scapegoated from the outside, divided on the inside and all but destroyed by aggressive employers' associations and court injunctions. And yet the ethic of cooperation and the practice of solidarity endured in the 1890s. New industrial unions of coal miners, hard-rock metal miners and railway laborers appeared and carried on the tradition of broad-based unionism in the nation's largest industries. Meanwhile, the contest for the political soul of the labor movement resumed. Socialists like George Schilling and his comrades offered a spirited challenge to the brand of unionism espoused by American Federation of Labor officials like Sam Gompers, who avoided visionary thinking and focused on immediate economic and political goals. Indeed, within the emerging labor movement, a majority of union leaders, whatever their partisan views, agreed that society "as presently constituted" was "corrupt and vicious" and required "complete reconstruction."[40]

Many of these activists believed unions on the shop floor were an embodiment of direct democracy and that the larger house of labor was a structure prefiguring a new kind of cooperative republic governed by the people, not ruled by the elite. The trade union was, said Gompers, "the germ of the future state which all will hail with glad acclaim." Albert Parsons and August Spies had died, but elements of their "Chicago idea" survived them.[41]

As the labor movement revived itself during the early 1890s, concern mounted in labor circles over the fate of the surviving carriers of the Chicago idea, the three Haymarket convicts languishing in Joliet Prison. George Schilling, Henry Lloyd and others active in the original Amnesty Association even held out hope that the last of the anarchists, Fielden, Schwab and Neebe, might be pardoned. In a revealing letter written to Lucy Parsons, Schilling warned against her continuing use of violent rhetoric that would roil the calming waters of Chicago politics. When Lucy wrote to him about a particularly violent speech she delivered to an enthusiastic group of Italian workers, Schilling replied, "The open espousal of physical force—especially when advocated by foreigners—as a remedy for social maladjustments can only lead to greater despotism." When the public was terrorized, policemen like Bonfield and "hangmen" like Judge Gary mounted their saddles and rode in like "saviors of society." Fear was not "the mother of progress" but of reaction, he added. Schilling told Lucy that her agitation still inspired such fear and could again call forth brutal men who would respond to forceful words with repressive actions. And then he added this sermon: "At Waldheim sleep five men—among them your beloved husband—who died in the hope that their execution might accelerate the emancipation of the world. Blessed be their memories and may future generations do full justice to their courage and motives, but I do not believe that the time will ever come when the judgment of an enlightened world will say that their methods were wise or correct. They worshipped at the shrine of force; wrote it and preached it; until finally they were overpowered by their own Gods and slain in their own temple."[42]

In the fall of 1892, Schilling and other reformers turned from talk to action when they helped elect John P. Altgeld governor of Illinois. Born in Germany and raised on an Ohio farm, Altgeld suffered a rough life on the road until he began a successful career as a Chicago lawyer in 1875. His law practice soon became lucrative, as did his endeavors in real estate. He began to participate in Democratic Party politics, expressing conventional, if not conservative, views. Yet, after he was elected to a judgeship, he revealed sympathies for the underdog when he advocated for prison reform, condemned police brutality and defended immigrants against the charge that foreigners were more inclined toward crime and disorder than native-born Americans. An unlikely figure for a politician, Altgeld had an oddly shaped head topped with matted hair and was afflicted with a harelip that impeded his heavily accented speech. He was often the subject of ridicule in the Yankee press, but when he campaigned with Schilling in the union halls and immigrant saloons, he seemed enormously attractive to the men in working clothes who embraced Pete Altgeld as one of their own. Despite vitriolic attacks on him by some Chicago newspapers, he won an impressive victory in 1892, in part because of the massive labor vote rung up in city wards by his friend Schilling and other union leaders.[43]

Labor activists were nearly as excited in the spring of 1893 when Carter Harrison miraculously returned from the oblivion to which he was assigned after Haymarket and won a fifth term as mayor, even after being red-baited with unprecedented severity. Once again the magician of Chicago politics brought his fellow citizens into a circle of civil discourse. Harrison's surprising election came at a time when American eyes were turned on Chicago, where the World's Fair opened on May 1, 1893—a day no doubt chosen to signal a new beginning for the city, if not to erase the memory of a troubled time seven years before when the Great Upheaval and the Haymarket crisis tore the city apart. To battle-weary activists like George Schilling, it suddenly seemed like the dark memories of the 1870s and 1880s might be erased by the bright lights that lit the grand buildings of the World's Columbian Exposition.

The fair was a colossal success, revealing to millions of Americans what Henry Demarest Lloyd called the possibilities of "social beauty, utility and harmony of which they have not been able even to dream." Carter Harrison, the mayor who had been driven from office for allowing free speech to anarchists, became the exposition's dominant personality, the embodiment of Chicago's tolerant soul and progressive spirit.[44]

The Haymarket case assumed a surprisingly prominent place in all this excitement. After John Peter Altgeld's inauguration as governor, Schilling, Lloyd and a young Ohio-born attorney named Clarence Darrow mounted a public campaign to pardon Fielden, Schwab and Neebe, on the ground that they had been denied a fair trial. Darrow, who had arrived in Chicago in 1888 and had plunged into Democratic politics on the West Side, became a follower of Henry George's brand of radicalism and an avid supporter of Pete Altgeld. His sympathy for the underdog and his interest in socialism and anarchism led him to investigate the case of the Haymarket anarchists in Joliet Prison and then to play a leading role in seeking their pardon. It was his first involvement in pleading the cases of notorious troublemakers—the beginning of a long and unparalleled career as "the attorney for the damned."[45]

So, during his first months in office, Altgeld was lobbied assiduously by two formidable advocates: Schilling, who helped engineer his election, and Darrow, a brilliant young legal talent who had become the governor's acolyte. Altgeld remained unmoved by their pleas until March, when he summoned Schilling to Springfield and asked him to gather, as secretly as possible, affidavits from jurymen, witnesses and victims of police violence whose testimony might be relevant in his review of the Haymarket case.[46]

In a few weeks, Schilling produced a huge stack of signed statements from citizens who had been beaten and shot by the Chicago police or who had been arrested without warrants and held without charges after the bombing. Among them were affidavits given by men to whom the police had offered their freedom, plus cash, for testifying against the indicted anarchists. Schilling also collected affidavits from members of the jury pool indicating that the special bailiff summoned only men who expressed prejudice toward the defendants. Altgeld now had all the ammunition he needed to fire off a legal salvo that would resound for decades to come.[47]

During the same month the fair opened in 1893, Lucy Parsons's effort to raise money for a monument on the martyrs' grave at Waldheim proceeded to its conclusion thanks to the efforts of the Pioneer Aid and Support Association, a group organized to care for the grave site and assist the families of the Haymarket anarchists. A sculptor, Albert Weinert, created a statue in forged bronze. Inspired by "La Marseillaise,"

Haymarket Martyrs' Monument, Waldheim Cemetery,
Forest Park, Illinois

the monument took the shape of a hooded woman placing a laurel on the head of a dying man. The female figure looks and strides forward assertively as if to protect the fallen worker at her feet. A parade of 1,000 people retraced part of the anarchists' funeral procession to attend the unveiling on June 25, 1893. The crowd included many visitors, native and foreign, who came to town for the World's Fair. During the day that followed, the *Tribune* reported that 8,000 more went out to Waldheim to view the monument.[48]

In the year after the fair it was estimated that almost as many people came to see the monument at Waldheim as to see the beautiful Saint-Gaudens statue of Abraham Lincoln in the lakeside park named after him. There was nothing like the Haymarket memorial in any other cemetery, park or city square in America. For the martyrs' followers, the Waldheim monument became a ritual site for preserving a sacred memory that, without commemorative vigilance, would soon be erased. The memorial provided an even more enduring symbol than Lucy Parsons and her supporters imagined; the haunting statue guarding the graves of the Haymarket anarchists also became a mecca, a kind of shrine for socialists and other pilgrims who came to visit from all over the world.[49]

The morning after the monument dedication Governor John Peter Altgeld announced that he was pardoning Fielden, Schwab and Neebe. His bluntly written statement declared that the trial of the Haymarket eight had been unfair and illegal because "a packed jury had been selected to convict," because "much of the evidence given at the trial was a pure fabrication," because the defendants were not proven guilty of the crime charged in the indictment, and finally, and most provocatively, because "the trial judge was either so prejudiced against the defendants or else so determined to win the applause of a certain class in the community, that he could not and did not grant a fair trial." Altgeld went even further, saying he believed the bomb thrower was not acting as a part of a conspiracy but as an individual seeking revenge against a police force that had been beating and shooting unarmed working people since the railroad strike of 1877.[50]

This gubernatorial opinion did not, however, bring an end to speculation about the bomb thrower's identity. City officials and many others, including historians, continued to believe the fugitive anarchist Schnaubelt was the perpetrator, even though the evidence against him was not credible. (Schnaubelt's odyssey had taken him from Chicago to the backwoods of Canada, where he lived among native people, then to England, where anarchists sheltered him, and finally to Argentina, where he became a successful manufacturer of farm equipment and lived a life of quiet respectability.) On the other hand, many working people, as well as advocates such as Captain Black and Henry Lloyd, continued to believe the bomber was either a Pinkerton agent who knew an attack on law officers would provoke a riot and a reaction against the eight-hour movement, or an off-duty policeman who was actually attempting to hurl his projectile into the crowd or at the speakers' wagon.[51]

Many years later the scholar Paul Avrich researched every lead in the case and tentatively concluded that the perpetrator was either a Chicago anarchist known to Dyer Lum or a German ultramilitant from New York. However, Lum, embittered beyond endurance by the fate of his comrades, committed suicide a few months before Altgeld issued his pardon and died without revealing the name of the individual he supposedly knew to be the bomber. The German suspect from New York died without ever being identified, except in a private conversation between two old anarchists.[52]

In any case, what mattered to Governor Altgeld was not the bomber's true identity, but the fact that the prosecution never charged anyone with committing the act and instead charged men with murder for allegedly having knowledge of an assassination plot. In giving his reasons for pardoning the Haymarket survivors, the governor vehemently objected to Judge Gary's ruling that the defendants could be tried for murder without proof that they had direct connection to the perpetrator. "No judge in a civilized country has laid down such a rule," he wrote. Altgeld concluded by agreeing with those who said Judge Gary had conducted the anarchists' trial with "malicious ferocity."[53]

The Haymarket case, already a prominent event in the minds of Americans and many Europeans, now became even more memorable because of this historic pardon and because of the way in which the governor of Illinois came out of his office and deliberately exposed himself to the thunderstorm of abuse that would follow his decision.

The next day, Darrow recalled, "a flood of vituperation and gall was poured out upon Altgeld's head." A United States Supreme Court justice compared the governor to the traitor Jefferson Davis, and Robert Todd Lincoln, an influential figure in the Pullman Company, declared Altgeld's pardon a disgrace to the state where his martyred father was buried. Newspaper editors far and wide joined the chorus of condemnation. The *Tribune*'s Joseph Medill, who despised Altgeld, now attacked him for issuing the pardon to pay off his electoral debt to socialist and anarchist voters. The governor "was not merely alien by birth but an alien by temperament and attitude" and an anarchist at heart.[54]

Altgeld had never shown the slightest degree of sympathy for anarchists, but he had expressed indignation when immigrants were stereotyped as lawless and disorderly. However, the governor's pardon statement was not motivated mainly by sympathy for fellow Germans but by what Clarence Darrow called his "patriotic love of liberty" and his belief that the methods used to convict the anarchists were a greater menace to the Republic than what they had done. Altgeld feared that when the law was bent to deprive immigrants of their civil liberties, it would later be bent to deprive native sons and daughters of theirs as well.[55]

Not everyone in Chicago condemned Altgeld, however. Three Chicago newspapers, including the Republican *Inter-Ocean,* defended his decision to pardon the anarchists. Some members of the city's legal and business communities who felt ashamed of the miscarriage of justice in 1886 also welcomed the pardon. One of them, a businessman named E. S. Dreyer, had headed the grand jury in the Haymarket case. After the trial he changed his mind about the case and signed the letter requesting

Governor John Peter Altgeld

clemency. When Governor Altgeld called Dreyer to the capital and asked him to take the pardon papers to Joliet Prison and present them to the three convicts, Dreyer broke down in tears.[56]

Arriving at the penitentiary, Dreyer found the anarchists soldiering away at their assigned tasks—Neebe serving food in the commissary, Schwab binding books, as he had done in Germany, and Fielden breaking stone in the sun, working on contract for the same firm that had employed him as a teamster when he was a free man. The three men were amazed by the tone of Altgeld's tough statement, and, in an outpouring of gratitude, they promised to live obscure lives, so much so that when they made their way back to Chicago, they jumped off their train in the freight yards to avoid the press.[57]

The three anarchists made good on their promises. Michael Schwab returned to the *Arbeiter-Zeitung,* where for two years he wrote articles friendly to the workingman. He then resigned and opened a shoe store, but he failed at this and died of tuberculosis three years later. Schwab asked to be buried at Waldheim with his old comrades. Oscar Neebe, whose first wife had died when he was in the Cook County Jail, married a German widow and quietly tended bar in her saloon near the stockyards until he died in 1916. He was interred next to his former partner August Spies. Sam Fielden inherited a small legacy from an English relative and moved to Colorado, where he lived a solitary, robust life in a log cabin until he died in 1922 at the age of seventy-four.[58]

Altgeld's pardon, for all the fury it caused in elite circles, removed a bone that had been sticking in the throats of liberal Chicagoans since the anarchist trial ended and the four bodies swung from the gallows. Now these concerned citizens could look forward more easily to a glorious summer when the Columbian Exposition would forecast the city's spectacular future of progress, reform and civic enlightenment. Indeed, before the summer ended, the miraculous White City erected on the lake had revealed Chicago's greatness to the world. The day before the fair closed in the fall of 1893, Mayor Harrison said this and more in a memorable speech predicting that the exposition would inaugurate a wonderful new era for Chicago.

THE EUPHORIC SPELL the fair cast over the city ended that same night, however, when a terrible event marred all the days of glory just past. The mayor was murdered in the living room of his mansion, felled by a bullet from the gun of a deranged office seeker. In death, even Carter Harrison's enemies extolled his virtues while all Chicago mourned his passing; it even seemed as though the mayor's legacy as a great unifier might inspire Chicagoans to maintain the civic solidarity and communal joy the fair had evoked. However, this wish would not come true, because in the next few months the city slid into another depression, and during the summer of 1894 its residents suffered another trauma produced by what seemed an unending and distressingly bloody conflict between labor and capital.

The trouble began unexpectedly on May 11 in George Pullman's model industrial town when 2,000 palace-car workers left their shops to protest drastic reductions in the workforce and a sharp wage cut of one-third for remaining employees. These losses were difficult to accept, because they came at a time when Pullman paid dividends to his stockholders. Furthermore, a piece-rate pay system, designed to boost output, alienated shop workers because they had to work faster and harder to make up for reduced wages and, at the same time, endure personal abuses from hard-driving foremen.

The strikers sought assistance from a new inclusive union of railroad workers whose leaders carried on the Knights' tradition of organizing all crafts and trades together. Led by Eugene V. Debs, a lanky organizer for the Brotherhood of Locomotive Firemen, the American Railway Union revived the spirit of 1886 on the railroads. Debs resisted pressure to call his members out in a sympathy strike, because he knew that Pullman and his corporate allies had formed an association of the twenty-four lines operating in and out of Chicago—perhaps the most powerful group of businessmen ever organized. Nonetheless, when Pullman refused to negotiate with his men, Debs ordered a boycott of trains hauling Pullman sleeping cars. In a few weeks a great sympathy strike had spread far and wide, paralyzing the nation's railroads west of Chicago, idling 50,000 workers and creating a panic among businessmen.[59]

Never before had a union exercised this kind of strategic power over the levers of commerce. Unable to break the strike, railroad managers attached U.S. Mail cars to trains carrying Pullman cars, so that when workers refused to haul them federal authorities could intervene. The U.S. attorney general, a railroad lawyer named Richard Olney, persuaded Democratic president Grover Cleveland to send army troops into Chicago to break the strike, because, he insisted, the country was once again on the "ragged edge of anarchy." In a short time, 15,000 regular army soldiers arrived from nearby Fort Sheridan, a base intended for just this kind of emergency by Marshall Field and his associates when they purchased the land on which it was constructed.

The battles that ensued in Chicago between troopers and strikers were the worst the country had seen since the bloodbath in Pittsburgh that began the great uprising in 1877. Hundreds of Chicago workers were wounded and at least thirty-four were killed before the fierce resistance was put down by army troops. Debs was arrested and later, after he was tried, sentenced to six months in jail for contempt of court because he had defied state authority. While he stood trial, he waited in a Cook County Jail cell next to the one where Albert Parsons had been held on similar charges.[60]

Debs and his union brothers had been utterly defeated by Pullman and his allies in the federal government. But the victory was a costly one for Chicago's most famous industrialist, one that cost him his reputation, and, some would say, his life. Pullman had created a model company town outside of Chicago, hoping to avoid its furies; he had resisted the winds of change when they penetrated the walls of his city during the upheaval of 1886 and when they came again eight years later, reaching hurricane force. Still, the violent events of 1894 signaled that the end was near for the great industrialist and his company town. In the aftermath a federal commission condemned Pullman for exploiting his own employees and for refusing to consider their grievances. Weakened by the strike, Pullman died of heart failure three years later in the midst of a legal battle with the state's attorney general to maintain his corporate charter and his private company houses. Family members commissioned a grand Corinthian column to top his grave, but also ordered that Pullman's iron-clad casket be buried in reinforced concrete because they feared that angry workers might vandalize his remains.[61]

The battle of 1894 also transformed Pullman's adversary, Eugene Debs, who, during his incarceration, decided that Americans were losing many of their precious liberties and that only radical measures could recover them. In fact, in response to the Pullman boycott federal courts had outlawed two of the most effective forms of labor solidarity to emerge from the Great Upheaval: the boycott and the sympathy strike. The following year the Illinois Supreme Court obliterated another vestige of 1886 when it struck down an eight-hour law covering women and children working in industry. These court actions initiated an era of extreme judicial hostility to nearly all forms of union organization and collective

George M. Pullman in the mid-1890s

labor activity, a time when some union leaders abandoned militant tactics and radical dreams in search of accommodation, while others turned to direct action and violent forms of resistance.[62]

Eugene Debs refused to take either course after he was released from prison in November of 1895. Instead, he embraced democratic socialism and took the lead in building a popular movement that he hoped would regain workers' lost liberties. Debs expressed no sympathy for anarchy in his jailhouse interviews or in the many speeches he delivered after his release from prison. However, when he came to Chicago two years later to found a new socialist group, Debs met with Lucy Parsons and made a pilgrimage to Waldheim, where he visited the graves of the men he regarded as "the first martyrs to the cause of industrial freedom."[63]

The Pullman disaster also led some influential Chicagoans to recall the Haymarket tragedy, and to reassess its meaning in light of current events. A year later, as Clarence Darrow pled Eugene Debs's case before the Supreme Court on First Amendment grounds, an impressive new history of Chicago was published. One of the editors, Joseph Kirkland, a noted writer, carefully reviewed the Haymarket case, which he regarded as the most decisive event in the city's history. Kirkland's detailed account of the trial reiterated the criticisms of the police, the bailiff, the prosecuting attorneys and the judge that Governor Altgeld had leveled against the same men in his famous pardon.[64]

The facts of the Haymarket case, wrote Kirkland, showed that the state had not only been unable to produce the bomber; it had failed to prove the existence of an anarchist conspiracy. Indeed, it was now known that much of the evidence given at the trial was "pure fabrication" and that prominent police officials had bribed some witnesses and even threatened to torture others unless they testified as they were told.[65] Kirkland's account of the Haymarket trial subverted the prosecution's case and vindicated the defense. George Schilling, William Dean Howells and others involved in the amnesty movement in 1887 had impatiently awaited the judgment of history; now it came, sooner than expected, reversing in almost every respect the legal judgment rendered by the court.

Kirkland closed the case in another way, however, one that gave no comfort to Lucy Parsons and the anarchist party of memory. As the years passed, he explained, the awful Haymarket tragedy had begun to fade from people's minds, just like "the cloud of Anarchism," which had once loomed in the sky like "a portentous menace to the peace of society," and then had passed into "an innocuous vapor." Now, he observed, the memory of the dead anarchists could only be "revived by their admiring disciples in feeble demonstrations on the anniversary of their execution."[66]

Indeed, every November 11, Lucy Parsons, Lizzie Holmes and other devoted custodians of the anarchists' memory faithfully gathered for the graveside ceremonies at Waldheim, where they sought to revive the martyrs' spirit with a passionate, almost religious, fervor. On one of these elegiac occasions, Emma Goldman proclaimed that these "martyrs of liberty" would continue to grow in their graves and "would live with us always unto all eternity." She also believed their memory would be revived by a resurgent anarchist movement in the next century, when humanity would enter a new time without warring nations, conflicting classes and dominating authorities. And so, in the years after Black Friday, anarchists gathered in little circles on November 11—not simply to mourn their heroes but also to venerate the men whose martyrdom would revive libertarian beliefs and inspire new believers around the world. This memorial day became an occasion for the faithful to express joy about the lives of the martyrs whose deaths mystically ensured the ultimate triumph of anarchism.[67]

And yet, as the nineteenth century ended with the trumpets of militarism and imperialism blaring in Cuba and the Philippines, and with the engines of corporate capitalism roaring from Pittsburgh to Chicago, even dedicated visionaries like Lizzie Holmes harbored doubts that anarchist beliefs were spreading. She and William had left Chicago for Denver, where their home became a refuge for traveling anarchists like Lucy Parsons and Emma Goldman. On these visits Lizzie and Lucy recalled the "stirring enthusiastic days" in Chicago, the loud rallies, colorful marches, the huge strikes and the desperate fight to save the lives of Albert and the other "Haymarket boys." Lizzie Holmes and her husband had remained as keenly devoted to their anarchist ideals as they had been "in the days when their faith was young and their hopes were high." As the November 11 memorial day of the Chicago anarchists approached in 1898, Lizzie wrote that she and William were "still looking longingly toward the east for the dawn of a new day for humanity." But at the next anniversary ceremony at Waldheim, she confessed that her hopes were fading. "As we clasp hands above their graves today," she said, "we cannot say the dawn is brighter, that mankind is happier and freer." As the nineteenth century drew to a close, Lizzie Holmes admitted that the anarchists buried at Waldheim no longer had a known following and that their lives and their ideas no longer held deep meaning for working people. A little more than a decade after the hangings on Black Friday, it appeared that the Haymarket martyrs had become lost in the past, forgotten and misunderstood.[68]

Epilogue

AT THE DAWN of the twentieth century few Americans had any reason to look backward to the dark age of bloody conflict marked by the Haymarket calamity. As Lizzie Holmes feared, no one but a small band of diehard anarchists seemed to remember her beloved comrades and their tragic story. As the century wore on, however, the Chicago anarchists were not so easily forgotten. Indeed, whether they were remembered as terrible criminals or revered as venerable martyrs, the five men buried at Waldheim were recalled quite often, not only on the American scene, but in faraway places as well. Even after the last of their cohorts passed away, even after the living memory of the anarchists faded into oblivion, Parsons, Spies and their comrades appeared again and again in poems, plays, novels and history books, in drawings and posters, as well as on banners carried at demonstrations, in speeches delivered at commemorative rituals and in editorials written on free speech.

The memory of the Haymarket anarchists endured not only because they became heroic figures in labor and radical folklore, but also because their words and actions, their trial and their execution raised so many critical questions about American society in the industrial age and after. Indeed, the most important issues raised by the Haymarket case— questions about equality and inequality, class and nationality, crime and punishment, free speech and public safety—remain as controversial in the twenty-first century as they ever were. All this is clear in retrospect, but in the two decades after the anarchists died, their story survived because a few radicals dedicated themselves to telling it and retelling it.

It was during this time that Lucy Parsons worked relentlessly, and at times single-handedly, to preserve the memory of her husband and his cause. Lucy's memorial work was always difficult, but at first it was an onerous and even dangerous task, especially in 1901 after Leon Czolgosz

Lucy Parsons in 1903

shot President William McKinley and it was revealed that the assassin had been in Chicago and that he claimed to be an anarchist. According to the *Tribune*, the Secret Service suspected the "Haymarket gang" of being involved in the crime. When the paper sent its reporters to interrogate Lucy Parsons, she told them she had never heard of the assassin and that the shooting of the president was the worst thing that could happen to the anarchist movement.[1] She was correct.

When President McKinley died, another red scare swept America, and the Haymarket-era image of the dangerous, anarchist immigrant reappeared. The new president, Theodore Roosevelt, set the tone, declaring that anarchism was "not the outgrowth of unjust social conditions but the daughter of degenerate lunacy, a vicious pest" that threatened "to uproot the very foundations of society" if it was "not speedily stamped out by death, imprisonment and deportation of all Anarchists."[2]

In 1903, President Roosevelt signed a pathbreaking law that barred anarchists from entry to the United States, along with paupers, prostitutes and the insane. The statute also allowed the government to deport any immigrants who converted to anarchism during their first three years in the country; this was the first time the federal government moved to exclude and deport certain immigrants because of their beliefs and associations.[3]

Nonetheless, Lucy Parsons plowed on with her publishing and speaking endeavors. She reprinted her collection of Albert's speeches and letters, and then set off on an exhausting road trip to promote the book. Although she was now overshadowed by the notorious Emma Goldman, the widow of Albert Parsons was still a revered figure in immigrant union halls around the country. Grief, hardship, poverty and advancing age (she was fifty years old in 1903) had not diminished her beauty. A stunning photograph of her appeared in the new edition of *The Life of Albert Parsons,* one that would become an iconic image when radicals rediscovered Lucy many decades later. She is standing erect, looking taller and younger than she was, delicately holding a paper scroll and wearing one of the formal dresses she made with her own hands. Her dark hair is short and curled. A light shines on her face as she looks out at the world with sad eyes.

By this time, Lucy Parsons had abandoned support for propaganda by deed, and had joined with the Socialist Party leader Eugene V. Debs and others who were trying to create a new labor movement, based largely on the "Chicago idea" of revolutionary unionism that her husband had espoused. And so it was fitting that Lucy appeared as an honored guest at the founding convention of the Industrial Workers of the World held at Chicago's Brandt's Hall in June 1905. Prominent among the 200 workers who attended the convention were the western hard-rock miners who followed their leader William D. Haywood to Chicago, carrying with them stories of the bloody battles they had fought in the Rocky Mountain metal-mining camps. Haywood, who had memorized the words of Spies and Parsons, convened the meeting of what he called the "Continental Congress of the working class." The aim of the assembly, Haywood declared, was to create a revolutionary labor movement, premised on the reality of class struggle around the world. The IWW would become a vehicle for organizing the vast army of immigrant machine tenders and common laborers into "one big union" that would one day engage in the ultimate general strike. Once the "wage slaves" felt their own transcendent power, it would be natural for them to want to seize control of their industries and run them cooperatively.[4]

Lucy Parsons's presence at the first IWW convention reminded the delegates of the Haymarket tragedy, which had ended the first great drive for revolutionary unionism in Chicago.[5] She told the assembled workingmen, and a few workingwomen, of how she came to Chicago twenty-seven years before as a young girl full of hope and animation, and how her life had been changed by her husband's ordeal. After the convention adjourned that day, Bill Haywood recalled, the delegates responded to a plea from Lucy and visited Waldheim Cemetery to lay wreaths on the graves of the Chicago martyrs.[6]

In the next dozen years, as the Chicago idea of one big union espoused by the Industrial Workers of the World began to catch on, Lucy found more and more workers eager to hear of her husband's words and deeds. This was an age of industrial violence, when employers mounted relentless union-busting drives, aided by local police and vigilantes, by private gunmen and state militiamen and by hostile judges who denied workers freedom of speech and freedom of association. Scores of unarmed workers were slain on picket lines during mass strikes that often seemed like rebellions. As a result, many of the new immigrants who had been pouring into the United States by the millions since 1890 were intimidated; some of them, however, were radicalized by these experiences and attracted by the IWW's embrace of all races, creeds and nationalities—"the wretched of the earth." Prominent among these alienated immigrant laborers were the peasants and laborers who came to "L'America" from the poor provinces of the Italian Mezzogiorno.

Common laborers and factory operatives from southern Italy played an outsized role in the mass strikes that exploded all over the United States between 1909 and 1919, notably in the "Uprising of the 20,000" women clothing workers of New York City; in the legendary strike for "Bread and Roses" at Lawrence, Massachusetts; and in the Colorado coalfield wars, which culminated in the infamous massacre of two women and eleven children at Ludlow. Deeply involved in all these battles, Italian workers gravitated to the IWW and to a special foreign-language federation of the Socialist Party; they also helped revive the anarchist movement in the United States by forming scores of groups in industrial cities and towns. All of these organizations celebrated May Day and enjoyed picnics, where immigrants danced, sang songs, listened to long speeches, watched performances of plays like *Primo Maggio,* written by the poet Pietro Gori, which began and ended with the singing of Verdi's operatic chorus "*Va, pensiero,*" and heard readings of poems like Gori's "Undici Novembre"—a tribute to those who died on Black Friday.[7] The main speaker on May 1 usually followed a common script that began with a reference to the first May Day and the grand struggle for freedom that cost the lives of the heroic Haymarket martyrs, innocent victims of so-called justice in America.[8]

The Chicago anarchists were recalled in especially grand fashion on May Day in 1913, during a huge strike of 25,000 Italian silk workers in Paterson, New Jersey, an anarchist stronghold. On that May 1, a monster demonstration wound its way through the city, led by women dressed entirely in red outfits with white IWW insignias. On this day, wrote a radical reporter, "the proletariat of Paterson raised the banner for which 26 years ago five of our comrades in Chicago were assassinated by the Republican Bourgeoisie."[9]

By this time, the memory of the Haymarket martyrs had taken on a new life of its own. References to the Chicago anarchists appeared across the United States in May Day marches, IWW mass strikes and anarchist picnics. The names of Parsons, Spies and the others also reappeared at various manifestations that took place in other nations, especially in Spain, France and Italy, as well as in Argentina, Cuba and Mexico, where revolutionary union federations led by anarchists became mass movements during the first two decades of the twentieth century. Many of the militants in these new anarchosyndicalist unions regarded the Chicago martyrs as pioneers and celebrated their memory in May Day job actions and demonstrations. In Mexico, for example, May Day was celebrated for the first time in 1913 with anarchist-inspired strikes for the eight-hour day, protests against the nation's military rulers and memorials to the heroes who gave their lives for the cause in 1887. From then on, Primero de Mayo became a national holiday in Mexico, known as the "Day of the Martyrs of Chicago."[10]

During these stirring times, the nearly forgotten widow of Albert Parsons regained her status as the leading player in a company of traveling anarchists dedicated to preserving the memory of Black Friday and the men who died that day. All the while, Lucy Parsons continued to struggle with local authorities over her right to speak freely. At one point Chicago police even denied her a permit to speak in Washington Square across from the Newberry Library, a site reserved for free speech at the request of the institution's founder—one of the few such places that existed in Chicago after Haymarket.[11] Lucy's numerous free-speech fights paralleled the IWW's massive civil disobedience campaigns on behalf of free expression for workers. At a time when the First Amendment was regarded as unenforceable, these radicals, known as Wobblies, challenged the courts in sharp ways and drew the attention of many complacent citizens to local authorities who regularly denied, and indeed mocked, the right to free speech for dissenters.[12]

Lucy Parsons and her radical comrades kept speaking and agitating until the United States entered World War I. Then, in 1917 and 1918, a patriotic fervor swept the land, and the government suppressed all types of protests, including strikes and May Day marches.[13] Eugene Debs and socialist opponents of the war were tried for sedition and imprisoned. The IWW was devastated by vigilante assaults and federal prosecutions. A third red scare followed the war, and in 1920, the Department of Justice conducted raids that led to the arrest of 10,000 people, whose civil liberties were abused by federal agents. That same year, Congress enacted a law that allowed the government to punish and deport aliens simply for possessing radical literature, for "advising, advocating or teaching" radical doctrines and for belonging to radical organizations.[14] By this time nearly every repressive measure called for during the post-Haymarket red scare had become federal law.

Under these circumstances, the nation's leading historians reopened the Haymarket case and retried the defendants. Of the prosecution and execution of the Chicago anarchists, one legal scholar remarked: "It may be that after all is said and done the end justified the means; it may be that our Government which today seems to be extremely lax in allowing Bolshevism and I.W.W. doctrines to be preached . . . might well study the result of the Chicago trial." The result was studied by historian James Ford Rhodes, who concluded in his influential *History of the United States* that "the punishment meted out to the anarchists was legally just." Another noted historian of the time wrote that "all seven anarchist wretches who assumed an impudent front during the trial" deserved to be hanged—even those whom Governor Altgeld had pardoned.[15]

Three decades after the hangings in Chicago, the memory of the Haymarket anarchists as heroic martyrs seemed to have survived mainly in the labor lore carried by itinerant Wobblies who constantly blew into the Windy City, where they roamed the "canyon stretching across the great west side from the Lake through the Loop on toward the setting sun." These never-ceasing streams of humanity created what one observer called "the largest number of homeless and hungry men that have ever been brought together anywhere in our land."[16] Some of these hoboes turned up regularly in the free-speech park at Washington Square, now called "Bughouse Square," where Lucy Parsons would speak about the old days and the men who gave their lives for the one-big-union idea.[17]

During the 1920s, Parsons joined the efforts of the Communist Party's International Labor Defense group and took up the case of Tom Mooney, then serving a life sentence for allegedly bombing a San Francisco military-preparedness parade. She also joined the worldwide campaign to save the lives of Nicola Sacco and Bartolomeo Vanzetti, the two Italian anarchists sentenced to death in Massachusetts after a sensational murder trial. The ordeal of Sacco and his comrade Vanzetti aroused the same objections from well-known writers and intellectuals that Henry Demarest Lloyd and William Dean Howells had made on behalf of Parsons, Spies and their comrades. Like the Chicago anarchists, the Italians were tried by a biased judge and a packed jury on charges of "general conspiracy" to commit murder, and they too were executed for their beliefs as much as for their actions; thus they became victims, one commentator wrote, of "a pattern of hate and fear toward radicals set in 1887."[18]

The fate of Sacco and Vanzetti, who were electrocuted on August 23, 1927, served as a reminder of what had happened to the Chicago anarchists four decades earlier; and so, when the Great Depression hit in 1929, stories of Haymarket had already resurfaced and floated out of the confines of Chicago's "hobohemia."[19] In the hard times that followed, the legions of unemployed people demanding bread or work, the scores of radicals risking their lives to organize immigrant factory workers and the numerous cases of policemen gunning down protesters and picketers recreated scenes that had been acted out in Chicago during the Great Upheaval decades earlier. As a result, Lucy Parsons had many occasions on which to call up the memories of the workers killed in 1886 and 1887.

Indeed, after many years of passing unnoticed, November 11 was celebrated once again as the Haymarket martyrs' memorial day in 1937, when Lucy Parsons addressed a mass meeting at the Amalgamated Hall on Ashland Avenue in Chicago. According to one observer, she stepped out on the platform, bent with age, almost totally blind, but still hurled curses at the powers that be and still called for the overthrow of capitalism.[20]

This fiftieth-anniversary ceremony occurred just five months after ten steelworkers were shot in the back and killed as they ran from Chicago police at the South Chicago plant of Republic Steel, where they had established a picket line. Known as the Memorial Day Massacre, the event aroused liberal Chicago in passionate protest against the police. History seemed to be repeating itself in 1937, as the city's police department re-created the bloody events of 1886 and the *Tribune* blamed the massacre on a riot caused by communists. Under these circumstances, the memory of the Haymarket tragedy fifty years earlier became useful to the militant organizers of the new industrial unions in Chicago. On May Day, 1938, local unionists trying to organize the old McCormick company (by now International Harvester) held a march from the South Side to Haymarket Square led by a float that featured a hooded man, identified as August Spies, who stood with a rope around his neck in a tableau meant to symbolize the ongoing suppression of workers' civil liberties by the Chicago police.[21]

The Haymarket affair was recalled during the bloody 1930s because it highlighted the agonizing dilemma violence presented for the American labor movement. Mainstream trade unionists like Sam Gompers had looked back in anger at the Chicago anarchists because their blatant advocacy of force played into the hands of labor's enemies, but other union activists, like Eugene Debs and Bill Haywood, admired Parsons and Spies for facing up to the brutal realities of American industrial life.[22] Even trade unionists opposed to the tactics and beliefs of the Chicago anarchists understood that workers' struggles had often been met with shocking repression, and that when violence bred violence, when powerless laboring people struck back in anger, they often paid with their lives. This is why, unsettling though it has been, the Haymarket case could never be forgotten within the labor movement.

The eminent American historian Richard Hofstadter once observed that, even with a minimum of radical activity and ideologically motivated class conflict, the United States has somehow experienced a maximum of industrial violence: at least 160 instances in which state and federal troops intervened in strikes, and at least 700 labor disputes in which deaths were recorded. He thought the reason for this lay more in the ethos of American capitalists than in that of the workers, because it was clear to him that most American violence had been initiated with a "conservative bias" by the "high dogs and the middle dogs" against radicals, workers and labor organizers, immigrants, blacks and other racial minorities who had, for their part, rarely taken forceful action against state authority. Writing in 1970, Hofstadter expressed dismay at the actions of young radicals like the Weathermen, who provoked violent confrontations to elicit repressive responses from authorities; he nonetheless concluded that there were far worse things in American history than the strikes and spontaneous riots that had erupted so often in the past. "After all," he noted, "the greatest and most calculating of killers is the national state, and this is true not only in international wars, but in domestic conflicts."[23]

During the years after the shocking 1937 Memorial Day Massacre in Chicago, the new industrial unions grew and used their political influence to curb the police and private armed forces that had been used against strikers and protesters over and over again for sixty years. The aged Lucy Parsons, whose life had been shaped by these violent episodes, was treated like a living saint by many trade unionists in Chicago, especially when Congress mandated the eight-hour day in the Fair Labor Standards Act of 1938, marking the end of the long struggle Albert and Lucy Parsons had helped to initiate. Lucy was a particularly important person to the radicals fighting to bring a union back to the old McCormick Reaper Works, where all the trouble began so many years ago. In 1941, at age eighty-eight, she braved the winter winds and spoke to workers on the Black Road, where a union affiliated with the new Congress of Industrial Organizations was conducting a campaign for votes at the old McCormick works. When the weather warmed up that spring, Lucy reappeared at a May Day parade, riding through the South Side as an honored guest sitting on top of a float sponsored by the Farm Equipment Workers Union. It would be her last May Day.[24]

Nine months later, on March 7, 1942, the stove in Lucy Parsons's little house caused a fire. Handicapped by her blindness, Lucy could not escape. She died of smoke inhalation. Her books, papers and letters from Albert and a host of others survived the fire, but were confiscated by police officers and never seen again. Lucy Parsons's ashes were placed at Waldheim, close to the remains of her beloved husband and her daughter, Lulu. Her quiet funeral was attended by many of the young radicals who carried on the union fight that had begun during the Great Upheaval of her youth.[25]

Lucy's final May Day in 1941 was also the last one celebrated in Chicago for many years. After the United States entered World War II, Communist Party leaders let May 1 pass without notice. They even disbanded their party organization and joined mainstream union leaders in taking a no-strike pledge for the duration of the war. The Chicago idea of militant unions taking mass action against capital and the state—the idea Parsons and Spies espoused until their last breaths—had simply vanished from the American labor scene.

After World War II the living memory of the Haymarket anarchists died, and their story survived only in literature—in the Chicago poems by Kenneth Rexroth; in a best-selling novel, *The American: A Middle Western Legend,* about the life of John Peter Altgeld written by the most popular leftist writer of the time, Howard Fast; and in Nelson Algren's prose poem to his hometown, *Chicago: City on the Make.*[26] Long ago, the famous novelist wrote, Chicago had been the town of "the great Lincolnian liberals," figures like John Peter Altgeld, "the ones who stuck out their stubborn necks in the ceaseless battle between the rights of Owners and the rights of Man." Algren loved this Chicago that was once the "most radical of all American cities: Gene Debs' town, Bill Haywood's town, the One Big Union town." But he also hated the place because it was the most brutal of all American cities, a "town of the hard and bitter strikes and the trigger happy cops," a town where "undried blood on the pavement" recalled the Haymarket tragedy. And so Chicago remained a city with "many bone-deep grudges to settle"—none greater, Algren thought, than the "big dark grudge cast by the four standing in white muslin robes, hands cuffed behind, at the gallows' head. For the hope of the eight hour day."[27]

AFTER ALGREN'S HARD-EDGED essay on Chicago appeared and then disappeared, the Haymarket story nearly vanished from literature during the Cold War years, when all manifestations of radicalism became deeply suspect. The May Day celebrations that had resumed briefly after World War II were banned. In 1955, May 1 was proclaimed Law Day in many states, and then designated as Loyalty Day throughout the country by presidential decree. The Congress of Industrial Organizations merged with the conservative American Federation of Labor that same year after nearly all radicals had been purged from union offices. The epic events in Chicago that gave birth to the first labor movement and the first May Day, as well as to the Haymarket tragedy, now became merely another chapter in "labor's untold story." Thus, it seemed that the memory of Haymarket would be effectively erased from the labor movement's history, even in Chicago.[28]

Elsewhere, however, particularly the Latin world, the Haymarket story was told and retold many times over. Indeed, no other event in United States history after the Civil War exerted the kind of hold the Haymarket tragedy maintained on the popular imagination of working people in other countries, particularly in Argentina, Chile, Cuba, Uruguay and Mexico, where exiled Spanish and Italian anarchists organized the first labor unions and led militant strikes and May Day marches in the decades after Haymarket.[29]

Even in Argentina, Bolivia, Chile and Uruguay, where military dictators destroyed unions, imprisoned their members, executed their leaders and suppressed all forms of oppositional writing and speaking during the 1970s, stories about the Haymarket martyrs were told and icons to their memory were preserved. While traveling in a remote tin-mining region of Bolivia during the 1980s, the writer Dan La Botz met a worker who invited him into his little home. As he was eating dinner with the miner and his family, La Botz noticed a small piece of cloth hanging in the window, an embroidery that in the United States might have read GOD BLESS OUR HOME. He moved closer to take a look and saw that it read LONG LIVE THE MARTYRS OF CHICAGO.[30]

IN 1985 THE URUGUAYAN AUTHOR Eduardo Galeano came to Chicago from Montevideo, where he had been a union activist and radical journalist until 1973, when a military coup sent him to prison and then into a long exile.[31] He fondly remembered the May Day marches that took place in his home city every year until the generals seized power; and so when Galeano came to Chicago during springtime, he wondered if May 1 would be celebrated in this city full of factories and workers. As soon as he arrived, he asked his hosts to take him to the Haymarket district to see the historic site, but when he arrived on Desplaines Street, he found nothing to mark the spot. No statue had "been erected in the memory of the martyrs of Chicago in the city of Chicago," he recalled. Not even a bronze plaque. Furthermore, May Day came and went without notice.

"May 1st is the only truly universal day of all humanity, the only day when all histories and all languages and religions and cultures of the world collide," Galeano wrote. "But in the United States, May 1st is a day like any other. On that day, people work normally and no one, or almost no one, remembers that the rights of the working class did not spring whole from the ear of a goat, or from the hand of God or the boss."[32]

Eduardo Galeano left Chicago without meeting those kindred spirits who did remember Haymarket and May Day—the old radicals and union veterans of the Depression-era struggles in the stockyards and steel mills who were custodians of the city's plebeian memories. Unbeknownst to Galeano, a small party of these people had been trying for more than fifteen years to erect a memorial in Haymarket Square to the workers who died there and to those who later swung from the gallows.

The most famous of them was Studs Terkel, a noted expert on jazz, a popular radio host, a much-loved raconteur and a keeper of the city's memory books. Terkel appeared on public television on May 1, 1986, to speak on the centennial of "one of the most traumatic moments in American labor history, the Haymarket tragedy." It was all about the fight for a freer workplace, he explained. Some young workers "bad-mouthed unions," he declared, but at the same time they accepted the freedom unions gained for workers "as a matter of course." But did they "know how it came about, how many blacklistings, how many busted heads, how many busted lives" it took? "Whatever benefits American working people have today didn't come from the big-heartedness of those who employed them," Terkel added. "They were hard-fought gains, through hard-fought battles."[33]

For sixteen years Terkel had been working with a small group of Chicagoans dedicated to preserving the memory of the workers who died during and after the riot in 1886. Studs first learned the Haymarket story from Wobblies who roomed in his mother's hotel and was reminded of it again and again, particularly on one memorable occasion in 1926 when he heard Lucy Parsons speak in Bughouse Square. For him the Haymarket saga was at the heart of Chicago's story as he knew it and told it.[34]

Terkel's preservation efforts took a public turn on May 4, 1970, when he addressed a small memorial meeting in Haymarket Square. He spoke that day of the duty to remember striking workers who came there to protest on May 4, 1886, and who deserved their monument, the same as the police who were memorialized by the old statue that still stood at the

Studs Terkel speaking at the Haymarket Memorial Committee rally on May 4, 1970, on the site where the speakers' wagon was located on May 4, 1886

end of the square, now hovering perilously close to an expressway that tore the West Side apart.[35]

The meeting took place in rough political waters still churning from violent events involving the Chicago police. After Martin Luther King's assassination in April 1968, angry black protesters appeared on the streets of the West Side, and 5,000 police officers massed to protect the downtown Loop. Once again blood flowed on those streets when patrolmen shot 48 African-Americans. Four of them died.[36]

A week later Mayor Richard J. Daley said the police had been too soft on the rioters and issued a militant "shoot to kill" order in cases involving arsonists and looters. The next day, in a speech observing May 1 as Law Day, Mayor Daley rephrased his controversial order, but he kept the police force on high alert and activated a special "Red Squad" to deal with black militants and the antiwar radicals planning to demonstrate at the Democratic National Convention in August.[37]

When protest groups applied for permits to march and rally at the event, they were denied them, but as the convention neared, demonstrators poured into the city anyway, expecting a showdown between "a police state and a people's movement." On the night the convention opened, the whole world watched on television as Chicago police furiously beat demonstrators and news reporters in front of the Hilton Hotel's Haymarket Bar and then pursued them into Grant Park.[38]

In the fall of 1969 tensions escalated again when the trial of the "Chicago Eight" began in the courtroom of Judge Julius Hoffman. Tom Hayden, Abbie Hoffman, Jerry Rubin and Black Panther leader Bobby Seale were among the eight radicals accused of conspiring to incite riots at the Democratic National Convention in a trial that conjured up the prosecution of the eight Haymarket anarchists eighty-three years before. Under the circumstances, the young revolutionaries who came to the city for the trial focused their anger on the Chicago police, whose history was symbolized by the police statue that still stood in Haymarket Square.[39]

The erection of public monuments had sometimes provoked controversy in the past, but no city experienced a conflict as explosive as the one that erupted in Chicago over the memorial legacy of Haymarket Square.[40] The Haymarket police statue had aroused resentment as soon as it was dedicated in 1889, and when it was moved to Union Park on the West Side a few years later, it was good riddance, according to the city's labor unionists. Then, in 1957, the Haymarket Businessmen's Association restored the monument and returned it to the square in an effort to promote tourism in a dingy part of town. And there it stood on Randolph Street until the night of October 6, 1969, when the monument was blown apart by several sticks of dynamite placed between the bronze patrolman's legs.

The explosion broke windows in nearby buildings and rained down pieces of metal on the Kennedy Expressway, but no one was hurt. "The blowing up of the only police monument in the United States . . ." was, according to the leader of the city's police sergeants, "an obvious declaration of war between the police, and the S.D.S. [Students for a Democratic Society] and other anarchist groups." In fact, the statue had been destroyed by members of the militant Weathermen faction of SDS, who knew the Haymarket story and regarded Spies and Parsons as heroic figures.[41] The explosion did nothing, however, to relieve the rage young revolutionaries felt toward the police—a rage that became an uncontrollable fury when two Black Panther leaders, Fred Hampton and Mark Clark, were killed by Chicago police officers during a nighttime raid on their apartment in December of 1969.[42]

Under these adverse circumstances, a small group of union veterans formed a Haymarket Memorial Committee to undertake the formidable task of erecting something in the square to honor the memory of the workers killed by police gunfire that night in 1886 and of the men who were tried and executed for the bombing. The committee's secretary, Leslie Orear, drew an explicit connection between past and present in his call for a new memorial. The Haymarket tragedy, he wrote, offered a useful analogy to the present because the conflicts that produced it were so much like the outbreaks of violence that caused bloodshed in the late 1960s.[43]

The memorial committee had no success, however, when it challenged what Les Orear called "a deliberate amnesia" on the part of city officials concerning the Haymarket tragedy. An even more serious problem was the police department's investment in its interpretation of violent events. "Our story is that the Haymarket was a police riot—nobody did a damn thing until the police came," Orear explained. "Their story is that they saved the city from anarchist terrorism." Mollie West, a Memorial Committee member who had nearly been killed by police gunfire during the Memorial Day Massacre in 1937, thought there could be a historical park in the Haymarket that would give the police a "fair shake" but also restore some balance to the site by honoring the protesters, though she realized that in Chicago this would be a hard act to complete.[44] West had no idea just how difficult this task would become over the next few turbulent years.

When city officials regularly rebuffed appeals for some marker to commemorate the worker casualties of Haymarket, preservationists found another way to remember them. On May 4, 1970, the same day that Mayor Daley unveiled the newly repaired police statue, Studs Terkel and other Illinois Labor History Society members pluckily gathered in the square to dedicate a small plaque honoring the union dead, which they placed on the wall of the Catholic Charities Building on Randolph Street; it was all they could get, because city officials refused to allow any such thing to be put in public space. Shortly after it was hung, the plaque was torn down. There would be nothing new mounted in the square to contest the police department's story of Haymarket, the story embodied so gallantly in the figure of the bronze patrolman with his hand raised in the air.

And then, on October 6, 1970, the Weathermen struck again, blowing up the police monument a second time.[45] Months later, when the battered statue was repaired and returned yet again to its concrete pedestal, the mayor ordered round-the-clock police protection at considerable cost and embarrassment to the city. At this point, Les Orear of the Labor History Society wrote to Daley and suggested that the monument be moved out of the violently contested space in the Haymarket to a more secure location. The metal policeman remained on his pedestal for two more years until the statue was quietly transferred to the lobby of the Central Police Station; it was later placed in a nearly hidden courtyard of the Chicago Police Training Academy, where it could be viewed only by special appointment.[46]

The square was now emptied of any physical reminder of the 1886 tragedy. This vacancy still seemed a shame to Orear, who had devoted years of work to memorializing the place. He had met people who visited the site and broke down in tears "when they found there was absolutely no demarcation there," and he had often led delegations of foreign travelers to the spot, pilgrims who came from all over the world to Chicago and who viewed the site "in awe, like it was a holy place."[47]

So Orear and his party of memory carried on until they finally achieved a victory in 1986, when the Illinois Labor History Society persuaded the new mayor of Chicago, Harold Washington (elected in 1983 as the city's first black mayor), to support a memorial park in the square that would honor the workers who died there, including the four anarchists who were later executed. On May 4, 1986, when the centennial of Haymarket was observed in various parts of the city, Mayor Washington issued a proclamation honoring the first May Day in 1886 as the beginning of "the movement towards the eight-hour day, union rights, civil rights, human rights" and describing the Chicago trial and execution that followed as "a tragic miscarriage of justice which claimed the lives of four labor activists."[48] However, when Mayor Washington died at the start of his second term in 1987, hopes for a memorial park expired with him. And so nothing existed in the Haymarket to recall the lives of anyone who died there, not the protesters and not the police.

ALTHOUGH HAYMARKET SQUARE lacked any visible reminders of the tragedy, the story of what happened there in 1886 and of what happened afterward gained more and more attention in the years after the centennial ceremonies. The old radical press in Chicago, the Charles H. Kerr Publishing Company, produced a rich documentary collection, reprinted William Adelman's popular walking tour of Haymarket sites, and published the music and lyrics to *Eight Hours,* a cabaret-style musical production. These centennial publications were followed by a parade of scholarly studies by historians interested in Haymarket as a watershed moment in U.S. history.[49] In 1998 historians at the Newberry Library achieved some public recognition of the event's significance when they persuaded the United States Park Service to make the martyrs' memorial at Waldheim a national landmark.[50] In addition, various artists and imaginative writers produced cultural interpretations and artistic representations of the story and its characters, most recently in a novel and in three plays about the ever intriguing lives of Albert and Lucy Parsons.[51] This continuing fascination with the Haymarket affair is based on the story's timeless qualities: its inherent drama, its tragic victims and larger-than-life characters, and its resonance with the political fears and moral concerns of the late-twentieth- and early-twenty-first-century world.[52]

ON SEPTEMBER 14, 2004, several hundred Chicagoans gathered to dedicate a memorial in Haymarket Square, finally erected as a result of persistent efforts by the Illinois Labor History Society and the officers of the Chicago Federation of Labor. The city's mayor, Richard M. Daley, the son of Richard J. Daley, approved the project, and the head of the city's police union spoke at the ceremony, even though both men seemed well aware of Haymarket Square's explosive history.[53]

There is a statue now on the exact spot where Sam Fielden stood speaking on a hay wagon when Captain Ward gave the order to disperse that night in 1886. Instead of naming the casualties of the Haymarket tragedy, the new monument on Desplaines Street offers the public a symbolic memorial: a figurative composition of rounded-off bronze figures with a reddish hue, shapes of people who are assembling, or perhaps disassembling, a wagon.[54] The base of the structure features a cautiously worded inscription that refers to the affair as "a powerful symbol for a diverse cross section of people, ideas and movements," which touched "on the issues of free speech, the right of public assembly, organized labor, the fight for the eight-hour workday, law enforcement, justice, anarchy, and the right of human beings to pursue an equitable and prosperous life."[55]

This language is nothing like what the fierce partisans of the Haymarket martyrs would have chosen. Rather, the inscribed words on the monument's base reflect a point of view carefully hammered out by a committee of citizens and local officials trying to mark a spot and an event that left a painfully conflicted memory as its legacy. So it took some time for citizens, advocates and officials to agree on an appropriate Haymarket memorial—thirty-five years after the idea was first raised by Studs Terkel and others. For all those years, said the city's cultural historian, the idea of commemorating Haymarket was impossible because the event aroused such strong emotions; it took a long time for Chicagoans to gain a perspective that allowed people "to look back on the Haymarket and see that it was everybody's tragedy."[56]

MANY PEOPLE ON ALL SIDES suffered, directly and indirectly, from the terrible events that unfolded in Chicago beginning on May 3, 1886. Besides the policemen and workers who lost their lives as a result, and scores of family members and friends who lost loved ones, other Americans sustained a different kind of loss—a loss of heart. This was particularly true in the case of many of the worker activists and labor reformers who imagined creating a new and better world on the eve of the Great Upheaval. In 1865 their forefathers, Andrew Cameron, William Sylvis and Ira Steward, believed that the Republic's sacrifices in the Civil War, including the death of their beloved president, had made it possible for the United States to become a more perfect union. With the slaves emancipated and the South under democratic reconstruction, union workers in Chicago and other cities began to anticipate their own emancipation from the endless workday and growing tyranny of wage labor. For nearly twenty years they clung to that dream despite their bitter disappointment with failed laws, despite their suffering in two crippling depressions and despite their bloody defeats in strike after strike. On May 1, 1886, all this was forgotten as workers celebrated their "emancipation day" and looked forward to a new era when, they believed, America would become a cooperative commonwealth, free of violence and coercion or "class rule of any kind." Three more days of hope followed, until the tragic bombing and shooting in Haymarket Square shattered the euphoria and unleashed the forces that led to Black Friday, when four workers in muslin robes dangled from ropes in Cook County Jail.

In the decades that followed, there would be other moments like May 1, 1886, when laboring people would strike and march and demonstrate their desire to create a new world of work, moments when they could even imagine the coming of a new cooperative society. But never again would there be anything quite like the feeling thousands of American workers experienced on that first May Day, that day when they believed that their dreams of freedom would really come true.

The nonviolent mass protests of May 1, 1886, could have marked a turning point in American history—a moment when our industrial relations could have developed in a different, less conflicted way, but instead the killings at the McCormick plant, the bombing in the Haymarket, along with the court proceedings and the hangings that followed, ushered in fifty years of recurrent industrial violence, a period when workers, especially immigrants, often found themselves at war with their employers, the courts, the police and the armed forces of their own government.

In this sense, the Haymarket affair was not "everybody's tragedy." The defeat of the eight-hour movement, the suppression of its radical wing and the extinction of the visionary Knights of Labor were great victories for employers in Chicago and other American industrial cities. Furthermore, the arrest, trial and execution of the anarchists were seen as moral and political victories for law and order, a series of events that were said to have saved the Republic from anarchy. The losers in the saga appeared at first to be merely a few maladjusted immigrant workers and the most militant troublemakers in their midst. But, in the long run, the losses were much broader.

The people of Chicago lost any chance for the social peace all classes desired; instead, they inherited the "bone deep grudges" that would rest on their shoulders for decades to come. The officers of the court, the police captains, the prosecuting attorneys, the judges and jurymen in the Haymarket case had seemed like heroes in 1887, but within a few years, they lost their lustrous reputations when members of the bar and other influential citizens throughout the state and elsewhere came to believe that the convictions of the anarchists were, in Clarence Darrow's words, "brought about through malice and hatred," and that the tactics used by the police and the prosecution constituted a "standing menace to the liberty of the citizen."[57] What is more, the execution of Spies, Parsons, Engel and Fischer came to be seen by many people in the United States and overseas not as a victory of democracy over anarchy, but as a travesty that betrayed the American ideal of liberty and justice for all. It is impossible to say exactly what might have been different if the police hadn't killed four strikers at McCormick's, if the police chief hadn't decided to break up the Haymarket meeting, if someone hadn't thrown the bomb, but it is clear that, in some sense, we are today living with the legacy of those long-ago events.

Notes

Prologue

1. Calculation based on 1880 and 1890 censuses of manufacturing, which calculated "value added" to manufacturing by subtracting the value of materials from the gross value of products. Figures from tables in Bessie Louise Pierce, *The Rise of the Modern City, 1871–1893*, Vol. 3 of *A History of Chicago* (New York: Knopf, 1957), pp. 534–35.

2. Bessie Louise Pierce, *From Town to City, 1848–1871*, Vol. 2 of *A History of Chicago* (New York: Knopf, 1940), pp. 67, 110; and *Chicago Tribune*, May 5, 6, 1886.

3. *Chicago Tribune*, May 3, 1886.

4. Donald L. Miller, *City of the Century: The Epic of Chicago and the Making of America* (New York: Simon & Schuster, 1996), pp. 225–26, 228. On Pullman, see Bessie Louise Pierce, ed., *As Others See Chicago: Impressions of Visitors, 1673–1933* (Chicago: University of Chicago Press, 1933), pp. 241–49. On Pullman building at Adams and Michigan, see Pierce, *Chicago*, Vol. 3, p. 232, n. 102.

5. Quote in Stanley Buder, *Pullman: An Experiment in Industrial Order and Community Planning, 1880–1930* (New York: Oxford University Press, 1967), p. 141.

6. All quotes describing the events of May 4 are from the *Chicago Tribune*, May 5, 1886, unless cited otherwise.

7. *New York Times*, May 6, 1886; and *Chicago Tribune*, May 6, 7, 1886. On the *Tribune* and its coverage, see Lloyd Wendt, *Chicago Tribune: The Rise of a Great American Newspaper* (Chicago: Rand McNally, 1969), pp. 282–85, 287–88.

8. On Medill, see Wendt, *Chicago Tribune;* Carl Sandburg, *Abraham Lincoln: The Prairie Years and the War Years* (New York: Harcourt, Brace & World, 1954), p. 57; Pierce, *Chicago*, Vol. 2, p. 86, and Vol. 3, p. 411; Gunther Barth, *City People: The Rise of Modern City Culture in Nineteenth-Century America* (New York: Oxford University Press, 1980), p. 98; and David Paul Nord, "The Public Community: The Urbanization of Journalism in Chicago," *Journal of Urban History* 11 (August 1985), p. 439.

9. *Chicago Tribune*, May 6, 1886.

10. Quotes from Henry David, *The History of the Haymarket Affair: A Study in the American Social-Revolutionary and Labor Movements* (New York: Russell & Russell, 1936), p. 179; Mary Jones, *The Autobiography of Mother Jones* (Chicago: Charles H. Kerr, 1925), p. 21; and Paul Avrich, *The Haymarket Tragedy* (Princeton: Princeton University Press, 1984), p. 218.

11. See Richard Sennett, "Middle-Class Families and Urban Violence: The Experience of a Chicago Community in the Nineteenth Century," in Stephan Thernstrom and

Richard Sennett, eds., *Nineteenth-Century Cities: Essays in the New Urban History* (New Haven: Yale University Press, 1969).

12. Quotes from Sven Beckert, *The Monied Metropolis: New York City and the Consolidation of the American Bourgeoisie, 1850–1896* (New York: Cambridge University Press, 2001), p. 276; and T. J. Jackson Lears, *No Place of Grace: Antimodernism and the Transformation of American Culture, 1880–1920* (Chicago: University of Chicago Press, 1994), p. 29.

13. Jeffory A. Clymer, *America's Culture of Terrorism: Violence, Capitalism, and the Written Word* (Chapel Hill: University of North Carolina Press, 2003), pp. 36–39; *New York Times,* May 6, 1886; and Paul Boyer, *Urban Masses and Moral Order in America, 1820–1920* (Cambridge: Harvard University Press, 1978), p. 126.

14. Reverend H. W. Thomas quoted in Carl Smith, *Urban Disorder and the Shape of Belief: The Great Chicago Fire, the Haymarket Bomb, and the Model Town of Pullman* (Chicago: University of Chicago Press, 1995), p. 169.

15. Ibid., p. 168.

16. Samuel Gompers, *Seventy Years of Life and Labor: An Autobiography* (New York: Dutton, 1925), pp. 238–39.

17. Quote from John Higham, *Strangers in the Land: Patterns of American Nativism, 1860–1925* (New York: Atheneum, 1977), p. 55. Also see Gary Gerstle, *American Crucible: Race and Nation in the Twentieth Century* (Princeton: Princeton University Press, 2001), p. 102; and Louis Joughin and Edmund M. Morgan, *The Legacy of Sacco and Vanzetti* (New York: Harcourt, Brace & World, 1948), pp. 208–9.

18. Quote from Edmund Wilson, *Letters on Literature and Politics* (New York: Farrar, Straus & Giroux, 1977), p. 154.

19. Martin J. Burke, *The Conundrum of Class: Public Discourse on the Social Order in America* (Chicago: University of Chicago Press, 1995), p. 161; and Boyer, *Urban Masses and Moral Order,* pp. 130–31.

20. George Pullman to Andrew Carnegie, May 5, 1886, Carnegie Papers, Vol. 9, Folio 1445, Library of Congress; and see Buder, *Pullman,* pp. 33, 37, 140–42. *Triumphant Democracy* quoted in *Chicago Tribune,* May 5, 1886.

21. On Oglesby, see Mark A. Plummer, *Lincoln's Rail-Splitter: Governor Richard J. Oglesby* (Urbana: University of Illinois Press, 2001), pp. 178, 190–91; and quote in Carl S. Smith, "Cataclysm and Cultural Consciousness: Chicago and the Haymarket Trial," *Chicago History* 15 (Summer 1986), p. 46.

Chapter One / For Once in Common Front

1. *Chicago Tribune,* May 2, 1865.

2. *Chicago Tribune,* May 2, 1865; Dorothy Meserve Kunhardt and Philip B. Kunhardt, Jr., *Twenty Days: A Narrative in Text and Pictures of the Assassination of Abraham Lincoln and the Twenty Days and Nights That Followed* (New York: Castle Books, 1993), p. 235; and quote from Sandburg, *Lincoln,* p. 740.

3. *Chicago Tribune,* May 2, 1865; Pierce, *Chicago,* Vol. 2, pp. 256, 504–5; Lincoln quoted in James McPherson, *Battle Cry of Freedom* (New York: Oxford University Press, 1988), p. 28.

4. *Chicago Tribune,* May 2, 1865.

5. Quote in Sandburg, *Lincoln,* p. 742.

6. First quote in Eric Foner, *The Story of American Freedom* (New York: Norton, 1998), p. 100. Second quote from *Chicago Tribune,* May 3, 1865.

7. James C. Sylvis, *The Life, Speeches, Labors and Essays of William H. Sylvis, Late President of the Iron-Moulders' International Union and also of the National Labor Union* (Philadelphia: Claxton, Remsen & Haffelfiner, 1872), pp. 129–30, 169.

8. Ibid., p. 129.

9. Ibid., p. 25. Also see David Montgomery, "William H. Sylvis and the Search for Working-Class Citizenship," in Melvyn Dubofsky and Warren Van Tine, eds., *Labor Leaders in America* (Urbana: University of Illinois Press, 1987), pp. 3–29.

10. Sylvis, *The Life*, pp. 31–32.

11. On antebellum labor history, see Norman Ware, *The Industrial Worker, 1840–1860* (Boston: Houghton Mifflin, 1924); and Philip S. Foner, *History of the Labor Movement in the United States* (New York: International Publishers, 1947), Vol. 1.

12. Bruce Laurie, *Artisans into Workers: Labor in Nineteenth-Century America* (New York: Hill & Wang, 1989), pp. 75–94, 103–6. In fact, no workers died in strike-related violence until 1850, when New York City police killed two German tailors. Edwin G. Burrows and Mike Wallace, *Gotham: A History of New York City to 1898* (New York: Oxford University Press, 1999), p. 771.

13. David Montgomery, *Beyond Equality: Labor and the Radical Republicans, 1862–1872* (New York: Knopf, 1967), pp. 94–96; Pierce, *Chicago*, Vol. 2, p. 157.

14. Sylvis, *The Life*, p. 15; and P. Foner, *Labor Movement*, Vol. 1, p. 340.

15. P. Foner, *Labor Movement*, Vol. 1, p. 348.

16. Robert Ozanne, *A Century of Labor-Management Relations at McCormick and International Harvester* (Madison: University of Wisconsin Press, 1967), p. 5; Philip S. Foner and David R. Roediger, *Our Own Time: A History of American Labor and the Working Day* (Westport, CT: Greenwood Press, 1989), p. 310, n. 46.

17. Quote in P. Foner, *Labor Movement*, Vol. 1, p. 361.

18. J. R. Green, *A Short History of the English People* (London: Macmillan, 1921), pp. 519, 616; G. D. H. Cole, *A Short History of the British Working-Class Movement, 1789–1947* (London: Allen & Unwin, 1948), pp. 95–96; Dorothy Thompson, *The Chartists: Popular Politics in the Industrial Revolution* (New York: Pantheon, 1984), pp. 116–21. Quote from E. P. Thompson, *Customs in Common: Studies in Traditional Popular Culture* (New York: New Press, 1991), p. 830.

19. On Andrew Cameron, see Allen Johnson et al., *Dictionary of American Biography* (New York: Scribner, 1937), pp. 433–34.

20. Ibid. Also see Richard Schneirov, "Political Cultures and the Role of the State in Labor's Republic: A View from Chicago," *Labor History* 32 (Summer 1991), pp. 387–93.

21. *Workingman's Advocate*, July 7, 1866.

22. *Workingman's Advocate*, April 28, 1866.

23. Montgomery, *Beyond Equality*, pp. 90–91.

24. P. Foner and Roediger, *Our Own Time*, p. 86. Also see Montgomery, *Beyond Equality*, pp. 254–55.

25. P. Foner, *Labor Movement*, Vol. 1, p. 364; Steward quoted in Montgomery, *Beyond Equality*, p. 251.

26. George McNeill, ed., *The Labor Movement: The Problem of Today* (Boston: A. M. Bridgman & Co., 1886), p. 128; and P. Foner and Roediger, *Our Own Time*, pp. 86, 108, 127.

27. Marx quoted in P. Foner and Roediger, *Our Own Time*, p. 82.

28. Pierce, *Chicago*, Vol. 2, pp. 168, 174; *Workingman's Advocate*, April 28, 1866.

29. Montgomery, *Beyond Equality*, p. 176; Sylvis, *The Life*, pp. 349–50.

30. Quotes from John R. Commons et al., eds., *Documentary History of American Industrial Society* (Cleveland: A. H. Clark, 1910), Vol. IX, p. 145.

31. E. Foner, *American Freedom*, pp. 99, 106.

32. Montgomery, *Beyond Equality*, p. 306; and Pierce, *Chicago*, Vol. 2, p. 175.

33. McNeill, ed., *The Labor Movement*, p. 130.

34. Quote in Pierce, *Chicago*, Vol. 2, p. 176.

35. *Boston Daily Evening Voice*, April 6, 1867, quoted in Montgomery, *Beyond Equality*, p. 307.

36. Quote in Montgomery, *Beyond Equality*, p. 254.

37. *Workingman's Advocate*, September 28, 1867.

38. Miller, *City of the Century*, p. 121.

Chapter Two / A Paradise for Workers and Speculators

1. *Chicago Tribune*, May 16, 1866.

2. Miller, *City of the Century*, p. 114; William Cronon, *Nature's Metropolis: Chicago and the Great West* (New York: Norton, 1991), p. 230.

3. Miller, *City of the Century*, p. 89; Cronon, *Nature's Metropolis*, p. 90; Pierce, *Chicago*, Vol. 2, p. 50.

4. Cronon, *Nature's Metropolis*, pp. 91–92.

5. Ibid., p. 91; Pierce, *Chicago*, Vol. 2, pp. 67, 71, 81–82, 110, 158, and quote on p. 103; John B. Jentz, "Class and Politics in an Emerging Industrial City: Chicago in the 1860s and 1870s," *Journal of Urban History* 17 (May 1991), p. 231; Robin Einhorn, *Property Rules: Political Economy in Chicago, 1833–1872* (Chicago: University of Chicago Press, 1991), p. 209; Ozanne, *Century*, p. 5; and Arthur C. Cole, *The Era of the Civil War* (Springfield: Illinois State Historical Society, 1919), pp. 381–82.

6. Miller, *City of the Century*, p. 114; *Chicago Tribune*, April 23, 1866; and see Cronon, *Nature's Metropolis*, pp. 149, 163, 230.

7. Pierce, *Chicago*, Vol. 2, p. 482; and Jentz, "Class and Politics," pp. 231–32.

8. Quote from Miller, *City of the Century*, pp. 143–44.

9. *Workingman's Advocate*, April 28, 1866.

10. Montgomery, *Beyond Equality*, pp. 231, 248, 254–57, 380–81.

11. Quote ibid., p. 308.

12. Description from *Illinois Staats-Zeitung*, May 2, 3, 1867, quoted in Hartmut Keil and John B. Jentz, "German Working Class Culture in Chicago," *Gulliver* 9 (1981), pp. 254–55, 257.

13. Ozanne, *Century*, pp. 6–7, including quote; and Montgomery, *Beyond Equality*, pp. 309–10.

14. Pierce, *Chicago*, Vol. 2, pp. 178, 258, 505; and Montgomery, *Beyond Equality*, p. 309.

15. Montgomery, *Beyond Equality*, p. 310.

16. Pierce, *Chicago*, Vol. 2, p. 179.

17. Montgomery, *Beyond Equality*, pp. 310–11; and Montgomery, "William H. Sylvis," p. 15.

18. Pierce, *Chicago*, Vol. 2, p. 179; Montgomery, *Beyond Equality*, pp. 226–27; and *Workingman's Advocate*, August 17, September 28, 1867.

19. Montgomery, *Beyond Equality*, p. 227.

20. P. Foner, *Labor Movement*, Vol. 1, pp. 376–77.

21. *Workingman's Advocate*, July 4, 1868.

22. Montgomery, *Beyond Equality*, p. 263.

23. Pierce, *Chicago*, Vol. 2, p. 185; and *Workingman's Advocate*, April 24, 1869.

24. Charlotte Todes, *William H. Sylvis and the National Labor Union* (New York: International Publishers, 1942), pp. 74–76.

25. Ibid., pp. 75, 106–9.

26. Pierce, *Chicago*, Vol. 2, pp. 18, 159; Jentz, "Class and Politics," pp. 235, 237–38, 241, 243; and see Richard Schneirov, *Labor and Urban Politics: Class Conflict and the Origins of Modern Liberalism in Chicago, 1864–97* (Urbana: University of Illinois Press, 1998), pp. 38–39, 54.

27. "Annual Report of the Agent of the German Society of Chicago," April 1, 1870, quoted in Hartmut Keil and John B. Jentz, eds., *German Workers in Chicago: A Documentary History of Working-Class Culture from 1850 to World War I* (Urbana: University of Illinois Press, 1998), p. 40.

28. Ibid., pp. 39–40; and Miller, *City of the Century*, p. 135.

29. Miller, *City of the Century*, p. 134.

30. Einhorn, *Property Rules*, Table 1, Property Ownership, p. 250. Mean total wealth in 1870 was $19,257 for native-born, $2,475 for German, $2,580 for Irish and $2,227 for Scandinavian. Edward Bubnys, "Nativity and the Distribution of Wealth: Chicago, 1870," *Explorations in Economic History* 19 (April 1982), Tables 2 and 3, pp. 104–5.

31. Miller, *City of the Century*, pp. 120, 127–31.

32. Alfred T. Andreas, *History of Chicago from the Earliest Period to the Present Time* (New York: Arno Press, 1975), Vol. 2, pp. 769, 775; Paul Andrew Hutton, *Phil Sheridan and His Army* (Lincoln: University of Nebraska Press, 1985), pp. 117, 153. Bismarck quoted in Miller, *City of the Century*, p. 131.

33. Quote in Miller, *City of the Century*, p. 121.

34. Twain's novel *The Gilded Age* was published in 1874. See H. Wayne Morgan, "An Age in Need of Reassessment," in H. Wayne Morgan, ed., *The Gilded Age: A Reappraisal* (Syracuse: Syracuse University Press, 1963), p. 1. Whitman quoted in John Tipple, "The Robber Baron in the Gilded Age," in Morgan, ed., *Gilded Age*, p. 32.

35. Walt Whitman, "Democratic Vistas," reprinted in Perry Miller, ed., *Major Writers of America* (New York: Harcourt, Brace & World, 1962), Vol. 1, pp. 1086–87, 1104.

36. Ibid., pp. 1087, 1100. Last Whitman quote in Robert Falk, "The Writers' Search for Lost Reality," in Morgan, ed., *Gilded Age*, p. 200.

Chapter Three / We May Not Always Be So Secure

1. See Frank Jellinek, *The Paris Commune of 1871* (1937; reprint, New York: Grosset & Dunlap, 1965), pp. 61–173; quote on p. 90.

2. Philip M. Katz, *From Appomattox to Montmarte: Americans and the Paris Commune* (Cambridge: Harvard University Press, 1998), pp. 18–19.

3. Quote ibid.

4. Jellinek, *Paris Commune*, pp. 338–70.

5. Katz, *From Appomattox*, pp. 69, 71, 75, 83, 85.

6. See Richard Slotkin, *Gunfighter Nation: The Myth of the Frontier in Twentieth-Century America* (New York: Atheneum, 1992), pp. 91–92.

7. Quote from Katz, *From Appomattox*, pp. 149, 153–54.

8. *Workingman's Advocate*, July 8, 1871.

9. *Workingman's Advocate*, July 8, 1871; and Karl Marx's *The Civil War in France*, in *Workingman's Advocate*, July 17, 1871.

10. *Workingman's Advocate*, July 8, August 19, 1871.

11. Pierce, *Chicago*, Vol. 3, p. 191.

12. Quotes in Miller, *City of the Century*, pp. 159, 171; and Karen Sawislak, *Smoldering City: Chicagoans and the Great Fire, 1871–1874* (Chicago: University of Chicago Press, 1995), p. 44.

13. Smith, *Urban Disorder* (see Prologue, n. 14), p. 49.

14. Quote ibid., p. 51. I have relied here upon Smith's discussion of the hanging rumors, ibid., pp. 53, 55–57.

15. See ibid., p. 34.

16. Ibid., pp. 33, 71, 73.

17. Miller, *City of the Century*, p. 164; and Einhorn, *Property Rules*, p. 234.

18. Sawislak, *Smoldering City*, pp. 79, 44; and Miller, *City of the Century*, p. 167.

19. Quotes in Katz, *From Appomattox*, pp. 124–25.

20. Quote ibid., p. 125.

21. Einhorn, *Property Rules*, pp. 235–36.

22. Sawislak, *Smoldering City*, p. 44. Also see Miller, *City of the Century*, pp. 134, 147–48.

23. Einhorn, *Property Rules*, p. 236.

24. Sawislak, *Smoldering City*, p. 93. On Medill, see Nord, "The Public Community," p. 423; Einhorn, *Property Rules*, p. 236.

25. Quote in Einhorn, *Property Rules*, p. 236.

26. Ibid., pp. 236, 239, 250.

27. John J. Flinn, *History of the Chicago Police from the Settlement of the Community to the Present Time* (Chicago: Police Book Fund, 1887), pp. 137–38, 140.

28. Quote from ibid., pp. 142, 144.

29. Jentz, "Class and Politics," p. 261.

30. Quote ibid., p. 248.

31. See Schneirov, *Labor and Urban Politics*, p. 61; Einhorn, *Property Rules*, pp. 219–21, 226–27.

32. Quote in Pierce, *Chicago*, Vol. 3, pp. 19, 194.

33. Katz, *From Appomattox*, p. 169.

34. Pierce, *Chicago*, Vol. 3, pp. 194, 196, 240–41.

35. Einhorn, *Property Rules*, pp. 233–34, Sawislak, *Smoldering City*, pp. 87–88, 97; and Miller, *City of the Century*, pp. 162–63.

36. Quote from Floyd Dell, "Socialism and Anarchism in Chicago," in J. Seymour Currey, ed., *Chicago: Its History and Its Builders* (Chicago: S. J. Clarke Publishing Co., 1912), p. 366.

37. Ibid., p. 365. Horace White quoted in Bruce C. Nelson, *Beyond the Martyrs: A Social History of Chicago's Anarchists* (New Brunswick, NJ: Rutgers University Press, 1988), p. 53.

38. Nelson, *Beyond the Martyrs*, p. 53; and quote in Herbert Gutman, "The Workers' Search for Power," in Morgan, ed., *Gilded Age*, pp. 61–63.

39. Schneirov, *Labor and Urban Politics*, p. 54; *Chicago Tribune*, December 23, 24, 25, 29, 1873, January 2, 1874.

40. Quotes from Schneirov, *Labor and Urban Politics*, p. 58; and Pierce, *Chicago*, Vol. 3, p. 345.

41. Nelson, *Beyond the Martyrs*, pp. 53–54.

42. Morris Hillquit, *History of Socialism in America* (New York: Russell & Russell, 1965), p. 186.

43. Nelson, *Beyond the Martyrs*, p. 54.

44. Jentz, "Class and Politics," p. 249.

45. See Schneirov, *Labor and Urban Politics*, p. 57; Ozanne, *Century*, p. 8; and quotes from Gutman, "Workers' Search," p. 45.

46. Quotes from Gutman, "Workers' Search," p. 45.

47. Schneirov, *Labor and Urban Politics*, p. 59.

Chapter 4 / A Liberty-Thirsty People

1. Michael J. Schaack, *Anarchy and Anarchists* (Chicago: Shulte & Co, 1889), p. 49.

2. On southern migrants to Chicago, see Pierce, *Chicago*, Vol. 3, p. 21.

3. On the Levee District, see Richard C. Lindberg, *Chicago Ragtime: Another Look at Chicago, 1880–1920* (South Bend, IN: Icarus Press, 1985), pp. 119–20.

4. Pierce, *Chicago*, Vol. 3, p. 408.

5. Nord, "The Public Community," pp. 416–17.

6. Ibid., pp. 419–21, and quote on pp. 431–32.

7. Albert R. Parsons, "Autobiography of Albert R. Parsons," in Philip S. Foner, ed., *The Autobiographies of the Haymarket Martyrs* (New York: Humanities Press, 1969), p. 30.

8. Ibid., p. 27.

9. Ibid., pp. 29–31.

10. See W. E. B. DuBois, *Black Reconstruction* (New York: Harcourt, Brace & Co., 1935), pp. 553, 556. By the middle of 1868 more than 400 Texas blacks had been killed in the violence, most of them murdered by white desperadoes. Some white men died as well, including some racists killed by army and militiamen, and some northerners, like seven men from Illinois murdered by a mob because they were carpetbaggers. See Randolph B. Campbell, *Grass-Roots Reconstruction in Texas, 1865–1880* (Baton Rouge: Louisiana State University Press, 1997), pp. 17–18, 165, 176–78, 184.

11. Albert Parsons to George A. Schilling, in Lucy Parsons, ed., *The Life of Albert R. Parsons* (Chicago: Lucy Parsons, 1903), p. 217; and A. Parsons, "Autobiography," p. 29.

12. Campbell, *Grass-Roots Reconstruction*, pp. 17–20.

13. Parsons to Schilling in L. Parsons, *The Life*, p. 216.

14. Campbell, *Grass-Roots Reconstruction*, pp. 19–20; A. Parsons to Schilling in L. Parsons, *The Life*, p. 218; and A. Parsons, "Autobiography," p. 29.

15. A. Parsons, "Autobiography," pp. 29–30.

16. Carolyn Ashbaugh, *Lucy Parsons: American Revolutionary* (Chicago: Charles H. Kerr, 1976), pp. 14, 268; and *Chicago Tribune*, July 22, 1886.

17. Ashbaugh, *Lucy Parsons*, pp. 14, 268; and Rima Lunin Schultz and Adele Hast, "Lucy Parsons," in Rima Lunin Schultz and Adele Hast, eds., *Women Building Chicago, 1790–1990: A Biographical Dictionary* (Bloomington: Indiana University Press, 2001), pp. 668–69.

18. Lucy Parsons quoted in Avrich, *Tragedy*, p. 11.

19. DuBois, *Black Reconstruction*, pp. 561, 624, 684, 708.

20. William J. Adelman, *Haymarket Revisited: A Tour Guide of Labor History Sites and Ethnic Neighborhoods Connected with the Haymarket Affair* (Chicago: Illinois Labor History Society, 1976), pp. 65–75; and Christine Harzig, "Chicago's German North Side, 1880–1900: The Structure of a Gilded Age Ethnic Neighborhood," in Hartmut Keil and John B. Jentz, eds., *German Workers in Industrial Chicago, 1850–1910: A Comparative Portrait* (DeKalb: Northern Illinois University Press, 1983), pp. 127–44.

21. United States Department of the Interior, Census Office, *Statistics of the Population of the United States at the Tenth Census, 1880* (Washington, DC: Government Printing Office, 1883), pp. 417, 448.

22. United States Department of the Interior, Census Office, *Statistics of the Population of the United States at the Eleventh Census, 1890* (Washington, DC: Government Printing Office, 1893), p. 374; United States Department of the Interior, Census Office, *Report on the Manufactures of the United States at the Tenth Census, 1880* (Washington, DC: Government Printing Office, 1883), p. 870. Quote in Bruce Carlan Levine, "Free Soil, Free Labor, and *Freimanner:* German Chicago in the Civil War Era," in Keil and Jentz, eds., *German Workers in Industrial Chicago,* pp. 176–77.

23. Hartmut Keil, "Chicago's German Working Class," in Keil and Jentz, eds., *German Workers in Industrial Chicago,* pp. 28, 31; Harzig, "Chicago's German North Side," p. 129.

24. The following account is based on August Spies, "Autobiography of August Spies," in P. Foner, *Autobiographies,* pp. 59–69.

25. Quotes ibid., p. 66.

26. *Manufactures at the Tenth Census,* p. 392.

27. Keil and Jentz, eds., *German Workers, Documentary,* pp. 170, 175–76; Hartmut Keil, "Immigrant Neighborhoods and American Society: German Immigrants on Chicago's Northwest Side in the Late Nineteenth Century," in Hartmut Keil, ed., *German Workers' Culture in the United States, 1850 to 1920* (Washington, DC: Smithsonian Institution Press, 1988), pp. 25–58.

28. Pierce, *Chicago,* Vol. 3, pp. 22–23; Keil and Jentz, eds., *German Workers, Documentary,* pp. 34, 170–71, 176.

29. Pierce, *Chicago,* Vol. 3, p. 23; and Keil and Jentz, eds., *German Workers, Documentary,* pp. 160–68, 176–81.

30. Avrich, *Tragedy,* p. 123.

31. Kathleen Neils Conzen, "Ethnicity as Festive Culture: Nineteenth-Century German America on Parade," in Werner Sollors, ed., *The Invention of Ethnicity* (New York: Oxford University Press, 1989), pp. 49–50.

32. Pierce, *Chicago,* Vol. 3, p. 489.

33. Hartmut Keil and Heinz Ickstadt, "Elements of German Working-Class Culture in Chicago, 1880 to 1990," and Christine Heiss, "Popular and Working-Class German Theater in Chicago, 1870–1910," in Keil, ed., *German Workers' Culture,* pp. 94–95, 181–202; Christa Carajal, "German-American Theater," in Maxine Schwartz Seller, ed., *Ethnic Theater in the United States* (Westport, CT: Greenwood Press, 1983), pp. 178–79, 183, 185.

34. *Manufactures at the Tenth Census,* p. 540; Pierce, *Chicago,* Vol. 3, p. 31; and Odd S. Lovoll, "A Scandinavian Melting Pot in Chicago," in Philip J. Anderson and Dag Blanck, eds., *Swedish-American Life in Chicago: Culture and Urban Aspects of an Immigrant People, 1850–1930* (Urbana: University of Illinois Press, 1992), p. 62.

35. Quote in Pierce, *Chicago,* Vol. 3, pp. 28–29; Lovoll, "Scandinavian Melting Pot," p. 63; S. N. D. North, *The Newspaper and Periodical Press at the Tenth Census, 1880* (Washington, DC: Government Printing Office, 1884), p. 221.

36. Lovoll, "Scandinavian Melting Pot," p. 60; and see Robert H. Wiebe, *Who We Are: A History of Popular Nationalism* (Princeton: Princeton University Press, 2002), pp. 65–72.

37. Conzen, "Ethnicity as Festive Culture," pp. 45, 63, 65.

38. Pierce, *Chicago,* Vol. 3, p. 345.

39. Schneirov, *Labor and Urban Politics,* pp. 53, 59; Flinn, *Chicago Police,* p. 148.

40. Schneirov, *Labor and Urban Politics,* p. 59; Pierce, *Chicago,* Vol. 3, p. 253; Christine Heiss, "German Radicals in Industrial America: The *Lehr-und-wehr Verein* in

Gilded Age Chicago," in Keil and Jentz, eds., *German Workers in Industrial Chicago*, pp. 211, 214, 224.

41. Heiss, "German Radicals," p. 214.

42. Spies, "Autobiography," p. 67.

43. Medill quoted in Wayne Andrews, *Battle for Chicago* (New York: Harcourt, Brace & Co., 1946), p. 68; A. Parsons, "Autobiography," pp. 30–31; Parsons quoted in John D. Lawson, ed., *American State Trials* (St. Louis: F. H. Thomas Law Book Co., 1919), p. 310.

44. George A. Schilling, "A History of the Labor Movement in Chicago," in L. Parsons, *The Life*, p. xxii.

45. Ibid., p. xxiii. On Schilling, see Hartmut Keil, "The German Immigrant Working Class of Chicago, 1875–90: Workers, Labor Leaders and the Labor Movement," in Dirk Hoerder, ed., *American Labor and Immigration History, 1877–1920s: Recent European Research* (Urbana: University of Illinois Press, 1983), pp. 165–66.

46. Avrich, *Tragedy*, p. 23. On southwestern humor, see Falk, "Writers' Search for Lost Reality," in Morgan, ed., *Gilded Age*, p. 215.

47. Avrich, *Tragedy*, p. 22; *Chicago Tribune*, quoted in Pierce, *Chicago*, Vol. 3, p. 244; A. Parsons, "Autobiography," p. 31.

Chapter Five / The Inevitable Uprising

1. Quotes from Flinn, *Chicago Police*, pp. 157–58, 202.

2. Advertisement in *Frank Leslie's Illustrated Newspaper*, April 7, 1877, reprinted in Joshua Freeman et al., *From the Gilded Age to the Present*, Vol. 2 of *Who Built America? Working People and the Nation's Economy, Politics, Culture, and Society* (New York: Pantheon, 1992), p. 26.

3. Pierce, *Chicago*, Vol. 3, p. 477.

4. *Chicago Tribune*, July 4, 1876.

5. William J. Adelman, *Pilsen and the West Side: A Tour Guide* (Chicago: Illinois Labor History Society, 1983), revised 1983 version, photocopy in the author's possession, courtesy of the Illinois Labor History Society.

6. Richard Schneirov, "Free Thought and Socialism in the Czech Community in Chicago, 1875–1887," in Dirk Hoerder, ed., *"Struggle a Hard Battle": Essays on Working-Class Immigrants* (DeKalb: Northern Illinois University Press, 1986), pp. 123–24, 127, 129, 133. Quote from Pierce, *Chicago*, Vol. 3, p. 33.

7. Schneirov, "Free Thought," pp. 125, 128, 133. On Czech socialist exiles in Chicago, see Thomas Capek, *The Czechs (Bohemians) in America: A Study of Their National, Cultural, Political, Social, Economic, and Religious Life* (New York: Houghton Mifflin, 1920), pp. 140, 148.

8. Schneirov, "Free Thought," p. 126; and Schneirov, *Labor and Urban Politics*, p. 103.

9. Flinn, *Chicago Police*, p. 151.

10. Ibid.; Schneirov, "Free Thought," p. 133.

11. Flinn, *Chicago Police*, pp. 151, 158.

12. Ibid., pp. 158–59.

13. Ibid.

14. Ibid., p. 159; Ashbaugh, *Lucy Parsons*, pp. 17–18.

15. Nelson, *Beyond the Martyrs*, p. 55; Schilling, "Labor Movement in Chicago," pp. xvi–xxvii.

16. Pierce, *Chicago*, Vol. 3, pp. 254, 346, 351, 539; Flinn, *Chicago Police*, p. 15; Schneirov, "Free Thought," p. 197; and Nelson, *Beyond the Martyrs*, pp. 103, 140.

17. Richard Digby-Junger, *The Journalist as Reformer: Henry Demarest Lloyd and Wealth Against Commonwealth* (Westport, CT: Greenwood Press, 1996), pp. 21–48; and John L. Thomas, *Alternative America: Henry George, Edward Bellamy, Henry Demarest Lloyd, and the Adversary Tradition* (Cambridge, MA: Belknap Press, 1983), p. 77.

18. See Robert V. Bruce, *1877: Year of Violence* (Indianapolis: Bobbs-Merrill, 1959), pp. 74–114.

19. Quotes from Flinn, *Chicago Police*, pp. 154, 159–60.

20. Ibid., p. 159.

21. Pierce, *Chicago*, Vol. 3, p. 246; Schneirov, *Labor and Urban Politics*, p. 71. Handbill reproduced in Schneirov, *Labor and Urban Politics*, following p. 98.

22. Flinn, *Chicago Police*, pp. 160–61; Schneirov, *Labor and Urban Politics*, p. 71.

23. Schilling, "Labor Movement in Chicago," p. xviii. See Avrich, *Tragedy*, pp. 29–30; Schneirov, *Labor and Urban Politics*, p. 72; and A. Parsons, "Autobiography," p. 31. Speech quoted in Adelman, *Pilsen*, p. 13.

24. The following account of the railroad strike in Chicago is based on Bruce, *1877*, pp. 235–53.

25. Miller, *City of the Century*, p. 232.

26. Bruce, *1877*, pp. 239–40; Flinn, *Chicago Police*, p. 165.

27. Schneirov, *Labor and Urban Politics*, p. 73.

28. Ibid., pp. 74, 105–10.

29. Quoted in Pierce, *Chicago*, Vol. 3, p. 250.

30. Spies, "Autobiography," p. 68.

31. Adelman, *Pilsen*, p. 50.

32. Miller, *City of the Century*, p. 233; Flinn, *Chicago Police*, pp. 199, 208.

33. Pierce, *Chicago*, Vol. 3, p. 251.

34. *Chicago Tribune* quoted in Flinn, *Chicago Police*, p. 203; and see Richard C. Marohn, "The Arming of the Chicago Police in the Nineteenth Century," *Chicago History* 11 (Spring 1982), pp. 42, 44, 46.

35. Wolfgang Abendroth, *A Short History of the European Working Class* (New York: Monthly Review Press, 1972), p. 40.

36. For a revealing study of how widespread the uprising of 1877 became and how it pulled thousands of nonstrikers from local communities into the protesting crowds, including many middle-class city dwellers who had been alienated from the railroad companies by their invasion and destruction of urban space, see David O. Stowell, *Streets, Railroads, and the Great Strike of 1877* (Chicago: University of Chicago Press, 1999).

37. McNeill, ed., *The Labor Movement*, pp. 459–60.

38. L. Parsons, *The Life*, p. 120; McNeill, ed., *The Labor Movement*, pp. 459–61.

39. Gompers, *Seventy Years* (see Prologue, n. 16), pp. 46–47.

40. The following account is from A. Parsons, "Autobiography," pp. 32–34.

Chapter Six / The Flame That Makes the Kettle Boil

1. Schilling, "Labor Movement in Chicago," p. xviii; and see Nelson, *Beyond the Martyrs*, pp. 57–58.

2. Quote in Nelson, *Beyond the Martyrs*, p. 58.

3. Ibid.

4. Ibid.

5. Heiss, "German Radicals in Industrial America" (see chap. 4, n. 40), pp. 216, 219–20. A. Parsons quoted in *Chicago Tribune*, April 26, 1878.

6. Quotes in Schneirov, *Labor and Urban Politics,* p. 87; and Nelson, *Beyond the Martyrs,* p. 59.

7. Ashbaugh, *Lucy Parsons,* p. 34.

8. Nelson, *Beyond the Martyrs,* p. 60.

9. Harzig, "Chicago's German North Side" (see chap. 4, n. 20), p. 218; and Schilling, "Labor Movement in Chicago," p. xix.

10. *Chicago Tribune,* March 23, 1879.

11. Nelson, *Beyond the Martyrs,* pp. 62–64; quote in Schilling, "Labor Movement in Chicago," p. xix.

12. Schneirov, *Labor and Urban Politics,* p. 91. The Socialistic Labor Party sent three more members to the Common Council, where they worked with Democratic aldermen to employ factory inspectors, to abolish labor for children under twelve years old, to open public baths and water closets and to gain funding for new public schools and reading rooms.

13. Meredith Tax, *The Rising of the Women: Feminist Solidarity and Class Conflict, 1880–1917* (New York: Monthly Review Press, 1981), p. 41; Avrich, *Tragedy,* p. 150; Blaine McKinley, "Holmes, Lizzie May Swank," in Schultz and Hast, eds., *Women Building Chicago* (see chap. 4, n. 17), p. 400.

14. See Ashbaugh, *Lucy Parsons,* pp. 33–36; Schilling, "Labor Movement in Chicago," p. xx; Nelson, *Beyond the Martyrs,* pp. 67–68; quote from A. Parsons, "Autobiography," p. 36.

15. Hartmut Keil, "German Working-Class Radicalism in the United States from the 1870s to World War I," in Hoerder, *"Struggle a Hard Battle,"* pp. 81–82; Nelson, *Beyond the Martyrs,* pp. 33–34.

16. Harzig, "Chicago's German North Side," pp. 217–18.

17. A. Parsons, "Autobiography," p. 36; and see August Spies, "The Right to Bear Arms," *Alarm,* January 9, 1886.

18. Oscar Neebe, "Autobiography of Oscar Neebe," in P. Foner, *Autobiographies,* p. 165.

19. Pierce, *Chicago,* Vol. 3, p. 259.

20. Quote in Avrich, *Tragedy,* p. 59.

21. James Joll, *The Anarchists* (London: Eyre & Spottswoode, 1963), pp. 120–24; Barbara Tuchman, *The Proud Tower: A Portrait of the World Before the War, 1890–1914* (New York: Macmillan, 1966), p. 76.

22. Joll, *The Anarchists,* pp. 124–25.

23. Avrich, *Tragedy,* p. 58.

24. *Population at the Eleventh Census,* p. 374; and see Einhorn, *Property Rules,* p. 249.

25. Quote in Nelson, *Beyond the Martyrs,* pp. 15–16. During the 1880s, Chicago's Bohemian population increased to 25,105, the Polish population to 24,086, the Norwegian to 21,835, the British and Scottish to 47,149, the Swedish to 43,032 and the German to 161,039. Furthermore, the Irish kept coming, increasing their numbers to 70,028; *Population at the Eleventh Census,* pp. 671–72. On Poles and Russian Jews, see Pierce, Vol. 3, pp. 34–39; Dominic A. Pacyga, *Polish Immigrants and Industrial Chicago: Workers on the South Side, 1880–1922* (Columbus: Ohio State University Press, 1991); and Edward Mazur, "Jewish Chicago: From *Shtetl* to Suburb," in Melvin G. Holli and Peter d'A. Jones, eds., *Ethnic Chicago* (Grand Rapids, MI: W. B. Eerdmans, 1977), pp. 73–75.

26. Nelson, *Beyond the Martyrs,* pp. 67, 69, 85, 96; Howard H. Quint, *The Forging of American Socialism* (Columbia: University of South Carolina Press, 1953), p. 35; Keil

and Jentz, eds., *German Workers, Documentary*, p. 407; Gary P. Steenson, *"Not One Man! Not One Penny!"*: *German Social Democracy, 1863–1914* (Pittsburgh: University of Pittsburgh Press, 1981), pp. 30–31.

27. See Schwab's life story in Michael Schwab, "Autobiography of Michael Schwab," in P. Foner, *Autobiographies*, pp. 99–121 (quote from p. 109).

28. Quotes in P. Foner, *Autobiographies*, pp. 112, 120–21, 123–24.

29. Avrich, *Tragedy*, p. 62.

30. Ibid., pp. 63–64; David Roediger and Franklin Rosemont, eds., *Haymarket Scrapbook* (Chicago: Charles H. Kerr, 1986), p. 137.

31. Avrich, *Tragedy*, p. 64.

32. Bruce, *1877*, pp. 193, 318.

33. Avrich, *Tragedy*, p. 24. And see Robert Weir, *Beyond Labor's Veil: The Culture of the Knights of Labor* (University Park: Pennsylvania State University Press, 1996), p. 32.

34. A. Parsons, "Autobiography," p. 37; P. Foner and Roediger, *Our Own Time*, pp. 132, 137, and quote on p. 121; "Statistics on German Bakers," *Arbeiter-Zeitung*, January 26, 1882, translation in Keil and Jentz, eds., *German Workers, Documentary*, p. 81; John R. Commons, *History of Labor in the United States* (New York: Macmillan, 1918), Vol. 2, p. 250, n. 8.

35. Quotes in Schneirov, *Labor and Urban Politics*, pp. 78, 128–29.

36. Ibid.

37. See Nelson, *Beyond the Martyrs*, p. 48; United States Department of the Interior, Census Office, *Report on Manufacturing Industries in the United States at the Eleventh Census, 1890* (Washington, DC: Government Printing Office, 1895), pp. 133–42; "The Fate of Women Workers," from *Arbeiter-Zeitung*, January 16, 1882, in Keil and Jentz, eds., *German Workers, Documentary*, p. 81; and Schneirov, *Labor and Urban Politics*, p. 197. On female carpet weavers and other "lady Knights," see Susan Levine, *Labor's True Woman: Carpet Weavers, Industrialization, and Labor Reform in the Gilded Age* (Philadelphia: Temple University Press, 1984).

38. *Harper's Weekly*, July 22, 1883; Henry F. May, *Protestant Churches and Industrial America* (New York: Harper, 1949), p. 97.

39. Schilling, "Labor Movement in Chicago," p. xxiii.

40. Norman Ware, *The Labor Movement in the United States, 1860–1895: A Study in Democracy* (New York and London: D. Appleton & Co., 1929), pp. 129, 131.

41. Schneirov, *Labor and Urban Politics*, p. 129; Nelson, *Beyond the Martyrs*, p. 39.

42. Quote from A. Parsons, "Autobiography," pp. 39–40.

43. Quote ibid., pp. 38–39, 41.

44. Quotes from Spies, "Autobiography," pp. 68–69, and from A. Parsons, "Autobiography," p. 47.

Chapter Seven / A Brutal and Inventive Vitality

1. On the railroads, see Miller, *City of the Century*, pp. 182, 241–42; and on the iron industry, the Union Steel Co. and other producers, see A. T. Andreas, *History of Chicago from the Earliest Period to the Present Time* (Chicago: A. T. Andreas, 1885), Vol. 2, pp. 673–700.

2. The value of capital invested in the city's ten leading industries rose from $40.5 million to $247.7 million, while the force of wage earners in these sectors grew from roughly 42,000 to 101,000. The value added by these manufacturing firms (after subtracting the value of materials) soared from $38.2 million to $810.7 million. Wages in the aggregate grew, but modestly, from a yearly average of $478 per worker in 1880 to $607

a decade later. If the cost of materials and the cost of wages are subtracted from the total value of manufactured goods, then "value added" multiplied twenty-seven times—from $27.7 million to $760.3 million, while wages paid grew from $19.3 million to $58 million. Based on census figures compiled in Nelson, *Beyond the Martyrs*, pp. 12–13, and Pierce, *Chicago*, Vol. 3, pp. 534–35. Quote from Sigfried Giedion, *Mechanization Takes Command: A Contribution to Anonymous History* (New York: Oxford University Press, 1948), p. 218.

3. Saul Bellow quoted in frontispiece of Miller, *City of the Century.*

4. Rudyard Kipling, *American Notes* (New York: F. F. Lovell, 1890), p. 149; Upton Sinclair, *The Jungle* (New York: Signet, 1905), pp. 39–42; and Giedion, *Mechanization Takes Command*, p. 218.

5. U.S. Department of the Interior, Census Office, *Report on the Manufactures of the United States at the Ninth Census, 1870* (Washington, DC: Government Printing Office, 1872), p. 849; *Manufactures at the Tenth Census*, pp. 391–93; *Report on Manufacturing, 1890*, Part I, Statistics of Cities, pp. 130–45; Pierce, *Chicago*, Vol. 3, p. 112, n. 11.

6. Miller, *City of the Century*, pp. 211–13; Giedion, *Mechanization Takes Command*, p. 218; Schneirov, *Labor and Urban Politics*, p. 107.

7. Miller, *City of the Century*, p. 223.

8. Ozanne, *Century*, pp. 5–7, 9–10.

9. Quote in Herbert Gutman, *Work, Culture and Society in Industrializing America* (New York: Knopf, 1976), p. 46.

10. Ibid., pp. 10–11; Schneirov, *Labor and Urban Politics*, pp. 187–90.

11. From Keil and Jentz, "German Working-Class Culture in Chicago," pp. 128–47. During the 1880s, capital investment grew from $8.4 million to $38.9 million in slaughtering, from $7.2 million to $14.7 million in men's clothing, from $4.5 million to $25.6 million in foundry and machine works. Pierce, *Chicago*, Vol. 3, pp. 534–35.

12. Nelson, *Beyond the Martyrs*, p. 13; Gutman, *Work, Culture and Society*, p. 37; Schneirov, *Labor and Urban Politics*, pp. 119, 189.

13. Nelson, *Beyond the Martyrs*, p. 24. Also see David Montgomery, *Workers' Control in America: Studies in the History of Work, Technology, and Labor Struggles* (New York: Cambridge University Press, 1979), pp. 9–19.

14. *Arbeiter-Zeitung* quoted in Keil and Jentz, eds., *German Workers, Documentary*, p. 78.

15. Ibid.; Nelson, *Beyond the Martyrs*, Table 4.3, p. 87, and Table 4.4, p. 89; Keil and Jentz, eds., *German Workers, Documentary*, p. 72.

16. Newspaper articles reprinted in Keil and Jentz, eds., *German Workers, Documentary*, pp. 56–57, 59, 72, 78–79, 81, 82, 88.

17. Montgomery, *Workers' Control in America*, pp. 12–13.

18. See ibid., first quote from p. 13. Also see Laurie, *Artisans into Workers* (see chap. 1, n. 12), pp. 102, 110–11, 162; and P. Foner, *Labor Movement* (see chap 1, n. 11), Vol. 2, pp. 56–74.

19. See David Montgomery, *Citizen Worker: The Experience of Workers in the United States with Democracy and the Free Market During the Nineteenth Century* (Cambridge: Cambridge University Press, 1993), pp. 130–62.

20. Gompers, *Seventy Years*, pp. 62, 72–73.

21. Ibid., p. 62; quote in Gutman, *Work, Culture and Society*, p. 37.

22. Franklin E. Coyne, *The Development of the Cooperage Industry in the United States, 1620–1940* (Chicago: Lumber Buyers Publishing Co., 1940), pp. 21–22; Gutman, *Work, Culture and Society*, p. 46.

23. Schwab, "Autobiography," p. 114.

24. *Arbeiter-Zeitung* quoted in Keil and Jentz, eds., *German Workers, Documentary,* pp. 55–56.

25. Quote in P. Foner, *Labor Movement,* Vol. 1, p. 514.

26. Nelson, *Beyond the Martyrs,* pp. 41–42, and quote p. 44.

27. Ibid., p. 95; Schneirov, "Free Thought," pp. 126–27. Also see Schneirov, *Labor and Urban Politics,* pp. 124–25; Weir, *Beyond Labor's Veil,* pp. 92–94.

28. Schneirov, "Free Thought," pp. 126–27; Schwab, "Autobiography," p. 103.

29. May, *Protestant Churches,* p. 83; Boyer, *Urban Masses and Moral Order* (see Prologue, n. 13), p. 136.

30. Josiah Strong, *Our Country* (1885; reprint, Cambridge, MA: Belknap Press, 1963), pp. 177–79, 186; also see May, *Protestant Churches,* pp. 114–15.

31. See Herbert Gutman, "Protestantism and the American Labor Movement: The Christian Spirit in the Gilded Age," reprinted in Gutman, *Work, Culture and Society,* pp. 79–118; and quote from McNeill, ed., *The Labor Movement,* p. 468.

32. Spies, "Autobiography," pp. 62–63.

33. Alan L. Sorkin, "The Depression of 1882–1885," in David Glasner, ed., *Business Cycles and Depressions: An Encyclopedia* (New York: Garland, 1997), pp. 149–51; Pierce, *Chicago,* Vol. 3, pp. 269–70.

34. On Lloyd, see Digby-Junger, *The Journalist as Reformer* (see chap. 5, n. 17), pp. 57–62, 67; and on George, see Thomas, *Alternative America* (see chap. 5, n. 17), pp. 140–41. Quotes from Henry George, *Social Problems* (Garden City, NY: Doubleday & Page, 1883), pp. 17–18, 35, 68–69.

35. "Workers' Lodgings: A Report by the Citizens Association," *Arbeiter-Zeitung,* September 3, 1883, in Keil and Jentz, eds., *German Workers, Documentary,* pp. 129–31. See Miller, *City of the Century,* p. 414.

36. Quote from Schaack, *Anarchy and Anarchists,* p. 77.

37. Nelson, *Beyond the Martyrs,* p. 141; A. Parsons quoted in Schaack, *Anarchy and Anarchists,* p. 77.

38. My interpretation of the political impact of hard times is based on Lawrence Goodwyn, *The Populist Moment: A Short History of the Agrarian Revolt in America* (New York: Oxford University Press, 1978), pp. 59, 61.

39. L. Parsons, *The Life,* pp. 25–27.

40. Ibid.

41. See Burke, *The Conundrum of Class* (see Prologue, n. 19), pp. 160–61.

42. Quote in John A. Garraty, ed., *Labor and Capital in the Gilded Age: Testimony Taken by the Senate Committee on the Relations Between Labor and Capital, 1883* (Boston: Little, Brown, 1968), p. 136.

43. Medill testimony ibid., pp. 7, 129.

44. Ozanne, *Century,* pp. 14–16. Quotes from J. Anthony Lukas, *Big Trouble: A Murder in a Small Western Town Sets Off a Struggle for the Soul of America* (New York: Knopf, 1997), p. 188. Also see Kevin Kenny, *Making Sense of the Molly Maguires* (New York: Oxford University Press, 1988), pp. 283–84.

45. Quote in Ozanne, *Century,* p. 13.

46. Pierce, *Chicago,* Vol. 3, p. 271; Ozanne, *Century,* p. 11, and quotes pp. 14–16.

47. Quote in Ozanne, *Century,* p. 19.

48. Schneirov, *Labor and Urban Politics,* pp. 109, 119–23, 130–34; Thomas N. Brown, *Irish-American Nationalism, 1870–1890* (Philadelphia: Lippincott, 1966), pp. 56–57, 102–3, 146–47; and Kenny, *Making Sense of the Molly Maguires,* pp. 280–81.

49. See Ozanne, *Century,* pp. 17–18 and quote p. 19.

50. Kathleen D. McCarthy, *Noblesse Oblige: Charity and Cultural Philanthropy in Chicago, 1849–1929* (Chicago: University of Chicago Press, 1982), pp. 113–14; Nettie Fowler McCormick quoted in Ozanne, *Century,* pp. 19–20.

51. Flinn, *Chicago Police,* p. 234; and quote in Plummer, *Lincoln's Rail-Splitter* (see Prologue, n. 21), p. 190.

52. L. Parsons, *The Life,* pp. 80–81, 86.

53. Quote in Ashbaugh, *Lucy Parsons,* pp. 59–60.

54. Flinn, *Chicago Police,* pp. 234, 236.

55. Ibid., pp. 239–40; and Schneirov, *Labor and Urban Politics,* p. 170.

56. Claudius O. Johnson, *Carter Henry Harrison I: Political Leader* (Chicago: University of Chicago Press, 1928), pp. 119, 120–21.

57. Ibid.

58. Ibid., pp. 131, 179.

59. Quote in Miller, *City of the Century,* p. 445.

60. Samuel P. McConnell, "The Chicago Bomb Case: Personal Recollections of an American Tragedy," *Harper's Magazine,* May 1934, p. 731.

61. Johnson, *Carter Henry Harrison,* pp. 131, 206; Pierce, *Chicago,* Vol. 3, p. 356; Miller, *City of the Century,* pp. 437, 443, 444–45; Schneirov, *Labor and Urban Politics,* pp. 167–69.

62. Quotes from Flinn, *Chicago Police,* pp. 346, 502, 508.

63. Samuel Walker, *A Critical History of Police Reform* (Lexington, MA: Lexington Books, 1977), pp. 17–18, 107–8; Sidney L. Harwood, *Policing a Class Society: The Experience of American Cities, 1895–1915* (New Brunswick, NJ: Rutgers University Press, 1983), pp. 50–55, 111, 113–17; Eric H. Monkkonen, *Police in Urban America, 1860–1920* (Cambridge: Cambridge University Press, 1981), pp. 87–88; Frank Donner, *Protectors of Privilege: Red Squads and Police Repression in Urban America* (Berkeley: University of California Press, 1990), pp. 10–14.

64. Quote in Flinn, *Chicago Police,* pp. 241, 243.

65. Charles Edward Russell quoted in Avrich, *Tragedy,* p. 97.

66. Avrich, *Tragedy,* pp. 97–98; Schneirov, *Labor and Urban Politics,* p. 170.

67. Quote in Flinn, *Chicago Police,* p. 248.

68. John Peter Altgeld, *Reasons for Pardoning the Haymarket Anarchists* (Chicago: Charles H. Kerr, 1893; reprint, 1986), pp. 36–37, 39, 45–46.

69. Ibid., p. 46.

70. Flinn, *Chicago Police,* p. 251.

Chapter Eight / The International

1. Avrich, *Tragedy,* pp. 92, 99, 109.

2. Ibid., p. 128; Nelson, *Beyond the Martyrs,* pp. 119–21, 125; and Renate Kiesewetter, "German-American Labor Press: The *Vorbote* and the *Chicagoer Arbeiter-Zeitung,*" in Keil, ed., *German Workers' Culture,* pp. 137–56.

3. Quote from E. P. Thompson, "18th Century English Society: Class Struggle Without Class?" *Social History* 3 (May 1978), pp. 154, 158.

4. First quote in Pierce, *Chicago,* Vol. 3, p. 80; Flinn, *Chicago Police,* p. 224; Miller, *City of the Century,* p. 186; and Digby-Junger, *The Journalist as Reformer,* pp. 64–65.

5. Flinn, *Chicago Police,* p. 230; Schaack, *Anarchy and Anarchists,* pp. 80–81; Avrich, *Tragedy,* p. 148.

6. Avrich, *Tragedy,* p. 471.

7. See Nelson, *Beyond the Martyrs*, p. 112.

8. Quote in Schaack, *Anarchy and Anarchists*, pp. 671–72.

9. Nelson, *Beyond the Martyrs*, pp. 154–55; A. Parsons, "Autobiography," p. 43.

10. Avrich, *Tragedy*, p. 173, and quotes from p. 73.

11. George Woodcock, *Anarchism: A History of Libertarian Ideas and Movements* (Cleveland: World Publishing Co., 1962), pp. 14, 122–24, 141–44. On the anarchist watchmakers in the Jura Mountains of Switzerland, see ibid., pp. 194–95. Also see Jellinek, *Paris Commune* (see chap. 3, n. 1), p. 14; on the hopes of Proudhon's Paris followers that other communes would form, see ibid., p. 388.

12. On the farmers' cooperative movement, see Goodwyn, *The Populist Movement*, pp. 25–30, 32–34. Also see Alan Dawley, "The International Working People's Association," in Roediger and Rosemont, eds., *Haymarket Scrapbook* (see chap. 6, n. 30), pp. 84–85.

13. A. Parsons, "Autobiography," p. 29; and Avrich, *Tragedy*, p. 115. For the particular influence of Thomas Paine on Albert Parsons, see Harvey J. Kaye, *Thomas Paine and the Promise of America* (New York: Hill & Wang, 2005), pp. 173–75.

14. Schaack, *Anarchy and Anarchists*, pp. 19–60; Slotkin, *Gunfighter Nation* (see chap. 3, n. 6), pp. 196, 204; *Chicago Tribune*, May 6, 1886.

15. See Albert Parsons, "What Is Anarchy?" in Roediger and Rosemont, eds., *Haymarket Scrapbook*, pp. 27–28.

16. For other expressions of popular disgust with Gilded Age greed and corruption, see Tipple, "The Robber Baron in the Gilded Age" (see chap. 2, n. 34), pp. 30–31; Montgomery, *Citizen Worker*, p. 146; and Leon Fink, *Workingmen's Democracy: The Knights of Labor and American Politics* (Urbana: University of Illinois Press, 1983), pp. 4–5.

17. Bruce C. Nelson, "Dancing and Picnicking Anarchists?" in Roediger and Rosemont, eds., *Haymarket Scrapbook*, pp. 76–78.

18. Quotes in Nelson, *Beyond the Martyrs*, pp. 135–37, 139.

19. Quote in L. Parsons, *The Life*, p. 77.

20. "Observing Thanksgiving Day, 1885," from *Alarm*, in L. Parsons, *The Life*, pp. 73–75.

21. Nelson, *Beyond the Martyrs*, pp. 133–34; and Heiss, "Popular and Working-Class German Theater in Chicago" (see chap. 4, n. 33), pp. 192–93.

22. Nelson, *Beyond the Martyrs*, p. 131.

23. *Chicago Times* quoted ibid., p. 135.

24. See Nelson, *Beyond the Martyrs*, pp. 144–45; and Friedrich A. Sorge, *Friedrich A. Sorge's Labor Movement in the United States: A History of the American Working Class from Colonial Times to 1890*, ed. Philip S. Foner and Brewster Chamberlin (Westport, CT: Greenwood Press, 1977), p. 71.

25. Avrich, *Tragedy*, pp. 99–104.

26. The account of Fielden's life is from "Autobiography of Samuel Fielden," in P. Foner, *Autobiographies*, pp. 131–55.

27. See Franklin Rosemont, "Anarchists and the Wild West," in Roediger and Rosemont, eds., *Haymarket Scrapbook*, pp. 101–2.

28. See Avrich, *Tragedy*, pp. 105–6.

29. Quote ibid., pp. 117–18.

30. Ibid., pp. 114–15.

31. Quote ibid., pp. 112–13.

32. Quote ibid., p. 117.

33. Nelson, *Beyond the Martyrs,* pp. 88–98.

34. Ibid., pp. 84 (Table 4.4), 89–90, 91, 103–5; Avrich, *Tragedy,* pp. 151–52, 235.

35. Nelson, *Beyond the Martyrs,* pp. 108–9; Perry Duis, *The Saloon: Public Drinking in Chicago and Boston, 1880–1920* (Urbana: University of Illinois Press, 1983), pp. 52, 61–62, 88–89, 148–49, 152, 180, 236–37, 243; Royal Melendy, "The Saloon in Chicago," *American Journal of Sociology* (November 1900), quoted in Freeman et al., *Who Built America?* (see chap. 5, n. 2), Vol. 2, p. 86. Also see Klaus Ensslen, "German-American Working-Class Saloons in Chicago," in Keil, ed., *German Workers' Culture,* pp. 157–80; and Sara M. Evans and Harry C. Boyte, *Free Spaces: The Sources of Democratic Change in America* (New York: Harper & Row, 1986).

36. Adolph Fischer, "Autobiography of Adolph Fischer," in P. Foner, *Autobiographies,* pp. 73–75; and see Avrich, *Tragedy,* pp. 150–51.

37. Quote in Avrich, *Tragedy,* p. 153.

38. Fischer, "Autobiography," p. 85.

39. Engel narrates his life in George Engel, "Autobiography of George Engel," in P. Foner, *Autobiographies,* pp. 92–96.

40. Ibid., p. 95; on *Der Vorbote,* see Paul Buhle, *Marxism in the United States* (London: Verso, 1979), pp. 38–39.

41. Engel, "Autobiography," pp. 95–96.

42. Avrich, *Tragedy,* pp. 97–98, 156.

43. See ibid., p. 165.

44. Quotes ibid., pp. 56–57, 169; and Dell, "Socialism and Anarchism in Chicago" (see chap. 3, n. 36), p. 388.

45. Dell, "Socialism and Anarchism in Chicago," p. 391.

46. Avrich, *Tragedy,* p. 175.

47. Louis Lingg, "Autobiography of Louis Lingg," in P. Foner, *Autobiographies,* p. 170.

48. See ibid., pp. 169–72; and Avrich, *Tragedy,* p. 157.

49. Lingg, "Autobiography," pp. 175–77; and quotes in Avrich, *Tragedy,* pp. 158–59.

50. Lingg, "Autobiography," p. 177.

51. Schaack, *Anarchy and Anarchists,* pp. 41–43; Brown, *Irish-American Nationalism,* pp. 147, 156, 162. Quotes in Michael F. Funchion, *Chicago's Irish Nationalists, 1881–1890* (New York: Arno Press, 1976), pp. 82–85; Clymer, *America's Culture of Terrorism* (see Prologue, n. 13), pp. 70–71, including last quote.

52. First quote from Avrich, *Tragedy,* pp. 176–77.

53. My interpretation of this escalating war of words is based on Avrich's account, ibid. Quote from Flinn, *Chicago Police,* p. 251.

Chapter Nine / The Great Upheaval

1. Florence Peterson, *Strikes in the United States, 1880–1936* (Washington, DC: U.S. Department of Labor, Bureau of Labor Statistics, 1938), Table 4, p. 29; and David Montgomery, "Machine Production in the Nineteenth Century," Table 1, p. 20, in Montgomery, *Workers' Control in America* (see chap. 7, n. 13).

2. Friedrich Engels to Friedrich Sorge, August 8, 1887, quoted in R. Laurence Moore, *European Socialists and the American Promised Land* (New York: Oxford University Press, 1970), p. 15.

3. P. Foner, *Labor Movement*, Vol. 2, pp. 103–4; and P. Foner and Roediger, *Our Own Time* (see chap. 1, n. 16), pp. 137–38.

4. Schilling, "Labor Movement in Chicago," p. xxiv.

5. Schneirov, *Labor and Urban Politics*, pp. 186–87.

6. Flinn, *Chicago Police*, pp. 253, 256.

7. Nelson, *Beyond the Martyrs*, p. 179.

8. Terence V. Powderly, *Thirty Years of Labor, 1859–1889* (Columbus, OH: Excelsior Publishing House, 1889), p. 495.

9. The following description is based on Ozanne, *Century*, pp. 20–22, and Schneirov, *Labor and Urban Politics*, pp. 191–92.

10. Schneirov, *Labor and Urban Politics*, p. 193; Buder, *Pullman* (see Prologue, n. 5), p. 140.

11. Jeremy Brecher, *Strike!* (San Francisco: Straight Arrow Books, 1972), pp. 32–33.

12. Quote from Garraty, *Labor and Capital* (see chap. 7, n. 42), p. 148.

13. McNeill, ed., *The Labor Movement*, p. 479; and Montgomery, *Citizen Worker*, pp. 39–49; Ware, *Labor Movement in the U.S.* (see chap. 6, n. 40), p. 146.

14. Montgomery, *Workers' Control*, Table 1, p. 20.

15. Quote from Selig Perlman, "Upheaval and Reorganisation," Part 6 of John R. Commons, *History of Labor in the United States* (New York: Macmillan, 1918), Vol. 2, pp. 250 (n. 8), 374.

16. Ozanne, *Century*, p. 22; Schneirov, *Labor and Urban Politics*, p. 192.

17. Quotes in Flinn, *Chicago Police*, pp. 263–64.

18. See P. Foner, *Labor Movement*, Vol. 2, p. 85; Brecher, *Strike!*, pp. 35–36; and Plummer, *Lincoln's Rail-Splitter*, pp. 190, 195.

19. Quote from Schneirov, *Labor and Urban Politics*, p. 197.

20. Pierce, *Chicago*, Vol. 3, p. 238.

21. "Memoranda of Cooperative Efforts Among Labor Organizations in Illinois," *Report of the Illinois Bureau of Labor Statistics, 1886* (Springfield, IL: H. W. Rokker, 1886), Table XLIX, pp. 455–56. Also see David Montgomery, *The Fall of the House of Labor: The Workplace, the State, and American Labor Activism, 1865–1925* (Cambridge: Cambridge University Press, 1987), pp. 146–47; P. Foner, *Labor Movement*, Vol. 2, p. 61.

22. Pierce, *Chicago*, Vol. 3, p. 38; and quotes in Abraham Bisno, *Abraham Bisno, Union Pioneer* (Madison: University of Wisconsin Press, 1967), pp. 66–71.

23. See E. P. Thompson, "Time, Work Discipline and Industrial Capitalism," in *Customs in Common* (see chap. 1, n. 18), p. 357.

24. Song lyrics quoted in P. Foner and Roediger, *Our Own Time*, p. 139.

25. Quote from Giuseppe Giacosa, "A City of Smoke," in Pierce, ed., *As Others See Chicago* (see Prologue, n. 4), p. 276.

26. On Chicago's industrial environment, see Waldo Frank, "The Soul of the City," in Pierce, ed., *As Others See Chicago*, pp. 478–79, 481; and Cronon, *Nature's Metropolis* (see chap. 2, n. 2), pp. 12–13.

27. Quote from Rudyard Kipling, "How I Struck Chicago and How Chicago Struck Me," in Pierce, ed., *As Others See Chicago*, p. 256.

28. Ware, *Labor Movement in the U.S.*, pp. 88–90, 303; P. Foner, *Labor Movement*, Vol. 2, p. 66.

29. Richard Oestreicher, "Terence Powderly, the Knights of Labor and Artisanal Republicanism," in Dubofsky and Van Tine, eds., *Labor Leaders in America* (see chap. 1, n. 9), pp. 56–59, 66; Craig Phelen, *Grand Master Workman: Terence Powderly and the Knights of Labor* (Westport, CT: Greenwood Press, 2000), pp. 47–51.

30. Schneirov, *Labor and Urban Politics*, p. 193.

31. Quote in Nelson, *Beyond the Martyrs*, pp. 179–80; P. Foner, *Labor Movement*, Vol. 2, pp. 88–89.

32. Schneirov, *Labor and Urban Politics*, pp. 196, 202.

33. Thomas J. Suhrbur, "Ethnicity and the Formation of the Chicago Carpenters Union, 1855–1890," in Keil and Jentz, eds., *German Workers in Industrial Chicago*, pp. 96–97.

34. P. Foner and Roediger, *Our Own Time*, p. 138.

35. Quote from Schilling, "Labor Movement in Chicago," p. xxiv.

36. Nelson, *Beyond the Martyrs*, pp. 181–82.

37. Schneirov, *Labor and Urban Politics*, p. 198.

38. Ibid., p. 195.

39. My interpretation of this point is based on Schneirov's account, ibid.

40. David Roediger, "Albert R. Parsons: The Anarchist as Trade Unionist," in Roediger and Rosemont, eds., *Haymarket Scrapbook*, pp. 31–32. "If workers could decree how long they would work, they could also dictate other terms of a renegotiated social contract," according to Richard Oestreicher. In the process of "taking normally unthinkable actions working people's capacity to envision future alternatives expanded." The idea of making May Day a moment for a coordinated general strike captivated workers whose prior experience with strikes was almost entirely one of engaging in isolated protests against wage cuts, job actions in which they were often fired and blacklisted if not injured or killed. By taking the offensive on a massive level, the eight-hour men promised to change the calculus of risk that always seemed to work against the strikers and their families. Richard Jules Oestreicher, *Solidarity and Fragmentation: Working People and Class Consciousness in Detroit, 1875–1900* (Urbana: University of Illinois Press, 1986), pp. 145–46, 149.

41. See Brecher, *Strike!*, p. 44; Perlman, "Upheaval and Reorganisation," p. 376; Schneirov, *Labor and Urban Politics*, p. 194; and Pierce, *Chicago*, Vol. 3, p. 264.

42. Flinn, *Chicago Police*, pp. 265, 269; P. Foner and Roediger, *Our Own Time*, p. 139; Schwab quoted in Lawson, *American State Trials* (see chap. 4, n. 43), Vol. 12, p. 106.

43. Quotes in Schneirov, *Labor and Urban Politics*, p. 199, Flinn, *Chicago Police*, p 265; and *Chicago Tribune*, May 1, 1886.

44. *Illinois State Register* quoted in David, *Haymarket Affair* (see Prologue, n. 10), p. 163.

45. Pierce, *Chicago*, Vol. 3, p. 190; and Nelson, *Beyond the Martyrs*, p. 186.

46. Quote in Flinn, *Chicago Police*, pp. 266–67.

47. Quote in Avrich, *Tragedy*, pp. 185–86.

Chapter Ten / A Storm of Strikes

1. The following account of events on May 1, and the quotations (unless indicated otherwise), are from the *Chicago Tribune*, May 1, 2, 1886.

2. Quote from Flinn, *Chicago Police*, p. 265.

3. Ibid., p. 269; Nelson, *Beyond the Martyrs*, p. 184; and see Schneirov, *Labor and Urban Politics*, p. 198.

4. Nelson, *Beyond the Martyrs*, p. 193; P. Foner and Roediger, *Our Own Time*, p. 139.

5. Quote from David Montgomery, "Strikes in Nineteenth-Century America," *Social Science Quarterly* 4 (February 1980), p. 95.

6. *Chicago Tribune*, May 2, 4, 1886.

7. *Chicago Tribune*, May 3, 5, 1886.

8. See Ozanne, *Century*, p. 23.

9. Goodwyn, *The Populist Moment* (see chap. 7, n. 38), p. 41.

10. Richard Boyer and Herbert Morais, *Labor's Untold Story* (New York: Cameron Associates, 1955), p. 92; Eric Hobsbawm, "Mass-Producing Traditions: Europe, 1870–1914," in Eric Hobsbawm and Terence Ranger, eds., *The Invention of Tradition* (Cambridge: Cambridge University Press, 1983), p. 283.

11. L. Parsons, *The Life*, pp. 121–22; quotes from Oscar Ameringer, *If You Don't Weaken: The Autobiography of Oscar Ameringer* (Norman: University of Oklahoma Press, 1983), pp. 44–45. And see Stephen J. Ross, *Workers on the Edge: Work, Leisure, and Politics in Industrializing Cincinnati, 1788–1890* (New York: Columbia University Press, 1985), p. 275.

12. Flinn, *Chicago Police*, p. 270.

13. All quotes on events of Sunday, May 2, are from *Chicago Tribune*, May 3, 1886, unless otherwise indicated.

14. *Chicago Tribune*, May 4, 1886; Schneirov, *Labor and Urban Politics*, p. 203; Miller, *City of the Century* (see Prologue, n. 4), pp. 260–61; and Pierce, *Chicago*, Vol. 3, pp. 178–83.

15. On Thomas, see Pierce, *Chicago*, Vol. 3, pp. 429, 432–33. Quote in *Chicago Tribune*, May 3, 1886.

16. Boyer, *Urban Masses and Moral Order* (see Prologue, n. 13), p. 136. Moody quoted in *Chicago Tribune*, May 3, 1886.

17. All quotes about events on May 3 are from the *Chicago Tribune*, May 4, 1886, unless otherwise indicated.

18. Flinn, *Chicago Police*, p. 271.

19. Buder, *Pullman* (see Prologue, n. 5), pp. 140–42.

20. *Chicago Tribune*, May 4, 1886; Ware, *Labor Movement in the U.S.* (see chap. 6, n. 40), p. 149.

21. *Chicago Tribune*, May 4, 1886; P. Foner, *Labor Movement*, Vol. 2, p. 85.

22. Flinn, *Chicago Police*, pp. 108, 114, 112, 222; and see Stanley Palmer, "Cops and Guns: Arming the American Force," *History Today* 28 (June 1978), pp. 386–89; Harwood, *Policing a Class Society* (see chap. 7, n. 63), pp. 104–14.

23. Spies's account in George McLean, *The Rise and Fall of Anarchy from Its Incipient Stage to the First Bomb Thrown in Chicago* (Chicago: R. G. Badoux & Co., 1890), pp. 87–88; and in Schaack, *Anarchy and Anarchists*, pp. 130–31.

24. McLean, *Rise and Fall of Anarchy*, pp. 88–89.

25. Roediger and Rosemont, eds. *Haymarket Scrapbook*, p. 14.

26. Dyer D. Lum, *A Concise History of the Great Trial of the Chicago Anarchists, 1886* (Chicago: Socialistic Publishing Co., 1886), pp. 164–68; Avrich, *Tragedy*, pp. 191–92.

27. Lum, *A Concise History*, p. 69.

28. *Chicago Tribune*, May 4, 5, 1886; Schaack, *Anarchy and Anarchists*, pp. 125–26. *Chicago Tribune* and police say mob was 8,000. Flinn, *Chicago Police*, pp. 275–76.

29. *Chicago Tribune*, May 4, 1886; Flinn, *Chicago Police*, p. 278.

30. Bonfield quoted in Flinn, *Chicago Police*, pp. 278, 280.

Chapter Eleven / A Night of Terror

1. Flinn, *Chicago Police*, p. 279.

2. All references and quotes to events of May 4, 1886, are from the *Chicago Tribune*, May 5, 1886, unless indicated otherwise.

3. Richard Ely quoted in Miller, *City of the Century*, p. 238.

4. Beckert, *The Monied Metropolis* (see Prologue, n. 12), pp. 273, 276, 290–91.

5. Ibid., pp. 282–83. First quote, ibid., p. 283; second quote in Plummer, *Lincoln's Rail-Splitter*, p. 193; and see Smith, "Cataclysm" (see Prologue, n. 21), p. 134.

6. Quote in Avrich, *Tragedy*, pp. 194–95.

7. Testimony of William Seliger in Lum, *A Concise History*, pp. 79–80.

8. McLean, *Rise and Fall of Anarchy*, p. 89; Avrich, *Tragedy*, p. 193.

9. Lum, *A Concise History*, p. 27.

10. Earlier in the day Adolph Fischer passed the Desplaines Street Police Station and saw the "police mounting five or six patrol wagons." Fischer thought the officers were replacements being sent out to McCormick's. It apparently did not occur to him that the police might be preparing to break up the rally that night. Lum, *A Concise History*, p. 70.

11. Flinn, *Chicago Police*, pp. 294, 296; and see Richard C. Lindberg, *To Serve and Collect: Chicago Politics and Police Corruption* (New York: Praeger, 1991), pp. 18–20.

12. Marohn, "The Arming of the Chicago Police" (see chap. 5, n. 34), pp. 41, 45.

13. Lucy Parsons, ed., *Famous Speeches of the Eight Chicago Anarchists in Court* (Chicago: Lucy E. Parsons, 1910; reprint, New York: Arno Press, 1969), p. 120; A. Parsons, "Autobiography," p. 48.

14. Ashbaugh, *Lucy Parsons*, p. 75.

15. Adelman, *Haymarket Revisited* (see chap. 4, n. 20), p. 32.

16. Quote in Keil and Jentz, eds., *German Workers, Documentary*, pp. 392–93, in a translated article in *Die Fackel*, June 19, 1910.

17. Lum, *A Concise History*, pp. 37–38; *Chicago Tribune*, May 5, 1886; McLean, *Rise and Fall of Anarchy*, p 91.

18. Parsons's summary of his speech on May 4 is quoted in Lum, *A Concise History*, pp. 39–42, 45–47.

19. Ibid., p. 46.

20. *Chicago Tribune*, May 5, 1886.

21. Harrison quoted in Lum, *A Concise History*, p. 30.

22. Ibid., pp. 131–32.

23. Ibid., pp. 29–30, 111.

24. Seliger testimony quoted ibid., pp. 79–80; and see David, *Haymarket Affair* (see Prologue, n. 10), p. 234.

25. *Chicago Tribune*, May 5, 1886.

26. George Brown, "The Police Riot: An Eye-Witness Account," in Roediger and Rosemont, eds., *Haymarket Scrapbook*, p. 75.

27. Fielden, "Autobiography," p. 158; Flinn, *Chicago Police*, p. 310.

28. *Chicago Tribune*, May 6, 1886.

29. Lum, *A Concise History*, p. 28.

30. Ibid.

31. *Chicago Tribune*, May 5, 1886.

32. Quote in Lum, *A Concise History*, p. 141.

33. Holmes quoted in Adelman, *Haymarket Revisited*, pp. 35–36.

34. See testimony of Lt. H. P. Stanton, *Illinois vs. August Spies et al. Trial Transcript*, Vol. 1, p. 220, Chicago Historical Society, Haymarket Digital Collection.

35. Bonfield and Ward quoted in *Chicago Tribune*, May 5, 6, 1886. Also see testimonies of other police officers in Lum, *A Concise History*, pp. 73–74, 76, 97, 133.

36. S. T. Ingram testimony in Lum, *A Concise History*, p. 133.

37. Testimony of Richter, Simonson and Ferguson, ibid., pp. 114–17. On Simonson's background, see ibid., p. 32.

38. *Chicago Herald* quoted in Avrich, *Tragedy*, p. 209; *Chicago Tribune*, May 5, 1886.

39. *Chicago Tribune*, June 27, 1886.

40. Lizzie Holmes's account quoted in Adelman, *Haymarket Revisited*, pp. 91–92.

41. Flinn, *Chicago Police*, p. 320; *Chicago Tribune*, May 5, 6, 1886.

42. *Chicago Tribune*, May 8, 1886; Avrich, *Tragedy*, pp. 210, 444.

43. See Avrich, *Tragedy*, p. 208. An eighth policeman wounded in the square died two years later, reportedly as a result of his wounds. *Chicago Tribune*, May 7, 8, 1886.

Chapter Twelve / The Strangest Frenzy

1. Quotes in Avrich, *Tragedy*, pp. 216–18; and *Chicago Tribune*, May 6, 1886.

2. *Chicago Tribune* and *Journal of the Knights of Labor*, May 8, 1886; Powderly quoted in Avrich, *Tragedy*, pp. 217, 219, 220.

3. Quotes in Avrich, *Tragedy*, p. 218; and *Chicago Tribune*, May 6, 1886.

4. *Chicago Tribune*, May 6, 1886.

5. *Chicago Tribune*, May 7, 8, 1886.

6. *Chicago Tribune*, May 7, 10, 1886; Schaack, *Anarchy and Anarchists*, p. 150.

7. McLean, *Rise and Fall of Anarchy*, p. 95; and see Avrich, *Tragedy*, p. 225.

8. Lindberg, *Chicago Ragtime*, pp. 18–19; Lindberg, *To Serve and Collect*, pp. 62–63.

9. Ashbaugh, *Lucy Parsons*, p. 81.

10. Ibid., pp. 82–83.

11. *Chicago Tribune*, May 6, 7, 1886; and see Avrich, *Tragedy*, p. 226.

12. See Marohn, "The Arming of the Chicago Police," p. 46.

13. Lindberg, *To Serve and Collect*, p. 63; Flinn, *Chicago Police*, pp. 560–61.

14. Quote in Avrich, *Tragedy*, p. 229.

15. *New York Times*, May 5, 1886.

16. *Chicago Tribune*, May 7, 8, 1886.

17. *Chicago Tribune*, May 6, 1886.

18. *Chicago Tribune*, May 6, 1886.

19. Taylor testimony in Lum, *A Concise History*, pp. 118–19.

20. *Chicago Tribune*, May 6, 1886; *New York Times*, May 8, 1886.

21. *Chicago Tribune*, May 8, 1886; *New York Times*, May 8, 1886; Ely quoted in Avrich, *Tragedy*, p. 222.

22. *Chicago Tribune*, May 7, 1886.

23. Brand Whitlock, *Forty Years of It* (New York: Appleton-Century, 1914), p. 73.

24. My description of popular sentiment at this moment relies on Smith, *Urban Disorder* (see Prologue, n. 14), pp. 7, 137, 139.

25. *Chicago Tribune*, May 10, 1886.

26. My interpretation draws upon that of Bryan Palmer, *Cultures of Darkness: Night Travels in the History of Transgression* (New York: Monthly Review Press, 2000), pp. 233, 235, 246.

27. *Chicago Tribune,* May 8, 1886.

28. *Chicago Tribune,* May 6, 8, 1886.

29. *Chicago Tribune,* May 5, 1886.

30. *Chicago Tribune,* May 5, 1886.

31. *Chicago Tribune,* May 7, 1886.

32. McConnell, "The Chicago Bomb Case" (see chap. 7, n. 60), p. 730.

33. Pierce, *Chicago,* Vol. 3, p. 356; *Chicago Tribune,* May 10, 1886.

34. *John Swinton's Paper,* May 8, 1886, quoted in David, *Haymarket Affair,* p. 185.

35. Ibid., p. 186.

36. *Chicago Tribune,* May 6, 8, 1886.

37. *Chicago Tribune,* May 6, 1886.

38. *Chicago Tribune,* May 6, 7, 1886.

39. See account by Abraham Bisno in Roediger and Rosemont, eds., *Haymarket Scrapbook,* p. 26.

40. *Chicago Tribune,* May 6, 1886.

41. *Chicago Tribune,* May 18, 19, 26, 27, 1886.

42. Avrich, *Tragedy,* pp. 231–32, 234.

43. *Chicago Tribune,* May 22, 1886. On Schnaubelt's release, see Richard Lindberg, *Chicago by Gaslight: A History of Chicago's Netherworld, 1880–1920* (Chicago: Academy Chicago Publishers, 1996), pp. 34–35.

44. Avrich, *Tragedy,* p. 231.

45. *Chicago Tribune,* May 17, 23, 25, 1886.

46. *Chicago Tribune,* May 8, 10, 26, 1886.

47. My interpretation of the drawing is based in part on that of Smith, *Urban Disorder,* pp. 125–26.

48. *Chicago Tribune,* May 21, 27, 28, 1886.

49. Lindberg, *Chicago by Gaslight,* pp. 32–33.

50. *Chicago Tribune,* May 26, 27, 28, 1886. See Avrich, *Tragedy,* p. 208.

51. *Chicago Times* quoted in Avrich, *Tragedy,* p. 233.

52. Quote in David, *Haymarket Affair,* p. 188.

Chapter Thirteen / Every Man on the Jury Was an American

1. *Chicago Tribune,* July 11, 1886.

2. David, *Haymarket Affair,* p. 198. On the German Jews in Chicago, see Pierce, *Chicago,* Vol. 3, pp. 40, 42; and Edward Herbert Mazur, *Minyans for a Prairie City: The Politics of Chicago Jewry, 1850–1940* (New York: Garland, 1990).

3. Avrich, *Tragedy,* p. 251.

4. Roediger and Rosemont, eds., *Haymarket Scrapbook,* p. 121; Lawson, ed., *American State Trials* (see chap. 4, n. 43), p. 18; Sigmund Zeisler, "Reminiscences of the Haymarket Case," *Illinois Law Review* 21 (November 1926), pp. 26–27.

5. Quoted in David, *Haymarket Affair,* pp. 197–98.

6. Ibid., p. 201.

7. Lawson, ed., *American State Trials,* p. 19.

8. Accounts of daily events in the trial are drawn from the reports of the *Chicago Tribune* from June 21 to August 22, 1886.

9. David, *Haymarket Affair,* p. 203; and Miller, *City of the Century,* p. 476.

10. David, *Haymarket Affair,* p. 204.

11. Altgeld, *Reasons* (see chap. 7, n. 68), pp. 25–26.

12. Ibid., p. 214.

13. *Chicago Tribune,* August 21, 1886.

14. Altgeld, *Reasons,* p. 12.

15. In the Supreme Court of the Illinois Grand Division, March Term, 1887, *August Spies et al. vs. the People of the State of Illinois, Brief on the Facts for the Defendants in Error* (Chicago: Barnard & Gunthorp Law Partners, 1887), in the Haymarket Collection, Yale University, Beinecke Rare Book and Manuscript Library, Box 4, Folder 79, pp. 38–140.

16. *Chicago Tribune,* June 27, 1886.

17. Lindberg, *To Serve and Collect,* p. 71; Schaack, *Anarchy and Anarchists,* pp. 184–85.

18. Quoted in David, *Haymarket Affair,* p. 217.

19. Ibid.

20. Ibid., pp. 218–19.

21. Melville Elijah Stone, *Fifty Years a Journalist* (New York: Doubleday, 1921), p. 173.

22. Lum, *A Concise History,* pp. 68–71; David, *Haymarket Affair,* pp. 222–23.

23. Quote in David, *Haymarket Affair,* p. 222.

24. *Chicago Tribune,* July 21, 1886.

25. *Chicago Tribune,* August 7, 1886.

26. *Chicago Tribune,* July 22, 1886.

27. *Chicago Tribune,* July 23, 24, 1886.

28. *Chicago Tribune,* July 24, 25, 1886.

29. McLean, *Rise and Fall of Anarchy,* pp. 32, 41, 42; *Chicago Tribune,* July 25, 27, 1886.

30. David, *Haymarket Affair,* pp. 229–30.

31. *Chicago Tribune,* July 29, 1886.

32. *Chicago Tribune,* July 27, 1886.

33. *Chicago Tribune,* July 30, 1886.

34. *Chicago Tribune,* July 30, 1886.

35. *Chicago Tribune,* August 1, 1886.

36. McLean, *Rise and Fall of Anarchy,* pp. 65–66; *Chicago Tribune,* August 3, 1886; David, *Haymarket Affair,* pp. 241–42.

37. McLean, *Rise and Fall of Anarchy,* pp. 67–68.

38. It is difficult to derive a clear picture of what happened in the Haymarket just after the explosion. The police clearly fabricated the story of Sam Fielden shooting at Captain Ward from the hay wagon. On the other hand, the patrolmen's testimony about taking fire from the crowd was corroborated by several civilian witnesses. However, other witnesses called by the defense team contradicted this testimony, and still others said it was clear that the police gunfire struck other officers on the densely packed streets. The doctors who examined the police victims and who testified on June 29, 1886, referred mainly to bomb wounds, without drawing any conclusions from the gunshot wounds about which guns the bullets had come from or from which direction the bullets had been shot. Two physicians said that three policemen had wounds from bullets shot in a downward trajectory, which might have indicated that bullets were fired from windows in nearby buildings or that the officers were kneeling down or ducking when they were hit by their fellow officers in the fusillade. Doctors' testimony in "Chicago Anarchists on Trial" (a digitized transcript of the trial proceedings available from the Library of Congress at http://memory.loc.gov/ammem/award98/ichihtml/haybuild.html); Doctors Bax-

ter, Murphy, Henrotin, Newman, Bluthardt and Flemming, Vol. K, pp. 617–19, 551–73, 640–45, 691–97, and Vol. M, pp. 179–266. Murphy and Bluthardt describe the trajectories in Vol. K, pp. 557–58, 570–71, 695.

Since the prosecution did not introduce ballistics tests into evidence, there is no way of knowing which guns fired the shots that hit officers. Even if reliable ballistics testing had been done, the results would have been dubious, because the police bought their own guns and were not issued standardized weapons by the department.

Even though Mayor Harrison and other objective observers saw no one in the crowd with firearms, it seems likely that some of the rallygoers were armed. Spies left his revolver on the North Side, but some of the others, fearing another assault like the one at the McCormick works the night before, would have been armed, at least for self-defense. It also seems quite possible that some civilians shot at the police after the officers opened fire in all directions when packed together in tight ranks; in such a formation and in a state of panic, it is also likely that the patrolmen would have hit one another with what was described as wild gunfire.

In any case, the state's case was built on the evidence that the bomb fragments killed Patrolman Degan. The argument that anarchists opened fire immediately after the bomb exploded was, of course, important to the allegation that a conspiracy had been planned to launch the attack, but the state's evidence relied on eyewitnesses whose testimony was contradicted by reliable reporters who had no connections to the anarchists or to the police.

39. *Chicago Tribune*, August 5, 1886.

40. *Chicago Tribune*, August 7–8, 10, 1886.

41. Ibid.

42. *Chicago Tribune*, August 12, 1886.

43. McLean, *Rise and Fall of Anarchy*, pp. 100, 102.

44. David, *Haymarket Affair*, pp. 258–59.

45. Quote ibid., pp. 103–4.

46. Quote in Lawson, *American State Trials*, pp. 175–76.

47. Ibid. The prosecution submitted expert testimony by chemists that was supposed to prove that the deadly bomb was similar in chemical composition to the bombs Lingg and Seliger made. David, *Haymarket Affair*, p. 235. Recently, a group of researchers conducted a new scientific analysis of the forensic evidence, including the tiny bomb fragments preserved in the Beinecke Library at Yale University. The conclusion of these scholars tends to confirm the testimony of the prosecution's expert witnesses at the Haymarket trial: that the fragments probably came from a bomb made by Lingg. The authors indicate, however, that firm conclusions cannot be drawn from this evidence (presumably about Lingg's involvement in the crime). Timothy Messer-Kruse, James O. Eckert, Jr., Pannee Burckel and Jeffery Dunn, "The Haymarket Bomb: Reassessing the Evidence," *Labor* 2 (Summer 2005), pp. 39–52.

Louis Lingg was not convicted for making bombs, however. He was convicted as an accessory to murder because he was allegedly part of a May 3 conspiracy meeting during which anarchists supposedly planned the May 4 bombing and because, as a part of this plot, Lingg "sent" some of his bombs to be used at the Haymarket. But the state never established any connection between Lingg and the alleged conspiracy meeting or the unknown bomb thrower.

And so, it makes no significant difference if more material evidence has been found indicating that Lingg (or Seliger) made the fatal bomb—even if the evidence is conclusive, which it is not, according to the authors of "The Haymarket Bomb." For a much more developed critique of this circumstantial evidence and how it is interpreted in the Messer-Kruse et al. article, see Bryan Palmer, "CSI Labor History: Haymarket and the Forensics of Forgetting," *Labor* 3 (Winter 2006), forthcoming.

48. Quote in Lawson, ed., *American State Trials*, pp. 207–8, 215, 221, 222; *Chicago Tribune*, August 17, 1886; McLean, *Rise and Fall of Anarchy*, p. 109.

49. McLean, *Rise and Fall of Anarchy*, pp. 112–13; *Chicago Tribune*, August 18, 1886.

50. This summary of how Black presented the case draws upon the account in Avrich, *Tragedy*, pp. 270–75.

51. Lawson, ed., *American State Trials*, p. 259.

52. Ibid., pp. 239–41, 248–49, 259–60.

53. Ibid., pp. 259–60.

54. *Chicago Tribune*, August 19, 20, 1886.

55. *Chicago Tribune*, August 20, 1886; McLean, *Rise and Fall of Anarchy*, pp. 120–21.

56. McLean, *Rise and Fall of Anarchy*, p. 121; *Chicago Tribune*, August 21, 1886.

57. McLean, *Rise and Fall of Anarchy*, pp. 121–22.

58. David, *Haymarket Affair*, p. 270; Miller, *City of the Century*, p. 477.

59. *Chicago Tribune*, August 21, 1886.

60. *Chicago Tribune*, August 21, 1886.

61. Quote in David, *Haymarket Affair*, pp. 271–72.

62. On the drama of murder trials and the way in which they were substituted for the drama of public hangings, see Stuart Banner, *The Death Penalty: An American History* (Cambridge: Harvard University Press, 2002), pp. 164–65; and quote from state's attorney in Lawson, *American State Trials*, p. 24.

63. David, *Haymarket Affair*, pp. 272, 274.

64. Quote ibid., p. 273.

65. *Workmen's Advocate* quoted ibid., p. 275.

66. *Chicago Express* quoted in Schneirov, *Labor and Urban Politics*, p. 215.

Chapter Fourteen / You Are Being Weighed in the Balance

1. Schneirov, *Labor and Urban Politics*, p. 215.

2. *Chicago Express* quoted in Ashbaugh, *Lucy Parsons*, p. 89. Also see McLean, *Rise and Fall of Anarchy*, p. 142; and Schneirov, *Labor and Urban Politics*, pp. 215, 217.

3. *Chicago Tribune*, September 2, 5, 28, 1886.

4. See Avrich, *Tragedy*, p. 293.

5. Lawson, *American State Trials*, p. 281. Also see Smith, *Urban Disorder*, pp. 157–75. Spies not only defended his citizenship in this impassioned address, he also asserted his manhood, as he had regularly urged workingmen to do in his speeches and writings, notably in the now-infamous "Workingmen to Arms" circular he wrote so furiously after witnessing the massacre at McCormick's on May 3. Spies's call to male pride was echoed by other anarchists in their final speeches, which asserted a passionate sense of working-class manhood against the more controlled expressions of middle-class manhood expressed by the attorney Grinnell, who seemed to reporters to be a strong, honorable man, wise and calm, dignified and refined, one who always stood firm in the midst of the nation's worst storms. In this sense the Haymarket trial could be seen as a contest over manhood that evoked the wounded pride of immigrant workingmen and the mental toughness of the city's "best men," who worried about losing control of the democracy to angry men of the lower classes. See Gail Bederman, *Manliness and Civi-*

lization: A Cultural History of Gender and Race in the United States, 1880–1917 (Chicago: University of Chicago Press, 1995), pp. 11–13.

6. McLean, *Rise and Fall of Anarchy*, pp. 149, 154; *The Accused and the Accusers: The Famous Speeches of the Eight Chicago Anarchists in Court on October 7th, 8th and 9th* (Chicago: Socialistic Publishing Co., 1886), p. 10.

7. McLean, *Rise and Fall of Anarchy*, pp. 157–59, 161–63.

8. Ibid., pp. 159–60.

9. Quote ibid., p. 173.

10. Quote ibid., p. 174. Also see Alan Calmer, *Labor Agitator: The Story of Albert R. Parsons* (New York: International Publishers, 1937) p. 111.

11. Lucy Parsons, ed., *Famous Speeches of the Eight Chicago Anarchists in Court* (1910; reprint, New York: Arno Press, 1969), p. 82.

12. Ibid., p. 102.

13. McLean, *Rise and Fall of Anarchy*, p. 176; L. Parsons, *Famous Speeches*, pp. 176–77.

14. L. Parsons, *Famous Speeches*, pp. 98, 111.

15. Ibid., p. 109.

16. Calmer, *Labor Agitator*, p. 112.

17. McLean, *Rise and Fall of Anarchy*, p. 177.

18. John Moses and Joseph Kirkland, eds., *The History of Chicago* (Chicago: Munsell & Co., 1895), pp. 199–200.

19. *Chicago Tribune*, October 13, 1886.

20. Schneirov, *Labor and Urban Politics*, pp. 221–22; *Chicago Tribune*, November 17, 1886.

21. Schneirov, *Labor and Urban Politics*, p. 237; Kim Voss, *The Making of American Exceptionalism: The Knights of Labor and Class Formation in the Nineteenth Century* (Ithaca: Cornell University Press, 1993), pp. 223, 225.

22. *Chicago Tribune*, October 18, 20, 1886; also see Ware, *Labor Movement in the U.S.* (see chap. 6, n. 40), pp. 152–54; and Avrich, *Tragedy*, p. 310.

23. Quote in Schneirov, *Labor and Urban Politics*, p. 223.

24. Richard Schneirov, "The Friendship of Bert Stewart and Henry Demarest Lloyd," in Roediger and Rosemont, eds., *Haymarket Scrapbook*, pp. 158–59.

25. Quoted in Schneirov, *Labor and Urban Politics*, p. 223.

26. *Chicago Tribune*, November 23–25, 1886.

27. Orvin Larson, *American Infidel: Robert G. Ingersoll* (New York: Citadel Press, 1962), pp. 219–20.

28. Ibid., p. 220.

29. Robert S. Eckley, "Leonard Swett: Lincoln's Legacy to the Chicago Bar," *Journal of the Illinois State Historical Society* 92 (1999), pp. 30–36.

30. Avrich, *Tragedy*, pp. 315–16; *Chicago Tribune*, November 6, 1887; and Edward Aveling and Eleanor Marx, *The Working-Class Movement in America* (London: Sonnenschein, 1886), p. 161.

31. Charles Edward Russell, *These Shifting Scenes* (New York: Hodder & Stoughton, 1914), pp. 94–95.

32. Ibid., p. 96.

33. Franklin Rosemont, "A Bomb-Toting, Long-Haired, Wild-Eyed Fiend: The Image of the Anarchist in Popular Culture," in Roediger and Rosemont, eds., *Haymarket Scrapbook*, p. 206; drawing of the Parsons family and quote from Art Young, ibid., pp. 100, 201.

34. Art Young, *On My Way: Being the Book of Art Young in Text and Pictures* (New York: Horace Liveright, 1928), p. 201; Russell, *These Shifting Scenes*, pp. 98–99; and see Franklin Rosemont, "The Most Dangerous Anarchist," in Roediger and Rosemont, eds., *Haymarket Scrapbook*, p. 51.

35. Russell, *These Shifting Scenes*, p. 100.

36. See Avrich, *Tragedy*, p. 324.

37. *Chicago Tribune*, January 14, 18, 19, 20, 1887; Van Zandt quoted in Avrich, *Tragedy*, p. 325.

38. *Chicago Tribune*, March 11, 13, 1887.

39. Aveling and Marx, *Working-Class Movement*, p. 167; L. Parsons, *The Life*, pp. 235–41.

40. *Chicago Tribune*, March 18, 1886.

41. Francis X. Busch, "The Haymarket Riot and the Anarchist Trial," *Journal of the Illinois State Historical Society* 48 (1935), p. 261; Swett and Oglesby quoted in Harry Barnard, *"Eagle Forgotten": The Life of John Peter Altgeld* (Indianapolis: Bobbs-Merrill, 1962), pp. 110, 198.

42. *Chicago Tribune*, November 4, 1886, and March 21, 1887.

43. Quote in *Chicago Tribune*, March 25, April 2, 5, 1887; Schneirov, *Labor and Urban Politics*, p. 228.

44. *Chicago Tribune*, April 6, 7, 1887.

45. *Chicago Tribune*, April 6, 7, 1887.

Chapter Fifteen / The Law Is Vindicated

1. *Chicago Tribune*, May 2, 1887.

2. *Chicago Tribune*, March 8, May 5, June 10, 1887. On the Merritt law, see David, *Haymarket Affair*, pp. 313–14.

3. McConnell, "The Chicago Bomb Case" (see chap. 7, n. 60), pp. 733–34; McLean, *Rise and Fall of Anarchy*, p. 182.

4. McLean, *Rise and Fall of Anarchy*, pp. 185–86.

5. Central Labor Union resolution quoted in David, *Haymarket Affair*, p. 347.

6. Ingersoll quoted in Avrich, *Tragedy*, p. 336, and in Larson, *American Infidel*, p. 220.

7. McLean, *Rise and Fall of Anarchy*, pp. 198–200; *Chicago Tribune*, September 22, 1886.

8. Avrich, *Tragedy*, pp. 304–5.

9. Digby-Junger, *The Journalist as Reformer* (see chap. 5, n. 17), pp. 80–81.

10. Avrich, *Tragedy*, pp. 303–4; Thomas, *Alternative America* (see chap. 5, n. 17), pp. 208, 232.

11. Quote in David, *Haymarket Affair*, pp. 345–46; *Chicago Tribune*, September 24, October 11, 21, 1887.

12. Quote in E. P. Thompson, *William Morris: Romantic to Revolutionary* (New York: Pantheon, 1976), p. 409; Beryl Ruehl, "From Haymarket Square to Trafalgar Square," in Roediger and Rosemont, eds., *Haymarket Scrapbook*, pp. 217, 220.

13. Moore, *European Socialists and the American Promised Land* (see chap. 9, n. 2), pp. 15, 33, 36–37; Marianne Debouzy, introduction to *In the Shadow of the Statue of Liberty: Immigrants, Workers, and Citizens in the American Republic, 1880–1920* (Urbana: University of Illinois Press, 1992), p. vii.

14. Marjorie Murphy, "And They Sang the *'Marseillaise'*: A Look at the French Left Press as It Responded to Haymarket"; Hubert Perrier et al., "The 'Social Revolution' in

America? European Reactions to the 'Great Upheaval' and to the Haymarket Affair";
and Raymond C. Sun, "Misguided Martyrdom: German Social Democratic Response to
the Haymarket Incident," in a special Haymarket centennial number of *International
Labor and Working Class History* 29 (Spring 1986), pp. 42–44, 53–60; George Richard
Esenwein, *Anarchist Ideology and the Working-Class Movement in Spain, 1868–1898*
(Berkeley: University of California Press, 1989), pp. 6–9, 125–27, 155–56. Quote in
Chicago Tribune, October 11, 1887.

15. Busch, "Haymarket Riot," p. 266. Butler made this argument about applying the
Fourteenth Amendment to state cases before a Supreme Court that had "rendered that
amendment innocuous as far as the Negro was concerned," wrote W. E. B. DuBois, and
made it instead into the "chief refuge" for corporations trying to avoid state regulation.
See DuBois, *Black Reconstruction* (see chap. 4, n. 10), p. 691.

16. Quote in McLean, *Rise and Fall of Anarchy,* pp. 207, 211.

17. David, *Haymarket Affair,* pp. 322–24; quoted in Busch, "Haymarket Riot,"
p. 267.

18. *Chicago Tribune,* November 3, 1887. Quotes in Avrich, *Tragedy,* p. 355.

19. L. Parsons, *The Life,* p. 230; Stone, *Fifty Years* (see chap. 13, n. 21), pp. 175–76.

20. *Chicago Tribune,* November 7, 1887; L. Parsons, *The Life,* pp. 183–86.

21. *Chicago Tribune,* November 5, 6, 7, 1887. On Trumbull, see McConnell, "The
Chicago Bomb Case," p. 735; Ralph J. Roske, *His Own Counsel: The Life and Times of
Lyman Trumbull* (Reno: University of Nevada Press, 1979), pp. 100–105, 113–16,
121–28; and Plummer, *Lincoln's Rail-Splitter,* p. 49.

22. Quoted in David, *Haymarket Affair,* p. 240.

23. Quotes from Garlin Sender, *Three American Radicals: John Swinton, Charles P.
Steinmetz and William Dean Howells* (Boulder, CO: Westview Press, 1991), pp. 107, 110.

24. Quote from Kenneth Lynn, *William Dean Howells: An American Life* (New York:
Harcourt, Brace & World, 1971), p. 291; Sender, *Three American Radicals,* pp. 127–38.

25. David, *Haymarket Affair,* pp. 336–38.

26. Quote ibid., p. 334. See Thomas, *Alternative America,* pp. 225–26, 230–31.

27. *Chicago Tribune,* November 7, 1887; Avrich, *Tragedy,* p. 353.

28. On Gage, see Pierce, *Chicago,* Vol. 3, p. 205. On the businessmen's meeting, see
David, *Haymarket Affair,* pp. 362–63; on Medill's view, see Plummer, *Lincoln's Rail-
Splitter,* p. 197.

29. *Chicago Tribune,* November 6, 8, 1887.

30. *Chicago Tribune,* November 11, 1887; Plummer, *Lincoln's Rail-Splitter,* p. 194.

31. *Chicago Tribune,* November 7, 8, 1887; Matson quote in Finis Farr, *Chicago: A
Personal History of America's Most American City* (New Rochelle, NY: Arlington House,
1973), p. 150.

32. *Chicago Tribune,* November 9, 1887.

33. David, *Haymarket Affair,* p. 367; Herman Raster to Richard J. Oglesby, November 7, 1887, Chicago, in Oglesby Papers, Abraham Lincoln Presidential Library, Springfield, IL; *Chicago Tribune,* November 10, 1887.

34. On Cora Richmond, see Avrich, *Tragedy,* pp. 371–72; quote about Oglesby in
David Herbert Donald, *Lincoln's Herndon* (New York: Knopf, 1948), p. 205. On literature
of reminiscence, see Merrill D. Peterson, *Lincoln and American Memory* (New York:
Oxford, 1994), pp. 158–63.

35. *Chicago Tribune,* November 10, 1887; Gompers, *Seventy Years* (see Prologue, n.
16), p. 238.

36. Quote in David, *Haymarket Affair,* p. 375.

37. Joseph R. Buchanan, *The Story of a Labor Agitator* (1903; reprint, Westport, CT: Greenwood Press, 1970), pp. 336–39.

38. *Chicago Tribune*, November 11, 1887; David, *Haymarket Affair*, pp. 364–66, 397; Avrich, *Tragedy*, pp. 367–71, 377.

39. Avrich, *Tragedy*, pp. 367–71, 377.

40. *Chicago Tribune*, November 11, 1887. Parsons's letter to his children is in L. Parsons, *The Life*, Appendix.

41. For the lyrics to "Annie Laurie," see http://www.ingeb.org/songs/annielau.html.

42. McLean, *Rise and Fall of Anarchy*, pp. 227–29.

43. Ibid., pp. 230–31.

44. Quotes from Farr, *Chicago: A Personal History*, p. 150; and Russell, *These Shifting Scenes*, pp. 103–4.

45. Russell, *These Shifting Scenes*, pp. 103–4.

46. *Chicago Tribune*, November 11, 1887; and see Ashbaugh, *Lucy Parsons*, pp. 35–36.

47. *Chicago Daily News*, November 11, 1887, quoted in McLean, *Rise and Fall of Anarchy*, pp. 232–33.

48. Ibid.

49. *Chicago Daily News*, quoted in McLean, *Rise and Fall of Anarchy*, pp. 234–37.

50. In 1886 a special committee of the English courts conducted a seminal study of execution by hanging and determined the ideal form of death by this means: sudden death caused by a broken neck instead of slow strangulation or decapitation, which sometimes resulted when a heavy body was dropped too far below the gallows platform. After various experiments in physics, it was determined that a man weighing 140 to 170 pounds, the weight range of the four men executed in Chicago, should fall at least 7½ feet below the platform in order for the neck to snap and death to occur most rapidly. These measurements would become the goal to which all subsequent Anglo-American judicial hangings aspired, but in November of 1887 such physics of death were not employed by the Cook County sheriff and the executioner: the four anarchists were given enough rope to fall only 4 feet below the gallows floor, and so they dangled at the ends of nooses for seemingly interminable minutes before finally choking to death. Timothy V. Kaufman-Osborn, *From the Noose to the Needle: Capital Punishment and the Late Liberal State* (Ann Arbor: University of Michigan Press, 2002), pp. 87–88, 112–13. Also see Charles Duff, *A Handbook of Hanging: Being a Short Introduction to the Fine Art of Execution* . . . (Boston: Hale, Cushman & Flint, 1929), pp. 62–63.

51. *Chicago Tribune*, November 11, 1887.

52. *Chicago Tribune*, November 11, 1887.

53. Buchanan, *Story of a Labor Agitator*, pp. 414–15; Avrich, *Tragedy*, p. 394; and Russell, *These Shifting Scenes*, p. 105.

54. *Chicago Tribune*, November 11, 1887.

55. Howells's letter quoted in Sender, *Three American Radicals*, pp. 122, 124, 129; and see Lynn, *William Dean Howells*, pp. 89, 109, 278, 290–92.

56. Abraham Cahan, *The Education of Abraham Cahan*, translated by Leon Stein, Abraham P. Conan and Lynn Davison (Philadelphia: Jewish Publication Society of America, 1969), p. 328; Morris U. Schappes, "Haymarket and the Jews," in Roediger and Rosemont, eds., *Haymarket Scrapbook*, pp. 119–120.

57. See Avrich, *Tragedy*, p. 407; and on Black's being haunted by Parsons's return, see ibid., p. 259. On Gompers, see Bernard Mandel, *Samuel Gompers, A Biography* (Yellow Springs, OH: Antioch Press, 1963), p. 57.

58. Schilling, "Labor Movement in Chicago," pp. xxvi–xxvii.

Chapter Sixteen / The Judgment of History

1. The following description of the funeral is drawn from the *Chicago Times*, November 14, 1887. Also see Ashbaugh, *Lucy Parsons*, pp. 137–39; and Avrich, *Tragedy*, pp. 395–96.

2. Avrich, *Tragedy*, pp. 395–96.

3. Russell, *These Shifting Scenes*, p. 105.

4. Roediger and Rosemont, eds., *Haymarket Scrapbook*, p. 121.

5. Avrich, *Tragedy*, p. 456.

6. See ibid., p. 409; and Esenwein, *Anarchist Ideology*, pp. 156–60.

7. David, *Haymarket Affair*, p. 395; McNeil, ed., *The Labor Movement*, pp. 467–68.

8. Emma Goldman, *Living My Life* (New York: Knopf, 1931), Vol. 1, p. 10.

9. Richard Drinnon, *Rebel in Paradise: A Biography of Emma Goldman* (Boston: Beacon Press, 1970), pp. 12–15; Goldman, *Living My Life*, Vol. 1, pp. 9–10, 23–42, 508; and also quote from a letter in Avrich, *Tragedy*, p. 434.

10. Bisno, *Abraham Bisno, Union Pioneer* (see chap. 9, n. 22), p. 90.

11. Jones, *Autobiography of Mother Jones* (see Prologue, n. 10), pp. 13–14; also see Elliot J. Gorn, *Mother Jones: The Most Dangerous Woman in America* (New York: Hill & Wang, 2001), pp. 263–65, 273–77.

12. William D. Haywood, *Bill Haywood's Book* (New York: International Publishers, 1929), p. 31.

13. Arthur Mann, *Yankee Reformers in the Urban Age* (Cambridge, MA: Belknap Press, 1954), p. 184.

14. Mary O. Furner, *Advocacy and Objectivity: A Crisis in the Professionalization of American Social Science, 1865–1905* (Lexington: University of Kentucky Press, 1975), pp. 134–37.

15. Zechariah Chafee, Jr., *Free Speech in the United States* (Cambridge: Harvard University Press, 1946), pp. 507–8.

16. Thomas, *Alternative America*, p. 214.

17. Edgar Lee Masters, *The Tale of Chicago* (New York: Putnam, 1933), p. 219.

18. May, *Protestant Churches* (see chap. 6, n. 38), pp. 100–102; Boyer, *Urban Masses and Moral Order* (see Prologue, n. 13), pp. 125–28, 131, 135, 242.

19. Quote from Flinn, *Chicago Police*, p. 222.

20. McLean, *Rise and Fall of Anarchy*, p. 20.

21. Schaack, *Anarchy and Anarchists*, p. 148.

22. William J. Adelman, "The Haymarket Monument at Waldheim," in Roediger and Rosemont, eds., *Haymarket Scrapbook*, p. 167.

23. Robert Wiebe, *Self-Rule: A Cultural History of American Democracy* (Chicago: University of Chicago Press, 1995), pp. 136–37.

24. William J. Adelman, "The Road to Fort Sheridan," in Roediger and Rosemont, eds., *Haymarket Scrapbook*, p. 130; Miller, *City of the Century* (see Prologue, n. 4), p. 476; Roy Turnbaugh, "Ethnicity, Civic Pride and Commitment: The Evolution of the Chicago Militia," *Journal of the Illinois State Historical Society* 72 (1979), pp. 111–22.

25. David, *Haymarket Affair*, p. 404; and Montgomery, *Citizen Worker* (see chap. 7, n. 19), pp. 102–4.

26. Barnard, *"Eagle Forgotten"* (see chap. 14, n. 41), p. 184; and see Rosemont, "A Bomb-Toting, Long-Haired, Wild-Eyed Fiend," p. 205.

27. Roediger and Rosemont, eds., *Haymarket Scrapbook*, p. 29.

28. For an insightful study of this popular literature, see Ann Fabian, *The Unvar-*

nished Truth: Personal Narratives in Nineteenth-Century America (Berkeley: University of California Press, 2000).

29. Smith, *Urban Disorder* (see Prologue, n. 14), pp. 137, 142–43.

30. Rudolph Vecoli, " 'Free Country': The American Republic Viewed by the Italian Left, 1880–1920," in Debouzy, ed., *In the Shadow of the Statue of Liberty,* p. 25.

31. Ashbaugh, *Lucy Parsons,* pp. 162–63, 175–76.

32. *Alarm,* December 8, 1888; Thompson, *William Morris,* pp. 506–7.

33. Quotes in Thompson, *William Morris,* pp. 487, 507.

34. Ibid., p. 487; also see pp. 489, 493–94.

35. Esenwein, *Anarchist Ideology,* pp. 6–9, 125–27, 156; quote on p. 159. Kropotkin quoted in Avrich, *Tragedy,* p. 412. Also see Lars-Goran Tedebrand, "America in the Swedish Press, 1880s to 1920s," in Debouzy, ed., *In the Shadow of the Stature of Liberty,* p. 55.

36. Gompers, *Seventy Years,* pp. 238–39.

37. Esenwein, *Anarchist Ideology,* p. 163; Andrea Panaccione, ed., *Sappi che Oggi e la tua Festa . . . per la Storia del l Maggio* [*May Day Celebration*] (Venice: Marsilio Editori, 1988); Eric Hobsbawm, "May Day," in Hobsbawm and Ranger, eds., *The Invention of Tradition* (see chap. 10, n. 10), p. 285.

38. *Chicago Tribune,* May 2, 1890.

39. Jane Addams, *Twenty Years at Hull House* (New York: Macmillan, 1934), pp. 177–78, and *My Friend, Julia Lathrop* (New York: Macmillan, 1935), quoted in "Haymarket, 1886!" *Chicago History* 15 (Summer 1986), p. 63.

40. See Richard Schneirov, "Voting as a Class: Haymarket and the Rise of the Democrat-Labor Alliance in Late Nineteenth-Century Chicago," *Labor History* 45 (Spring–Summer 2004), pp. 6–20, and Schneirov, *Labor and Urban Politics,* pp. 284–86, 307; Leon Fink, "The New Labor History and the Power of Historical Pessimism: Consensus, Hegemony and the Case of the Knights of Labor," *Journal of American History* 75 (June 1988), p. 132; David Brody, "Shaping a Labor Movement," in Brody, *In Labor's Cause* (New York: Oxford University Press, 1989), pp. 87–88. On the socialist challenge to Gompers led by Chicago machinist Tommy Morgan, see P. Foner, *Labor Movement,* Vol. 1, pp. 279–310. Quote from Chicago activist George Detwiler in Schneirov, *Labor and Urban Politics,* p. 318.

41. Quote in Christopher L. Tomlins, *The State and the Unions: Labor Relations, Law, and the Organized Labor Movement in America, 1880–1960* (New York: Cambridge University Press, 1985), pp. 30, 49, 57.

42. Schilling to Lucy Parsons, December 1, 1893, in George Schilling Papers, quoted in Ashbaugh, *Lucy Parsons,* p. 191.

43. Barnard, *"Eagle Forgotten,"* pp. 1–18, 23–39, 43, 133, 159–62; and Pierce, *Chicago,* Vol. 3, p. 452.

44. See Erik Larson, *The Devil in the White City: Murder, Magic, and Madness at the Fair That Changed America* (New York: Vintage, 2004); quote from Lloyd on p. 374.

45. Clarence Darrow, *The Story of My Life* (New York: Scribner, 1932), pp. 41–55, 96–104.

46. See Barnard, *"Eagle Forgotten,"* quotes on pp. 183, 187, and see pp. 204–8, 250–56.

47. Ibid., pp. 208, 218–19.

48. Adelman, "The Haymarket Monument," p. 171. Also see Melissa Dabakis, *Visualizing Labor in American Sculpture: Monuments, Manliness, and the Work Ethic, 1880–1935* (Cambridge: Cambridge University Press, 1999), pp. 60–61.

49. Dabakis, *Visualizing Labor,* p. 61. On sites of memory that encourage "commemorative vigilance," see Pierre Nora, "Between Memory and History: *Les Lieux de Memoire,*" *Representations* 26 (Spring 1989), pp. 8–22; and James Green, "Crime Against Memory at Ludlow," *Labor* 1 (Spring 2004), pp. 9–16.

50. Quotes from Altgeld, *Reasons* (see chap. 7, n. 68), pp. 11–12, 35, 46, 36–37, 39.

51. Avrich, *Tragedy,* pp. 238–39, 439–41. Author's interview with Tim Samuelson, Chicago, December 5, 2004.

52. On Lum, see Avrich, *Tragedy,* pp. 408, 442–45, and Paul Avrich, "The Bomb Thrower—A New Candidate," in Roediger and Rosemont, eds. *Haymarket Scrapbook,* pp. 71–73.

53. Altgeld, *Reasons,* pp. 35, 46; also see pp. 36–37, 39.

54. See Barnard, *"Eagle Forgotten,"* pp. 240–41; David, *Haymarket Affair,* p. 246; and Darrow, *Story of My Life,* p. 101.

55. On Altgeld's criticism of those who associated immigrants with crime and disorder, see Barnard, *"Eagle Forgotten,"* pp. 132–33. On his love of liberty, see quotes from Clarence Darrow's eulogy for Altgeld in Arthur Weinberg, ed., *Attorney for the Damned: Clarence Darrow in the Courtroom* (Chicago: University of Chicago Press, 1989), p. 544, and from Ray Ginger in *Altgeld's America: The Lincoln Ideal vs. Changing Realities* (New York: Funk & Wagnalls, 1958), p. 87. Altgeld did not live to see his prophecy fulfilled. He died in 1902, one year before a federal law banned alien anarchists from entering the United States and paved the way for the wartime suspension of civil liberties for all American radicals, native-born and foreign-born. For a contemporary version of Altgeld's argument that the targeting of immigrants as potential terrorists leads to broader attacks on civil liberties, see the syndicated column by Molly Ivins, "Mr. Ashcroft, Let's Not Repeat Past Mistakes," *Boston Globe,* November 21, 2001, and the more extensive version of the argument in David Cole, *Enemy Aliens: Double Standards and Constitutional Freedoms in the War on Terrorism* (New York: New Press, 2003).

56. David, *Haymarket Affair,* pp. 412–13. And see Barnard, *"Eagle Forgotten,"* p. 214, and quotes on p. 248.

57. Barnard, *"Eagle Forgotten,"* pp. 236–38.

58. Avrich, *Tragedy,* pp. 446–48.

59. Buder, *Pullman* (see Prologue, n. 5), pp. 170–71, 179–81; Ginger, *Altgeld's America,* p. 100; Addams, *Twenty Years at Hull House,* p. 160.

60. Miller, *City of the Century,* pp. 546–49; Barnard, *"Eagle Forgotten,"* p. 298; Roediger and Rosemont, eds., *Haymarket Scrapbook,* p. 185; Ginger, *Altgeld's America,* pp. 192–93.

61. Miller, *City of the Century,* pp. 546–47.

62. Nick Salvatore, *Eugene V. Debs: Citizen and Socialist* (Urbana: University of Illinois Press, 1982), pp. 152–55; Ray Ginger, *Eugene V. Debs: The Making of an American Radical* (1949; reprint, New York: Collier, 1962), pp. 64, 108, 192–93; William E. Forbath, *Law and the Shaping of the American Labor Movement* (Cambridge: Harvard University Press, 1989), pp. 42–43, 75–77, 168; Tomlins, *The State and the Unions,* pp. 30, 49, 57.

In the age of industrial violence that followed the Pullman conflict, dynamite bombs exploded with a frequency even August Spies and Louis Lingg could not have predicted. The bombs were not used as weapons in pitched battles between strikers and the National Guard as the Chicago anarchists imagined, but rather in secret campaigns waged by embattled trade unionists against antiunion employers and their hired gunmen. For example, in Rocky Mountain metal-mining districts, battles between union miners and the armed forces of the operators led to the deaths of sixty people, most of them as a result of the brutal conflict that erupted around the Cripple Creek mining district in Colorado. Many of the casualties were members of the Western Federation of Miners, a union organized by militant socialists like William D. Haywood, an admirer of Albert Parsons and August Spies. In addition to the union casualties, two mine foremen and thirteen strikebreakers died in dynamite explosions. The authorities blamed the blasts on "socialist dynamiters" like Haywood, but no one was ever charged in any of the Colorado killings. See Rhodri Jeffreys-Jones, *Violence and Reform in American History* (New York: New Viewpoints, 1978), pp. 8–78; and Elizabeth Jameson, *All That Glitters: Class, Conflict, and Community in Cripple Creek* (Urbana: University of Illinois Press, 1998), pp. 218–25, 244–47.

63. Quote in Ginger, *Eugene V. Debs*, p. 66; Ashbaugh, *Lucy Parsons*, pp. 199–200.

64. Joseph Kirkland, "Some Notable Trials," in Moses and Kirkland, eds., *History of Chicago* (see chap. 14, n. 18), p. 208. Joseph Kirkland was a practicing lawyer in Chicago as well as a novelist whose book *Zury: The Meanest Man in Spring County* (published the year of the Haymarket executions) focused on the life of a tightfisted farmer who became a hardheaded Chicago businessman devoted entirely to the pursuit of wealth. Kirkland was a leading figure in the city's genteel literary circles, but his 1887 novel was anything but genteel; it was the first realist novel produced by what would become the Chicago school of novelists devoted to exposing the brutal conflicts that seemed to overwhelm the city's residents. Timothy B. Spears, *Chicago Dreaming: Midwesterners and the City, 1871–1919* (Chicago: University of Chicago Press, 2005), pp. 53–54.

65. Kirkland, "Some Notable Trials," p. 208.

66. Ashbaugh, *Lucy Parsons*, p. 182; quote in Kirkland, "Some Notable Trials," p. 204.

67. Quotes in Blaine McKinley, "A Religion in a New Time: Anarchists' Memorials to the Haymarket Martyrs," *Labor History* 28 (Summer 1997), pp. 391, 395–96. Holmes and Goldman quoted in Avrich, *Tragedy*, p. 449.

68. Quotes in McKinley, "A Religion in a New Time," p. 399.

Epilogue

1. Ashbaugh, *Lucy Parsons*, p. 211.

2. Quoted in Gerstle, *American Crucible*, p. 70; and see Eric Rauchway, *Murdering McKinley: The Making of Theodore Roosevelt's America* (New York: Hill & Wang, 2003).

3. Gerstle, *American Crucible*, pp. 54–55; William Preston, *Aliens and Dissenters: Federal Suppression of Radicals, 1903–1933* (Cambridge: Harvard University Press, 1963), pp. 29, 31.

4. Joyce L. Kornbluh, ed., *Rebel Voices: An I.W.W. Anthology* (Chicago: Charles H. Kerr, 1988), pp. 1–12.

5. Melvyn Dubofsky, *We Shall Be All: A History of the Industrial Workers of the World* (Chicago: Quadrangle Books, 1969), p. 81; and Roediger and Rosemont, eds., *Haymarket Scrapbook*, pp. 189, 193.

6. *Proceedings of the Founding Convention of the Industrial Workers of the World* (New York: Merit Publishers, 1969), pp. 56–57, 167–68, 171; Haywood, *Bill Haywood's Book*, p. 187. For an impressive argument that the IWW was strongly influenced by anarchists, see Salvatore Salerno, *Red November, Black November: Culture and Community in the Industrial Workers of the World* (Albany: State University Press of New York, 1989).

7. Robert D'Attilio, *"Primo Maggio:* Haymarket as Seen by Italian Anarchists in America," in Roediger and Rosemont, eds. *Haymarket Scrapbook,* pp. 229–32; Rudolph Vecoli, *"Primo Maggio:* May Day Observances Among Italian Immigrant Workers," *Labor's Heritage* 7 (Spring 1966), p. 35.

8. Vecoli, *"Primo Maggio,"* pp. 30–31, 40.

9. Rudolph Vecoli, *"Primo Maggio:* An Invented Tradition of the Italian Americans," in Panaccione, *May Day Celebration,* p. 70.

10. On the important, and sometimes dominant, role of anarchists in forming militant trade unions in Italy, France, Spain, Argentina, Chile and Mexico, see Woodcock, *Anarchism* (see chap. 8, n. 11), pp. 270–71, 370–80, 426; Esenwein, *Anarchist Ideology,* pp. 172, 189, 191, 197, 202–3; Robert J. Alexander, *A History of Organized Labor in Argentina* (Westport, CT: Praeger, 2003), pp. 10, 12, 26–27; Peter De Shazo, *Urban Workers and Labor Unions in Chile, 1902–1927* (Madison: University of Wisconsin Press, 1983), p. 133, 158; and John M. Hart, *Anarchism and the Mexican Working Class, 1860–1931* (Austin: University of Texas Press, 1978), pp. 83–94, 108–11.

11. Ashbaugh, *Lucy Parsons,* p. 227.

12. E. Foner, *American Freedom* (see chap. 1, n. 6), pp. 163–64, 168; Ashbaugh, *Lucy Parsons,* p. 245.

13. Philip S. Foner, *May Day: A Short History of the International Workers' Holiday, 1886–1986* (New York: International Publishers, 1986), pp. 76–79, 87–90; John Bodnar, *Remaking America: Public Memory, Commemoration and Patriotism in the Twentieth Century* (Princeton: Princeton University Press, 1992), pp. 83, 85–88, 93; Francis Russell, *A City in Terror: 1919, the Boston Police Strike* (New York: Viking Press, 1975), p. 21.

14. Ginger, *Eugene V. Debs,* pp. 372–413; Dubofsky, *We Shall Be All,* pp. 430–36, 459; and Preston, *Aliens and Dissenters,* pp. 220–29.

15. Lawson, ed., *American State Trials,* p. vi.; James Ford Rhodes and Ellis Paxson Oberholtzer, quoted in David, *Haymarket Affair,* p. 446, from Rhodes's *History of the United States from the Compromise of 1850 to the McKinley-Bryan Campaign of 1896* (New York: Macmillan, 1920) and Oberholtzer's *A History of the United States Since the Civil War* (New York: Macmillan, 1917).

16. Quote from Frank O. Beck, *Hobohemia: Emma Goldman, Lucy Parsons, Ben Reitman and Other Agitators and Outsiders in the 1920s and 1930s* (1956; reprint, Chicago: Charles H. Kerr, 2000), p. 35.

17. See Franklin Rosemont's introduction to ibid., pp. 7–9.

18. Quote from Joughin and Morgan, *Legacy of Sacco and Vanzetti* (see Prologue, n. 17), pp. 208–9. Also see Upton Sinclair, *Boston: A Documentary Novel of the Sacco-Vanzetti Case* (1928; reprint, Boston: Robert Bentley, 1978), p. 754.

19. The Haymarket story also appeared in books written by young writers on the left born to immigrant parents. See Anthony Bimba, *The History of the American Working Class* (New York: International Publishers, 1927), pp. 188, 314; and Louis Adamic, *Dynamite: The Story of Class Violence in America* (New York: Viking Press, 1934), pp. 65–85. On Adamic and second-generation ethnic writers with radical politics, see Michael Denning, *The Cultural Front: The Laboring of American Culture in the Twentieth Century* (London: Verso, 1997), pp. 447–48.

20. Sam Dolgoff quoted in Roediger and Rosemont, eds., *Haymarket Scrapbook,* p. 246.

21. Toni Gilpin and Steve Rosswurm, "The Haymarket Tradition," *Haymarket: Chicago's Progressive Journal of Politics and Arts* 21 (May 1986), p. 21.

22. Jeffreys-Jones, *Violence and Reform,* pp. 18–19, 35, 40–44.

23. Richard Hofstadter, "Reflections on Violence," in Richard Hofstadter and Michael Wallace, eds., *American Violence: A Documentary History* (New York: Knopf, 1970), pp. 6, 11, 19–20, 39–40. Statistics from Philip Taft and Philip Ross, "American Labor Violence: Its Causes, Character and Outcome," in Hugh Davis Graham and Ted R. Gurr, eds., *Violence in America: Historical and Comparative Perspectives, A Report to the National Commission on the Causes and Prevention of Violence* (New York: Bantam Books, 1969), p. 270.

24. Lizabeth Cohen, *Making a New Deal: Industrial Workers in Chicago, 1919–1939* (Cambridge: Cambridge University Press, 1990), p. 299; Gilpin and Rosswurm, "The Haymarket Tradition," p. 21; Ashbaugh, *Lucy Parsons,* p. 262.

25. Cohen, *Making a New Deal,* p. 300; Ashbaugh, *Lucy Parsons,* pp. 262–64; and Studs Terkel, *Chicago* (New York: Pantheon, 1986), p. 35.

26. See Kenneth Rexroth, "Again at Waldheim," in Sam Hamill and Bradford Morrow, eds., *The Complete Poems of Kenneth Rexroth* (Port Townsend, WA: Copper Canyon Press, 2003), p. 221, in which the poet reflects on the death of Emma Goldman and her burial at Waldheim near the Haymarket anarchists. Rexroth's poem reads in part: "What memory lasts Emma of you / Or the intrepid comrades of your grave . . . / Against the iron-clad, flame throwing / Course of time?" Howard Fast, *The American: A Middle Western Legend* (New York: Duell, Sloan & Pearce, 1946). On Howard Fast as a Popular Front writer, see Denning, *The Cultural Front,* p. 248, and Priscilla Murolo, "History in the Fast Lane," *Radical History Review* 31 (December 1984), pp. 22–31. On Algren and Chicago, see H. E. F. Donahue, *Conversations with Nelson Algren* (New York: Hill & Wang, 1964), pp. 61–64, 88.

27. Nelson Algren, *Chicago: City on the Make* (1951; reprint, Chicago: University of Chicago Press, 2001), pp. 23, 48, 52, 62–64, 66.

28. The story did appear in a few other books, in the pages of Ray Ginger's fine collection of essays in *Altgeld's America* (chap. 2) and in the chapters of a few labor histories written by leftist authors, published by small presses and read mainly by curious workers in independent labor unions who had learned to keep their heads down while the winds of McCarthyism raged about them. See Boyer and Morais, *Labor's Untold Story,* pp. 84–86; and P. Foner, *Labor Movement,* Vol. 2, pp. 105–14. On the suppression of May Day and the impact of the Cold War on workers' consciousness, see P. Foner, *May Day,* pp. 135–37, 145; James Green, *The World of the Worker: Labor in Twentieth-Century America* (New York: Hill & Wang, 1980), pp. 133–209; Marianne Debouzy, "In Search of Working-Class Memory: Some Questions and a Tentative Assessment," *History and Anthropology* 2 (Spring 1986), pp. 275–78; Bruno Cartoiso, "Memoria Privata e Memoria Pubblica nella Storiografico del Movimento Operaio," *Studi Storici* 38 (Inverno 1997), pp. 897–910; and Michael Kammen, *Mystic Chords of Memory: The Transformation of Tradition in American Culture* (New York: Knopf, 1991), p. 517.

29. P. Foner, *May Day,* pp. 74, 80; and James Green, "Globalization of Memory: The Enduring Remembrance of the Haymarket Martyrs Around the World," *Labor* 2 (Fall 2005), pp. 5–15.

30. Dan LaBotz to Jim Green, e-mail, November 18, 2004. The memory also survived in China, even in a year, 1987, when the Communist government held no May Day celebrations. "Yesterday is the holiday for the working class," a friend wrote to me from Beijing on May 2, 1987. "Though we did not hold any grand meeting or some parade, yet the mighty struggle for the eight hour day is ingrained in our minds." In the past "we paid great tribute to these heroes who sacrificed their lives for the benefit of the working

class. May First is one of the most important holidays; on this day we pay tribute to the Haymarket martyrs." Huang Shao-xiang to Jim Green, May 2, 1987, Beijing, PRC.

31. In 1976 Galeano escaped Argentina for Barcelona, the historic center of Spanish anarchism, where citizens and workers were still celebrating the death of dictator Francisco Franco and his fascist regime. There, in Catalonia, Galeano began to write his magnum opus, the trilogy *Memoria del fuego,* an epic prose poem dedicated to the people of the Americas and their bloody histories—memory books that transcended existing literary genres. "I am a writer obsessed with remembering," he said, "with remembering the past of America, above all that of Latin America, intimate land condemned to amnesia." Galeano's obsession with the past remains obvious in the third volume of the trilogy, finished in 1986, the year after he came to Chicago. In *Century of the Wind* he offers yearly calendar scenes that begin at Montevideo in 1900 with a new century being born as "the time of anybodies," a time when "[t]he people want democracy and trade unions." Biography of Eduardo Galeano from the Web site www.kirjasto.sci.fi/galeano.htm, including first quote; second quote from Eduardo Galeano, *Century of the Wind* (1986; English trans., New York: Norton, 1988), p. 4. Also see Luis Roniger, Luis Sznajder, and Mario Sznajder, "The Politics of Memory in Redemocratized Argentina and Uruguay," *Memory and History* 10, no. 1 (Spring 1998), pp. 155–56.

32. Eduardo Galeano, *The Book of Embraces* (New York: Norton, 1991), p. 118.

33. "Forgotten Battle," transcript of Studs Terkel television interview on the *McNeill-Lehrer News Hour,* Public Broadcasting System, May 1, 1986, pp. 13–14. Thanks to Martin Blatt for a copy of this transcript.

34. Studs Terkel, *Talking to Myself: A Memoir of My Time* (New York: Pantheon, 1971), pp. 48–49, 58, 197; Studs Terkel, *Division Street: America* (New York: Pantheon, 1967), p. xxii; Terkel, *Chicago,* p. 28; and the author's tape-recorded interview with Studs Terkel, Chicago, July 11, 2003.

35. Jeff Huebner, "Haymarket Revisited," *Chicago Reader,* December 10, 1993, pp. 1, 14; press release from the Haymarket Square Workers Memorial Committee, April 25, 1969, signed by Leslie Orear, in Carolyn Ashbaugh Collection, Charles H. Kerr Papers, Newberry Library, Chicago.

36. David Farber, *Chicago '68* (Chicago: University of Chicago Press, 1988), pp. 140–43.

37. Ibid., pp. 145–48.

38. James Miller, *Democracy Is in the Streets: From Port Huron to the Siege of Chicago* (New York: Simon & Schuster, 1987), pp. 298–99; Farber, *Chicago '68,* pp. 161, 165, 179–80, 182–83, 199–201.

39. The Chicago Eight became the Chicago Seven after the case of Black Panther Bobby Seale was severed from the rest. See J. Anthony Lukas, *The Barnyard Epithet and Other Obscenities: Notes on the Chicago Conspiracy Trial* (New York: Harper & Row, 1970).

40. For an earlier example of a public controversy over a monument to revolutionary martyrs (the victims of the Boston Massacre of 1770), see Dennis B. Ryan, *Beyond the Ballot Box: A Social History of the Boston Irish* (Amherst: University of Massachusetts Press, 1983), p. 132.

41. Huebner, "Haymarket Revisited," pp. 2, 20; Miller, *Democracy,* p. 308. The bombing of the police statue was a symbolic act to inaugurate the Days of Rage, when young radicals planned to bring the Vietnam War home with violent attacks on war-related institutions. One of these Weathermen, Bill Ayers, wrote later about being there that night as he watched a comrade blow up the police monument in Haymarket Square.

"Terry," who set off the dynamite, had committed the story of the Haymarket anarchists to memory, Ayers recalled, and could quote what August Spies said to the court about "a subterranean fire about to blaze up." The Weathermen had come to Chicago that October after whipping themselves up in a kind of frenzy, as Ayers put it, remaking themselves "into street fighters and persuading ourselves against all evidence that working-class youth were with us, that our uncompromising militancy was winning them over, and that Chicago would be the wild, unruly embodiment of the Revolutionary Youth Movement." If the Weathermen brought the Vietnam War home to the streets of Chicago, Ayers thought, "August Spies and Albert Parsons would smile on us from their graves, and rest just a wee bit easier." But when the urban guerrilla fighter and his comrades raged through the city streets, broke windows, set fires and fought with police, no one joined them. Worse, they were beaten, shot, maced and brutally interrogated by law officers. Ayers somehow escaped arrest and rejoined a few street fighters at a prearranged spot. When the battered Weathermen gathered at the charred base of the Haymarket police statue for their final march, they were surrounded by cordons of infuriated police, he recalled. The curtain then fell on what Ayers called their "theater of revolution." Bill Ayers, *Fugitive Days: A Memoir* (New York: Penguin, 2003), pp. 162–63, 165, 168, 176.

42. On the killing of Hampton and Clark, who died in a hail of seventy-nine bullets from police revolvers, see Henry Hampton and Steve Fayer, *Voices of Freedom: An Oral History of the Civil Rights Movement from the 1950s Through the 1980s* (New York: Bantam Books, 1990) pp. 520–38.

43. Press release from the Haymarket Square Workers Memorial Committee, April 25, 1969.

44. Huebner, "Haymarket Revisited," p. 16.

45. Jonah Raskin, ed., *The Weather Eye: Communiqués from the Weather Underground, May 1970–May 1974* (New York: Union Square Press, 1974), p. 5.

46. Huebner, "Haymarket Revisited," pp. 16, 22.

47. Quote ibid., p. 14.

48. This official reference to the Haymarket martyrs as "activists," not as anarchists—along with everything else that transpired during the centennial ceremonies—enraged a band of 200 neo-anarchists who gathered in Chicago for the events, complete with black flags and banners with slogans such as "Eat the Rich, Feed the Poor." Smith, *Urban Disorder* (see Prologue, n. 14), p. 277.

49. The collection of documents and images is Roediger and Rosemont's *Haymarket Scrapbook.* The walking tour is in Adelman, *Haymarket Revisited* (see chap. 4, n. 20). Warren Lemming's cabaret production was published as *Cold Chicago: A Haymarket Fable* (Chicago: Charles H. Kerr, 2001). Scholarly publications include special issues of *International Labor and Working Class History* 29 (Spring 1986), edited by David Montgomery, and *Chicago History* 15 (Summer 1986), edited by Russell Lewis; Bruce C. Nelson's impressively researched monograph on the Chicago anarchist movement, *Beyond the Martyrs* (see chap. 3, n. 37); Charnan Simon's *The Story of the Haymarket Riot* (Chicago: The Children's Press of Regensteiner Printing Enterprises, 1988); as well as chapters on the case in P. Foner, *May Day* (see Epilogue, n. 13); Udo Achten, Mathias Reichelt and Reinhard Schultz, eds., *Mein Vaterland 1st International* (Berlin: Asso Verlag, 1986); and Roediger and E. Foner, *Our Own Time* (see chap. 1, n. 16). In 1993, a researcher found 1,000 articles and books in which the case was discussed (not simply mentioned) and another 200 "imaginative works" that involved the Haymarket characters and events. Robert W. Glenn, *The Haymarket Affair: An Annotated Bibliography* (Westport, CT: Greenwood Press, 1993). Since then, other writers who have devoted

chapters to the story include Smith, *Urban Disorder and the Shape of Belief* (1995); Miller, *City of the Century* (1996); Schneirov, *Labor and Urban Politics* (1998); Marco d'Eramo, *Il maiale e il grattacielo* (Milan: Feltrinelli Editore, 1999), translated into English as *The Pig and the Skyscraper: Chicago, A History of Our Future* (London: Verso, 2002); James Green, *Taking History to Heart: The Power of the Past in Building Social Movements* (Amherst: University of Massachusetts Press, 2000); Palmer, *Cultures of Darkness* (see chap. 12, n. 26); Clymer, *America's Culture of Terrorism* (2003); and various entries in two superb encyclopedias of Chicago history: Schultz and Hast, eds., *Women Building Chicago* (see chap. 4, n. 17), and James R. Grossman, Ann Durkin Keating and Janice L. Reiff, eds., *The Encyclopedia of Chicago* (Chicago: University of Chicago Press, 2004). Now researchers may also consult the Web site "The Dramas of Haymarket" (www.chicagohistory.org/dramas), created by the Chicago Historical Society and designed by the historian Carl Smith, and the Library of Congress digital transcript of the Haymarket trial at http://www.memory.loc.gov/ammem/award98/ichihtml/haybuild.html.

50. The landmark status came as a result of a Newberry Library project directed by James Grossman. The Waldheim site study was written by Robin Bachin, who argued that the memorial provided a symbol through which various groups could share pride in their radical heritage. "Haymarket Martyrs Monument," National Historic Landmark Nomination by Robin Bachin for the Newberry Library, photocopy in author's possession. Also see Robin Bachin, "Structuring Memory—The Haymarket Martyrs' Memorial," *Cultural Resources Management* 21 (1998), pp. 45–46; and Green, *Taking History to Heart*, pp. 130–32, 142–43.

The ceremony held to rededicate the martyrs' monument attracted 500 people to Waldheim on May 3, 1998, and, like nearly everything else about the case, it aroused protest and controversy. The whole affair infuriated some anarchists in attendance, who shouted protests against the very idea that the U.S. government would grant any kind of state recognition to men who died fighting against it. One critic bitterly noted that the labor union speakers all referred to Spies, Parsons and their comrades not as revolutionaries, but "as 'labor activists' who died for 'workers' rights, good American trade unionists who died in the fight for an eight-hour day, a fair day's work for a fair day's pay, mom and apple pie." G. L. Doebler, "The Contest for Memory: Haymarket Through a Revisionist Looking Glass," reprint from *Fifth Estate*, Winter 1999, in a leaflet produced by the Louis Lingg League of Chicago, copies in author's possession.

The disaffected anarchists made a valid point. The memory of the Haymarket anarchists had been tamed when it was stripped of meaningful references to their revolutionary beliefs, violent speeches and confrontational tactics. Official commemorative efforts placed the Chicago anarchists within a legal discourse honoring dissenters who sacrificed themselves to expand civil liberties—freedoms granted by the very state the anarchists aimed to dismantle. This redemptive narrative of Haymarket, common in the telling of other national tales of catastrophe, seemed to modern anarchists to be a betrayal of the martyrs' memory and a perversion of history. On a similar taming of Emma Goldman's memory, as part of constitutional history, see Oz Frankl, "What Ever Happened to 'Red' Emma? Emma Goldman, From American Rebel to American Icon," *Journal of American History* 83, no. 3 (December 1996), pp. 903–42; quotes on pp. 931, 939.

Nonetheless, the labor movement's memory of Parsons, Spies and their mates as free-speech fighters and fearless organizers had truth on its side as well. After all, the International did call the rally in the Haymarket to make a peaceful protest against the killing of unarmed strikers who had been denied the right to picket. The anarchists did put themselves in harm's way time and again to exercise their freedoms of speech and

assembly, because they knew that without such liberties they could not succeed in organizing the kind of mass movement they thought would change America.

51. A variety of artistic works about Haymarket appeared after the 1986 centennial.
In Chicago, filmmakers made two videos on the case, an artist fought a three-year battle
with the Park District to create a public memorial to Lucy Parsons in Wicker Park using
May Stevens's well-known portrait of Lucy and the city's Steppenwolf Theater produced
Haymarket Eight, written by Derek Goldman and Jessica Thebus. The videos, produced
by Labor Beat in Chicago, are *The Road to Haymarket* and *Train Wreck of Ideologies*
(laborbeat@findourinfo.com). On the spiral artwork dedicated to Lucy Parsons and its
designer, Marjorie Woodruff, see Jeff Huebner, *Haymarket and Beyond: A Guide to
Wicker Park's Labor History Sites*, pamphlet published by the Near Northwest Side Arts
Council, 1996 (copy in author's possession), p. 8; and "Dangerous Women," *Chicago
Reader*, September 8, 1985, p. 1. May Stevens's painting featuring the 1903 photo of
Lucy Parsons overlaid with her own handwritten words ("Women are the slaves of
slaves") is reproduced in *Images of Labor*, edited by Moe Foner (New York: Pilgrim
Press, 1981), facing p. 35. On the Steppenwolf production, see *Northwestern University
Alumni Magazine*, Fall 2000, pp. 39–42. Other interpretive works of note include
Harold A. Zlotnik, *Toys of Desperation: A Haymarket Mural in Verse* (Interlaken, NY:
Heart of the Lakes Press, 1987); and *Haymarket Heritage: The Memoirs of Irving S.
Abrams*, edited by David Roediger and Phyllis Boanes (Chicago: Charles H. Kerr, 1989).
A new fictional version of the story also appeared in Martin Duberman's evocative *Hay-
market: A Novel* (New York: Seven Stories Press, 2003). Greg Guma's play *Inquisitions
and Other Unamerican Activities* was performed in Burlington, Vermont, in May 2003 (a
CD can be purchased at the Web site www.towardfreedom.com). Zayd Dohrn's play *Haymarket* was performed in Boston in November 2003. Another play, *Day of Reckoning*,
written by Melody Cooper (who also plays the role of Lucy Parsons), was performed in
New York in February 2005; it was reviewed in the *New York Times*, February 10, 2005.

52. The Haymarket affair marked Americans' first experience with what would today
be called terrorism, even though the scale of what happened on May 4, 1886, is difficult
to compare with mass murders of civilians that have taken place in modern times.
Nonetheless, the anarchists did make serious threats to use dynamite against their enemies in order to terrorize the authorities and the public—and this was clearly a result of
the Haymarket bombing. It thus makes sense to return to the affair as the starting point
for studying how Americans first reacted to the fear of bombings and then how they
responded when suspects, particularly aliens, were accused of conspiring to commit
such violent acts. Indeed, some commentators believe the Haymarket affair should be
regarded as a warning to citizens who allow the civil liberties of immigrants to be violated in the name of fighting terrorism. See Clymer, *America's Culture of Terrorism*, pp.
38, 211; Ivins, "Mr. Ashcroft, Let's Not Repeat Past Mistakes" (see chap. 16, n. 55); and
Studs Terkel, "Constitution Abuse," *Chicago Tribune*, July 11, 2003.

The term "terrorist" had not yet been invented in 1886, but the press, the police and
prosecutors, and most members of the public regarded the Haymarket bomber very
much like the public of today regards terrorists whose bombs kill civilians, even though
the victims in 1886 were armed police officers who had shown no hesitation about
attacking unarmed civilians. The bomber, whether or not he was an anarchist, clearly
had no concern about harming civilians when he threw that hand grenade into a crowded
street. Yet it seems likely, as Governor Altgeld suggested, that his act was one of revenge
aimed directly at the police. In any case, the Chicago anarchists advocated the use of

force as a defensive strategy for workers involved in life-or-death struggles with armed forces, not as a means of inspiring terror through indiscriminate killing.

Despite the ways in which the story of the Haymarket affair resonates in an age preoccupied with a "war on terror," I have not placed the Chicago anarchists and their activities within a discourse dominated by contemporary definitions of terrorism. The crime of murder committed with a bomb on May 4, 1886, whether it was intended as an act of revenge or was the work of an agent provocateur, seems, in retrospect, like the kind of terrorist attack that has became tragically common in the last few decades. However, the violence that came before and after the event on May 4 is better understood not as an early chapter in the history of terrorism, but as an episode in a different tradition of violent struggle between immigrant workers and their unions and the armed forces deployed against them.

53. Lara Kelland, "Putting Haymarket to Rest?" *Labor* 2 (Spring 2005), pp. 31–38.

54. Deanna Isaacs, "A Monumental Effort Pays Off," *Chicago Reader,* January 16, 2004, p. 22.

55. Stephen Kinzer, "In Chicago, an Ambiguous Memorial to the Haymarket Attack," *New York Times,* September 15, 2004, including quote from the city's cultural historian, Tim Samuelson.

56. Ibid.

57. Darrow, *The Story of My Life* (see chap. 16, n. 45), p. 99.

Acknowledgments

My editor, Andrew Miller, initially approached me about writing a new narrative history of the Haymarket affair, one that situated the event in a large social context and re-created the tensions and passions surrounding the birth of the first labor movement. The challenge was an exciting one. Andrew has supported my efforts to meet that challenge at every critical step in the process. His attention to detail, structure and flow in several drafts of the manuscript helped me to improve it in many important ways.

Howard Zinn persuaded me to undertake this project. And I am very happy that he did. Howard offered his own special brand of encouragement all along the way, and did me a good turn at first when he referred me to his agent, John Taylor Williams. Ike Williams agreed to represent me and has done so very well.

Several of my Boston friends have read the manuscript at various stages and offered many helpful suggestions, especially Jim O'Brien and Michael Kenney, who waded through a first draft with me and helped me chart a smoother course to my final destination. Jim also helped me with the epilogue. Christopher Daly read the manuscript with the eyes of a journalist and a historian, and offered me many valuable suggestions. John Hess and Robert d'Attilio read through these pages as well and gave me the benefit of their exceptional knowledge of anarchists and anarchism. Martin Blatt also read the entire manuscript and added a rewarding installment to our long and valuable dialogue about doing movement history. My research assistant in Boston, Jacob Carliner Remes, not only made excellent research notes for me; he also helped me clarify my thinking about the anarchists' trial and provided me with insightful suggestions about other critical aspects of my account. Ron Joseph, a former student, reappeared in my life a few years ago and offered to help me with this book: he has done so with great effect by carefully proofreading the text, by making editorial suggestions, by organizing and checking the citations, and by solving the mysteries of creating endnotes in Microsoft Word. My thanks also to Ellen Feldman and Dixon Gaines at Pantheon Books for additional editing.

I am also deeply indebted to three historians whose own scholarship in labor and working-class history I respect and admire enormously. Bruce Laurie, David Montgomery and David Roediger each brought their own impressive knowledge of nineteenth-century social history to bear on my treatment of subjects they have studied in far greater depth.

Any historian who seeks to retell an old story for a new time naturally relies upon the work of those who told the tale in earlier times. The Haymarket case is discussed in hundreds of books and articles and is examined exhaustively in three scholarly studies: in a pioneering political and legal study by Henry David; in a richly detailed account by Paul Avrich, the noted scholar of anarchism; and then, more recently, in an insightful cultural interpretation by Carl Smith. Anyone interested in the affair also owes a great debt to David Roediger and Franklin Rosemont for compiling and editing the superb *Haymarket Scrapbook* for Charles H. Kerr. Since my account is also a story of Chicago, its immigrant workers and their organizations, I have relied upon the excellent historical work on the city, first of all the three volumes authored by the wonderful writer Bessie Louise Pierce, and then all those who followed her. I am especially indebted to the valuable research about Chicago's immigrant workers and their struggles produced by John B. Jentz, Hartmut Keil, Bruce C. Nelson, Richard Schneirov and Karen Sawislak.

I have also returned again and again to the work of four great historians—Herbert Gutman, David Montgomery, Edward Thompson and Eric Hobsbawm—whose pioneering scholarship in social history informs this account of Gilded Age wage earners and their struggles. I trust the citations in my endnotes adequately express my debt to these historians and many others who have widened and deepened my understanding of the Gilded Age and its cities, its industries, its politics and its working people.

One of my desires in telling this story was to re-create scenes and characters by borrowing a few of the approaches novelists and playwrights use when they turn to historical subjects. I was, therefore, fascinated by Martin Duberman's exciting novel on Haymarket and by Zayd Dohrn's gripping play on the lives of Albert and Lucy Parsons. Martin and Zayd both met with me in New York City to talk about the story that fascinates us all. Zayd also responded with helpful comments on my nonfiction treatment of characters and scenes he has dramatized.

I owe many thanks to those in Chicago who assisted me when I visited there: to James Grossman, Alfred Young and Tobias Higbie of the incomparable Newberry Library, who made me welcome as a summer fellow in 2004, when I was just beginning to think about the book, and then offered me a chance to speak to a knowledgeable public audience about my work in progress; to William Adelman, who took me on a personalized tour of the Haymarket sites and brought his own unrivaled knowledge of the case to his reading of a draft; to Leslie Orear, Mollie West, Mike Matejka and the folks at the Illinois Labor History Society, who have supported my work in various important ways; to Tim Samuelson, the city's cultural historian, for providing me with his account of the struggle to create a memorial in the square; to Mary Brogger, the Chicago sculptor, for sharing her artist's sense of how she has represented the Haymarket events in a public monument; and, most of all, to Studs Terkel, who granted me an unforgettable interview in his home in July of 2003 and told me his version of the Haymarket story in his inimitable voice.

I am indebted to others in Chicagoland as well. During one visit my aunt and uncle, Ann and Bob DiVall, welcomed me back to their home and reminded me of my boyhood days when I ventured out of my little hometown of Carpentersville to see the big-city sites they selected: the ones we all remembered best were Union Station, Wrigley Field and the Chicago Historical Society—the source of many of the illustrations used in this book.

In addition to the professionals at the Newberry Library and the Historical Society in Chicago, I owe other debts for research assistance. Elaine Bernard, director of the Harvard Trade Union Program, and the outstanding professionals at Harvard's Widener, Littauer and Lamont libraries unlocked the doors to the treasure of books and documents in their care. Special thanks to David Cobb in the map room at Pusey Library for helping me find the superb Railway Terminal and Industrial Map of Chicago from 1886 and for putting me in touch with Jonathan Wyss and Kelly Sandefer of Topaz Maps in Watertown, Massachusetts, who made the attractive and illustrative maps for this book. I would also like to acknowledge the professionals who staff the Beinecke Rare Book and Manuscript Library at Yale University; they helped me search the newly acquired Haymarket Collection.

During the writing of this book I entered into a partnership with Leon Fink, who, as editor of the new journal *Labor: Studies of Working-Class History in the Americas,* proposed that the publication become the official journal of the Labor and Working-Class History Association, this at a time when I had just assumed the presidency of LAWCHA. Thanks to Leon, a portion of the epilogue of this book appeared in article form in *Labor* 2 (Fall 2005), and is reprinted here by permission. Leon perked my interest in writing a book like this some time ago when he asked why scholars of labor history weren't tackling the large, epic stories as the journalist J. Anthony Lukas had done in his book *Big Trouble.* He also helped more directly by referring me to his graduate student, Aaron Max Berkowitz, who has worked as my capable research assistant in Chicago. Aaron has been especially helpful in finding and copying many of the illustrations that appear in this book.

I also owe *ringraziamenti* to many friends and associates in Italy, where I spent a month working on the manuscript in the fall of 2004 at Centro Studi Liguri in Bogliasco, near Genoa. I thank the Fondazione Bogliasco for awarding me a valuable fellowship and affording me several weeks of time to write in a well-equipped studio on a hill above the Mediterranean Sea. As enchanting as the vistas were, as delightful as the meals were, as engaging as the company of the other writers and artists was, I was only moderately distracted from my writing, and so my time in Bogliasco was therefore extremely productive. So *grazie mille* to the staff at the Centro and to the other fellows, especially to my novelist friends from Germany, Beate Rygiert and Danny Bachmann, who took an interest in my Chicago Germans and helped me prepare a reading based on six episodes in the life of August Spies. My return to Genoa was enriched, as it always is, by my friends Nando Fasce and Carla Viale, who took such good care of me, as they always do. Nando was especially helpful in shaping my thinking about the memory of Haymarket in a walk around the Porto Antico and on a train ride to Milano. So helpful too was *mio amico* Bruno Cartosio, who invited me to Bergamo and shared his own insights on the legacy of Haymarket and the mysteries of *la memoria pubblica e la memoria privata.*

Closer to home I owe thanks to my faculty colleagues and the administrators of the University of Massachusetts Boston who awarded me a sabbatical leave and a post-tenure review award, which supported the research costs for this project, and to Susan Moir, director of the Labor Resource Center, for a grant to cover travel and copying costs. I also wish to express appreciation to all the workers and union members who have supported me at UMass-Boston in the library, in the offices of the College of Public and Community Service, in the mail room, in the computer labs and in the copy centers.

Even closer to home are the various members of my extended family who showed their interest and encouragement during this bookmaking process, especially my sister Beth Kress, her son Simon, and my parents, Mary Kaye and Gerald Green, who first took me to Chicago when I was a boy.

Finally, I express my love and gratitude to the two people who mean the most to me: my wife, Janet Lee Grogan, and my son, Nicholas James Green. Janet and Nick have both understood what doing this work means to me and have supported my effort to do it in many important ways, even though it has taken me away from them too often and too long. Janet read the entire manuscript with her own perceptive eyes and helped me improve it. Nick turned his mind and his red pen on the prologue and the epilogue and let me know how a student feels reading a marked-up essay. He also offered me sage bits of advice about making good word choices and avoiding poor metaphors, usually in conversations we had on the way to and from his school. It has been a special pleasure to write this book; this would not have been the case but for the love and peace of mind Janet and Nick have given me. So, for these priceless gifts, and for many others as well, I dedicate this book to them.

Somerville, Massachusetts
May 15, 2005

Illustration Credits

Credit for all images reproduced from John J. Flinn, *A History of the Chicago Police,* and Michael J. Schaack, *Anarchy and Anarchists,* goes to the University Library, Rare Book Collection, University of Illinois at Chicago. Thanks also to the Imaging Services, Harvard College Widener Library; the Beinecke Rare Book and Manuscript Library, Yale University; the Library of Congress Photo Duplication Service; and the University of Michigan libraries.

17 *President Lincoln's funeral hearse in Chicago:* Photograph by S. M. Fassett. Library of Congress, USZ62-2454.
22 *William H. Sylvis:* From James Sylvis, *The Life of William Sylvis.*
34 Workingman's Advocate *advertisement:* From Sylvis, *The Life of William Sylvis.*
43 *A drawing from* Frank Leslie's Illustrated Newspaper: From *Frank Leslie's Illustrated Newspaper,* October 28, 1871. Chicago Historical Society, ICHi-02909.
45 *Joseph Medill:* Chicago Historical Society, ICHi-16828.
55 *Socialist-led march:* Chicago Historical Society, ICHi-19695.
62 *Thalia Hall:* From Michael J. Schaack, *Anarchy and Anarchists.*
64 *German Turner gymnasium:* Chicago Historical Society, ICHi-14858.
72 *Chicago's lumberyard district:* From *Harper's Weekly,* October 20, 1883.
79 *Police attacking cabinetmakers:* Chicago Historical Society, ICHi-14018.
82 *The Battle of the Viaduct:* From *Harper's Weekly,* August 18, 1877.
87 *Albert Parsons:* Chicago Historical Society, ICHi-03695.
92 *August Spies and Oscar Neebe:* From Lucy Parsons, *The Life of Albert Parsons.*
96 *Johann Most:* From Schaack, *Anarchy and Anarchists.*
103 *Map of Chicago during the early 1880s:* From the Railway Terminal and Industrial Map of Chicago, Chicago: Industrial World Co., 1886. Map Room, Pusey Library, Harvard University. Mapmakers: Jonathan Wyss and Kelly Sandefer, Topaz Maps, Inc.
105 *McCormick Reaper Works:* From A. T. Andreas, *History of Chicago,* Vol. II (1885).
117 *Cyrus McCormick, Jr.:* From John Moses and Joseph Kirkland, eds., *The History of Chicago,* Vol. II (1895).
120 *Mayor Carter H. Harrison:* Chicago Historical Society, IHCi-19662.
123 *Captain John Bonfield:* From John J. Flinn, *A History of the Chicago Police* (1887).
129 Arbeiter-Zeitung *building:* From Schaack, *Anarchy and Anarchists.*
133 *Anarchist banners:* From Schaack, *Anarchy and Anarchists.*

138 *A group of worker militiamen:* From Schaack, *Anarchy and Anarchists.*

150 The Strike: From *Harper's Weekly,* May 1, 1886.

155 *Terence V. Powderly:* From George McNeill, ed., *The Labor Movement: The Problem of Today* (1886).

162 *Workers at Horn Brothers:* From Chicago Historical Society, ICHi-20069.

170 *Painting of August Spies:* From Schaack, *Anarchy and Anarchists.*

175 *Map of Chicago with strike locations:* From the Railway Terminal and Industrial Map of Chicago, Chicago: Industrial World Co., 1886. Map Room, Pusey Library, Harvard University. Mapmakers: Jonathan Wyss and Kelly Sandefer, Topaz Maps, Inc. Strike locations were originally identified on a map produced for the Newberry Library by Michael Conzen and Christopher Thale, in James R. Grossman, Ann Durkin Keating and Janice L. Reiff, eds., *The Encyclopedia of Chicago* (Chicago: University of Chicago Press, 2004).

179 *Haymarket circular:* From Haymarket Collection, Beinecke Rare Book and Manuscript Library, Yale University.

187 *Map of Haymarket Square:* Based on map in Schaack, *Anarchy and Anarchists.*

194 *Patrolman Mathias J. Degan:* Chicago Historical Society, ICHi-31340.

197 *Samuel Fielden and Michael Schwab:* From Schaack, *Anarchy and Anarchists.*

200 *Bohemian workers arrested by police:* From Schaack, *Anarchy and Anarchists.*

205 *Lucy Parsons after one of her arrests:* From Schaack, *Anarchy and Anarchists.*

207 *Thure de Thulstrup's depiction of events at the Haymarket:* From *Harper's Weekly,* May 15, 1886.

215 *Julius S. Grinnell:* From George N. McLean, *The Rise and Fall of Anarchy in America* (1890).

218 *Captain William Black and his wife, Hortensia:* From McLean, *The Rise and Fall of Anarchy in America.*

222 *"The Great Trial":* From Schaack, *Anarchy and Anarchists.*

227 *Judge Joseph E. Gary:* Chicago Historical Society, ICHi-18750.

233 *August Spies:* Chicago Historical Society, ICHi-03702.

236 *Albert Parsons:* Beinecke Rare Book and Manuscript Library, Yale University.

242 *George Engel and Adolph Fischer:* Chicago Historical Society, ICHi-03703 and ICHi-03692.

244 *Nina Van Zandt:* From McLean, *The Rise and Fall of Anarchy in America.*

249 *Cook County Jail cells at visiting time:* Chicago Historical Society, ICHi-03688.

252 *Samuel Gompers and John Swinton:* From McNeill, *The Labor Movement.*

256 *George Schilling and Henry Demarest Lloyd:* Labadie Collection, University of Michigan, and Chicago Historical Society, ICHi-21779.

258 *William Dean Howells:* From *Harper's Weekly,* June 19, 1886.

261 *Governor Richard J. Oglesby:* Chicago Historical Society, ICHi-31331.

265 *Louis Lingg:* Bienecke Rare Book and Manuscript Library, Yale University.

268 *"The Execution":* From Schaack, *Anarchy and Anarchists.*

281 *Police statue in Haymarket Square:* Chicago Historical Society, ICHi-14452.

290 *Haymarket Martyrs' Monument at Waldheim:* Illinois Labor History Society.

293 *Governor John Peter Altgeld:* From L. Parsons, *The Life of Albert Parsons.*

297 *George M. Pullman:* Chicago Historical Society, ICHi-32204.

302 *Lucy Parsons in 1903:* From L. Parsons, *The Life of Albert Parsons.*

313 *Studs Terkel speaking at Haymarket rally:* Illinois Labor History Society.

Index

Italicized page numbers indicate illustrations.

A NOTE ABOUT THE AUTHOR

JAMES GREEN was born in Oak Park, Illinois, raised in Carpentersville, a small factory town outside of Chicago, and educated at Northwestern University. He studied American history with C. Vann Woodward at Yale University and earned his Ph.D. there in 1972. Five years later he joined the faculty at the University of Massachusetts Boston, where he currently teaches history. Green has also held lectureships at Warwick University in England; at University of Genoa in Italy, where he was a Fulbright Senior Fellow; and at Harvard University, where he has taught in the Trade Union Program since 1987. He has served as research coordinator for the PBS documentary film series *The Great Depression* and as president of the Labor & Working-Class History Association. The author of five books on U.S. labor and social history, including *Taking History to Heart*, Jim Green lives in Somerville, Massachusetts, with his wife and son. He can be reached at JamesGreenWorks.com.

A NOTE ON THE TYPE

THIS BOOK was set in Bodoni, a typeface named after Giambattista
Bodoni (1740–1813), the celebrated printer and type designer of
Parma. The Bodoni types of today were designed not as faithful
reproductions of any one of the Bodoni fonts but rather as a compos-
ite, modern version of the Bodoni manner. Bodoni's innovations in
type style included a greater degree of contrast in the thick and thin
elements of the letters and a sharper and more angular finish of
details.

Composed by North Market Street Graphics,
Lancaster, Pennsylvania
Printed and bound by Berryville Graphics,
Berryville, Virginia
Designed by Virginia Tan